TOTAL BASIC SKILLS
Grade 5

School Specialty
Children's Publishing

Copyright © 2004 by School Specialty Children's Publishing. Published by American Education Publishing, an imprint of School Specialty Children's Publishing, a member of the School Specialty Family.

Printed in the United States of America. All rights reserved. Except as permitted under the United States Copyright Act, no part of this publication may be reproduced or distributed in any form or by any means, or stored in a database or retrieval system, without prior written permission from the publisher, unless otherwise indicated.

Send all inquiries to:
School Specialty Children's Publishing
8720 Orion Place
Columbus, OH 43240-2111

ISBN 0-7696-3645-4

1 2 3 4 5 6 7 8 9 10 VHJ 09 08 07 06 05 04

Table of Contents

Reading
Spelling: Digraphs ... 6
Spelling: Listening for Sounds ... 7
Spelling: The j and ch Sounds ... 8
Spelling: Words With Silent Letters ... 9
Spelling: Syllables ... 10
Writing: Sounding Out Syllables ... 11
Writing: Word Families ... 12–13
Spelling: Double Consonants ... 14
Writing: Verb Forms ... 15
Spelling: Math Plurals ... 16
Spelling: More Plurals ... 17
Spelling: Finding Mistakes ... 18
Spelling: Proofreading Practice ... 19
Adding Suffixes ... 20
Adding Prefixes ... 21
Synonyms ... 22–23
Antonyms ... 24–25
Homophones ... 26–27
Similes ... 28
Metaphors ... 29
Using a Dictionary ... 30–32
Learning New Words ... 33
Using a Thesaurus ... 34–35
Classifying ... 36–37
Analogies ... 38–39
Facts and Opinions ... 40–41
Cause and Effect ... 42
Main Idea ... 43
Reading Skills: Skimming ... 44
Reading Skills: Maps ... 45
Following Directions: Continents ... 46
Reading a Recipe ... 47
Reading Skills: Labels ... 48
Reading Skills: Newspapers ... 49
Reading Skills: Schedules ... 50
Context Clues: Remember Who You Are ... 51
Context Clues: Kids' Books Are Big Business ... 52

Reading Comprehension
Using Prior Knowledge: Music ... 54
Main Idea: Where Did Songs Come From? ... 55
Comprehension: Facts About Folk Music ... 56
Recalling Details: Woodwinds ... 57
Comprehension: Harp Happenings ... 58
Comprehension: Brass Shows Class ... 59
Comprehension: Violins ... 60
Using Prior Knowledge: Art ... 61
Main Idea: Creating Art ... 62
Comprehension: Leonardo da Vinci ... 63
Context Clues: Leonardo da Vinci ... 64
Comprehension: Michelangelo ... 65
Comprehension: Rembrandt ... 66
Using Prior Knowledge: Big Cats ... 67
Comprehension: Jaguars ... 68
Comprehension: Leopards ... 69
Comprehension: Lynxes ... 70
Comprehension: Pumas ... 71
Comprehension: Tigers ... 72
Comprehension: Lions ... 73
Using Prior Knowledge: Cooking ... 74
Following Directions: Chunky Tomato and Green Onion Sauce ... 75
Comprehension: Cooking With Care ... 76
Sequencing: Chocolate Chunk Cookies ... 77
Comprehension: Eating High-Fiber Foods ... 78
Main Idea: New Corn ... 79

Comprehension: The French Eat Differently ... 80
Comprehension: Chinese Cabbage ... 81
Recognizing Details: The Coldest Continent ... 82
Reading Comprehension: The Arctic Circle ... 83
Main Idea: The Polar Trail ... 84
Reading Skills: Research ... 85
Recognizing Details: The Frozen Continent ... 86
Reading Comprehension: Polar Bears ... 87
Context Clues: Seals ... 88
Reading Comprehension: Walruses ... 89
Main Idea: Penguins ... 90

Grammar and Punctuation
Nouns ... 92
Proper and Common Nouns ... 93
Abstract and Concrete Nouns ... 94
Verbs ... 95–96
Verb Tenses ... 97
Writing: Verb Forms ... 98
Writing: Future-Tense Verbs ... 99
Irregular Verbs ... 100
"Be" as a Helping Verb ... 101
"Be" as a Linking Verb ... 102
Transitive and Intransitive Verbs ... 103
Subjects and Predicates ... 104
Which Noun Is the Subject? ... 105
Subjects and Verbs ... 106
Writing: Subjects and Verbs ... 107
Complete Sentences ... 108
Direct Objects ... 109
Indirect Objects ... 110
Prepositions ... 111
Pronouns ... 112
Singular and Plural Pronouns ... 113
Possessive Pronouns ... 114
Writing: Possessive Pronouns ... 115
Indefinite Pronouns ... 116
Interrogative and Relative Pronouns ... 117
Gender and Number of Pronouns ... 118
Writing: Pronouns ... 119
Pronouns as Subjects ... 120
Pronouns as Direct Objects ... 121
Pronouns as Indirect Objects and Objects of Prepositions ... 122
Adjectives ... 123
Writing: Comparatives ... 124
"Good" and "Bad" ... 125
Demonstrative and Indefinite Adjectives ... 126
Interrogative and Possessive Adjectives ... 127
Prepositional Phrases as Adjectives ... 128
Adverbs ... 129
Prepositional Phrases as Adverbs ... 130
Writing: Adjectives and Adverbs ... 131
Placement of Adjective and Adverb Phrases ... 132
Writing: Parts of Speech Story ... 133
Writing: Parts of Speech ... 134
Conjunctions ... 135
Writing: Conjunctions ... 136
Statements and Questions ... 137–138
Commands, Requests, and Exclamations ... 139–140
Writing: Four Kinds of Sentences ... 141
Compound Subjects/Compound Predicates ... 142
Combining Subjects ... 143
Combining Predicates ... 144
Writing: Using Commas Correctly ... 145
Run-On Sentences ... 146
Commas ... 147–148
Combining Sentences ... 149

Total Basic Skills Grade 5

Punctuation	150
Quotation Marks	151
Capitalization/Punctuation	152
Capitalization	153
"Who" Clauses	154
"Which" Clauses	155
"That" Clauses	156
"That" and "Which" Clauses	157
Combining Sentences	158
"Who's" and "Whose"	159
"Their," "There" and "They're"	160
"Teach" and "Learn"	161
"Lie" and "Lay"	162
"Rise" and "Raise"	163
"All Right," "All Ready" and "Already"	164

Writing

Writing: Topic Sentences	166
Writing: Supporting Sentences	167
Writing: Building Paragraphs	168
Writing: Sequencing	469
Sequencing	170
Author's Purpose	171–172
Writing: Descriptive Details	173
Descriptive Sentences	174
Writing: Descriptive Details	175
Personal Narratives	176–177
Advantages and Disadvantages	178
Complete the Story	179
Writing Fiction	180
Writing: Point of View	181
Friendly Letters	182–183
Writing: Supporting Your Opinion	184
Writing From a Prompt: An Opinion Essay	185
Writing a Summary	186–187
Comparing and Contrasting	188
News Writing	189
News Writing: Inverted Pyramid Style	190
Writing: Just the Facts	191
Writing: You're the Reporter	192
Writing: Personification	193
Similes	194
Writing: Common Similes	195
Metaphors	196
How to Write a Book Report	197
Book Report: A Book I Devoured	198
Library Research	199–200
Fiction, Nonfiction and Biographies	201
Reports: Choosing a Topic	202
Reports: Doing Research	203
Reports: Taking Notes	204
Encyclopedia Skills: Taking Notes	205
Reports: Making an Outline	206
Reports: Writing the Paper	207
Editing	208–213
Proofreading	214–215
Editing: Check Your Proofreading Skills	216
Ancient Egypt	217
Taking Notes: Egyptian Mummies	218
Outlining	219
Outlining: Egyptian Pyramids	220
Summarizing	221
Summarizing: King Tut	222

Math

Place Value	224–225
Addition	226–229
Subtraction	230–231
Checking Subtraction	232
Addition and Subtraction	233–234
Rounding	235
Estimating	236
Rounding and Estimating	237
Prime Numbers	238–239
Multiples	240
Factors	241
Factor Trees	242–243
Greatest Common Factor	244
Least Common Multiple	245
Multiplication	246–247
Division	248–249
Checking Division	250
Multiplication and Division	251
Adding and Subtracting Like Fractions	252
Adding and Subtracting Unlike Fractions	253
Reducing Fractions	254
Improper Fractions	255
Mixed Numbers	256
Adding Mixed Numbers	257
Subtracting Mixed Numbers	258
Comparing Fractions	259
Ordering Fractions	260
Multiplying Fractions	261
Multiplying Mixed Numbers	262
Dividing Fractions	263
Dividing Whole Numbers by Fractions	264
Decimals	265
Decimals and Fractions	266
Adding and Subtracting Decimals	267
Multiplying Decimals	268
Dividing With Decimals	269
Dividing Decimals by Decimals	270
Geometry	271–272
Similar, Congruent and Symmetrical Figures	273
Perimeter and Area	274
Volume	275
Perimeter and Area	276
Perimeter, Area and Volume	277
Circumference	278–279
Diameter, Radius and Circumference	280
Triangle Angles	281
Area of a Triangle	282
Space Figures	283
Length	284
Length: Metric	285
Weight	286
Weight: Metric	287
Capacity	288
Capacity: Metric	289
Comparing Measurements	290
Temperature: Fahrenheit	291
Temperature: Celsius	292
Review	293
Ratio	294
Percent	295
Probability	296
Using Calculators to Find Percent	297
Finding Percents	298
Locating Points on a Grid	299
Graphs	300–302
Answer Key	303–352

Total Basic Skills Grade 5

READING

Spelling: Digraphs

A **digraph** is two consonants pronounced as one sound.

Examples: **sh** as in **shell**, **ch** as in **chew**, **th** as in **thin**

Directions: Write **sh**, **ch** or **th** to complete each word below.

1. _____ reaten
2. _____ ill
3. _____ ock
4. _____ iver
5. _____ aw

6. _____ allenge
7. peri _____
8. _____ ield
9. _____ art
10. _____ rive

Directions: Complete these sentences with a word, or form of the word, from the list above.

1. A trip to the South Pole would really be a (**ch**) _____ .

2. The ice there never (**th**) _____ because the temperature averages –50°C.

3. How can any living thing (**th**) _____ or even live when it's so cold?

4. With 6 months of total darkness and those icy temperatures, any plants would soon (**sh**) _____ .

5. Even the thought of that numbing cold makes me (**sh**) _____ .

6. The cold and darkness (**th**) _____ the lives of explorers.

7. The explorers take along maps and (**ch**) _____ to help them find their way.

8. Special clothing helps protect and (**sh**) _____ them from the cold.

9. Still, the weather must be a (**sh**) _____ at first.

10. Did someone leave a door open? Suddenly I feel a (**ch**) _____ .

Total Basic Skills Grade 5   6   Reading

Spelling: Listening for Sounds

Not every word spelled with **ow** is pronounced **ou** as in **powder** and **however**. In the same way, not every word spelled with **ou** is pronounced **ou** as in **amount** and **announce**. The letters **ou** can be pronounced a number of ways.

Directions: Write the word from the box that rhymes with each of the words or phrases below. Some words are used twice.

| doubt | amount | avoid | annoy | announce |
| choice | poison | powder | soil | however |

joys in _____

shout _____

a boy _____

employed _____

now never _____

voice _____

a bounce _____

enjoyed _____

two counts _____

loyal _____

crowd her _____

Joyce _____

a count _____

employ _____

louder _____

trout _____

Spelling: The j and ch Sounds

The **j** sound can be spelled with a **j** as in **jump**, with a **g** before **e** or **i** as in **agent** and **giant**, or with **ge** at the end of a word as in **page**.

The **ch** sound is often spelled with the letters **ch** but can also be spelled with a **t** before **u**, as in **nature**.

Directions: Use words from the box to complete the exercises below.

| statue | imagination | jealous | future | arrangements |
| furniture | stranger | project | justice | capture |

1. Say each word and then write it in the correct row, depending on whether it has the **j** or **ch** sound.

   j _____ _____ _____

   _____ _____ _____

   ch _____ _____ _____ _____

2. Write a word from the box that belongs to the same word family as each word below.

   imagine _____   arranging _____

   strangely _____   furnish _____

   just _____   jealousy _____

Directions: Complete each sentence with a word containing the given sound.

1. What is your group's (**j**) _____ this week?

2. There is a (**ch**) _____ of George Washington in front of our school.

3. She used her (**j**) _____ to solve the problem.

4. My sister keeps rearranging the (**ch**) _____ in our room.

Total Basic Skills Grade 5 — 8 — Reading

Spelling: Words With Silent Letters

Some letters in words are not pronounced, such as the **s** in **island**, the **t** in **listen**, the **k** in **knee**, the **h** in **hour** and the **w** in **write**.

Directions: Use words from the box to complete the exercises below.

wrinkled	honest	aisle	knife	wrist
rhyme	exhaust	glisten	knowledge	wrestle

1. Write each word beside its silent letter. Two words have two silent letters—write them twice.

   s _____

   t _____ _____

   h _____ _____ _____

   w _____ _____ _____ _____

   k _____ _____ _____

2. Write in the missing letter or letters for each word.

   __ res __ le   ex __ aust   __ nife   glis __ en   ai __ le

   __ nowledge   __ rinkle   r __ yme   __ onest   __ rist

Directions: Complete each sentence with a word that has the given silent letter. Use each word only once.

1. He always tells the truth. He's very (**h**) _____.

2. I like (**s**) _____ seats in airplanes.

3. I need a sharper (**k**) _____ to cut this bread.

4. I think a long hike might (**h**) _____ me.

5. Did you sleep in that shirt? It is so (**w**) _____!

6. The snow seemed to (**t**) _____ in the sunlight.

7. To play tennis, you need a strong (**w**) _____.

Reading

Total Basic Skills Grade 5

Spelling: Syllables

A **syllable** is a part of a word with only one vowel sound. Some words have only one syllable, like **cat**, **leaf** and **ship**. Some words have two or more syllables. **Be-lief** and **trac-tor** have two syllables, **to-ge-ther** and **ex-cel-lent** have three syllables and **con-ver-sa-tion** has four syllables. Some words can have six or more syllables! The word **ex-tra-ter-res-tri-al**, for example, has six syllables.

Directions: Follow the instructions below.

1. Count the syllables in each word below, and write the number of syllables on the line.

   a. badger _____   f. grease _____

   b. location _____   g. relationship _____

   c. award _____   h. communication _____

   d. national _____   i. government _____

   e. necessary _____   j. Braille _____

2. Write four words with four syllables each in the blanks.

   a. _____   c. _____

   b. _____   d. _____

3. Write one word with five syllables and one with six syllables. If you need help, use a dictionary.

   Five syllables: _____

   Six syllables: _____

Writing: Sounding Out Syllables

Directions: Use words from the box to complete the exercises below.

| decision | division | pressure | addition | ancient |
| subtraction | confusion | multiplication | social | correction |

1. Write each word in the row showing the correct number of syllables.

   Two: _____ _____ _____

   Three: _____ _____ _____

   _____ _____ _____

   Five: _____

2. Write in the missing syllables for each word.

   __ __ cial   sub __ __ __ tion   mul __ __ pli __ __ tion   pres __ __ __

   di __ __ sion   an __ __ __ __   deci __ __ __   ad __ __ tion

   __ __ fusion   cor __ __ __ tion

3. Beside each word below, write a word with the same number of syllables. Use each word from the box only once.

   daily _____   challenging _____

   syllable _____   election _____

   decreasing _____   threaten _____

   advantage _____   shivering _____

   title _____   experimenting _____

Writing: Word Families

A **word family** is a group of words based on the same word. For example, **playful**, **playground** and **playing** are all based on the word **play**.

Directions: Use words from the box to complete the exercises below.

decision	division	pressure	addition	create
subtraction	confusion	multiplication	social	correction

1. Write the word that belongs to the same word family as each word below.

    correctly _____   confused _____

    divide _____   subtracting _____

    pressing _____   society _____

    multiply _____   decide _____

    added _____   creativity _____

2. Complete each sentence by writing the correct form of the given word.

    Example: Have you (decide) <u>decided</u> what to do? Did you make a (decide) <u>decision</u> yet?

    I am (add) _____ the numbers right now. Would you check my (add) _____ ?

    This problem has me (confuse) _____ . Can you clear up my (confuse) _____ ?

    This is a (press) _____ problem. We feel (press) _____ to solve it right away.

    Is he (divide) _____ by the right number? Will you help him with his (divide) _____ ?

    Try to answer (correct) _____ . Then you won't have to make any (correct) _____ on your paper later on.

Total Basic Skills Grade 5

Writing: Word Families

Directions: Write the word that belongs to the same word family as each word below.

| doubt | amount | avoid | annoy | announce |
| choice | poison | powder | soil | however |

avoidance _____   annoyance _____

doubtful _____   soiled _____

announcement _____   poisonous _____

choose _____   amounted _____

powdery _____   whenever _____

Directions: Complete each sentence by writing the correct form of the given word.

Example: Are you (doubt) <u>doubting</u> my word? You never (doubt) <u>doubted</u> it before.

1. The teacher is (announce) _____ the next test. Did you hear what he (announce) _____?

2. This stream was (poison) _____ by a chemical from a factory nearby.

3. Is the chemical (poison) _____ any other water supply? How many (poison) _____ does the factory produce?

4. My cat always (annoy) _____ our dog.

5. Last night, Camie (annoy) _____ Lucas for hours.

6. I think Carrie is (avoid) _____ me. Yesterday, she (avoid) _____ walking home with me.

Spelling: Double Consonants

When adding endings such as **ing** and **ed** to verbs, use the following rule: Double the final consonant of verbs that have short vowel sounds and end with only one consonant. For example, **rip** becomes **ripped** and **beg** becomes **begging**. However, do not double the final consonant in words that end in double consonants. For example, **rock** ends with two consonants, **ck**. So even though it has a short vowel sound, **rock** becomes **rocked**.

Directions: Add **ed** to the verbs below. Remember, when a verb ends with **e**, drop the **e** before adding an ending (**taste**, **tasting**). The first one has been done for you.

top _____topped_____   rip _____

pet _____   punch _____

sob _____   rinse _____

brag _____   stock _____

scrub _____   lack _____

flip _____   dent _____

Directions: Add **ing** to the verbs below. The first one has been done for you.

flap _____flapping_____   snack _____

scrub _____   flip _____

stock _____   rinse _____

dent _____   brag _____

pet _____   lack _____

sob _____   punch _____

Writing: Verb Forms

Directions: In the following story, some of the verbs are missing. Write the proper form of the verbs shown, adding **ed** or **ing** when necessary.

Yesterday, I was (brag) _____ to my brother about how much I (help) _____ our mother around the house. I had (scrub) _____ the kitchen floor, (wipe) _____ off all the counters and (rinse) _____ out the sink. I was (pour) _____ the dirty water out of the bucket when our mother came in. She looked around the kitchen and (smile) _____ . "Who did all this work?" she (ask) _____ .

I was (get) _____ ready to tell her what I had done when my brother (interrupt) _____ me. "We both did! We've been (work) _____ very hard!" he said. "He's not (tell) _____ the truth!" I said to Mom. "I did everything!" My brother (glare) _____ at me.

"Is that true?" asked Mom. My brother (look) _____ at the floor and (nod) _____ . He was (think) _____ about all the trouble he would get into. Instead, Mom smiled again. "Well, that's okay," she said. "The rest of the house needs to be (clean) _____ , too. You can get (start) _____ right away!"

Spelling: Math Plurals

To make most nouns plural, add **s**. When a noun ends with **s**, **ss**, **sh**, **ch** or **x**, add **es**: bus—bus**es**, cross—cross**es**, brush—brush**es**, church—church**es**, box—box**es**. When a noun ends with a consonant and **y**, change the **y** to **i** and add **es**: berry—berr**ies**. For some words, insteading of adding **s** or **es**, the spelling of the word changes: man—men, mouse—mice.

Directions: Write the correct plural or singular form of the words in these math problems. Write whether the problem requires addition (**A**), subtraction (**S**), multiplication (**M**) or division (**D**). The first one has been done for you.

1. 3 (box) __boxes__ − 2 (box) __boxes__ = __1 box__ __S__
2. 2 (supply) _____ + 5 (supply) _____ = _____ ___
3. 4 (copy) _____ x 2 (copy) _____ = _____ ___
4. 6 (class) _____ ÷ 2 (class) _____ = _____ ___
5. 5 (factory) _____ − 3 (factory) _____ = _____ ___
6. 3 (daisy) _____ x 3 (daisy) _____ = _____ ___
7. 8 (sandwich) _____ + 4 (sandwich) _____ = _____ ___
8. 3 (child) _____ − 1 (child) _____ = _____ ___
9. 10 (brush) _____ ÷ 5 (brush) _____ = _____ ___
10. 4 (goose) _____ + 1 (goose) _____ = _____ ___
11. 3 (mouse) _____ + 1 (mouse) _____ = _____ ___

Spelling: More Plurals

Remember, in some words, an **f** changes to a **v** to make the plural form.

Examples: life — li**v**es   wife — wi**v**es   knife — kni**v**es   leaf — lea**v**es

Directions: Complete these sentences by writing the correct plural form of the given word. Also, circle the spelling errors and write the words correctly on the lines to the right.

1. The (leaf) _____ are dry and rinkled. _____

2. The (knife) _____ glisened in the sun. _____

3. I think the (child) _____ in this school are honist. _____

4. The (supply) _____ were stacked in the isle. _____

5. (mouse) _____ rimes with twice. _____

6. Some people feel exausted all their (life) _____. _____

7. The (class) _____ were trying to gain more knowlege about Olympic athletes. _____

8. The kittens were wresling in the (bush) _____. _____

9. Jamie nearly broke his rist trying to carry all those (box) _____. _____

10. Some kings had several (wife) _____ who new about each other. _____

11. (Daisy) _____ are knot expensive. _____

12. Right your name on both (copy) _____. _____

13. We watched the (monkey) _____ play on the swings for ours. _____

14. Do you like (strawberry) _____ hole or sliced? _____

Spelling: Finding Mistakes

Directions: Circle the four spelling mistakes in each paragraph. Then write the words correctly on the lines below.

Last nite, our family went to a nice restaurant. As we were lookking at the menus, a waiter walked in from the kichen carrying a large tray of food. As he walked by us, he triped, and the tray went flying! The food flew all over our table and all over us, too!

_____ _____

_____ _____

Last week, while my dad was washing the car, our dog Jack dicided to help. He stuck his nose in the pale of soapy water, and it tiped over and soaked him! As he shook himself off, the water from his fur went all over the car. "Look!" Dad laffed. "Jack is doing his part!"

_____ _____

_____ _____

For our next feild trip, my class is going to the zoo. We have been studying about animals in sceince class. I'm very eksited to see the elephants, but my freind Karen really wants to see the monkeys. She has been to the zoo before, and she says the monkeys are the most fun to watch.

_____ _____

_____ _____

It seems the rain will never stop! It has been rainning for seven days now, and the sky is always dark and clowdy. Everyone at school is in a bad mood, because we have to stay inside during resess. Will we ever see the son again?

_____ _____

_____ _____

Total Basic Skills Grade 5   18   Reading

Spelling: Proofreading Practice

Directions: Circle the six spelling and pronoun mistakes in each paragraph. Write the words correctly on the lines below.

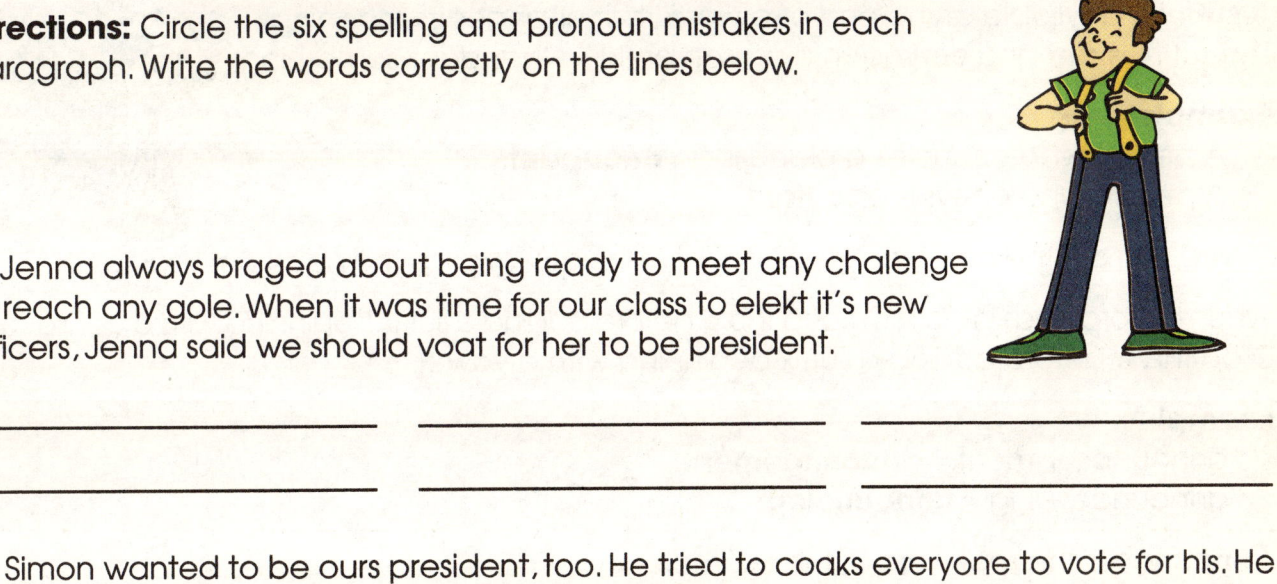

Jenna always braged about being ready to meet any chalenge or reach any gole. When it was time for our class to elekt it's new officers, Jenna said we should voat for her to be president.

_____ _____ _____

_____ _____ _____

Simon wanted to be ours president, too. He tried to coaks everyone to vote for his. He even lowned kids money to get their votes! Well, Jenna may have too much pryde in herself, but I like her in spit of that. At least she didn't try to buy our votes!

_____ _____ _____

_____ _____ _____

Its true that Jenna tried other ways to get us to vote for hers. She scrubed the chalkboards even though it was my dayly job for that week. One day, I saw her rinseing out the paintbrushes when it was Peter's turn to do it. Then she made sure we knew about her good deeds so we would praize her.

_____ _____ _____

_____ _____ _____

We held the election, but I was shalked when the teacher releesed the results. Simon won! I wondered if he cheeted somehow. I feel like our class was robed! Now Simon is the one who's braging about how great he is. I wish he knew the titel of president doesn't mean anything if no one wants to be around you!

_____ _____ _____

_____ _____ _____

Reading

Adding Suffixes

A **suffix** is a syllable at the end of a word that changes its meaning. The suffixes **ant** and **ent** mean a person or thing that does something.

Examples:
A person who occupies a place is an **occupant**.
A person who obeys is **obedient**.

A **root word** is the common stem that gives related words their basic meanings.

When a word ends in silent **e**, keep the **e** before adding a suffix beginning with a consonant. Drop the **e** before adding a suffix beginning with a vowel.

Examples:
announce + ment = **announcement**
announce + ing = **announcing**

Announce is the root word in this example.

Directions: Combine each root word and suffix to make a new word. The first one has been done for you.

Root word	Suffix	New word
observe	ant	observant
contest	ant	_____
please	ant	_____
preside	ent	_____
differ	ent	_____

Directions: Use the meanings in parentheses to complete the sentences with one of the above new words. The first one has been done for you.

1. To be a good scientist, you must be very __observant__. (pay careful attention)

2. Her perfume had a strong but very _____ smell. (nice)

3. Because the bridge was out, we had to find a _____ route home. (not the same)

4. The game show _____ jumped up and down when she won the grand prize. (person who competes)

5. Next week we will elect a new student council _____ . (highest officer)

Adding Prefixes

A **prefix** is a syllable at the beginning of a word that changes its meaning. The prefixes **il**, **im**, **in** and **ir** all mean not.

Examples:
Illogical means not logical or practical.
Impossible means not possible.
Invisible means not visible.
Irrelevant means not relevant or practical.

Directions: Divide each word into its prefix and root word. The first one has been done for you.

	Prefix	**Root Word**
illogical	il	logical
impatient	_____	_____
immature	_____	_____
incomplete	_____	_____
insincere	_____	_____
irresponsible	_____	_____
irregular	_____	_____

Directions: Use the meanings in parentheses to complete the sentences with one of the above words.

1. I had to turn in my assignment _____ because I was sick last night. (not finished)

2. It was _____ for Jimmy to give me his keys because he can't get into his house without them. (not practical)

3. Sue and Joel were _____ to leave their bikes out in the rain. (not doing the right thing)

4. I sometimes get _____ waiting for my ride to school. (restless)

5. The boys sounded _____ when they said they were sorry. (not honest)

6. These towels didn't cost much because they are _____. (not straight or even)

Reading

Total Basic Skills Grade 5

Synonyms

A **synonym** is a word with the same or similar meaning as another word.

Examples: bucket — pail   happy — cheerful   dirty — messy

Directions: Match the words on the left with their synonyms on the right. The first one has been done for you.

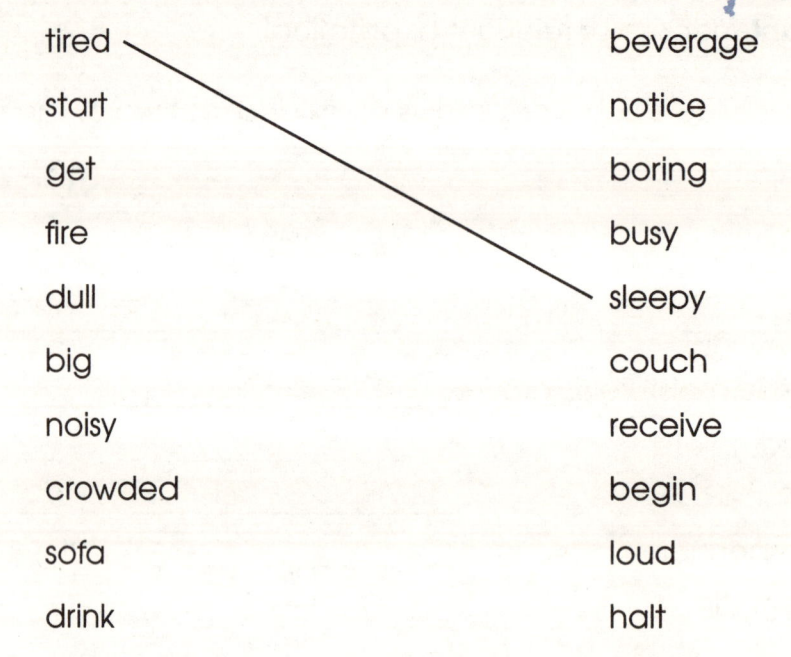

tired	beverage
start	notice
get	boring
fire	busy
dull	sleepy
big	couch
noisy	receive
crowded	begin
sofa	loud
drink	halt
sign	large
stop	flames

Directions: Rewrite the sentences below using synonyms for the bold words.

1. Because the road was **rough**, we had a **hard** time riding our bikes on it.

   _____

2. After the accident, the driver appeared to be **hurt**, so someone **ran** to call an ambulance.

   _____

3. Yesterday everyone stayed after school to pick up litter, and now the school yard is **nice** and **clean**.

Total Basic Skills Grade 5   22   Reading

Synonyms

Directions: Circle a word or a phrase in each sentence that is a synonym for a word in the box. Write the synonym on the line.

challenged	shocked	thaw	chart	frighten
perish	chill	shivering	thrive	shield

Example: The writing was in an (old) code.   _____ancient_____

1. A fish out of water will quickly die.   _____

2. The ice carving is beginning to melt.   _____

3. I was amazed when I saw how he looked.   _____

4. The puppy was trembling with excitement.   _____

5. Ferns need moisture to grow well.   _____

6. Are you trying to scare me?   _____

7. Let the salad get cold in the refrigerator.   _____

8. She tried to protect him from the truth.   _____

9. He made a list of different kinds of birds.   _____

10. They dared us to enter the contest.   _____

Directions: Write your own sentences using five words from the box. If you're not sure what a word means, look it up in a dictionary.

_____

_____

_____

_____

Reading   23   Total Basic Skills Grade 5

Antonyms

An **antonym** is a word with the opposite meaning of another word.

Examples: hot — cold
up — down
start — stop

Directions: Match the words on the left with their antonyms on the right. The first one has been done for you.

asleep	sloppy
sit	shut
excited	full
north	awake
wild	tame
hairy	stand
open	bored
quick	bald
neat	south
hungry	slow

Directions: In the sentences below, replace each bold word with a synonym or an antonym so that the sentence makes sense. Write the word on the line. Then, write either **synonym** or **antonym** to show its relationship to the given word. The first one has been done for you.

1. If the weather stays warm, all the plants will **perish**. <u>live — antonym</u>

2. Last night, mom made my favorite meal, and it was **delicious**. _____

3. The test was **difficult**, and everyone in the class passed it. _____

4. The music from the concert was so **loud** we could hear it in the parking lot! _____

5. The bunks at camp were **comfortable**, and I didn't sleep very well. _____

Total Basic Skills Grade 5   24   Reading

Antonyms

Antonyms are words that mean the opposite.

Examples:
  tall and short
  high and low
  top and bottom

Directions: Write an antonym for each word. Then use it in a sentence. Use a dictionary if you are unsure of the meaning of a word.

1. tired _____
   _____

2. bright _____
   _____

3. sparkling _____
   _____

4. tame _____
   _____

5. fresh _____
   _____

6. elegant _____
   _____

7. real _____
   _____

8. odd _____
   _____

9. unruly _____
   _____

10. valor _____
    _____

Homophones

Homophones are words that sound alike but have different spellings and meanings. The words **no** and **know** are homophones. They sound alike, but their spellings and meanings are very different.

Directions: Use words from the box to complete the exercises below.

hour	wring	knot	whole	knew
wrap	knight	piece	write	

1. Write each word beside its homophone.

   peace _____   new _____   ring _____

   hole _____   rap _____   night _____

   not _____   right _____ our _____

2. Write three words that have a silent **k**. _____ _____ _____

3. Write one word that has a silent **h**. _____

Directions: Circle the misused homophones in each sentence. Then rewrite the sentences, using the correct homophones.

1. By the time knight fell, I new she was knot coming.
   _____

2. I would never have any piece until I new the hole story.
   _____

3. He spent an our righting down what had happened.
   _____

4. I could see write through the whole in the night's armor.
   _____

Total Basic Skills Grade 5   Reading

Homophones

Directions: Complete the story below by writing the correct homophones for the words in parentheses.

Last Saturday, I went to (meat) _____ my friend, Andrea, at the mall.

When I got there, I noticed she looked a little (pail) _____ .

"What's wrong?" I asked her.

She (side) _____ . "I'm (knot) _____ feeling so (grate) _____ ," she said. "I don't (no) _____ what's wrong with me."

"Maybe you (knead) _____ to take some aspirin," I said. "Let's go to the drugstore. It's this (weigh) _____ ."

As we were walking, we passed a (flour) _____ shop, and I bought (sum) _____ roses for my mother. Then we found the drugstore, and Andrea bought some aspirin and took (too) _____ of them. An (our) _____ later, she felt much better.

That (knight) _____ , I gave the roses to my mother. "You shouldn't (waist) _____ your money on (presence) _____ for me!" she said, but she was smiling. I (new) _____ she was pleased.

"That's okay, Mom, I wanted to buy them for you," I said. "But now I'm broke. How about a (lone) _____ ?"

Similes

A **simile** uses the words **like** or **as** to compare two things.

Examples:
　　The snow glittered **like** diamonds.
　　He was **as** slow **as** a turtle.

Directions: Circle the two objects being compared in each sentence.

1. The kittens were like gymnasts performing tricks.

2. My old computer is as slow as molasses.

3. When the lights went out in the basement, it was as dark as night.

4. The sun was like a fire, heating up the earth.

5. The young girl was as graceful as a ballerina.

6. The puppy cried like a baby all night.

7. He flies that airplane like a daredevil.

8. The girl was as pretty as a picture.

9. The snow on the mountain tops was like whipped cream.

10. The tiger's eyes were like emeralds.

Directions: Complete the simile in each sentence.

11. My cat is as _____ as _____ .

12. He was as _____ as _____ .

13. Melissa's eyes shone like _____ .

14. The paints were like _____ .

15. The opera singer's voice was as _____ as _____ .

16. My friend is as _____ as _____ .

Metaphors

A **metaphor** is a direct comparison between two things. The words **like** or **as** are not used in a metaphor.

Example: The **sun** is a **yellow ball** in the sky.

Directions: Underline the metaphor in each sentence. Write the two objects being compared on the line.

1. As it bounded toward me, the dog was a quivering furball of excitement.
   _____

2. The snow we skied on was mashed potatoes.
   _____

3. John is a mountain goat when it comes to rock climbing.
   _____

4. The light is a beacon shining into the dark basement.
   _____

5. The famished child was a wolf, eating for the first time in days.
   _____

6. The man's arm was a tireless lever as he fought to win the wrestling contest.
   _____

7. The flowers were colorful circles against the green of the yard.
   _____

Using a Dictionary

Directions: Read about dictionaries. Then answer the questions.

Dictionaries are books that give definitions of words. Dictionaries list words in alphabetical order. **Guide words** at the top of each page show the first and last words listed on the page. All other words on the page are listed in alphabetical order between the guide words. This helps you locate the word you want quickly and easily.

In addition to definitions, dictionaries also show the following: how to pronounce, or say, each word; the individual syllables found in each word; the part of speech for each word; and the plural form or verb forms if the base word changes.

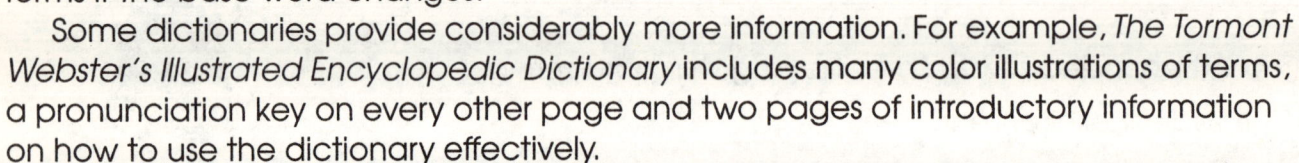

Some dictionaries provide considerably more information. For example, *The Tormont Webster's Illustrated Encyclopedic Dictionary* includes many color illustrations of terms, a pronunciation key on every other page and two pages of introductory information on how to use the dictionary effectively.

Other highlights of the *Tormont Webster* are **historic labels** that tell the history of words no longer in common use; **geographic labels** that tell in what part of the world uncommon words are used; **stylistic labels** that tell whether a word is formal, informal, humorous or a slang term; and **field labels** that tell what field of knowledge—such as medicine—the word is used in.

1. Where are guide words found? _____

2. What is the purpose of guide words? _____

3. Which label tells if a word is a slang term? _____

4. Which label tells the history of a word? _____

5. Which type of information is not provided for each word in the dictionary?

☐ definition
☐ part of speech
☐ picture

Using a Dictionary

Directions: Use the dictionary entry below to answer the questions.

ad-he-sive (ad-he'-siv) *adj.* 1. Tending to adhere; sticky. 2. Gummed so as to adhere. *n.* 3. An adhesive substance such as paste or glue. **ad-he-sive-ly** *adv.* **ad-he-sive-ness** *n.*

1. Based on the first definition of **adhesive**, what do you think **adhere** means?
   _____
   _____

2. Which definition of **adhesive** is used in this sentence? The tape was so adhesive that we couldn't peel it loose. _____
   _____

3. Which part of speech is **adhesive** used as in this sentence? We put a strong adhesive on the package to keep is sealed. _____

4. How many syllables does **adhesive** have? _____

5. Is **adhesive** used as a noun or an adjective in this sentence? The adhesive we chose to use was not very gummy. _____

6. **Adhesive** and variations of the word can be used as what parts of speech? _____
   _____

Directions: Write sentences using these words.

7. adhesiveness _____
   _____

8. adhesively _____
   _____

9. adhere _____
   _____

Reading   31   Total Basic Skills Grade 5

Using the Dictionary

Guide words are the words that appear at the top of dictionary pages. They show the first and last words on each page.

Directions: Read the guide words on each dictionary page below. Then look around for objects whose names come between the guide words. Write the names of the objects, and then number them in alphabetical order.

babble	buzz

magic	myself

cabin	cycle

pea	puzzle

dairy	dwarf

scar	sword

feast	future

tack	truth

Learning New Words

Directions: Write a word from the box to complete each sentence. Use a dictionary to look up words you are unsure of.

bouquet	unconscious	inspire	disability
inherit	hovering	assault	enclosure
commotion	criticize		

1. He was knocked _____ by the blow to his head.

2. Megan never let her _____ stand in the way of accomplishing what she wanted.

3. The teacher burst into the noisy room and demanded to know what all the _____ was about.

4. He offered her a _____ of flowers as a truce after their argument.

5. The zoo was in the process of building a new _____ for the elephants.

6. The mother was _____ over her sick child.

7. The movie was meant to _____ people to do good deeds.

8. My friend will eventually _____ a fortune from his grandmother.

9. Not many people enjoy having someone _____ their work.

10. The female leopard led the _____ on the herd of zebras.

Using a Thesaurus

A **thesaurus** is a type of reference book that lists words in alphabetical order followed by their synonyms and antonyms. **Synonyms** are words that mean the same. **Antonyms** are words that mean the opposite.

A thesaurus is an excellent tool for finding "just the right word." It is also a valuable resource for finding a variety of synonyms and/or antonyms to make your writing livelier.

Each main entry in a thesaurus consists of a word followed by the word's part of speech, its definition, an example, a list of related words and other information.

Here is a typical entry in a thesaurus, with an explanation of terms below:

SLOW
ADJ **SYN** deliberate, dilatory, laggard, leisurely, unhasty, unhurried
REL lateness, limited, measured, slowish, steady, unhurrying, slow-footed, plodding, pokey, straggling, snail-like **IDIOM** as slow as molasses in January; as slow as a turtle **CON** blitz, quick, rapid, swift **ANT** fast

ADJ means adjective
CON means contrasted words
SYN means synonym
ANT means antonym
REL means related words
idiom means a common phrase that is not literal

Directions: Use the thesaurus entry to answer the questions.

1. What is the antonym listed for **slow**? _____

2. How many contrasting words are listed for **slow**? _____

3. How many synonyms are listed for **slow**? _____

4. What is **slow** compared to in the two idioms listed? _____

5. What is the last related word listed for **slow**? _____

Total Basic Skills Grade 5   Reading

Using a Thesaurus

Directions: Use a thesaurus to list as many synonyms (SYN) as possible for the following words.

1. calm _____
2. hunt _____
3. quilt _____
4. tender _____
5. vacate _____

Directions: Use a thesaurus to list as many related words (REL) as possible for the following words.

6. value _____
7. difference _____
8. enable _____

Directions: Use a thesaurus to list one idiom for each of the following words.

9. beauty _____
10. cake _____

dog
pooch
canine
puppy
cur
bow wow
mongrel
mutt

Classifying

Classifying means putting items into categories based on similar characteristics.

Example: Apple pie, cookies and ice cream could be classified as desserts.

Directions: Cross out the word in each group that does not belong. Then add a word of your own that does belong. The first one has been done for you.

1. wren   robin   ~~feather~~
   sparrow   eagle   **bluebird**
2. sofa   stool   chair
   carpet   bench   _____
3. lettuce   salad   corn
   broccoli   spinach   _____
4. pencil   chalk   crayon
   pen   drawing   _____
5. perch   shark   penguin
   bass   tuna   _____
6. rapid   quick   unhurried
   swift   speedy   _____
7. lemon   daisy   melon
   lime   grapefruit   _____

Directions: Write a category name above each group of words. Then write a word of your own that belongs in each group.

_____   _____
blizzard   ankle
hurricane   shin
thunder   thigh

_____   _____

_____   _____
antenna   hockey
speaker   ice skating
battery   bobsledding

_____   _____

Total Basic Skills Grade 5   Reading

Classifying

Directions: Write three objects which could belong in each category.

1. whales _____ _____ _____
2. songs _____ _____ _____
3. sports stars _____ _____ _____
4. fruit _____ _____ _____
5. schools _____ _____ _____
6. teachers _____ _____ _____
7. tools _____ _____ _____
8. friends _____ _____ _____
9. books _____ _____ _____
10. mammals _____ _____ _____
11. fish _____ _____ _____
12. desserts _____ _____ _____
13. cars _____ _____ _____
14. hobbies _____ _____ _____
15. vegetables _____ _____ _____
16. insects _____ _____ _____

Reading

Analogies

An **analogy** is a way of comparing objects to show how they relate.

Example: Nose is to smell as tongue is to taste.

Directions: Write the correct word on the blank to fill in the missing part of each analogy. The first one has been done for you.

1. <u>Scissors</u> are to paper as saw is to wood.   fold   (scissors)   thin
2. Man is to boy as woman is to _____ .   mother   girl   lady
3. _____ is to cellar as sky is to ground.   down   attic   up
4. Rag is to dust as _____ is to sweep.   floor   straw   broom
5. Freezer is to cold as stove is to _____ .   cook   hot   recipe
6. Car is to _____ as book is to bookshelf.   ride   gas   garage
7. Window is to _____ as car is to metal.   glass   clear   house
8. Eyes are to seeing as feet are to _____ .   legs   walking   shoes
9. Gas is to car as _____ is to lamp.   electricity   plug   cord
10. Refrigerator is to food as _____ is to clothes.   fold   material   closet
11. Floor is to down as ceiling is to _____ .   high   over   up
12. Pillow is to soft as rock is to _____ .   dirt   hard   hurt
13. Carpenter is to house as poet is to _____ .   verse   novel   writing
14. Lamp is to light as clock is to _____ .   time   hands   numbers
15. _____ is to hand as sole is to foot.   wrist   finger   palm

Total Basic Skills Grade 5   Reading

Analogies

Directions: Write your own words on the blanks to complete each analogy. The first one has been done for you.

1. Fuse is to firecracker as wick is to __candle__ .
2. Wheel is to steering as _____ is to stopping.
3. Scissors are to _____ as needles are to sew.
4. Water is to skiing as rink is to _____ .
5. Steam shovel is to dig as tractor is to _____ .
6. Stick is to hockey as _____ is to baseball.
7. Watch is to television as _____ is to radio.
8. _____ are to goose as children are to child.
9. Multiply is to multiplication as _____ is to subtraction.
10. Milk is to cow as egg is to _____ .
11. Yellow is to banana as _____ is to tomato.
12. _____ is to slow as day is to night.
13. Pine is to tree as _____ is to flower.
14. Zipper is to jacket as _____ is to shirt.
15. Museum is to painting as library is to _____ .
16. Petal is to flower as branch is to _____ .
17. Cow is to barn as car is to _____ .
18. Dresser is to bedroom as _____ is to kitchen.
19. Teacher is to _____ as doctor is to patient.
20. Ice is to cold as fire is to _____ .

Reading

Total Basic Skills Grade 5

Facts and Opinions

A **fact** is information that can be proved.

Example: Hawaii is a state.

An **opinion** is a belief. It tells what someone thinks. It cannot be proved.

Example: Hawaii is the prettiest state.

Directions: Write **f** (fact) or **o** (opinion) on the line by each sentence. The first one has been done for you.

____f____ 1. Hawaii is the only island state.
_____ 2. The best fishing is in Michigan.
_____ 3. It is easy to find a job in Wyoming.
_____ 4. Trenton is the capital of New Jersey.
_____ 5. Kentucky is nicknamed the Bluegrass State.
_____ 6. The friendliest people in the United States live in Georgia.
_____ 7. The cleanest beaches are in California.
_____ 8. Summers are most beautiful in Arizona.
_____ 9. Only one percent of North Dakota is forest or woodland.
_____ 10. New Mexico produces almost half of the nation's uranium.
_____ 11. The first shots of the Civil War were fired in South Carolina on April 12, 1861.
_____ 12. The varied geographical features of Washington include mountains, deserts, a rainforest and a volcano.
_____ 13. In 1959, Alaska and Hawaii became the 49th and 50th states admitted to the Union.
_____ 14. Wyandotte Cave, one of the largest caves in the United States, is in Indiana.

Directions: Write one fact and one opinion about your own state.

Fact: _____

Opinion: _____

Total Basic Skills Grade 5   Reading

Facts and Opinions

A **fact** is a statement based on truth. It can be proven. **Opinions** are the beliefs of an individual that may or may not be true.

Examples:
   Fact: Alaska is a state.
   Opinion: Alaska is the most magnificent state.

Directions: Write **F** if the statement is a fact. Write **O** if the statement is an opinion.

1. _____ The Grand Canyon is the most scenic site in the United States.

2. _____ Dinosaurs roamed Earth millions of years ago.

3. _____ Scientists have discovered how to clone sheep.

4. _____ All people should attend this fair.

5. _____ Purebreds are the best dogs to own because they are intelligent.

6. _____ Nobody likes being bald.

7. _____ Students should be required to get straight A's to participate in extracurricular activities.

8. _____ Reading is an important skill that is vital in many careers.

9. _____ Snakes do not make good pets.

10. _____ Many books have been written about animals.

11. _____ Thomas Edison invented the lightbulb.

12. _____ Most people like to read science fiction.

13. _____ Insects have three body parts.

Cause and Effect

A **cause** is an event or reason which has an effect on something else.

Example:
The heavy rains produced flooding in Chicago.
Heavy rains were the **cause** of the flooding in Chicago.

An **effect** is an event that results from a cause.

Example:
Flooding in Chicago was due to the heavy rains.
Flooding was the **effect** caused by the heavy rains.

Directions: Read the paragraphs. Complete the charts by writing the missing cause (reason) or effect (result).

Club-footed toads are small toads that live in the rainforests of Central and South America. Because they give off a poisonous substance on their skins, other animals cannot eat them.

Cause:
They give off a poisonous substance.

Effect:
_____

Civets (siv its) are weasel-like animals. The best known of the civets is the mongoose, which eats rats and snakes. For this reason, it is welcome around homes in its native India.

Cause:
_____

Effect:
It is welcome around homes in its native India.

Bluebirds can be found in most areas of the United States. Like other members of the thrush family of birds, young bluebirds have speckled breasts. This makes them difficult to see and helps them hide from their enemies. The Pilgrims called them "blue robins" because they are much like the English robin. They are the same size and have the same red breast and friendly song as the English robin.

Cause:
Young bluebirds have speckled breasts.

_____

Effect:
_____

The Pilgrims called them "blue robins."

Main Idea

The **main idea** is the most important idea, or main point, in a sentence, paragraph or story.

Directions: Read the paragraphs below. For each paragraph, underline the sentence that tells the main idea.

Sometimes people think they have to choose between exercise and fun. For many people, it is more fun to watch television than to run 5 miles. Yet, if you don't exercise, your body gets soft and out of shape. You move more slowly. You may even think more slowly. But why do something that isn't fun? Well, there are many ways to exercise and have fun.

One family solved the exercise problem by using their TV. They hooked up the television to an electric generator. The generator was operated by an exercise bike. Anyone who wanted to watch TV had to ride the bike. The room with their television in it must have been quite a sight!

Think of the times when you are just "hanging out" with your friends. You go outside and jump rope, play ball, run races, and so on. Soon you are all laughing and having a good time. Many group activities can provide you with exercise and be fun, too.

Maybe there aren't enough kids around after school for group games. Perhaps you are by yourself. Then what? You can get plenty of exercise just by walking, biking or even dancing. In the morning, walk the long way to the bus. Ride your bike to and from school. Practice the newest dance by yourself. Before you know it, you will be the fittest dancer of all your friends!

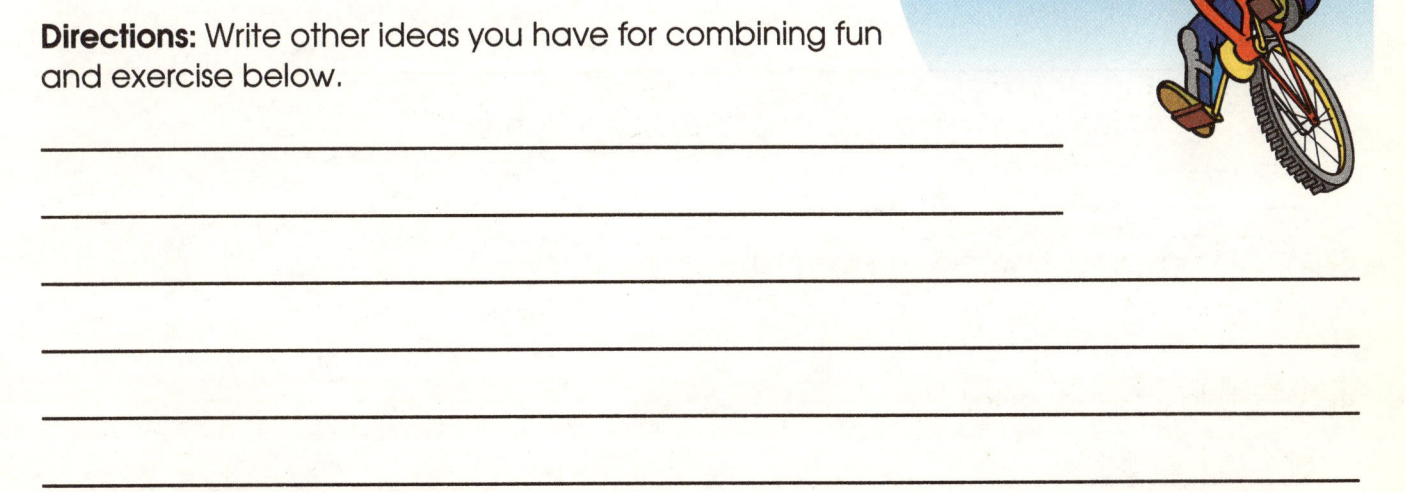

Directions: Write other ideas you have for combining fun and exercise below.

_____

_____

_____

_____

_____

_____

Reading Skills: Skimming

Skimming an article means to read quickly, looking for headings and key words to give an overall idea of the content of an article or to find a particular fact. When skimming for answers, read the questions first. Then look for specific words that will help locate the answers.

Directions: Skim the paragraph to answer this question.

1. What "marvel" is the paragraph about? _____

   In America, there is so much magnificent scenery. Perhaps the most stunning sight of all is the Grand Canyon. This canyon is in northern Arizona. It is the deepest, widest canyon on Earth. The Grand Canyon is 217 miles long, 4 to 18 miles wide and, in some places, more than a mile deep. The rocks at the bottom of the steep walls are at least 500 million years old. Most of the rocks are sandstone, limestone and shale. By studying these rocks, scientists know that this part of the world was once under the sea.

Directions: Skim the paragraph again to find the answers to these questions.

1. How deep are the lowest points in the Grand Canyon?

   _____

2. How old are the rocks at the bottom of the Grand Canyon?

   _____

3. What kinds of rocks would you find in the Grand Canyon?

   _____

4. What do these rocks tell us?

   _____

Total Basic Skills Grade 5 Reading

Reading Skills: Maps

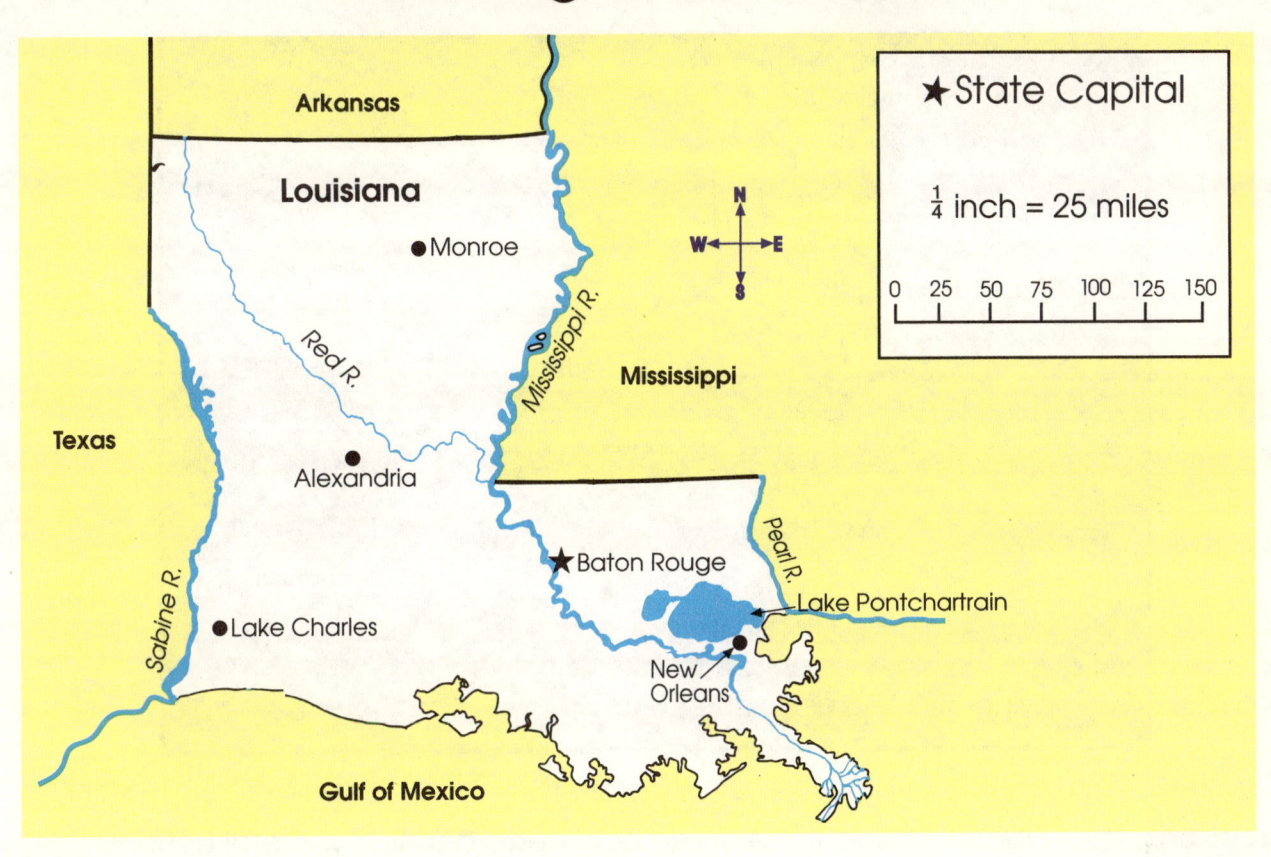

Directions: Use this map to answer the questions.

1. What state borders Louisiana to the north?

2. What is the state capital of Louisiana?

3. What cities are located near Lake Pontchartrain?

4. In which direction would you be traveling if you drove from Monroe to Alexandria?

5. About how far is it from Alexandria to Lake Charles?

6. Besides Arkansas, name one other state that borders Louisiana.

Following Directions: Continents

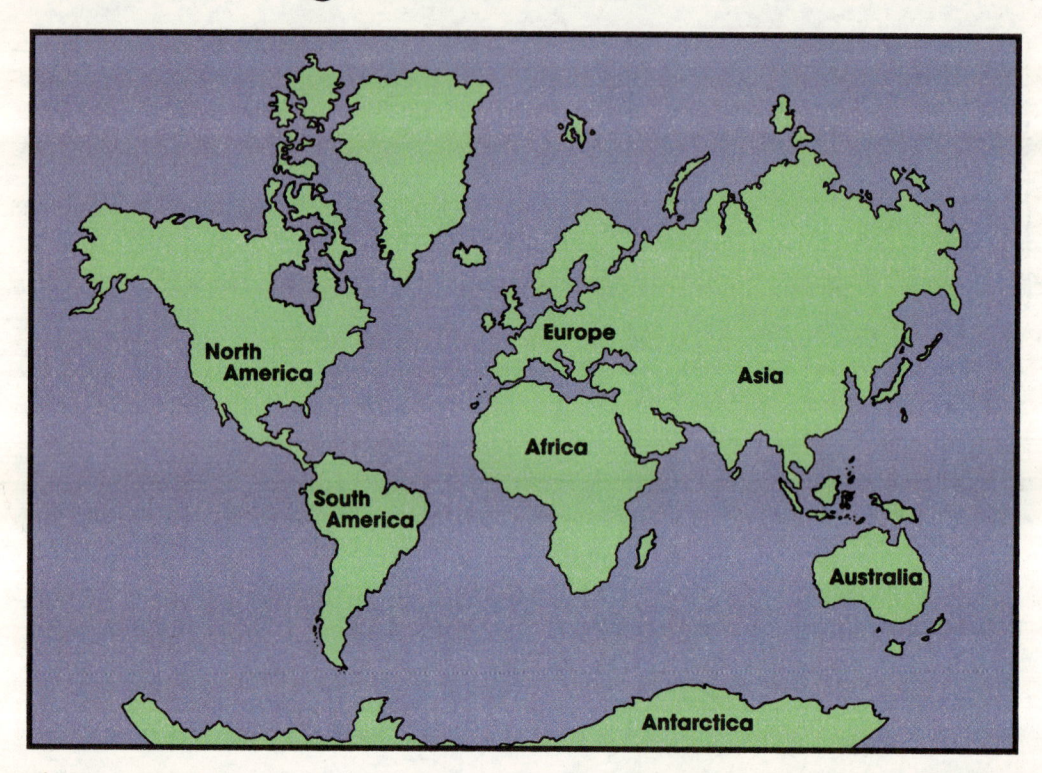

Directions: Read the facts about the seven continents and follow the directions.

1. Asia is the largest continent. It has the largest land mass and the largest population. Draw a star on Asia.
2. Africa is the second largest continent. Write a **2** on Africa.
3. Australia is the smallest continent in area: 3 million square miles, compared to 17 million square miles for Asia. Write **3,000,000** on Australia.
4. Australia is not a very crowded continent, but it does not rank lowest in population. That honor goes to Antarctica, which has no permanent population at all! This ice-covered continent is too cold for life. Write **zero** on Antarctica.
5. Australia and Antarctica are the only continents entirely separated by water. Draw circles around Australia and Antarctica.
6. North America and South America are joined together by a narrow strip of land. It is called Central America. Write an **N** on North America, an **S** on South America and a **C** on Central America.
7. Asia and Europe are joined together over such a great distance that they are sometimes called one continent. The name given to it is Eurasia. Draw lines under the names of the two continents in Eurasia.

Reading a Recipe

Directions: Read the recipe. Then answer the questions.

Graham Cracker Smoothies

Graham crackers

Icing:
  2 T. peanut butter
  2 T. butter
  2 c. powdered sugar
  milk

Break graham crackers in half. Mix peanut butter, butter and powdered sugar with a spoon. Add enough milk to make creamy icing. Stir vigorously until no lumps remain. Spread on graham cracker half and top with another graham cracker half, sandwich style. Enjoy!
The smoothie icing will keep in the refrigerator for two days.

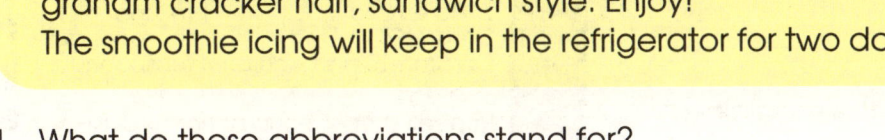

1. What do these abbreviations stand for?

   T. _____

   c. _____

2. Number the steps in the correct order.

   ___ Spread icing on graham crackers.

   ___ Add milk and stir until creamy.

   ___ Break graham crackers in half.

   ___ Eat and enjoy.

   ___ Mix the peanut butter, butter and powdered sugar together.

3. Why is it important to follow the correct sequence when cooking?

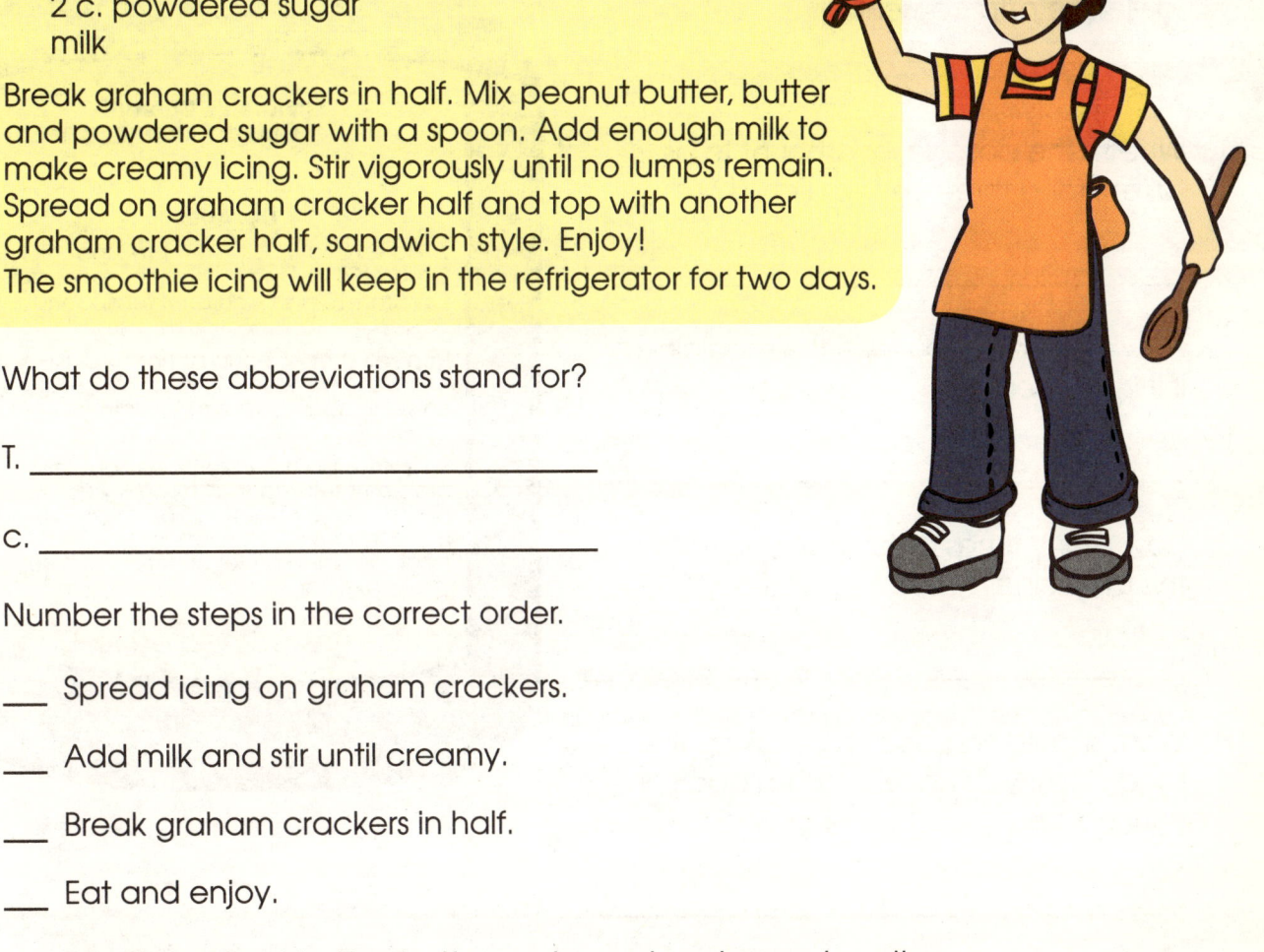

   _____

Reading Skills: Labels

Labels provide information about products.

Directions: Read the label on the medicine bottle. Answer the questions.

Remember: Children should never take medicines without their parents' knowledge and consent.

1. What is the dosage, or amount to be taken, for a three-year-old child?

   _____

2. How often can you take this medicine if it is needed?

   _____

3. How many times a day can you take this medicine?

   _____

4. What should you do before taking the medicine if you have a rash in addition to your cough?

   _____

5. Will this medicine help you if you are sneezing?

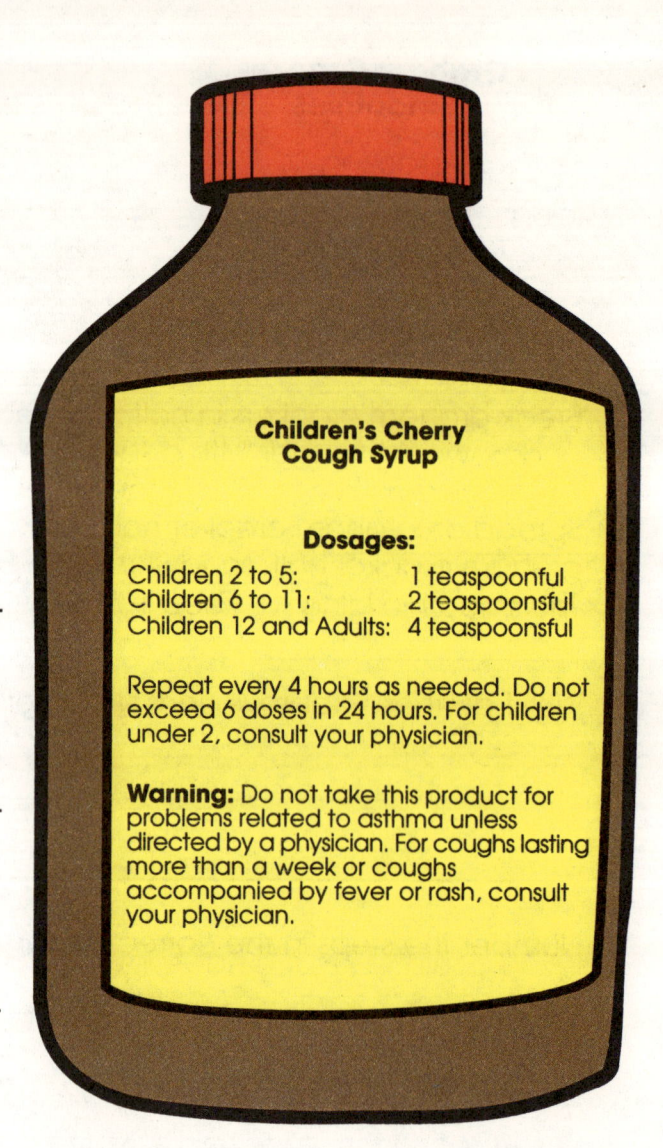

   _____

6. What is the dosage for an adult?

   _____

Children's Cherry Cough Syrup

Dosages:

Children 2 to 5: 1 teaspoonful
Children 6 to 11: 2 teaspoonsful
Children 12 and Adults: 4 teaspoonsful

Repeat every 4 hours as needed. Do not exceed 6 doses in 24 hours. For children under 2, consult your physician.

Warning: Do not take this product for problems related to asthma unless directed by a physician. For coughs lasting more than a week or coughs accompanied by fever or rash, consult your physician.

Reading Skills: Newspapers

Directions: Write the answers.

1. What is the name of your daily local newspaper?
   _____

2. List the sections included in your local newspaper.
   _____

3. What sections of the newspaper do you read on a regular basis?
   _____

4. Ask a parent which sections he or she reads on a regular basis.
   _____

5. Find the editorial section of your newspaper. An editorial is the opinion of one person. Write the main idea of one editorial. _____
   _____
   _____
   _____

6. If you could work at a newspaper, which job would you like? Why?
   _____
   _____
   _____

Directions: Read a copy of *USA Today*. You can find a copy in most libraries. Compare it to your local paper.

7. How are they alike? _____
   _____

8. How are they different? _____
   _____

Reading Skills: Schedules

A **schedule** lists events or programs by time, date and place or channel.
Example:

Packer Preseason Games

August 14	7 P.M.	NY Jets at Green Bay
August 23	7 P.M.	Denver Broncos at Madison
August 28	3 P.M.	Saints at New Orleans
September 2	Noon	Miami Dolphins at Green Bay

Directions: Use this newspaper television schedule to answer the questions.

Evening
- 6:00
  - 3 Let's Talk! Guest: Animal expert Jim Porter
  - 5 Cartoons
  - 8 News
  - 9 News
- 7:00
  - 3 Farm Report
  - 5 Movie. *A Laugh a Minute* (1955) James Rayburn. Comedy about a boy who wants to join the circus.
  - 8 Spin for Dollars!
  - 9 Cooking with Cathy. Tonight: Chicken with mushrooms
- 7:30
  - 3 Double Trouble (comedy). The twins disrupt the high school dance.
  - 8 Wall Street Today: Stock Market Report
- 8:00
  - 3 NBA Basketball. Teams to be announced.
  - 8 News Special. "Saving Our Waterways: Pollution in the Mississippi."
  - 9 Movie. *At Day's End* (1981). Michael Collier, Julie Romer. Drama set in World War II.

1. What two stations have the news at 6:00? _____
2. What time would you turn on the television to watch a funny movie? _____
   What channel? _____
3. What could you watch if you are a sports fan? _____
   What time and channel is it on? _____
4. Which show title sounds like it could be a game show? _____
5. What show might you want to watch if you are interested in the environment?
   _____
   What time and channel is it on? _____

Context Clues: Remember Who You Are

Directions: Read each paragraph. Then use context clues to figure out the meanings of the bold words.

During the 1940s, Esther Hautzig lived in the town of Vilna, which was then part of Poland. Shortly after the **outbreak** of World War II, she and her family were **deported** to Siberia by Russian communists who hated Jews. She told what happened to her and other Polish Jews in a book. The book is called *Remember Who You Are: Stories About Being Jewish*.

1. Choose the correct definition of **deported**.

    ☐ sent away   ☐ asked to go   ☐ invited to visit

2. Choose the correct definition of **outbreak**.

    ☐ a sudden occurrence   ☐ to leave suddenly

Remember Who You Are: Stories About Being Jewish is a nonfiction book that tells true stories. An interesting **fiction** book is *Leave the Cooking to Me* by Judie Angell. It tells the story of a girl named Shirley, who learns about cooking from her best friend's mother. Shirley gets very good at making fancy food. Most young people have a hard time finding jobs that pay well, but Shirley's cooking skills help her land a **lucrative** summer job.

3. Choose the correct definition of **fiction**.

    ☐ stories that are true   ☐ stories that are not true

4. Choose the correct definition of **lucrative**.

    ☐ interesting   ☐ profitable   ☐ nearby

Context Clues: Kids' Books Are Big Business

Between 1978 and 1988, the number of children's books published in the United States doubled. The publishing industry, which prints, promotes and sells books, does not usually move this fast. Why? Because if publishers print too many books that don't sell, they lose money. They like to wait, if they can, to see what the "public demand" is for certain types of books. Then they accept manuscripts from writers who have written the types of books the public seems to want. More than 4,600 children's books were published in 1988, because publishers thought they could sell that many titles. Many copies of each title were printed and sold to bookstores and libraries. The publishers made good profits and, since then, the number of children's books published each year has continued to grow.

The title of a recent new book for children is *The Wild Horses of Sweetbriar* by Natalie Kinsey-Warnock. It is the story of a girl and a band of wild horses that lived on an island off the coast of Massachusetts in 1903. The story sounds very exciting! Wild horses can be quite dangerous. The plot of *The Wild Horses of Sweetbriar* is probably filled with danger and suspense.

Directions: Answer these questions about how interest in writing, reading and selling children's books has grown.

1. Use context clues to choose the correct definition of **industry**.

   ☐ booksellers   ☐ writers   ☐ entire business

2. If 4,600 books were sold in 1988, how many books were sold in 1978? _____

3. The number of children's books published in the United States doubled between 1978 and 1988.   Fact   Opinion

4. *The Wild Horses of Sweetbriar* is the story of a girl and a band of wild horses that lived on an island in 1903.   Fact   Opinion

5. The story sounds very exciting!   Fact   Opinion

6. The plot of *The Wild Horses of Sweetbriar* is probably filled with danger and suspense.   Fact   Opinion

READING COMPREHENSION

Using Prior Knowledge: Music

Using **prior knowledge** means being able to use what one already knows to find an answer or get information.

Directions: Before reading about music in the following section, answer these questions.

1. In your opinion, why is music important to people?
   _____
   _____
   _____

2. Name as many styles of music as you can.
   _____
   _____
   _____

3. What is your favorite type of music? Why?
   _____
   _____
   _____

4. If you could choose a musical instrument to play, what would it be? Why?
   _____
   _____
   _____

5. Name a famous musician and describe what you know about him/her.
   _____
   _____
   _____
   _____

Main Idea: Where Did Songs Come From?

Historians say the earliest music was probably connected to religion. Long ago, people believed the world was controlled by a variety of gods. Singing was among the first things humans did to show respect to the gods.

Singing is still an important part of most religions. Buddhists (bood-ists), Christians and Jews all use chants and/or songs in their religious ceremonies. If you have ever sung a song—religious or otherwise—you know that singing is fun. The feeling of joy that comes from singing must also have made ancient people feel happy.

Another time people sang was when they worked. Egyptian slaves sang as they carried the heavy stones to build the pyramids. Soldiers sang as they marched into battle. Farmers sang one song as they planted and another when they harvested. Singing made the work less burdensome. People used the tunes to pace themselves. Sometimes they followed instructions through songs. For example, "Yo-oh, heave ho!/Yo-oh, heave ho!" was sung when sailors pulled on a ship's ropes to lift the sails. **Heave** means "to lift," and that is what they did as they sang the song. The song helped sailors work together and pull at the same time. This made the task easier.

Directions: Answer these questions about music.

1. Circle the main idea:

    Singing is fun, and that is why early people liked it so much.

    Singing began as a way to show respect to the gods and is still an important part of most religious ceremonies.

    Traditionally, singing has been important as a part of religious ceremonies and as inspiration to workers.

2. Besides religious ceremonies, what other activity fostered singing? _____

    _____

3. When did farmers sing two different songs? _____

4. How did singing "Yo-oh, heave ho!" help sailors work? _____

    _____

Comprehension: Facts About Folk Music

Folk music literally means music "of the folks," and it belongs to everyone. The names of the musicians who composed most folk music have long been forgotten. Even so, folk music has remained popular because it tells about the lives of people. Usually, the tune is simple, and even though folk songs often have many verses, the words are easy to remember. Do you know the words to "She'll Be Comin' 'Round the Mountain"?

Although no one ever says who "she" is, the verses tell you that she will be "riding six white horses" and that "we'll go out to greet her." The song also describes what will be eaten when she comes (chicken and dumplings) and what those singing will be wearing (red pajamas).

"Clementine" is a song that came out of the California gold rush in the mid-1800s. It tells the story of a woman who was "lost and gone forever" when she was killed. ("In a cavern, in a canyon, excavating for a mine/Met a miner '49er and his daughter, Clementine.")

Another famous folk song is "Swing Low, Sweet Chariot." This song was sung by slaves in the United States and today is sung by people of all races. The words "Swing low, sweet chariot, coming for to carry me home . . ." describe the soul being united with God after death. Like other folk songs that sprang from slaves, "Swing Low, Sweet Chariot" is simple, moving and powerful.

Directions: Answer these questions about folk music.

1. What is the purpose of folk music? _____
_____

2. What food is sung about in "She'll Be Comin' 'Round the Mountain"? _____
_____

3. Where did Clementine live?

    ☐ Florida   ☐ Mississippi   ☐ California

4. Where in the United States do you think "Swing Low, Sweet Chariot" was first sung?

    ☐ the North   ☐ the West   ☐ the South

Recalling Details: Woodwinds

There are four kinds of woodwind instruments in modern bands. They are flutes, oboes, clarinets and bassoons. They are called "woodwind" instruments for two sensible reasons. In the beginning, they were all made of wood. Also, the musician's breath, or "wind," was required to play them.

Although they are all woodwinds, these instruments look different and are played differently. To play an oboe, the musician blows through a mouthpiece on the front of the instrument. The mouthpiece, called a reed, is made of two flat pieces of a kind of wood called cane. Clarinet players also blow into a reed mouthpiece. The clarinet has only one reed in its mouthpiece.

To play the flute, the musician blows across a hole near one end of the instrument. The way the breath is aimed helps to make the flute's different sounds. The bassoon is the largest woodwind instrument. Bassoon players blow through a mouthpiece that goes through a short metal pipe before it goes into the body of the bassoon. It makes a very different sound from the clarinet or the oboe.

Woodwind instruments also have keys—but not the kind of keys that open locks. These keys are more like levers that the musician pushes up and down. The levers cover holes. When the musician pushes down on a lever, it closes that hole. When he/she lifts his/her finger, it opens the hole. Different sounds are produced by controlling the amount of breath, or "wind," that goes through the holes.

Directions: Answer these questions about woodwind instruments.

1. What instruments are in the woodwind section? _____

2. Why are some instruments called woodwinds? _____

3. How is a flute different from the other woodwinds? _____

4. What happens when a musician pushes down on a woodwind key? _____

5. How would a woodwind musician open the holes on his/her instrument?
_____

Comprehension: Harp Happenings

If you have ever heard a harpist play, you know what a lovely sound a harp makes. Music experts say the harp is among the oldest of instruments. It probably was invented several thousand years ago in or near Egypt.

The first harps are believed to have been made by stretching a string tightly between an empty tortoise shell and a curved pole. The empty shell magnified the sound the string made when it was plucked. More strings were added later so that more sounds could be made. Over the centuries, the shape of the harp gradually was changed into that of the large, graceful instruments we recognize today.

Here is how a harpist plays a harp. First, he/she leans the harp against his/her right shoulder. Then, the harpist puts his/her hands on either side of the harp and plucks its strings with both hands.

A harp has seven pedals on the bottom back. The audience usually cannot see these pedals. Most people are surprised to learn about them. The pedals are connected to the strings. Stepping on a particular pedal causes certain strings to tighten. The tightening and loosening of the strings makes different sounds; so does the way the strings are plucked with the hands.

At first glance, harps look like simple instruments. Actually, they are rather complicated and difficult to keep in tune. A harpist often spends as long as half an hour before a performance tuning his/her harp's strings so it produces the correct sounds.

Directions: Answer these questions about harps.

1. When were harps invented? _____

2. Where were harps invented? _____

3. What is a person called who plays the harp? _____

4. The harpist leans the harp against his/her
   ☐ right shoulder.   ☐ left shoulder.   ☐ left knee.

5. How many pedals does a harp have?
   ☐ five   ☐ six   ☐ seven

6. Harps are easy to play.
   ☐ yes   ☐ no

Comprehension: Brass Shows Class

If you like band music, you probably love the music made by brass instruments. Bright, loud, moving and magnificent—all these words describe the sounds made by brass.

Some of the earliest instruments were horns. Made from hollowed-out animal horns, these primitive instruments could not possibly have made the rich sounds of modern horns that are made of brass.

Most modern brass bands have three instruments—tubas, trombones and trumpets. Combined, these instruments can produce stirring marches, as well as haunting melodies.

The most famous composer for brass instruments was John Phillip Sousa. Born in Washington, D.C., in 1854, Sousa was a military band conductor and composer. He died in 1932, but his music is still very popular today. One of Sousa's most famous tunes for military bands is "Stars and Stripes Forever."

Besides composing band music, Sousa also invented a practical band instrument—the sousaphone. The sousaphone is a huge tuba that makes very low noises. Because of the way it curls around the body, a sousaphone is easier to carry than a tuba, especially when the musician must march. This is exactly why John Phillip Sousa invented it!

Directions: Answer these questions about brass instruments.

1. Who invented the sousaphone? _____

2. What were the first horns made from? _____

3. Where was John Phillip Sousa born? _____

4. When did John Phillip Sousa die? _____

5. Why did Sousa invent the sousaphone? _____

_____

6. What types of instruments make up a modern brass band? _____

_____

Comprehension: Violins

If you know anything about violin music, chances are you have heard the word **Stradivarius** (Strad-uh-vary-us). Stradivarius is the name for the world's most magnificent violins. They are named after their creator, Antonio Stradivari.

Stradivari was born in northern Italy and lived from 1644 to 1737. Cremona, the town he lived in, was a place where violins were manufactured. Stradivari was very young when he learned to play the violin. He grew to love the instrument so much that he began to make them himself.

Violins were new instruments during Stradivari's time. People made them in different sizes and shapes and of different types of wood. Stradivari is said to have been very particular about the wood he selected for his violins. He took long walks alone in the forest to find just the right tree. He is also said to have used a secret and special type of varnish to put on the wood. Whatever the reasons, his violins are the best in the world.

Stradivari put such care and love into his violins that they are still used today. Many of these are in museums. But some wealthy musicians, who can afford the thousands and thousands of dollars they cost, own Stradivarius violins.

Stradivari passed his methods on to his sons. But the secrets of making Stradivarius violins seem to have died out with the family. Their rarity, as well as their mellow sound, make Stradivarius violins among the most prized instruments in the world.

Directions: Answer these questions about Stradivarius violins.

1. Where did Stradivari live? _____

2. Why did he begin making violins? _____

3. Why are Stradivarius violins special? _____
_____

4. Where can Stradivarius violins be found today? _____
_____

5. How did Stradivari select the wood for his violins? _____
_____

6. Who else knew Stradivari's secrets for making such superior violins? ____

Using Prior Knowledge: Art

Directions: Before reading about art in the following section, answer these questions.

1. Write a short paragraph about a famous artist of your choice.

   _____
   _____
   _____

2. Many artists paint realistic scenes. Other artists paint imaginary scenes. Which do you prefer? Why?

   _____
   _____

3. Although we often think of art as painting and drawing, art also includes sculpture, fabric weavings and metalwork. Are you talented at a particular type of art? If so, what type? If not, what would you like to learn?

   _____
   _____
   _____

4. Why are art museums important to society?

   _____
   _____
   _____

5. Why do you think some artwork is worth so much money? Would you pay several thousand dollars for a piece of artwork? Why or why not?

   _____
   _____
   _____

Reading Comprehension   Total Basic Skills Grade 5

Main Idea: Creating Art

No one knows exactly when the first human created the first painting. Crude drawings and paintings on the walls of caves show that humans have probably always expressed themselves through art. These early cave pictures show animals being hunted, people dancing and other events of daily life. The simplicity of the paintings reflect the simple lifestyles of these primitive people.

The subjects of early paintings also help to make another important point. Art is not created out of nothing. The subjects an artist chooses to paint reflect the history, politics and culture of the time and place in which he/she lives. An artist born and raised in New York City, for example, is not likely to paint scenes of the Rocky Mountains. An artist living in the Rockies is not likely to paint pictures of city life.

Of course, not all paintings are realistic. Many artists choose to paint pictures that show their own "inner vision" as opposed to what they see with their eyes. Many religious paintings of earlier centuries look realistic but contain figures of angels. These paintings combine the artist's inner vision of angels with other things, such as church buildings, that can be seen.

Directions: Answer these questions about creating art.

1. Circle the main idea:

   Art was important to primitive people because it showed hunting and dancing scenes, and is still important today.

   Through the ages, artists have created paintings that reflect the culture, history and politics of the times, as well as their own inner visions.

2. Why is an artist living in the Rocky Mountains less likely to paint city scenes?

   _____

   _____

3. In addition to what they see with their eyes, what do some artists' paintings also show?

   _____

   _____

Comprehension: Leonardo da Vinci

Many people believe that Leonardo da Vinci, an Italian artist and inventor who lived from 1452 to 1519, was the most brilliant person ever born. He was certainly a man ahead of his time! Records show that da Vinci loved the earth and was curious about everything on it.

To learn about the human body, he dissected corpses to find out what was inside. In the 15th and 16th centuries, dissecting the dead was against the laws of the Catholic church. Leonardo was a brave man!

He was also an inventor. Leonardo invented a parachute and designed a type of helicopter—5 centuries before airplanes were invented! Another of da Vinci's major talents was painting. You have probably seen a print, or copy, of one of his most famous paintings. It is called *The Last Supper*, and shows Jesus eating his final meal with his disciples. It took da Vinci 3 years to paint *The Last Supper*. The man who hired da Vinci to do the painting was upset. He went to da Vinci to ask why it was taking so long. The problem, said da Vinci, was that in the painting, Jesus has just told the disciples that one of them would betray him. He wanted to get their expressions exactly right as each cried out, "Lord, am I the one?"

Another famous painting by da Vinci is called the *Mona Lisa*. Have you seen a print of this painting? Maybe you have been lucky enough to see the original hanging in a Paris art museum called the Louvre (Loov). If so, you know that Mona Lisa has a wistful expression on her face. The painting is a real woman, the wife of an Italian merchant. Art historians believe she looks wistful because one of her children had recently died.

Directions: Answer these questions about Leonardo da Vinci.

1. How old was da Vinci when he died? _____

2. Name two of da Vinci's inventions. _____

3. Name two famous paintings by da Vinci. _____

4. In which Paris museum does *Mona Lisa* hang? ☐ Lourre ☐ Loure ☐ Louvre

Context Clues: Leonardo da Vinci

Directions: Read the sentences below. Use context clues to figure out the meaning of the bold words.

1. Some people are **perplexed** when they look at *The Last Supper*, but others understand it immediately.

    ☐ unhappy ☐ happy ☐ puzzled

2. Because his model felt **melancholy** about the death of her child, da Vinci had music played to lift her spirits as he painted the *Mona Lisa*.

    ☐ sad ☐ unfriendly ☐ hostile

3. Because da Vinci's work is so famous, many people **erroneously** assume that he left behind many paintings. In fact, he left only 20.

    ☐ rightly ☐ correctly ☐ wrongly

4. Leonardo da Vinci was not like most other people. He didn't care what others thought of him—he led an interesting and **unconventional** life.

    ☐ dull ☐ not ordinary ☐ ordinary

5. The **composition** of *The Last Supper* is superb. All the parts of the painting seem to fit together beautifully.

    ☐ the picture frame ☐ parts of the picture

6. Leonardo's **genius** set him apart from people with ordinary minds. He never married, he had few friends and he spent much of his time alone.

    ☐ great mental abilities ☐ great physical abilities
    ☐ improper way to do things ☐ proper way to do things

7. Because he was a loner, da Vinci worried no one would come to his funeral when he died. In his will, he set aside 70 cents each to hire 60 **mourners** to accompany his body to his grave.

    ☐ friends ☐ people who grieve ☐ people who smile

Comprehension: Michelangelo

Another famous painter of the late 14th and early 15th centuries was Michelangelo Buonarroti. Michelangelo, who lived from 1475 to 1564, was also an Italian. Like da Vinci, his genius was apparent at a young age. When he was 13, the ruler of his hometown of Florence, Lorenzo Medici (Muh-dee-chee), befriended Michelangelo and asked him to live in the palace. There Michelangelo studied sculpture and met many artists.

By the time he was 18, Michelangelo was a respected sculptor. He created one of his most famous religious sculptures, the *Pieta* (pee-ay-tah), when he was only 21. Then the Medici family abruptly fell from power and Michelangelo had to leave Florence.

Still, his work was well known and he was able to make a living. In 1503, Pope Julius II called Michelangelo to Rome. He wanted Michelangelo to paint the tomb where he would someday be buried. Michelangelo preferred sculpting to painting, but no one turned down the pope! Before Michelangelo finished his painting, however, the pope ordered Michelangelo to begin painting the ceiling of the Sistine Chapel inside the Vatican. (The Vatican is the palace and surrounding area where the pope lives in Rome.)

Michelangelo was very angry! He did not like to paint. He wanted to create sculptures. But no one turns down the pope. After much complaining, Michelangelo began work on what would be his most famous project.

Directions: Answer these questions about Michelangelo.

1. How old was Michelangelo when he died? _____

2. What was the first project Pope Julius II asked Michelangelo to paint?

   _____

3. What is the Vatican? _____

4. What was the second project the pope asked Michelangelo to do?

   ☐ paint his tomb's ceiling   ☐ paint the Sistine Chapel's ceiling

Comprehension: Rembrandt

Most art critics agree that Rembrandt (Rem-brant) was one of the greatest painters of all time. This Dutch artist, who lived from 1606 to 1669, painted some of the world's finest portraits.

Rembrandt, whose full name was Rembrandt van Rijn, was born in Holland to a wealthy family. He was sent to a fine university, but he did not like his studies. He only wanted to paint. He sketched the faces of people around him. During his lifetime, Rembrandt painted 11 portraits of his father and nearly as many of his mother. From the beginning, the faces of old people fascinated him.

When he was 25, Rembrandt went to paint in Amsterdam, a large city in Holland where he lived for the rest of his life. There he married a wealthy woman named Saskia, whom he loved deeply. She died from a disease called tuberculosis (ta-bur-ku-lo-sis) after only 8 years, leaving behind a young son named Titus (Ty-tuss).

Rembrandt was heartbroken over his wife's death. He began to spend all his time painting. But instead of painting what his customers wanted, he painted exactly the way he wanted. Unsold pictures filled his house. They were wonderful paintings, but they were not the type of portraits people wanted. Rembrandt could not pay his debts. He and his son were thrown into the streets. The creditors took his home, his possessions and his paintings. One of the finest painters on Earth was treated like a criminal.

Directions: Answer these questions about Rembrandt.

1. How old was Rembrandt when he died? _____

2. In what city did he spend most of his life? _____

3. How many children did Rembrandt have? _____

4. Rembrandt's wife was named

    ☐ Sasha.   ☐ Saskia.   ☐ Saksia.

5. These filled his house after his wife's death.

    ☐ friends   ☐ customers   ☐ unsold paintings

Using Prior Knowledge: Big Cats

Directions: Before reading about big cats in the following section, answer these questions.

1. Name at least four big wild cats.

   _____   _____

   _____   _____

2. Compare and contrast a house cat with a wild cat.

   _____

   _____

   _____

   _____

3. What impact might the expansion of human population and housing have on big cats?

   _____

   _____

   _____

4. Do you have a cat? What are the special qualities of this pet? Write about your cat's name and its personality traits. If you don't have a cat, write about a cat you would like to have.

   _____

   _____

   _____

   _____

Comprehension: Jaguars

The jaguar is a large cat, standing up to 2 feet tall at the shoulder. Its body can reach 73 inches long, and the tail can be another 30 inches long. The jaguar is characterized by its yellowish-red coat covered with black spots. The spots themselves are made up of a central spot surrounded by a circle of spots.

Jaguars are not known to attack humans, but some ranchers claim that jaguars attack their cattle. This claim has given jaguars a bad reputation.

The jaguar can be found in southern North America, but is most populous in Central and South America. Jaguars are capable climbers and swimmers, and they eat a wide range of animals.

Female jaguars have between one and four cubs after a gestation of 93 to 105 days. Cubs stay with the mother for 2 years. Jaguars are known to have a life expectancy of at least 22 years.

Directions: Use context clues for these definitions.

1. populous: _____

2. reputation: _____

3. gestation: _____

Directions: Answer these questions about jaguars.

4. Describe the spots on a jaguar's coat.

   _____

   _____

5. Why would it be to a jaguar's advantage to have spots on its coat?

   _____

   _____

Comprehension: Leopards

The leopard is a talented nocturnal hunter and can see very well in the dark. Because of its excellent climbing ability, the leopard is able to stalk and kill monkeys and baboons. Leopards are also known to consume mice, porcupines and fruit.

Although the true leopard is characterized by a light beige coat with black spots, some leopards can be entirely black. These leopards are called black panthers. Many people refer to other cat species as leopards. Cheetahs are sometimes referred to as hunting leopards. The clouded leopard lives in southeastern Asia and has a grayish spotted coat. The snow leopard, which has a white coat, lives in Central Asia. A leopard's spots help to camouflage (cam-o-floj) it as it hunts.

True leopards can grow to over 6 feet long, not including their 3-foot-long tail. Leopards can be found in Africa and Asia.

Directions: Use context clues for these definitions.

1. consume: _____

2. ability: _____

3. nocturnal: _____

Directions: Answer these questions about leopards.

4. List three differences between the leopard and the jaguar.

_____
_____
_____
_____
_____
_____

5. What makes a leopard able to hunt monkeys and baboons?

_____

Comprehension: Lynxes

Lynxes are strange-looking cats with very long legs and large paws. Their bodies are a mere 51 inches in length, and they have short little tails. Most lynxes have a clump of hair that extends past the tip of their ears.

Lynxes not only are known to chase down their prey, but also to leap on them from a perch above the ground. They eat small mammals and birds, as well as an occasional deer.

There are four types of lynxes. Bobcats can be found in all areas of the United States except the Midwest. The Spanish lynx is an endangered species. The Eurasian lynx, also known as the northern lynx, and the Canadian lynx are two other kinds of lynxes.

Directions: Use context clues for these definitions.

1. prey: _____

2. perch: _____

Directions: Answer these questions about lynxes.

3. What are the four types of lynxes? _____
_____

4. Use the following words in a sentence of your own.

   mammal _____

   endangered _____

5. Do you believe it is important to classify animals as "endangered" to protect a species that is low in population? Explain your answer.

_____

_____

_____

Total Basic Skills Grade 5   Reading Comprehension

Comprehension: Pumas

The puma is a cat most recognized by the more popular names of "cougar" or "mountain lion." Just like other large cats, the puma is a carnivore. It feeds on deer, elk and other mammals. It can be found in both North and South America.

Pumas have small heads with a single black spot above each eye. The coat color ranges from bluish-gray (North America) to reddish-brown (South America). The underside of the body, as well as the throat and muzzle, are white. The puma's body can be almost 6 feet long, not including the tail.

Female pumas give birth to two to four young. When first born, pumas have brown spots on their backs, and their tails are lined with dark brown rings.

As with the jaguar, pumas are blamed for killing cattle. Because of this, pumas are either nonexistent in some areas or are endangered.

Directions: Answer these questions about pumas.

1. What is a muzzle? _____

2. As the population increases in North America, predict what might happen to pumas.

    _____

    _____

    _____

3. What are two other popular names for the puma? _____

4. What other cat besides the puma is blamed for killing cattle? _____

5. Reviewing the sizes of cats discussed so far, write their names in order, from smallest to largest.

    1) _____   2) _____

    3) _____   4) _____

Reading Comprehension   71   Total Basic Skills Grade 5

Comprehension: Tigers

Tigers live on the continent of Asia. The tiger is the largest cat, often weighing over 500 pounds. Its body can grow to be 9 feet long and the tail up to 36 inches in length.

There are three types of tigers. The Siberian tiger is very rare and has a yellow coat with dark stripes. The Bengal tiger can be found in southeastern Asia and central India. Its coat is more orange and its stripes are darker. There is a tiger that lives on the island of Sumatra as well. It is smaller and darker in color than the Bengal tiger.

Tigers lead solitary lives. They meet with other tigers only to mate and share food or water. Tigers feed primarily on deer and cattle but are also known to eat fish and frogs. If necessary, tigers will also eat dead animals.

Female tigers bear one to six cubs at a time. The cubs stay with their mother for almost 2 years before going out on their own.

Because tiger parts are in high demand for use in Chinese medicine and recipes, tigers have been hunted almost to extinction. All tigers are currently listed as endangered.

Directions: Use context clues for these definitions.

1. rare: _____

2. solitary: _____

3. extinction: _____

Directions: Answer these questions about tigers.

4. Why have tigers been hunted almost to extinction?

_____

_____

5. Name the three types of tigers.

_____

Comprehension: Lions

The lion, often referred to as the king of beasts, once commanded a large territory. Today, their territory is very limited. Lions are savanna-dwelling animals, which has made them easy targets for hunters. The increasing population of humans and their livestock has also contributed to the lion's decreased population.

Lions are heavy cats. Males weigh over 500 pounds and can grow to be over 8 feet in length, with a tail over 36 inches long. Males are characterized by a long, full mane that covers the neck and most of the head and shoulders. Females do not have a mane and are slightly smaller in size. Both males and females have beige coats, hooked claws and powerful jaws. Their roars can be heard up to 5 miles away!

Lions tend to hunt in the evening and spend the day sleeping. They prefer hunting zebra or giraffe but will eat almost anything. A lion is capable of eating over 75 pounds of meat at a single kill and then going a week without eating again. Generally, female lions do the hunting, and the males come to share the kill.

Lions live in groups called prides. Each pride has between 4 and 37 lions. Females bear one to four cubs approximately every 2 years.

Directions: Answer these questions about lions.

1. What are the differences between male and female lions? _____

2. Why would living on a savanna make the lion an "easy target"? _____

Directions: Use context clues for these definitions.

3. pride: _____

4. territory: _____

5. savanna: _____

6. capable: _____

Using Prior Knowledge: Cooking

Before reading about cooking in the following section, answer these questions.

1. What is your favorite recipe? Why?

   _____
   _____
   _____

2. What do you most like to cook? Why?

   _____
   _____
   _____

3. Have you tried food from cultures other than your own? If so, which type of food do you like most? Why?

   _____
   _____
   _____

4. Why is it important to follow the correct sequence when preparing a recipe?

   _____
   _____
   _____

5. What safety precautions must be followed when working in a kitchen?

   _____
   _____
   _____

Following Directions: Chunky Tomato and Green Onion Sauce

Following directions means to do what the directions say to do, step by step, in the correct order.

Directions: Read the recipe for chunky tomato and green onion sauce. Answer the questions below.

Ingredients:
- 2 tablespoons corn oil
- 2 cloves of garlic, finely chopped
- 1½ pounds plum tomatoes, cored, peeled, seeded, then coarsely chopped
- 3 green onions, cut in half lengthwise, then thinly sliced
- salt
- freshly ground pepper

Heat oil in a heavy skillet over medium heat. Add garlic and cook until yellow, about 1 minute. Stir in tomatoes. Season with salt and pepper. Cook until thickened, about 10 minutes. Stir in green onions and serve.

1. What is the last thing the cook does to prepare the tomatoes before cooking them?
   _____

2. What kind of oil does the cook heat in the heavy skillet? _____

3. How long should the garlic be cooked? _____

4. What does the cook do to the tomatoes right before removing the seeds?
   _____

5. Is the sauce served hot or cold? _____

Comprehension: Cooking With Care

People are so busy these days that many have no time to cook. This creates a problem, because most families love home cooking! The food tastes good and warm, and a family meal brings everyone together. In some families, meals are often the only times everyone sees one another at the same time.

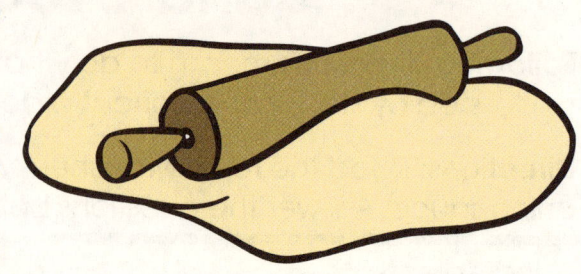

Another reason people enjoy home cooking is that it is often a way of showing love. A parent who bakes a batch of chocolate chip cookies isn't just satisfying a child's sweet tooth. He/she is sending a message. The message says, "I care about you enough to spend an hour making cookies that you will eat up in 15 minutes if I let you!"

There's also something about the smell of good cooking that appeals to people of all ages. It makes most of us feel secure and loved—even if we are the ones doing the cooking! Next time you smell a cake baking, stop for a moment and pay attention to your mood. Chances are, the good smell is making you feel happy.

Real estate agents know that good cooking smells are important. They sometimes advise people whose homes are for sale to bake cookies or bread if prospective buyers are coming to see the house. The good smells make the place "feel like home." These pleasant smells help convince potential buyers that the house would make a good home for their family, too!

Directions: Answer these questions about good cooking.

1. Why do fewer people cook nowadays? _____

2. Why are family meals important? _____

3. What do homemade cookies do besides satisfy a child's sweet tooth?

   _____

4. Real estate agents often advise home sellers holding open houses to

   ☐ clean the garage.   ☐ bake cookies or bread.

5. The smell of baking at open houses may encourage buyers to

   ☐ bake cookies.   ☐ buy the house.   ☐ bake bread.

Sequencing: Chocolate Chunk Cookies

These chocolate chunk cookies require only five ingredients. Before you combine them, preheat the oven to 350 degrees. Preheating the oven to the correct temperature is always step number one in baking.

Now, into a large mixing bowl, empty an $18\frac{1}{4}$-ounce package of chocolate fudge cake mix (any brand). Add a 10-ounce package of semi-sweet chocolate, broken into small pieces, two $5\frac{1}{8}$-ounce packages of chocolate fudge pudding mix (any brand) and $1\frac{1}{2}$ cups chopped walnuts.

Use a large wooden spoon to combine the ingredients. When they are well-mixed, add $1\frac{1}{2}$ cups mayonnaise and stir thoroughly. Shape the dough into small balls and place the balls 2 inches apart on an ungreased cookie sheet. Bake 12 minutes. Cool and eat!

Directions: Number in correct order the steps for making chocolate chunk cookies.

_____ Place $1\frac{1}{2}$ cups of mayonnaise in the bowl.

_____ Shape dough into small balls and place them on a cookie sheet.

_____ Empty the package of chocolate fudge cake mix into the bowl.

_____ Bake the dough for 12 minutes.

_____ Place two $5\frac{1}{8}$-ounce packages of chocolate fudge pudding in the bowl.

_____ Put $1\frac{1}{2}$ cups chopped walnuts in the bowl.

_____ Preheat the oven to 350 degrees.

_____ Place the 10-ounce package of semi-sweet chocolate pieces in the bowl.

_____ Stir everything thoroughly.

Comprehension: Eating High-Fiber Foods

Have you heard your parents or other adults talk about "high-fiber" diets? Foods that are high in fiber, like oats and other grains, are believed to be very healthy. Here's why: The fiber adds bulk to the food the body digests and helps keep the large intestines working properly. Corn, apples, celery, nuts and other chewy foods also contain fiber that helps keep the body's systems for digesting and eliminating food working properly.

Researchers at the University of Minnesota have found another good reason to eat high-fiber food, especially at breakfast. Because fiber is bulky, it absorbs a lot of liquid in the stomach. As it absorbs the liquid, it swells. This "fools" the stomach into thinking it's full. As a result, when lunchtime comes, those who have eaten a high-fiber breakfast are not as hungry. They eat less food at lunch. Without much effort on their parts, dieters eating a high-fiber breakfast can lose weight.

The university researchers say a person could lose 10 pounds in a year just by eating a high-fiber breakfast! This is good news to people who are only slightly overweight and want an easy method for losing that extra 10 pounds.

Directions: Answer these questions about eating high-fiber foods.

1. Why is fiber healthy? _____

_____

2. How does fiber "fool" the stomach? _____

_____

3. How does "fooling" the stomach help people lose weight? _____

_____

4. How many pounds could a dieter eating a high-fiber breakfast lose in a year?

    ☐ 20 pounds   ☐ 30 pounds   ☐ 10 pounds

5. The university that did the research is in which state?

    ☐ Michigan   ☐ Minnesota   ☐ Montana

Main Idea: New Corn

I will clothe myself in spring clothing
And visit the slopes of the eastern hill.
By the mountain stream, a mist hovers,
Hovers a moment and then scatters.
Then comes a wind blowing from the south
That brushes the fields of new corn.

Directions: Answer these questions about this ancient poem, which is translated from Chinese.

1. Circle the main idea:

    The poet will dress comfortably and go to where the corn grows so he/she can enjoy the beauty of nature.

    The poet will dress comfortably and visit the slopes of the eastern hill, where he/she will plant corn.

2. From which direction does the wind blow? _____

3. Where does the mist hover? _____

4. What do you think the poet means by "spring clothing"? _____
_____

Reading Comprehension   79   Total Basic Skills Grade 5

Comprehension: The French Eat Differently

Many people believe that French people are very different from Americans. This is certainly true where eating habits are concerned! According to a report by the World Health Organization, each year the French people eat four times more butter than Americans. The French also eat twice as much cheese! In addition, they eat more vegetables, potatoes, grain and fish.

Yet, despite the fact that they eat larger amounts of these foods, the French take in about the same number of calories each day as Americans. (French and American men consume about 2,500 calories daily. French and American women take in about 1,600 calories daily.)

How can this be? If the French are eating more of certain types of foods, shouldn't this add up to more calories? And why are so few French people overweight compared to Americans? The answer—Americans consume 18 times more refined sugar than the French and drink twice as much whole milk!

Although many Americans believe the French end each meal with grand and gooey desserts, this just isn't so. Except for special occasions, dessert in a typical French home consists of fresh fruit or cheese. Many American families, on the other hand, like to end their meals with a bowl or two of ice cream or another sweet treat.

It's believed that this difference in the kind of calories consumed—rather than in the total number of calories taken in—is what causes many Americans to be chubby and most French people to be thin.

Directions: Answer these questions about the eating habits of French and American people.

1. How many calories does the average French man eat each day? _____

2. How much whole milk does the average French person drink compared to the average American? _____

3. How much more refined sugar do Americans eat than the French?

☐ 2 times more   ☐ 18 times more   ☐ 15 times more

4. What do French families usually eat for dessert?

☐ refined sugar   ☐ ice cream   ☐ fruit and cheese

Comprehension: Chinese Cabbage

Many Americans enjoy Chinese food. In big cities, like New York and Chicago, many Chinese restaurants deliver their food in small boxes to homes. It's just like ordering a pizza! Then the people who ordered the "take-out" food simply open it, put it on their plates and eat it while it's hot.

Because it tastes so good, many people are curious about the ingredients in Chinese food. Siu choy and choy sum are two types of Chinese cabbage that many people enjoy eating. Siu choy grows to be 2 to 3 feet! Of course, it is chopped into small pieces before it is cooked and served. Its leaves are light green and soft. It is not crunchy like American cabbage. Siu choy is used in soups and stews. Sometimes it is pickled with vinegar and other ingredients and served as a side dish to other courses.

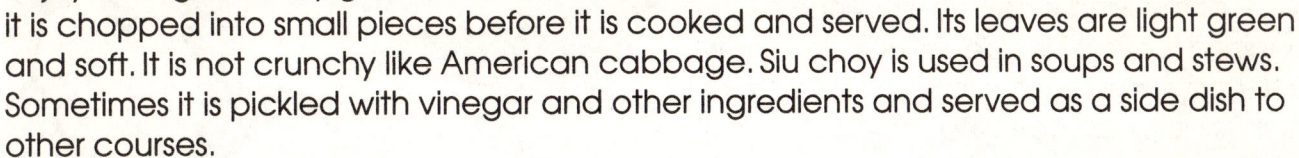

Choy sum looks and tastes different from siu choy. Choy sum grows to be only 8 to 10 inches. It is a flowering cabbage that grows small yellow flowers. The flowers are "edible," which means they can be eaten. Its leaves are long and bright green. After its leaves are boiled for 4 minutes, choy sum is often served as a salad. Oil and oyster sauce are mixed together and poured over choy sum as a salad dressing.

Directions: Answer these questions about Chinese cabbage.

1. Which Chinese cabbage grows small yellow flowers? _____

2. Which Chinese cabbage is served as a salad? _____

3. Is siu choy crunchy? _____

4. What ingredients are in the salad dressing used on choy sum?

   _____

5. To what size does siu choy grow? _____

6. Name two main dishes in which siu choy is used. _____

Recognizing Details: The Coldest Continent

Directions: Read the information about Antarctica. Then answer the questions.

Antarctica lies at the South Pole and is the coldest continent. It is without sunlight for months at a time. Even when the sun does shine, its angle is so slanted that the land receives little warmth. Temperatures often drop to 100 degrees below zero, and a fierce wind blows almost endlessly. Most of the land is covered by snow heaped thousands of feet deep. The snow is so heavy and tightly packed that it forms a great ice cap covering more than 95 percent of the continent.

Considering the conditions, it is no wonder there are no towns or cities in Antarctica. There is no permanent population at all, only small scientific research stations. Many teams of explorers and scientists have braved the freezing cold since Antarctica was sighted in 1820. Some have died in their effort, but a great deal of information has been learned about the continent.

From fossils, pieces of coal and bone samples, we know that Antarctica was not always an ice-covered land. Scientists believe that 200 million years ago it was connected to southern Africa, South America, Australia and India. Forests grew in warm swamps, and insects and reptiles thrived there. Today, there are animals that live in and around the waters that border the continent. In fact, the waters surrounding Antarctica contain more life than oceans in warmer areas of the world.

1. Where is Antarctica? _____

2. How much of the continent is covered by an ice cap? _____

3. When was Antarctica first sighted by explorers? _____

4. What clues indicate that Antarctica was not always an ice-covered land?

   _____

5. Is Antarctica another name for the North Pole?   Yes   No

Reading Comprehension: The Arctic Circle

Directions: Read the article about the Arctic Circle. Then answer the questions.

On the other side of the globe from Antarctica, at the northernmost part of the Earth, is another icy land. This is the Arctic Circle. It includes the North Pole itself and the northern fringes of three continents—Europe, Asia and North America, including the state of Alaska—as well as Greenland and other islands.

The seasons are opposite at the two ends of the Earth. When it is summer in Antarctica, it is winter in the Arctic Circle. In both places, there are very long periods of sunlight in summer and very long nights in the winter. On the poles themselves, there are six full months of sunlight and six full months of darkness each year.

Compared to Antarctica, the summers are surprisingly mild in some areas of the Arctic Circle. Much of the snow cover may melt, and temperatures often reach 50 degrees in July. Antarctica is covered by water—frozen water, of course—so nothing can grow there. Plant growth is limited in the polar regions not only by the cold, but also by wind, lack of water and the long winter darkness.

In the far north, willow trees grow but only become a few inches high! The annual rings, the circles within the trunk of a tree that show its age and how fast it grows, are so narrow in those trees that you need a microscope to see them.

A permanently frozen layer of soil, called "permafrost," keeps roots from growing deep enough into the ground to anchor a plant. Even if a plant could survive the cold temperatures, it could not grow roots deep enough or strong enough to allow the plant to get very big.

1. What three continents have land included in the Arctic Circle?

   _____   _____   _____

2. Is the Arctic Circle generally warmer or colder than Antarctica?

   _____

3. What is "permafrost"? _____

4. Many tall pine trees grow in the Arctic Circle.   Yes   No

Main Idea: The Polar Trail

Directions: Read the information about explorers to Antarctica.

A recorded sighting of Antarctica, the last continent to be discovered, was not made until the early nineteenth century. Since then, many brave explorers and adventurers have sailed south to conquer the icy land. Their achievements once gained as much world attention as those of the first astronauts.

Long before the continent was first spotted, the ancient Greeks suspected there was a continent at the bottom of the Earth. Over the centuries, legends of the undiscovered land spread. Some of the world's greatest seamen tried to find it, including Captain James Cook in 1772.

Cook was the first to sail all the way to the solid field of ice that surrounds Antarctica every winter. In fact, he sailed all the way around the continent but never saw it. Cook went farther south than anyone had ever gone. His record lasted 50 years.

Forty years after Cook, a new kind of seamen sailed the icy waters. They were hunters of seals and whales. Sailing through unknown waters in search of seals and whales, these men became explorers as well as hunters. The first person known to sight Antarctica was an American hunter, 21-year-old Nathaniel Brown Palmer in 1820.

Directions: Draw an **X** on the blank for the correct answer.

1. The main idea is:
   ____ Antarctica was not sighted until the early nineteenth century.
   ____ Many brave explorers and adventurers have sailed south to conquer the icy land.

2. The first person to sail to the ice field that surrounds Antarctica was:
   ____ Nathaniel Brown Palmer
   ____ Captain James Cook
   ____ Neal Armstrong

3. His record for sailing the farthest south stood for:
   ____ 40 years
   ____ 50 years
   ____ 500 years

4. The first person known to sight Antarctica was:
   ____ an unknown ancient Greek
   ____ Captain James Cook
   ____ Nathaniel Brown Palmer

5. His profession was:
   ____ hunter
   ____ ship captain
   ____ explorer

Reading Skills: Research

To learn more about the explorers to Antarctica, reference sources like encyclopedias, CD-ROMs, the Internet and history books are excellent sources for finding more information.

Directions: Use reference sources to learn more about Captain James Cook and Captain James Clark Ross. Write an informational paragraph about each man.

1. Captain James Cook

   _____
   _____
   _____
   _____
   _____
   _____

2. Captain James Clark Ross

   _____
   _____
   _____
   _____
   _____
   _____

3. What dangers did both these men and their teams face in their attempts to reach the South Pole?

   _____
   _____
   _____
   _____

Recognizing Details: The Frozen Continent

Directions: Read the information about explorers. Then answer the questions.

By the mid-1800s, most of the seals of Antarctica had been killed. The seal hunters no longer sailed the icy waters. The next group of explorers who took an interest in Antarctica were scientists. Of these, the man who took the most daring chances and made the most amazing discoveries was British Captain James Clark Ross.

Ross first made a name for himself sailing to the north. In 1831, he discovered the North Magnetic Pole—one of two places on Earth toward which a compass needle points. In 1840, Ross set out to find the South Magnetic Pole. He made many marvelous discoveries, including the Ross Sea, a great open sea beyond the ice packs that stopped other explorers, and the Ross Ice Shelf, a great floating sheet of ice bigger than all of France!

The next man to make his mark exploring Antarctica was British explorer Robert Falcon Scott. Scott set out in 1902 to find the South Pole. He and his team suffered greatly, but they were able to make it a third of the way to the pole. Back in England, Scott was a great hero. In 1910, he again attempted to become the first man to reach the South Pole. But this time he had competition: an explorer from Norway, Roald Amundsen, was also leading a team to the South Pole.

It was a brutal race. Both teams faced many hardships, but they pressed on. Finally, on December 14, 1911, Amundsen became the first man to reach the South Pole. Scott arrived on January 17, 1912. He was bitterly disappointed at not being first. The trip back was even more horrible. None of the five men in the Scott expedition survived.

1. After the seal hunters, who were the next group of explorers interested in Antarctica?
   _____

2. What great discovery did James Ross make before ever sailing to Antarctica?
   _____

3. What were two other great discoveries made by James Ross?
   _____ _____

4. How close did Scott and his team come to the South Pole in 1902?
   _____

5. Who was the first person to reach the South Pole?_____

Reading Comprehension: Polar Bears

Directions: Read the information about polar bears. Then answer the questions by circling **Yes** or **No**.

Some animals are able to survive the cold weather and difficult conditions of the snow and ice fields in the Arctic polar regions. One of the best known is the polar bear.

Polar bears live on the land and the sea. They may drift hundreds of miles from land on huge sheets of floating ice. They use their great paws to paddle the ice along. Polar bears are excellent swimmers, too. They can cross great distances of open water. While in the water, they feed mostly on fish and seals.

On land, these huge animals, which measure 10 feet long and weigh about 1,000 pounds, can run 25 miles an hour. Surprisingly, polar bears live as plant-eaters rather than hunters while on land. Unlike many kinds of bears, polar bears do not hibernate. They are active the whole year.

Baby polar bears are born during the winter. At birth, they are pink and almost hairless. These helpless cubs weigh only two pounds—less than one-third the size of most human infants. The mother bears raise their young in dens dug in snowbanks. By the time they are 10 weeks old, polar bear cubs are about the size of puppies and have enough white fur to protect them in the open air. The mothers give their cubs swimming, hunting and fishing lessons. By the time autumn comes, the cubs are left to survive on their own.

1. Polar bears can live on the land and the sea.　　　　Yes　　No

2. Polar bears are excellent swimmers.　　　　Yes　　No

3. Polar bears hibernate in the winter.　　　　Yes　　No

4. A newborn polar bear weighs more than a newborn human baby.　　　　Yes　　No

5. Mother polar bears raise their babies in caves.　　　　Yes　　No

6. Father polar bears give the cubs swimming lessons.　　　　Yes　　No

Context Clues: Seals

Directions: Read the information about seals. Use context clues to determine the meaning of the bold words. Check the correct answers.

Seals are **aquatic** mammals that also live on land at times. Some seals stay in the sea for weeks or months at a time, even sleeping in the water. When seals go on land, they usually choose **secluded** spots to avoid people and other animals.

The 31 different kinds of seals belong to a group of animals often called pinnipeds meaning "fin-footed." Their fins, or flippers, make them very good swimmers and divers. Their nostrils close tightly when they dive. They have been known to stay **submerged** for as long as a half-hour at a time!

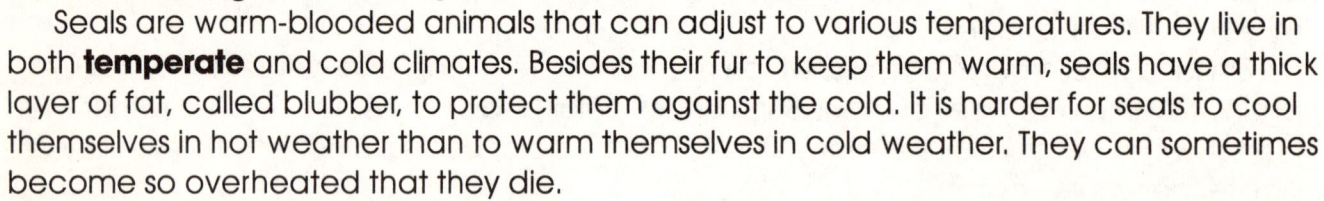

Seals are warm-blooded animals that can adjust to various temperatures. They live in both **temperate** and cold climates. Besides their fur to keep them warm, seals have a thick layer of fat, called blubber, to protect them against the cold. It is harder for seals to cool themselves in hot weather than to warm themselves in cold weather. They can sometimes become so overheated that they die.

1. Based on other words in the sentence, what is the correct definition of **aquatic**?

    ____ living on the land

    ____ living on or in the sea

    ____ living in large groups

2. Based on other words in the sentence, what is the correct definition of **submerged**?

    ____ under the water

    ____ on top of the water

    ____ in groups

3. Based on other words in the sentence, what is the correct definition of **secluded**?

    ____ rocky

    ____ private or hidden

    ____ near other animals

4. Based on other words in the sentence, what is the correct definition of **temperate**?

    ____ rainy

    ____ measured on a thermometer

    ____ warm

Total Basic Skills Grade 5   Reading Comprehension

Reading Comprehension: Walruses

Directions: Read the information about walruses. Then answer the questions.

A walrus is actually a type of seal that lives only in the Arctic Circle. It has two huge upper teeth, or tusks, which it uses to pull itself out of the water or to move over the rocks on land. It also uses its tusks to dig clams, one of its favorite foods, from the bottom of the sea. On an adult male walrus, the tusks may be three and a half feet long!

A walrus has an unusual face. Besides its long tusks, it has a big, bushy mustache made up of hundreds of movable, stiff bristles. These bristles also help the walrus push food into its mouth. Except for small wrinkles in the skin, a walrus has no outer ears.

Like a seal, the walrus uses its flippers to help it swim. Its front flippers serve as paddles, and while swimming, it swings the back of its huge body from side to side. A walrus looks awkward using its flippers to walk on land, but don't be fooled! A walrus can run as fast as a man.

Baby walruses are born in the early spring. They stay with their mothers until they are two years old. There is a good reason for this—they must grow little tusks, at least three or four inches long, before they can catch their own food from the bottom of the sea. Until then, they must stay close to their mothers to eat. A young walrus that is tired from swimming will climb onto its mother's back for a ride, holding onto her with its front flippers.

1. The walrus is a type of seal found only _____.

2. List two ways the walrus uses its tusks.

   _____   _____

3. A walrus cannot move quickly on land.   Yes   No

4. A walrus has a large, bushy mustache.   Yes   No

5. A baby walrus stays very close to
   its mother until it is two years old.   Yes   No

6. Baby walruses are born late in fall.   Yes   No

Main Idea: Penguins

Directions: Read the information about penguins.

People are amused by the funny, duck-like waddle of penguins and by their appearance because they seem to be wearing little tuxedos. Penguins are among the best-liked animals on Earth, but are also a most misunderstood animal. People may have more wrong ideas about penguins than any other animal.

For example, many people are surprised to learn that penguins are really birds, not mammals. Penguins do not fly, but they do have feathers, and only birds have feathers. Also, like other birds, penguins build nests and their young hatch from eggs. Because of their unusual looks, though, you would never confuse them with any other bird!

Penguins are also thought of as symbols of the polar regions, but penguins do not live north of the equator, so you would not find a penguin on the North Pole. Penguins don't live at the South Pole, either. Only two of the seventeen **species** of penguins spend all of their lives on the frozen continent of Antarctica. You would be just as likely to see a penguin living on an island in a warm climate as in a cold area.

Directions: Draw an **X** on the blank for the correct answer.

1. The main idea is:

   ____ Penguins are among the best-liked animals on earth.
   ____ The penguin is a much misunderstood animal.

2. Penguins live

   ____ only at the North Pole.
   ____ only at the South Pole.
   ____ only south of the equator.

3. Based on the other words in the sentence, what is the correct definition of the word **species**?

   ____ number
   ____ bird
   ____ a distinct kind

Directions: List three ways penguins are like other birds.

_____

ENGLISH

Metaphor:
Don't be a crab!

Simile:
The wet floor was as slippery as an eel.

Nouns

A **noun** is a word that names a person, place or thing.

Examples:
- **person** — friend
- **place** — home
- **thing** — desk

Nouns are used many ways in sentences. They can be the subjects of sentences.

Example: Noun as subject: Your high-topped **sneakers** look great with that outfit.

Nouns can be direct objects of a sentence. The **direct object** follows the verb and completes its meaning. It answers the question **who** or **what**.

Example: Noun as direct object: Shelly's family bought a new **car**.

Nouns can be indirect objects. An **indirect object** comes between the verb and the direct object and tells **to whom** or **for whom** something was done.

Example: Noun as indirect object: She gave **Tina** a big hug.

Directions: Underline all the nouns. Write **S** above the noun if it is a subject, **DO** if it is a direct object or **IO** if it is an indirect object. The first one has been done for you.

1. Do <u>alligators</u> eat <u>people</u>? (S, DO)

2. James hit a home run, and our team won the game.

3. The famous actor gave Susan his autograph.

4. Eric loaned Keith his bicycle.

5. The kindergarten children painted cute pictures.

6. Robin sold David some chocolate chip cookies.

7. The neighbors planned a going-away party and bought a gift.

8. The party and gift surprised Kurt and his family.

9. My scout leader told our group a funny joke.

10. Karen made her little sister a clown costume.

Proper and Common Nouns

Proper nouns name specific people, places or things.

Examples: Washington, D.C., Thomas Jefferson, Red Sea

Common nouns name nonspecific people, places or things.

Examples: man, fortress, dog

Directions: Underline the proper nouns and circle the common nouns in each sentence.

1. My friend, Josephine, loves to go to the docks to watch the boats sail into the harbor.
2. Josephine is especially interested in the boat named *Maiden Voyage*.
3. This boat is painted red with yellow stripes and has several large masts.
4. Its sails are white and billow in the wind.
5. At Misty Harbor, many boats are always sailing in and out.
6. The crews on the boats rush from bow to stern working diligently to keep the sailboats moving.
7. Josephine has been invited aboard *Maiden Voyage* by its captain.
8. Captain Ferdinand knew of her interest in sailboats, so he offered a tour.
9. Josephine was amazed at the gear aboard the boat and the skills of the crew.
10. It is Josephine's dream to sail the Atlantic Ocean on a boat similar to *Maiden Voyage*.
11. Her mother is not sure of this dangerous dream and urges Josephine to consider safer dreams.
12. Josephine thinks of early explorers like Christopher Columbus, Amerigo Vespucci and Leif Ericson.
13. She thinks these men must have been brave to set out into the unknown waters of the world.
14. Their boats were often small and provided little protection from major ocean storms.
15. Josephine believes that if early explorers could challenge the rough ocean waters, she could, too.

English | 93 | Total Basic Skills Grade 5

Abstract and Concrete Nouns

Concrete nouns name something that can be touched or seen.
Abstract nouns name an idea, a thought or a feeling which cannot be touched or seen.

Examples:
   concrete nouns: house, puppy, chair
   abstract nouns: love, happiness, fear

Directions: Write **concrete** or **abstract** in the blank after each noun.

1. loyalty _____
2. light bulb _____
3. quarter _____
4. hope _____
5. satellite _____
6. ability _____
7. patio _____

8. door _____
9. allegiance _____
10. Cuba _____
11. Michael Jordan _____
12. friendship _____
13. telephone _____
14. computer _____

Directions: Write eight nouns for each category.

Concrete	Abstract
1. _____	1. _____
2. _____	2. _____
3. _____	3. _____
4. _____	4. _____
5. _____	5. _____
6. _____	6. _____
7. _____	7. _____
8. _____	8. _____

Total Basic Skills Grade 5   English

Verbs

A **verb** tells what something does or that something exists.

Examples:
Tim **has shared** his apples with us.
Those apples **were** delicious.
I hope Tim **is bringing** more apples tomorrow.
Tim **picked** the apples himself.

Directions: Underline the verbs.

1. Gene moved here from Philadelphia.
2. Now he is living in a house on my street.
3. His house is three houses away from mine.
4. I have lived in this house all my life.
5. I hope Gene will like this town.
6. I am helping Gene with his room.
7. He has a lot of stuff!
8. We are painting his walls green.
9. He picked the color himself.
10. I wonder what his parents will say.

Directions: Write verbs to complete these sentences.

11. We _____ some paintbrushes.
12. Gene already _____ the paint.
13. I _____ my old clothes.
14. There _____ no furniture in his room right now.
15. It _____ several hours to paint his whole room.

Verbs

A **verb** is the action word in a sentence. It tells what the subject does (**build**, **laugh**, **express**, **fasten**) or that it exists (**is**, **are**, **was**, **were**).

Examples: Randy **raked** the leaves into a pile.
　　　　　　I **was** late to school today.

Directions: In the following sentences, write verbs that make sense.

1. The quarterback _____ the ball to the receiver.
2. My mother _____ some cookies yesterday.
3. John _____ newspapers to make extra money.
4. The teacher _____ the instructions on the board.
5. Last summer, our family _____ a trip to Florida to visit relatives.

Sometimes, a verb can be two or more words. Verbs used to "support" other verbs are called **helping verbs**.

Examples: We **were** listening to music in my room.
　　　　　　Chris **has been** studying for over 2 hours.

Directions: In the following sentences, write helping verbs along with the correct form of the given verbs. The first one has been done for you.

1. Michelle (write) __is writing__ a letter to her grandmother right now.
2. My brother (have) _____ trouble with his math homework.
3. When we arrived, the movie (start) _____ already.
4. My aunt (live) _____ in the same house for 30 years.
5. Our football team (go) _____ to win the national championship this year.
6. My sister (talk) _____ on the phone all afternoon!
7. I couldn't sleep last night because the wind (blow) _____ so hard.
8. Last week, Pat was sick, but now he (feel) _____ much better.
9. Tomorrow, our class (have) _____ a bake sale.
10. Mr. Smith (collect) _____ stamps for 20 years.

Total Basic Skills Grade 5　　　　　　　　　　　　　　　　　　　　　　English

Verb Tenses

Verbs have different forms to show whether something already happened, is happening right now or will happen.

Examples:
   Present tense: I **walk**.
   Past tense: I **walked**.
   Future tense: I **will walk**.

Directions: Write **PAST** if the verb is past tense, **PRES** for present tense or **FUT** for future tense. The first one has been done for you.

<u>PRES</u> 1. My sister Sara works at the grocery store.

_____ 2. Last year, she worked in an office.

_____ 3. Sara is going to college, too.

_____ 4. She will be a dentist some day.

_____ 5. She says studying is difficult.

_____ 6. Sara hardly studied at all in high school.

_____ 7. I will be ready for college in a few years.

_____ 8. Last night, I read my history book for 2 hours.

Directions: Complete these sentences using verbs in the tenses listed. The first one has been done for you.

9. take: future tense   My friends and I <u>will take</u> a trip.

10. talk: past tense   We _____ for a long time about where to go.

11. want: present tense   Pam _____ to go to the lake.

12. want: past tense   Jake _____ to go with us.

13. say: past tense   His parents _____ no.

14. ride: future tense   We _____ our bikes.

15. pack: past tense   Susan and Jared already _____ lunches for us.

English   Total Basic Skills Grade 5

Writing: Verb Forms

Present-tense verbs tell what is happening right now. To form present-tense verbs, use the "plain" verbs or use **is** or **are** before the verb and add **ing** to the verb.

Examples: We **eat**. We **are eating**.
He **serves**. He **is serving**.

Directions: Complete each sentence with the correct verb form, telling what is happening right now. Read carefully, as some sentences already have **is** or **are**.

Examples: Scott is (loan) loaning Jenny his math book.
Jenny (study) is studying for a big math test.

1. The court is (release) _____ the prisoner early.
2. Jonah and Jill (write) _____ their notes in code.
3. Are you (vote) _____ for Baxter?
4. The girls are (coax) _____ the dog into the bathtub.
5. The leaves (begin) _____ to fall from the trees.
6. My little brother (stay) _____ at his friend's house tonight.
7. Is she (hide) _____ behind the screen?

To tell what already happened, or in the **past tense**, add **ed** to many verbs or use **was** or **were** and add **ing** to the verb.

Example: I **watched**. I **was watching**.

Directions: Complete each sentence with the correct verb form. This time, tell what already happened.

Examples: We (walk) walked there yesterday.
They were (talk) talking.

1. The government was (decrease) _____ our taxes.
2. Was anyone (cheat) _____ in this game?
3. We were (try) _____ to set goals for the project.

Total Basic Skills Grade 5   English

Writing: Future-Tense Verbs

Future-tense verbs tell about things that will happen in the future. To form future-tense verbs, use **will** before the verb.

Example: Tomorrow I **will walk** to school.

When you use **will**, you may also have to add a helping verb and the ending **ing**.

Example: Tomorrow I **will be walking** to school.

Directions: Imagine what the world will be like 100 years from now. Maybe you think robots will be doing our work for us, or that people will be living on the moon. What will our houses look like? What will school be like? Write a paragraph describing what you imagine. Be sure to use future-tense verbs.

_____
_____
_____
_____
_____
_____
_____
_____
_____
_____
_____
_____

Irregular Verbs

Irregular verbs change completely in the past tense. Unlike regular verbs, the past tense forms of irregular verbs are not formed by adding **ed**.

Examples:
Chung **eats** the cookies.
Chung **ate** them yesterday.
Chung **has eaten** them for weeks.

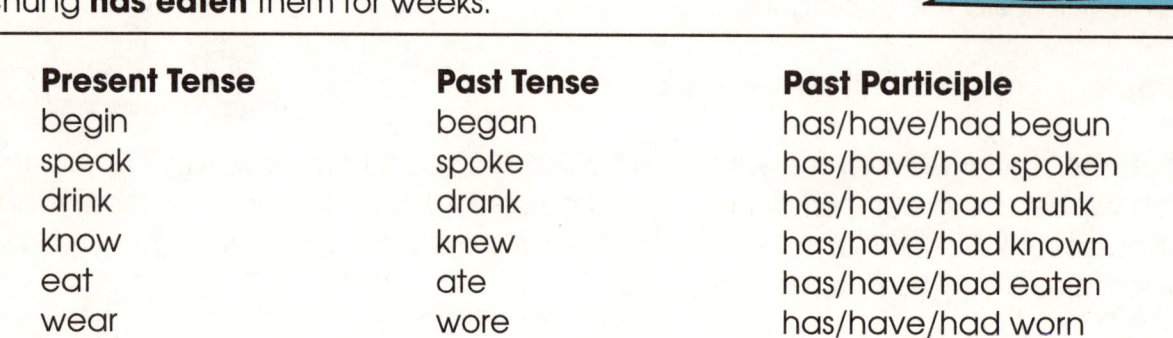

Present Tense	Past Tense	Past Participle
begin	began	has/have/had begun
speak	spoke	has/have/had spoken
drink	drank	has/have/had drunk
know	knew	has/have/had known
eat	ate	has/have/had eaten
wear	wore	has/have/had worn

Directions: Rewrite these sentences once using the past tense and again using the past participle of each verb.

1. Todd begins football practice this week.
   _____
   _____

2. She wears her hair in braids.
   _____
   _____

3. I drink two glasses of milk.
   _____
   _____

4. The man is speaking to us.
   _____
   _____

5. The dogs are eating.
   _____
   _____

"Be" as a Helping Verb

A **helping verb** tells when the action of a sentence takes place. The helping verb **be** has several forms: **am**, **is**, **are**, **was**, **were** and **will**. These helping verbs can be used in all three tenses.

Examples:
   Past tense: Ken **was** talking. We **were** eating.
   Present tense: I **am** coming. Simon **is** walking. They **are** singing.
   Future tense: I **will** work. The puppies **will** eat.

In the present and past tense, many verbs can be written with or without the helping verb **be**. When the verb is written with a form of **be**, add **ing**. **Was** and **is** are used with singular subjects. **Were** and **are** are used with plural subjects.

Examples:
   Present tense: Angela **sings**. Angela **is singing**. The children **sing**. They **are singing**.
   Past tense: I **studied**. I **was studying**. They **studied**. They **were studying**.

The helping verb **will** is always needed for the future tense, but the **ing** ending is not used with **will**. **Will** is both singular and plural.

Examples:
   Future tense: I **will eat**. We **will watch**.

Directions: Underline the helping verbs.

1. Brian is helping me with this project.
2. We are working together on it.
3. Susan was painting the background yesterday.
4. Matt and Mike were cleaning up.
5. Tomorrow, we will present our project to the class.

Directions: Rewrite the verbs using a helping verb. The first one has been done for you.

6. Our neighborhood plans a garage sale.   _is planning_

7. The sale starts tomorrow.   _____

8. My brother Doug and I think about things we sell.   _____

9. My grandfather cleans out the garage.   _____

10. Doug and I help him.   _____

English

"Be" as a Linking Verb

A **linking verb** links a noun or adjective in the predicate to the subject. Forms of the verb **be** are the most common linking verbs. Linking verbs can be used in all three tenses.

Examples:
   Present: My father **is** a salesman.
   Past: The store **was** very busy last night.
   Future: Tomorrow **will be** my birthday.

In the first sentence, **is** links the subject (father) with a noun (salesman). In the second sentence, **was** links the subject (store) with an adjective (busy). In the third sentence, **will be** links the subject (tomorrow) with a noun (birthday).

Directions: Circle the linking verbs. Underline the two words that are linked by the verb. The first one has been done for you.

1. Columbus (is) the capital of Ohio.

2. By bedtime, Nicole was bored.

3. Andy will be the captain of our team.

4. Tuesday is the first day of the month.

5. I hate to say this, but we are lost.

6. Ask him if the water is cold.

7. By the time I finished my paper, it was late.

8. Spaghetti is my favorite dinner.

9. The children were afraid of the big truck.

10. Karen will be a good president of our class.

11. These lessons are helpful.

12. Was that report due today?

Transitive and Intransitive Verbs

An **intransitive verb** can stand alone in the predicate because its meaning is complete. In the examples below, notice that each short sentence is a complete thought.

Examples: Intransitive verbs: The tree **grows**. The mouse **squeaked**. The deer **will run**.

A **transitive verb** needs a direct object to complete its meaning. The meaning of a sentence with a transitive verb is not complete without a direct object.

Examples: Transitive verbs: The mouse **wants** seeds. The deer **saw** the hunter. The tree **will lose** its leaves.

The direct object **seeds** tells what the mouse wants. **Leaves** tells what the tree will lose and **hunter** tells what the deer saw.

Both transitive and intransitive verbs can be in the past, present or future tense.

Directions: Underline the verb in each sentence. Write **I** if the sentence has an intransitive verb or **T** if it has a transitive verb.

_____ 1. The snake slid quietly along the ground.

_____ 2. The snake scared a rabbit.

_____ 3. The rabbit hopped quickly back to its hole.

_____ 4. Safe from the snake, the rabbit shivered with fear.

_____ 5. In the meantime, the snake caught a frog.

_____ 6. The frog was watching flies and didn't see the snake.

Directions: Complete these sentences with intransitive verbs.

7. Our friends _____

8. The movie _____

Directions: Complete these sentences with transitive verbs and direct objects.

9. My family _____

10. The lightning _____

Subjects and Predicates

The **subject** tells who or what a sentence is about. The **predicate** tells what the subject does, did or is doing. All complete sentences must have a subject and a predicate.

Examples:
Subject	Predicate
Hamsters	are common pets.
Pets	need special care.

Directions: Circle the subjects and underline the predicates.

1. Many children keep hamsters as pets.
2. Mice are good pets, too.
3. Hamsters collect food in their cheeks.
4. My sister sneezes around furry animals.
5. My brother wants a dog instead of a hamster.

Directions: Write subjects to complete these sentences.

6. _____ has two pet hamsters.
7. _____ got a new pet last week.
8. _____ keeps forgetting to feed his goldfish.

Directions: Write predicates to complete these sentences.

9. Baby hamsters _____.
10. Pet mice _____.
11. I _____.

Directions: Write **S** if the group of words is a sentence or **NS** if the group of words is not a sentence.

12. _____ A new cage for our hamster.
13. _____ Picked the cutest one.
14. _____ We started out with two.
15. _____ Liking every one in the store.

Which Noun Is the Subject?

A **noun** is a word that names a person, place or thing.

Examples: Andy, Mrs. Henderson, doctor, child, house, shirt, dog, freedom, country

Often a noun is the subject of a sentence. The **subject** tells who or what the sentence is about. In this sentence, the subject is **Sara**: Sara drank some punch. A sentence can have several nouns, but they are not all subjects.

Directions: Underline each noun in the sentences below. Then circle the noun that is the subject of the sentence.

Example: (Benny) caught a huge fish in a small net.

1. Anna bragged about her big brother.
2. The car has a dent in the fender.
3. Our school won the city spirit award.
4. The cook scrubbed the pots and pans.
5. The quarter flipped onto the floor.
6. My sister rinsed her hair in the sink.
7. Our neighbor has 12 pets.
8. The cross country team ran 5 miles at practice.
9. Jo walked to the store on the corner.
10. A farmer stocks this pond with fish.

Directions: Each sentence below has two subjects. Underline all the nouns, as you did above. Then circle both subjects.

Example: (Joe) and (Peter) walked to school.

1. Apples and peaches grow in different seasons.
2. The chair and table matched the other furniture.

English   Total Basic Skills Grade 5

Subjects and Verbs

Directions: Underline the subject and verb in each sentence below. Write **S** over the subject and **V** over the verb. If the verb is two words, mark them both.

                    S   V   V

Examples: <u>Dennis</u> <u>was</u> <u>drinking</u> some punch.

                        S   V

              The <u>punch</u> <u>was</u> too sweet.

1. Hayley brags about her dog all the time.

2. Mrs. Thomas scrubbed the dirt off her car.

3. Then her son rinsed off the soap.

4. The teacher was flipping through the cards.

5. Jenny's rabbit was hungry and thirsty.

6. Your science report lacks a little detail.

7. Chris is stocking the shelves with cans of soup.

8. The accident caused a huge dent in our car.

Just as sentences can have two subjects, they can also have two verbs.

                  S   S V   V

Example: <u>Jennifer</u> and <u>Amie</u> <u>fed</u> the dog and <u>gave</u> him clean water.

Directions: Underline all the subjects and verbs in these sentences. Write **S** over the subjects and **V** over the verbs.

1. Mom and Dad scrubbed and rinsed the basement floor.

2. The men came and stocked the lake with fish.

3. Someone broke the window and ran away.

4. Carrie punched a hole in the paper and threaded yarn through the hole.

5. Julie and Pat turned their bikes around and went home.

Writing: Subjects and Verbs

Directions: Make each group of words below into a sentence by adding a subject, a verb, or a subject and a verb. Then write **S** over each subject and **V** over each verb.

Example: the dishes in the sink

           S   V

    The dishes in the sink were dirty.

1. a leash for your pet

   _____

2. dented the table

   _____

3. a bowl of punch for the party

   _____

4. rinsed the soap out

   _____

5. a lack of chairs

   _____

6. bragging about his sister

   _____

7. the stock on the shelf

   _____

8. with a flip of the wrist

   _____

English   Total Basic Skills Grade 5

Complete Sentences

A sentence which does not contain both a subject and a predicate is called a **fragment**.

Directions: Write **C** if the sentence is complete or **F** if it is a fragment.

1. _____ My mother and I hope to go to the mall this afternoon.
2. _____ To get shoes.
3. _____ We both need a new pair of tennis shoes.
4. _____ Maybe blue and white.
5. _____ Mom wants a pair of white shoes.
6. _____ That seems rather boring to me.
7. _____ There are many shoe stores in the mall.
8. _____ Sure to be a large selection.
9. _____ Tennis shoes are very expensive.
10. _____ My last pair cost $72.00!

Directions: Write the missing subject or predicate for these sentences.

11. _____ decided to go for hamburgers.

12. We _____.

13. My parents _____.

14. One day soon, I _____.

15. My favorite subject in school _____.

16. _____ went fishing on Sunday.

Direct Objects

A **direct object** is a word or words that follow a transitive verb and complete its meaning. It answers the question **whom** or **what**. Direct objects are always nouns or pronouns.

Examples:
We built a **doghouse**. **Doghouse** is the direct object. It tells **what** we built.
I called **Mary**. **Mary** is the direct object. It tells **whom** I called.

Directions: Underline the direct objects.

1. Jean drew a picture of the doghouse.
2. Then we bought some wood at the store.
3. Erin measured each board.
4. Who will saw the wood into boards?
5. Chad hammered nails into the boards.
6. He accidentally hit his thumb with the hammer.
7. Kirsten found some paint in the basement.
8. Should we paint the roof?
9. Will you write Sparky's name above the door?
10. Spell his name correctly.

Directions: Write direct objects to complete these sentences.

11. Will Sparky like _____?
12. When we were finished, we put away _____.
13. We washed out _____.
14. We threw away _____.
15. Then, to celebrate, we ate _____.

English

Total Basic Skills Grade 5

Indirect Objects

An **indirect object** is a word or words that come between the verb and the direct object. An indirect object tells **to whom** or **for whom** something has been done. Indirect objects are always nouns or pronouns.

Examples:
She cooked **me** a great dinner. **Me** is the indirect object. It tells **for whom** something was cooked.
Give the **photographer** a smile. **Photographer** is the indirect object. It tells **to whom** the smile should be given.

Directions: Circle the indirect objects. Underline the direct objects.

1. Marla showed me her drawing.
2. The committee had given her an award for it.
3. The principal offered Marla a special place to put her drawing.
4. While babysitting, I read Timmy a story.
5. He told me the end of the story.
6. Then I fixed him some hot chocolate.
7. Timmy gave me a funny look.
8. Why didn't his mother tell me?
9. Hot chocolate gives Timmy a rash.
10. Will his mom still pay me three dollars for watching him?

Directions: Write indirect objects to complete these sentences.

11. I will write _____ a letter.
12. I'll give _____ part of my lunch.
13. Show _____ your model.
14. Did you send _____ a card?
15. Don't tell _____ my secret.

Total Basic Skills Grade 5   English

Prepositions

A **preposition** is a word that comes before a noun or pronoun and shows the relationship of that noun or pronoun to other words in the sentence.

The **object of a preposition** is a noun or pronoun that follows a preposition and completes its meaning. A **prepositional phrase** includes a preposition and the object(s) of the preposition.

Examples:
   The girl **with red hair** spoke first.
   With is the preposition.
   Hair is the object of the preposition.
   With red hair is a prepositional phrase.

In addition to being subjects, direct and indirect objects and nouns and pronouns can also be objects of prepositions.

Prepositions						
across	behind	from	near	over	to	on
by	through	in	around	off	with	of
after	before	for	between	beyond	at	into

Directions: Underline the prepositional phrases in these sentences. Circle the prepositions. The first sentence has been done for you.

1. The name (of) our street is Redsail Court.
2. We have lived in our house for three years.
3. In our family, we eat a lot of hamburgers.
4. We like hamburgers on toasted buns with mustard.
5. Sometimes we eat in the living room in front of the TV.
6. In the summer, we have picnics in the backyard.
7. The ants crawl into our food and into our clothes.
8. Behind our house is a park with swings.
9. Kids from the neighborhood walk through our yard to the park.
10. Sometimes they cut across Mom's garden and stomp on her beans.
11. Mom says we need a tall fence without a gate.
12. With a fence around our yard, we could get a dog!

Pronouns

A **pronoun** is a word used in place of a noun. Instead of repeating a noun again and again, use a pronoun.

Examples: I you he she them us
me your him her they it
my our his we their its

Each pronoun takes the place of a certain noun. If the noun is singular, the pronoun should be singular. If the noun is plural, the pronoun should be plural.

Examples: John told **his** parents **he** would be late.
The girls said **they** would ride **their** bikes.

Directions: In the sentences below, draw an arrow from each pronoun to the noun it replaces.

Example: Gail needs the salt. Please pass it to her.

1. The workers had faith they would finish the house in time.

2. Kathy fell and scraped her knees. She put bandages on them.

3. The teacher told the students he wanted to see their papers.

Directions: Cross out some nouns and write pronouns to replace them.

Example: Dan needed a book for ~~Dan's~~ his book report.

1. Brian doesn't care about the style of Brian's clothes.

2. Joy dyed Joy's jeans to make the jeans dark blue.

3. Faith said Faith was tired of sharing a bedroom with Faith's two sisters. Faith wanted a room of Faith's own.

4. Bathe babies carefully so the soap doesn't get in the babies' eyes and make the babies cry.

5. When the children held up the children's pictures, we could see the pride in the children's eyes.

Singular and Plural Pronouns

Directions: Rewrite the sentences so the pronouns match the nouns they replace in gender and number. Change the verb form if necessary. The first one has been done for you.

1. Canada geese are the best-known geese in North America. It was here when the first settlers came from Europe.

   <u>Canada geese are the best-known geese in North America. They were here when the first settlers came from Europe.</u>

2. A Canada goose has a white patch from their chin to a spot behind their eyes.

3. Canada geese can harm farmland when it grazes in fields.

4. Geese have favorite fields where it likes to stop and eat.

5. While most of the flock eats, some geese stand guard. He warns if there is any danger.

6. Each guard gets their turn to eat, too.

7. Female geese usually lay five or six eggs, but she may lay as many as eleven.

8. While the female goose sits on the eggs, the male goose guards their mate.

English 113 Total Basic Skills Grade 5

Possessive Pronouns

A **possessive pronoun** shows ownership. A possessive pronoun can be used with the name of what is owned or by itself.

Examples:
This is **my** book. The book is **mine**.
This is **your** sandwich. It is **yours**.
This is **our** room. The room is **ours**.

The possessive pronouns are **my**, **your**, **our**, **his**, **her**, **their**, **its**, **mine**, **yours**, **ours**, **hers** and **theirs**. Possessive pronouns do not have apostrophes.

Directions: Complete the sentences with the correct possessive pronouns.

1. I entered _____ picture in the contest. That farm scene is _____.

2. Shelby entered _____ picture, too. Do you see _____?

3. Hal didn't finish _____ drawing. He left _____ at home.

4. Did you enter _____ clay pot? That looks like _____.

5. One picture has fallen off _____ stand.

6. Brian and Kendell worked together on a chalk drawing. That sketch by the doorway is _____.

7. The judges have made _____ choices.

8. We both won! They picked both of _____!

9. Here come the judges with our ribbons in _____ hands.

10. Your ribbon is the same as _____.

Writing: Possessive Pronouns

A **possessive pronoun** shows ownership. Instead of writing "That is Jill's book," write "That is her book" or "That is hers." Instead of "I lost my pencil," write "I lost mine." Use possessive pronouns to name what is possessed.

Examples: my (book)   our (car)   your (hat)   his (leg)
her (hair)   their (group)   its (team)

Use **mine**, **ours**, **yours**, **his**, **hers** and **theirs** when you do not name what is possessed. Notice that possessive pronouns don't use apostrophes.

Directions: Complete these sentences with the correct possessive pronoun.

Example: This book belongs to Jon. It is _____his_____.

1. I brought my lunch. Did you bring _____?

2. I can't do my homework. I wonder if Nancy figured out _____.

3. Jason saved his candy bar, but I ate _____.

4. Our team finished our project, but the other team didn't finish _____.

5. They already have their assignment. When will we get _____?

It's easy to confuse the possessive pronoun **its** with the contraction for **it is**, which is spelled **it's**. The apostrophe in **it's** shows that the **i** in **is** has been left out.

Directions: Write **its** or **it's** in each sentence below.

Examples: The book has lost its cover. It's going to rain soon.

1. _____ nearly time to go.

2. The horse hurt _____ leg.

3. Every nation has _____ share of problems.

4. What is _____ name?

5. I think _____ too warm to snow.

6. The teacher said _____ up to us.

English · 115 · Total Basic Skills Grade 5

Indefinite Pronouns

Indefinite pronouns often end with **body**, **one** or **thing**.

Examples:
   Everybody is going to be there.
   No one wants to miss it.

Indefinite pronouns do not change form when used as subjects or objects. They are always singular.

Example:
   Incorrect: Everyone must bring **their** own lunches.
   Correct: All students must bring **their** own lunches.
      Everyone must bring **his or her** own lunch.
      Everyone must bring **a** lunch.

Directions: Write twelve indefinite pronouns by matching a word from column A with a word from column B.

Column A	Column B
any	thing
every	one
no	body
some	

1. _____
2. _____
3. _____
4. _____
5. _____
6. _____
7. _____
8. _____
9. _____
10. _____
11. _____
12. _____

Directions: Write all the indefinite pronouns that would make sense in the sentence below.
_____ can come.

13. _____

Directions: Rewrite this sentence correctly.

14. Everybody has their books.

_____

Interrogative and Relative Pronouns

An **interrogative pronoun** is used when asking a question. The interrogative pronouns are **who**, **what** and **which**. Use **who** when referring to people. Use **what** when referring to things. **Which** can be used to refer to people or things.

Directions: Circle the interrogative pronouns. Write whether the pronoun refers to people or things.

1. Who brought this salad for the picnic?
   _____

2. Which car will we drive to the movies?
   _____

3. Which girl asked the question?
   _____

4. What time is it?
   _____

5. What will we do with the leftover food?
   _____

6. Who is going to the swim meet?
   _____

Relative pronouns refer to the noun or pronoun which comes before them. The noun or pronoun to which it refers is called the **antecedent**. The relative pronouns are **who**, **whom**, **which** and **that**. **Who** and **whom** refer to people. **Which** refers to things or animals. **That** can refer to people, animals or things.

Directions: Circle the relative pronouns and underline the antecedents.

1. My dog, which is very well-behaved, never barks.
2. The story was about a girl who wanted a horse of her own.
3. The bookcase, which was full, toppled over during the night.
4. The man to whom I spoke gave me complicated directions.
5. The book that I wanted had already been checked out of the library.

English · Total Basic Skills Grade 5

Gender and Number of Pronouns

Pronouns that identify males are **masculine gender**. The masculine pronouns are **he**, **his** and **him**. Pronouns that identify females are **feminine gender**. The feminine pronouns are **she**, **her** and **hers**. Pronouns that identify something that is neither male nor female are **neuter gender**. The neuter pronouns are **it** and **its**.

The plural pronouns **they** and **them** are used for masculine, feminine or neuter gender.

Examples:

Noun	Pronoun	Noun	Pronoun
boot	it	woman	she
man	he	John's	his
travelers	they	dog's	its

Directions: List four nouns that each pronoun could replace in a sentence. The first one has been done for you.

1. she   _mother_   _doctor_   _girl_   _friend_
2. he   _____   _____   _____   _____
3. it   _____   _____   _____   _____
4. they   _____   _____   _____   _____
5. hers   _____   _____   _____   _____
6. its   _____   _____   _____   _____

Singular pronouns take the place of singular nouns. Plural pronouns take the place of plural nouns. The singular pronouns are **I**, **me**, **mine**, **he**, **she**, **it**, **its**, **hers**, **his**, **him**, **her**, **you** and **yours**. The plural pronouns are **we**, **you**, **yours**, **they**, **theirs**, **ours**, **them** and **us**.

Directions: Write five sentences. Include a singular and a plural pronoun in each sentence.

1. _____
2. _____
3. _____
4. _____
5. _____

Writing: Pronouns

Sometimes, matching nouns and pronouns can be difficult.

Example: A teacher should always be fair to their students.

Teacher is singular, but **their** is plural, so they don't match. Still, we can't say "A teacher should always be fair to his students," because teachers are both men and women. "His or her students" sounds awkward. One easy way to handle this is to make **teacher** plural so it will match **their**.

Example: Teachers should always be fair to their students.

Directions: Correct the problems in the following sentences by crossing out the incorrect words and writing in the correct nouns and pronouns. (If you make the noun plural, make the verb plural, too.)

Examples: Ron's school won ~~their~~ *its* basketball game.

You can tell if ~~a cat is~~ *cats are* angry by watching their tails.

1. A student should try to praise their friends' strong points.
2. The group finished their work on time in spite of the deadline.
3. A parent usually has a lot of faith in their children.
4. The company paid their workers once a week.
5. The train made their daily run from Chicago to Detroit.
6. Each student should have a title on their papers.

Directions: Complete these sentences with the correct pronouns.

1. Simon fell out of the tree and scraped _____ arm.
2. The citizens felt a deep pride in _____ community.
3. Heather and Sheila wear _____ hair in the same style.
4. I dyed some shirts, but _____ didn't turn out right.
5. The nurse showed the mother how to bathe _____ baby.
6. Our school made $75 from _____ carnival.

Pronouns as Subjects

A **pronoun** is a word that takes the place of a noun. The pronouns **I**, **we**, **he**, **she**, **it**, **you** and **they** can be the subjects of a sentence.

Examples:
  I left the house early.
  You need to be more careful.
  She dances well.

A pronoun must be singular if the noun it replaces is singular. A pronoun must be plural if the noun it replaces is plural. **He**, **she** and **it** are singular pronouns. **We** and **they** are plural pronouns. **You** is both singular and plural.

Examples:
  Tina practiced playing the piano. **She** plays well.
  Jim and I are studying Africa. **We** made a map of it.
  The children clapped loudly. **They** liked the clown.

Directions: Write the correct pronouns.

1. Bobcats hunt at night. _____ are not seen during the day.

2. The mother bobcat usually has babies during February or March. _____ may have two litters a year.

3. The father bobcat stays away when the babies are first born. Later, _____ helps find food for them.

4. We have a new assignment. _____ is a project about bobcats.

5. My group gathered pictures of bobcats. _____ made a display.

6. Jennifer wrote our report. _____ used my notes.

Directions: Circle the pronouns that do not match the nouns they replace. Then write the correct pronouns on the lines.

7. Two boys saw a bobcat. He told us what happened. _____

8. Then we saw a film. They showed bobcats climbing trees. _____

Pronouns as Direct Objects

The pronouns **me**, **you**, **him**, **her**, **it**, **us** and **them** can be used as direct objects.

Examples:
I heard Grant. Grant heard **me**.
We like the teacher. The teacher likes **us**.
He saw the dog. The dog saw **him**.

A pronoun used as a direct object must be plural if the noun is plural and singular if the noun is singular.

Directions: Write the correct pronouns.

1. Goldfish come from China. The Chinese used to eat _____ like trout.

2. The prettiest goldfish were kept as pets. The Chinese put _____ in small bowls and ponds.

3. My sister, brother and I have goldfish. Grandpa took _____ to the store to get them.

4. They come to the top when I am around. I think they like _____ .

5. My sister's fish was white. She kept _____ for 3 weeks.

6. She claimed the fish splashed _____ when she fed it.

Directions: Circle pronouns that do not match the nouns they replace. Rewrite the sentences using the correct pronouns. Change the verbs after the pronouns if necessary.

7. Goldfish often die because kids don't feed it.
_____

8. Some goldfish live a long time because it is well cared for.
_____

9. A wild goldfish will eat anything they think looks good.
_____

10. Birds eat wild goldfish. It likes the young ones best.
_____

English   Total Basic Skills Grade 5

Pronouns as Indirect Objects and Objects of Prepositions

The pronouns **me**, **you**, **him**, **her**, **it**, **us** and **them** can be used as indirect objects and objects of prepositions.

Examples:
　Pronouns as indirect objects: Shawn showed **me** his new bike. The teacher gave **us** two more days to finish our reports.
　Pronouns as objects of prepositions: It's your turn after **her**. I can't do it without **them**.

A pronoun used as an indirect object or an object of a preposition must be singular if the noun it replaces is singular and plural if the noun it replaces is plural.

Directions: Write the correct pronouns. Above the pronoun, write **S** if it is the subject, **DO** if it is the direct object, **IO** if it is the indirect object or **OP** if it is the object of a preposition.

1. Markos is coming to our party. I gave _____ the directions.

2. Janelle and Eldon used to be his friends. Is he still friends with _____?

3. Kevin and I like each other, but _____ are too young to go steady.

4. We listened closely while she told _____ what happened to _____.

5. My brother hurt his hand, but I took care of _____.

6. A piece of glass cut him when _____ dropped _____.

7. When Annalisa won the race, the coach gave _____ a trophy.

8. We were hot and sweaty, but a breeze cooled _____ off.

Adjectives

An **adjective** describes a noun or pronoun. There are three types of adjectives. They are **positive**, **comparative** and **superlative**.

Examples:

Positive	Comparative	Superlative
big	bigger	biggest
beautiful	more beautiful	most beautiful
bright	less bright	least bright

Directions: Write the comparative and superlative forms of these adjectives.

Positive	Comparative	Superlative
1. happy		
2. kind		
3. sad		
4. slow		
5. low		
6. delicious		
7. strong		
8. straight		
9. tall		
10. humble		
11. hard		
12. clear		
13. loud		
14. clever		

Writing: Comparatives

Comparatives are forms of adjectives or adverbs used to compare different things. With adjectives, you usually add **er** to the end to make a comparative. If the adjective ends in **y**, drop the **y** and add **ier**.

Examples:	**Adjective**	**Comparative**
	tall	taller
	easy	easier

With adverbs, you usually add **more** before the word to make a comparative.

Examples:	**Adverb**	**Comparative**
	quickly	more quickly
	softly	more softly

Directions: Using the given adjective or adverb, write a sentence comparing the two nouns.

Example: clean   my room   my sister's room

<u>My room is always cleaner than my sister's room.</u>

1. cold   Alaska   Florida
   _____

2. neatly   Maria   her brother
   _____

3. easy   English   Math
   _____

4. scary   book   movie
   _____

5. loudly   the drummer   the guitarist
   _____

6. pretty   autumn   winter
   _____

"Good" and "Bad"

When the adjectives **good** and **bad** are used to compare things, the entire word changes.

Examples:

	Comparative	Superlative
good	better	best
bad	worse	worst

Use the comparative form of an adjective to compare two people or objects. Use the superlative form to compare three or more people or objects.

Examples:
This is a **good** day.
Tomorrow will be **better** than today.
My birthday is the **best** day of the year.

This hamburger tastes **bad**.
Does it taste **worse** than the one your brother cooked?
It's the **worst** hamburger I have ever eaten.

Directions: Write the correct words in the blanks to complete these sentences.

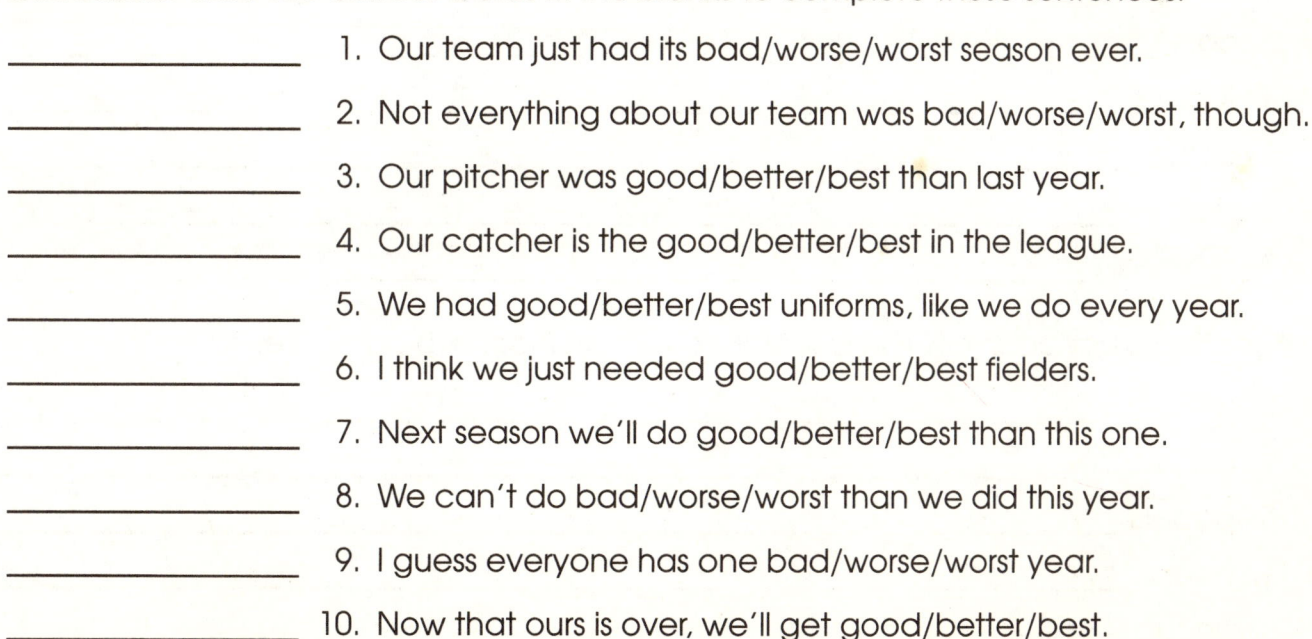

_____ 1. Our team just had its bad/worse/worst season ever.

_____ 2. Not everything about our team was bad/worse/worst, though.

_____ 3. Our pitcher was good/better/best than last year.

_____ 4. Our catcher is the good/better/best in the league.

_____ 5. We had good/better/best uniforms, like we do every year.

_____ 6. I think we just needed good/better/best fielders.

_____ 7. Next season we'll do good/better/best than this one.

_____ 8. We can't do bad/worse/worst than we did this year.

_____ 9. I guess everyone has one bad/worse/worst year.

_____ 10. Now that ours is over, we'll get good/better/best.

Demonstrative and Indefinite Adjectives

A **demonstrative adjective** identifies a particular person, place or thing. **This**, **these**, **that** and **those** are demonstrative adjectives.

Examples:
- **this** pen
- **that** chair
- **these** earrings
- **those** books

An **indefinite adjective** does not identify a particular person, place or thing but rather a group or number. **All**, **any**, **both**, **many**, **another**, **several**, **such**, **some**, **few** and **more** are indefinite adjectives.

Examples:
- **all** teachers
- **both** girls
- **another** man
- **any** person
- **many** flowers
- **more** marbles

Directions: Use each noun in a sentence with a demonstrative adjective.

1. dishes _____
2. clothes _____
3. cats _____
4. team _____
5. apples _____
6. stereo _____
7. mountain _____

Directions: Use each noun in a sentence with an indefinite adjective.

8. reporters _____
9. decisions _____
10. papers _____
11. pears _____
12. occupations _____
13. friends _____

Total Basic Skills Grade 5   English

Interrogative and Possessive Adjectives

An **interrogative adjective** is used when asking a question. The interrogative adjectives are **what** and **which**.

Examples:
　　What kind of haircut will you get?
　　Which dog snarled at you?

A **possessive adjective** shows ownership. The possessive adjectives are **our**, **your**, **her**, **his**, **its**, **my** and **their**.

Examples:
　　That is **my** dog.
　　He washed **his** jeans.
　　Our pictures turned out great.

Directions: Write six sentences containing interrogative adjectives and six sentences containing possessive adjectives.

Interrogative Adjectives

1. _____
2. _____
3. _____
4. _____
5. _____
6. _____

Possessive Adjectives

1. _____
2. _____
3. _____
4. _____
5. _____
6. _____

English　　　　　　　　　　　　　　　　　　　　　　Total Basic Skills Grade 5

Prepositional Phrases as Adjectives

An adjective can be one word or an entire prepositional phrase.

Examples:
 The **new** boy **with red hair**
 The **tall** man **in the raincoat**
 The **white** house **with green shutters**

Directions: Underline the prepositional phrases used as adjectives.

1. The boy in the blue cap is the captain.
2. The house across the street is 100 years old.
3. Jo and Ty love cookies with nuts.
4. I lost the book with the green cover.
5. Do you know the girl in the front row?
6. I like the pony with the long tail.
7. The dog in that yard is not friendly.
8. The picture in this magazine looks like you.

Directions: Complete these sentences with prepositional phrases used as adjectives.

9. I'd like a hamburger _____.

10. Did you read the book _____?

11. The dog _____ is my favorite.

12. The woman _____ is calling you.

13. I bought a shirt _____.

14. I'm wearing socks _____.

15. I found a box _____.

Total Basic Skills Grade 5   English

Adverbs

Adverbs modify verbs. Adverbs tell **when**, **where** or **how**. Many, but not all adverbs, end in **ly**.

Adverbs of time answer the questions **how often** or **when**.

Examples:
  The dog escapes its pen **frequently**.
  Smart travelers **eventually** will learn to use travelers' checks.

Adverbs of place answer the question **where**.

Example: The police pushed bystanders **away** from the accident scene.

Adverbs of manner answer the questions **how** or **in what manner**.

Example: He **carefully** replaced the delicate vase.

Directions: Underline the verb in each sentence. Circle the adverb. Write the question each adverb answers on the line.

1. My grandmother walks gingerly to avoid falls.

2. The mice darted everywhere to escape the cat.

3. He decisively moved the chess piece.

4. Our family frequently enjoys a night at the movies.

5. Later, we will discuss the consequences of your behavior.

6. The audience glanced up at the balcony where the noise originated.

7. The bleachers are already built for the concert.

8. My friend and I study daily for the upcoming exams.

English — Total Basic Skills Grade 5

Prepositional Phrases as Adverbs

An adverb can be one word or an entire prepositional phrase.

Examples:
They'll be here **tomorrow**.
They always come **on time**.
Move it **down**.
Put it **under the picture**.
Drive **carefully**.
He drove **with care**.

Directions: Underline the adverb or prepositional phrase used as an adverb in each sentence. In the blank, write **how**, **when** or **where** to tell what the adverb or prepositional phrase explains.

1. Don't go swimming without a buddy. _____

2. Don't go swimming alone. _____

3. I wish you still lived here. _____

4. I wish you still lived on our street. _____

5. I will eat lunch soon. _____

6. I will eat lunch in a few minutes. _____

7. He will be here in a few hours. _____

8. He will be here later. _____

9. I'm going outside. _____

10. I'm going in the backyard. _____

11. She smiled happily. _____

12. She smiled with happiness. _____

Writing: Adjectives and Adverbs

An **adjective** is a describing word. It describes nouns. Adjectives can tell:
• Which one or what kind — the dog's **floppy** ears, the **lost** child
• How many — **three** wagons, **four** drawers

An **adverb** is also a describing word. It describes verbs, adjectives or other adverbs. Adverbs can tell:
• How — ran **quickly**, talked **quietly**
• When — finished **prompty**, came **yesterday**
• Where — lived **there**, drove **backward**
• How often — sneezed **twice**, **always** wins

Directions: The adjectives and adverbs are bold in the sentences below. Above each, write **ADJ** for adjective or **ADV** for adverb. Then draw an arrow to the noun the adjective describes or to the verb the adverb describes.

Example: A girl in a **green** jacket **quickly** released the birds into the sky. (ADJ, ADV)

1. An **old** mayor was elected **twice**.

2. He **carefully** put the **tall** screen between our desks.

3. The **new** boy in our class moved **here** from Phoenix.

4. **Today**, our **soccer** team **finally** made its **first** goal.

5. The woman **gently** coaxed the **frightened** kitten out of the tree.

Directions: Use adjectives and adverbs to answer the questions below.

Example: The boy talked. (Which boy? How?)
The nervous boy talked loudly.

1. The plant grew. (Which plant? How?)

2. The birds flew. (How many? What kind? Where?)

English   Total Basic Skills Grade 5

Placement of Adjective and Adverb Phrases

Adjectives and adverbs, including prepositional phrases, should be placed as close as possible to the words they describe to avoid confusion.

Example:
   Confusing: The boy under the pile of leaves looked for the ball.
       (Is the boy or the ball under the pile of leaves?)
   Clear: The boy looked under the pile of leaves for the ball.

Directions: Rewrite each sentence by moving the prepositional phrase closer to the word or words it describes. The first one has been done for you.

1. A bird at the pet store bit me in the mall.
   A bird at the pet store in the mall bit me.

2. The woman was looking for her dog in the large hat.

3. This yard would be great for a dog with a fence.

4. The car hit the stop sign with the silver stripe.

5. My cousin with a big bow gave me a present.

6. The house was near some woods with a pond.

7. I'll be back to wash the dishes in a minute.

8. We like to eat eggs in the morning with toast.

9. He bought a shirt at the new store with short sleeves.

10. We live in the house down the street with tall windows.

Writing: Parts of Speech Story

Directions: Play the following game with a partner. In the story below, some of the words are missing. Without letting your partner see the story, ask him/her to provide a word for each blank. Each word should be a noun, verb, adjective or adverb, as shown. Then read the story aloud. It might not make sense, but it will make you laugh!

Last night, as I was _____ through the _____, a
                           (verb + ing)   (noun)

_____ _____ fell from the ceiling and landed on my
(adjective)   (noun)

head! "Yikes!" I shrieked. I _____ _____ through the
                           (past-tense verb)   (adverb)

_____, trying to get rid of the thing. Finally, it fell off, and it started
(noun)

_____ around the _____. I tried to hit it with a _____,
(verb + ing)   (noun)   (noun)

but it was too _____. I _____ managed to _____
              (adjective)   (adverb)   (verb)

it out of the house, where it quickly climbed the nearest _____.
                                                                           (noun)

Writing: Parts of Speech

Directions: Write each word from the box in the column that names its part of speech. Some words can be listed in two columns.

Example: a chair **behind** me   he was walking **behind** me
           ADJ   ADV

code	young	slowly	today	finally	screen
thirsty	praise	loan	broken	decrease	slowly
nearby	twenty	Monday	town	faithful	red
coax	goal	bathe	release	cheat	there

Noun	Verb	Adjective	Adverb
___	___	___	___
___	___	___	___
___	___	___	___
___	___	___	___
___	___	___	___
___	___	___	___

Directions: Write four sentences, using at least three words from the box in each one. Mark each word as a noun (**N**), verb (**V**), adjective (**ADJ**) or adverb (**ADV**).

Example: **Twenty** people **slowly** walked through the **town**.
           ADJ   ADV   N

_____

_____

_____

_____

Total Basic Skills Grade 5   134   English

Conjunctions

A **conjunction** joins words or groups of words in a sentence. The most commonly used conjunctions are **and**, **but** and **or**.

Examples: My brother **and** I each want to win the trophy.
Tonight, it will rain **or** sleet.
I wanted to go to the party, **but** I got sick.

Directions: Circle the conjunctions.

1. Dolphins and whales are mammals.
2. They must rise to the surface of the water to breathe, or they will die.
3. Dolphins resemble fish, but they are not fish.
4. Sightseeing boats are often entertained by groups of dolphins or whales.
5. Whales appear to effortlessly leap out of the water and execute flips.
6. Both whale and dolphin babies are born alive.
7. The babies are called calves and are born in the water, but must breathe air within a few minutes of birth.
8. Sometimes an entire pod of whales will help a mother and calf reach the surface to breathe.
9. Scientists and marine biologists have long been intrigued by these ocean animals.
10. Whales and dolphins do not seem to be afraid of humans or boats.

Directions: Write six sentences using conjunctions.

11. _____
12. _____
13. _____
14. _____
15. _____
16. _____

English Total Basic Skills Grade 5

Writing: Conjunctions

Too many short sentences make writing seem choppy. Short sentences can be combined to make writing flow better. Words used to combine sentences are called **conjunctions**.

Examples: but, before, after, because, when, or, so, and

Directions: Use **or**, **but**, **before**, **after**, **because**, **when**, **and** or **so** to combine each pair of sentences. The first one has been done for you.

1. I was wearing my winter coat. I started to shiver.

    <u>I was wearing my winter coat, but I started to shiver.</u>

2. Animals all need water. They may perish without it.
    _____

3. The sun came out. The ice began to thaw.
    _____

4. The sun came out. The day was still chilly.
    _____

5. Will the flowers perish? Will they thrive?
    _____

6. The bear came closer. We began to feel threatened.
    _____

7. Winning was a challenge. Our team didn't have much experience.
    _____

8. Winning was a challenge. Our team was up to it.
    _____

Directions: Write three sentences of your own. Use a conjunction in each sentence.

Statements and Questions

A **statement** is a sentence that tells something. It ends with a period (.).

A **question** is a sentence that asks something. It ends with a question mark (?).

Examples:
   Statement: Shari is walking to school today.
   Question: Is Shari walking to school today?

In some questions, the subject comes between two parts of the verb. In the examples below, the subjects are underlined. The verbs and the rest of the predicates are bold.

Examples:
   Is Steve **coming with us**?
   Who **will be there**?
   Which one did you **select**?

To find the predicate, turn a question into a statement.

Example: Is Steve coming with us? Steve is coming with us.

Directions: Write **S** for statement or **Q** for question. Put a period after the statements and a question mark after the questions.

_____ 1. Today is the day for our field trip
_____ 2. How are we going to get there
_____ 3. The bus will take us
_____ 4. Is there room for everyone
_____ 5. Who forgot to bring a lunch
_____ 6. I'll save you a seat

Directions: Circle the subjects and underline all parts of the predicates.

7. Do you like field trips?
8. Did you bring your coat?
9. Will it be cold there?
10. Do you see my gloves anywhere?
11. Is anyone sitting with you?
12. Does the bus driver have a map?
13. Are all the roads this bumpy?

English   Total Basic Skills Grade 5

Statements and Questions

Directions: Write 10 statements and 10 questions.

Statements

1. _____
2. _____
3. _____
4. _____
5. _____
6. _____
7. _____
8. _____
9. _____
10. _____

Questions

1. _____
2. _____
3. _____
4. _____
5. _____
6. _____
7. _____
8. _____
9. _____
10. _____

Commands, Requests and Exclamations

A **command** is a sentence that orders someone to do something. It ends with a period or an exclamation mark (!).

A **request** is a sentence that asks someone to do something. It ends with a period or a question mark (?).

An **exclamation** is a sentence that shows strong feeling. It ends with an exclamation mark (!).

Examples:
  Command: Stay in your seat.
  Request: Would you please pass the salt?
    Please pass the salt.
  Exclamation: Call the police!

In the first and last two sentences in the examples, the subject is not stated. The subject is understood to be **you**.

Directions: Write **C** if the sentence is a command, **R** if it is a request and **E** if it is an exclamation. Put the correct punctuation at the end of each sentence.

_____ 1. Look both ways before you cross the street

_____ 2. Please go to the store and buy some bread for us

_____ 3. The house is on fire

_____ 4. Would you hand me the glue

_____ 5. Don't step there

_____ 6. Write your name at the top of the page

_____ 7. Please close the door

_____ 8. Would you answer the phone

_____ 9. Watch out

_____ 10. Take one card from each pile

Commands, Requests and Exclamations

Directions: Write six sentences for each type listed.

Command

1. _____
2. _____
3. _____
4. _____
5. _____
6. _____

Request

1. _____
2. _____
3. _____
4. _____
5. _____
6. _____

Exclamation

1. _____
2. _____
3. _____
4. _____
5. _____
6. _____

Writing: Four Kinds of Sentences

There are four kinds of sentences used in writing. Different punctuation is used for different kinds of sentences.

A **statement** tells something. A period is used after statements.

Examples: I jogged five miles yesterday.
We are going to have a spelling test on Friday.

A **question** asks something. A question mark is used after questions.

Examples: What are you wearing to the dance?
Will it ever stop raining?

An **exclamation** shows strong feeling or excitement. An exclamation mark is used after exclamations.

Examples: Boy, am I tired!
What a beautiful painting!

A **command** tells someone to do something. A period or an exclamation mark is used after a command, depending on how strong it is.

Examples: Please hand me that pen. Don't touch the stove!

Directions: Write the correct punctuation mark at the end of each sentence below. Then write whether the sentence is a statement, question, exclamation or command.

Example: I didn't have time to finish my homework last night. __statement__

1. Why didn't she come shopping with us _____
2. Somebody call an ambulance _____
3. He's been watching TV all morning _____
4. How did you do on the quiz _____
5. Go sit in the third row _____
6. I have to go to the dentist tomorrow _____
7. I've never been so hungry _____
8. Who tracked mud all over the house _____
9. That restaurant is too expensive _____

English 141 Total Basic Skills Grade 5

Compound Subjects/Compound Predicates

A **compound subject** has two or more nouns or pronouns joined by a conjunction. Compound subjects share the same predicate.

Examples:
    Suki and Spot walked to the park in the rain.
    Cars, buses and trucks splashed water on them.
    He and I were glad we had our umbrella.

A **compound predicate** has two or more verbs joined by a conjunction. Compound predicates share the same subject.

Examples:
    Suki **went** in the restroom **and wiped** off her shoes.
    Paula **followed** Suki **and waited** for her.

A sentence can have a compound subject and a compound predicate.

Example: Tina and Maria went to the mall **and shopped** for an hour.

Directions: Circle the compound subjects. Underline the compound predicates.

1. Steve and Jerry went to the store and bought some gum.
2. Police and firefighters worked together and put out the fire.
3. Karen and Marsha did their homework and checked it twice.
4. In preschool, the boys and girls drew pictures and colored them.

Directions: Write compound subjects to go with these predicates.

5. _____ ate peanut butter sandwiches.
6. _____ left early.
7. _____ don't make good pets.
8. _____ found their way home.
9. _____ are moving to Denver.

Directions: Write compound predicates to go with these subjects.

10. A scary book _____
11. My friend's sister _____
12. The shadow _____
13. The wind _____
14. The runaway car _____

Total Basic Skills Grade 5   English

Combining Subjects

Too many short sentences make writing sound choppy. Often, we can combine sentences with different subjects and the same predicate to make one sentence with a compound subject.

Example:
   Lisa tried out for the play. Todd tried out for the play.
   Compound subject: Lisa and Todd tried out for the play.

When sentences have different subjects and different predicates, we cannot combine them this way. Each subject and predicate must stay together. Two short sentences can be combined with a conjunction.

Examples:
   Lisa got a part in the play. Todd will help make scenery.
   Lisa got a part in the play, and Todd will help make scenery.

Directions: If a pair of sentences share the same predicate, combine them with compound subjects. If the sentences have different subjects and predicates, combine them using **and**.

1. Rachel read a book about explorers. Eric read the same book about explorers.
   _____

2. Rachel really liked the book. Eric agreed with her.
   _____

3. Vicki went to the basketball game last night. Dan went to the basketball game, too.
   _____

4. Vicki lost her coat. Dan missed his ride home.
   _____

5. My uncle planted corn in the garden. My mother planted corn in the garden.
   _____

6. Isaac helped with the food drive last week. Amy helped with the food drive, too.
   _____

English   143   Total Basic Skills Grade 5

Combining Predicates

If short sentences have the same subject and different predicates, we can combine them into one sentence with a compound predicate.

Example:
Andy got up late this morning.
He nearly missed the school bus.
Compound predicate: Andy got up late this morning and nearly missed the school bus.

The pronoun **he** takes the place of Andy in the second sentence, so the subjects are the same and can be combined.

When two sentences have different subjects and different predicates, we cannot combine them this way. Two short sentences can be combined with a conjunction.

Examples:
Andy got up late this morning. Cindy woke up early.
Andy got up late this morning, but Cindy woke up early.

Directions: If the pair of sentences share the same subject, combine them with compound predicates. If the sentences have different subjects and predicates, combine them using **and** or **but**.

1. Kyle practiced pitching all winter. Kyle became the pitcher for his team.

2. Kisha studied two hours for her history test. Angela watched TV.

3. Jeff had an earache. He took medicine four times a day.

4. Nikki found a new hair style. Melissa didn't like that style.

5. Kirby buys his lunch every day. Sean brings his lunch from home.

Writing: Using Commas Correctly

A **comma** tells a reader where to pause when reading a sentence. Use commas when combining two or more *complete* sentences with a joining word.

Examples: We raked the leaves, and **we put them into bags**.
Brian dressed quickly, but **he still missed the school bus**.

Do not use commas if you are not combining complete sentences.

Examples: We raked the leaves and put them into bags.
Brian dressed quickly but still missed the school bus.

If either part of the sentence does not have both a subject and a verb, do not use a comma.

Directions: Read each sentence below and decide whether or not it needs a comma. If it does, rewrite the sentence, placing the comma correctly. If it doesn't, write **O.K.** on the line.

1. The cat stretched lazily and walked out of the room.

   _____

2. I could use the money to buy a new shirt or I could go to the movies.

   _____

3. My sister likes pizza but she doesn't like spaghetti.

   _____

4. Mom mixed the batter and poured it into the pan.

   _____

5. The teacher passed out the tests and she told us to write our names on them.

   _____

6. The car squealed its tires and took off out of the parking lot.

   _____

7. The snow fell heavily and we knew the schools would be closed the next day.

   _____

8. The batter hit the ball and it flew over the fence.

   _____

Run-On Sentences

A **run-on sentence** occurs when two or more sentences are joined together without the correct punctuation. A run-on sentence must be divided into two or more separate sentences.

Example:
Run-on: On Tuesday my family went to the amusement park but unfortunately it rained and we got wet and it took hours for our clothes to dry.
Correct: On Tuesday, my family went to the amusement park. Unfortunately, it rained and we got wet. It took hours for our clothes to dry.

Directions: Rewrite these run-on sentences correctly.

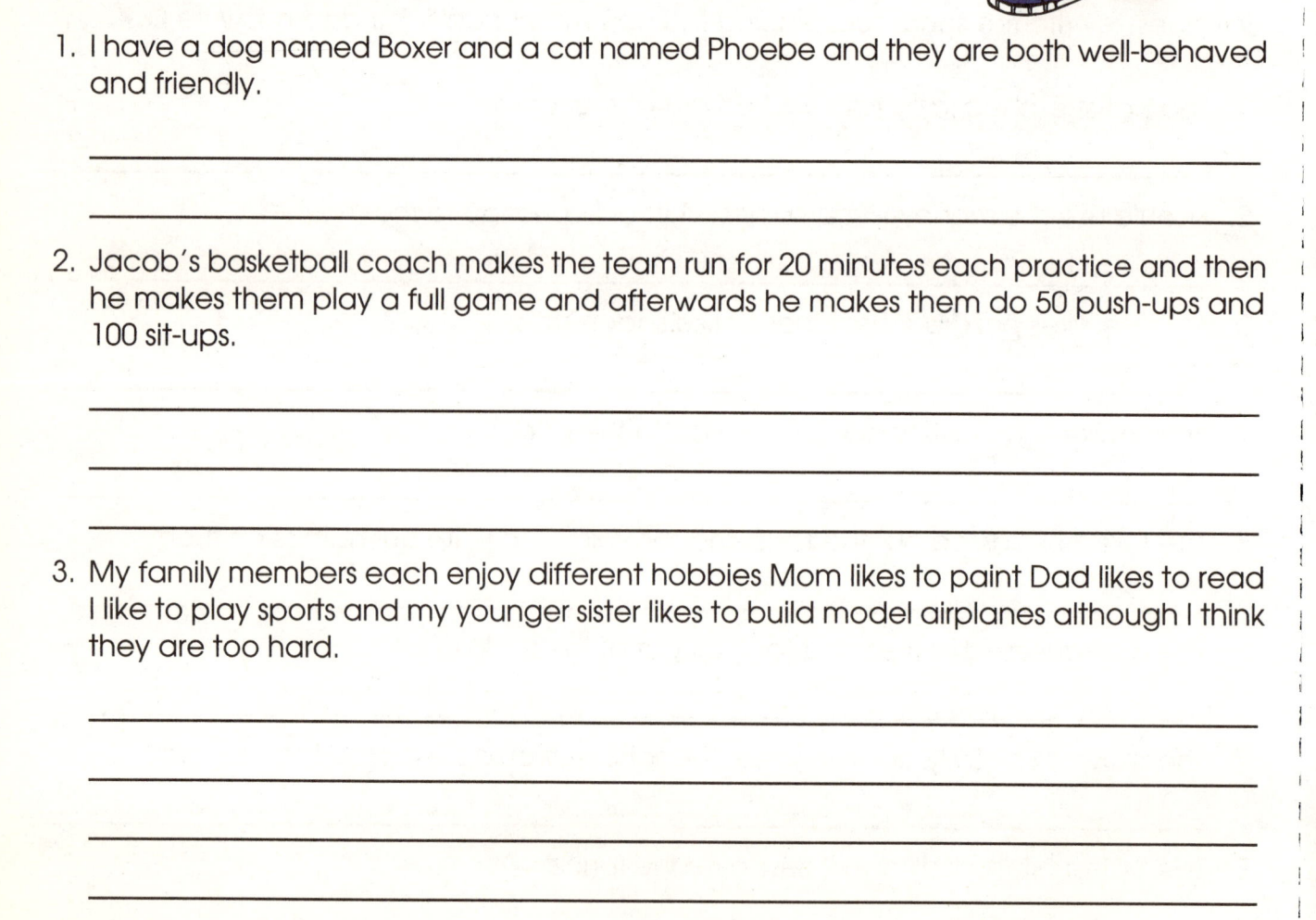

1. I have a dog named Boxer and a cat named Phoebe and they are both well-behaved and friendly.

   _____
   _____

2. Jacob's basketball coach makes the team run for 20 minutes each practice and then he makes them play a full game and afterwards he makes them do 50 push-ups and 100 sit-ups.

   _____
   _____
   _____

3. My family members each enjoy different hobbies Mom likes to paint Dad likes to read I like to play sports and my younger sister likes to build model airplanes although I think they are too hard.

   _____
   _____
   _____
   _____

Commas

Commas are used to separate items in a series. Both examples below are correct. A final comma is optional.

Examples:
    The fruit bowl contains oranges, peaches, pears, and apples.
    The fruit bowl contains oranges, peaches, pears and apples.

Commas are also used to separate geographical names and dates.

Examples:
    Today's date is January 13, 2000.
    My grandfather lives in Tallahassee, Florida.
    I would like to visit Paris, France.

Directions: Place commas where needed in these sentences.

1. I was born on September 21 1992.
2. John's favorite sports include basketball football hockey and soccer.
3. The ship will sail on November 16 2004.
4. My family and I vacationed in Salt Lake City Utah.
5. I like to plant beans beets corn and radishes in my garden.
6. Sandy's party will be held in Youngstown Ohio.
7. Periods commas colons and exclamation marks are types of punctuation.
8. Cardinals juncos blue jays finches and sparrows frequent our birdfeeder.
9. My grandfather graduated from high school on June 4 1962.
10. The race will take place in Burlington Vermont.

Directions: Write a sentence using commas to separate words in a series.

11. _____

Directions: Write a sentence using commas to separate geographical names.

12. _____

Directions: Write a sentence using commas to separate dates.

13. _____

Commas

Commas are used to separate a noun or pronoun in a direct address from the rest of the sentence. A noun or pronoun in a **direct address** is one that names or refers to the person addressed.

Examples:
   John, this room is a mess!
   This room, **John,** is a disgrace!
   Your room needs to be more organized, **John**.

Commas are used to separate an appositive from the rest of the sentence. An **appositive** is a word or words that give the reader more information about a previous noun or pronoun.

Examples:
   My teacher, **Ms. Wright**, gave us a test.
   Thomas Edison, **the inventor of the lightbulb**, was an interesting man.

Directions: Place commas where needed in these sentences. Then write **appositive** or **direct address** on the line to explain why the commas were used.

1. Melissa do you know the answer? _____

2. John the local football hero led the parade through town. _____

3. Cancun a Mexican city is a favorite vacation destination. _____

4. Please help me move the chair Gail. _____

5. My great-grandfather an octogenarian has witnessed many events. _____

6. The president of the company Madison Fagan addressed his workers. _____

7. My favorite book *Anne of Green Gables* is a joy to read. _____

8. Your painting Andre shows great talent. _____

Total Basic Skills Grade 5   148   English

Combining Sentences

When the subjects are the same, sentences can be combined by using appositives.

Examples:
Tony likes to play basketball. Tony is my neighbor.
Tony, **my neighbor**, likes to play basketball.

Ms. Herman was sick today. Ms. Herman is our math teacher.
Ms. Herman, **our math teacher**, was sick today.

Appositives are set off from the rest of the sentence with commas.

Directions: Use commas and appositives to combine the pairs of sentences.

1. Julie has play practice today. Julie is my sister.

   _____

2. Greg fixed my bicycle. Greg is my cousin.

   _____

3. Mr. Scott told us where to meet. Mr. Scott is our coach.

   _____

4. Tiffany is moving to Detroit. Tiffany is my neighbor.

   _____

5. Kyle has the flu. Kyle is my brother.

   _____

6. My favorite football team is playing tonight. Houston is my favorite team.

   _____

7. Bonnie Pryor will be at our school next week. Bonnie Pryor is a famous author.

   _____

8. Our neighborhood is having a garage sale. Our neighborhood is the North End.

   _____

English

Punctuation

Directions: Add commas where needed. Put the correct punctuation at the end of each sentence.

1. My friend Jamie loves to snowboard

2. Winter sports such as hockey skiing and skating are fun

3. Oh what a lovely view

4. The map shows the continents of Asia Africa Australia and Antarctica

5. My mother a ballet dancer will perform tonight

6. What will you do tomorrow

7. When will the plane arrive at the airport

8. Jason do you know what time it is

9. Friends of ours the Watsons are coming for dinner

10. Margo look out for that falling rock

11. The young child sat reading a book

12. Who wrote this letter

13. My sister Jill is very neat

14. The trampoline is in our backyard

15. We will have chicken peas rice and salad for dinner

16. That dog a Saint Bernard looks dangerous

Quotation Marks

When a person's exact words are used in a sentence, **quotation marks** (" ") are used to identify those words. Commas are used to set off the quotation from the rest of the sentence. End punctuation is placed inside the final quotation mark.

Examples:
"When are we leaving?" Joe asked.
Marci shouted, "Go, team!"

When a sentence is interrupted by words that are not part of the quotation (he said, she answered, etc.), they are not included in the quotation marks. Note how commas are used in the next example.

Example: "I am sorry," the man announced, "for my rude behavior."

Directions: Place quotation marks, commas and other punctuation where needed in the sentences below.

1. Watch out yelled Dad.
2. Angela said I don't know how you can eat Brussels sprouts, Ted
3. Put on your coats said Mom. We'll be leaving in 10 minutes
4. Did you hear the assignment asked Joan.
5. Jim shouted This game is driving me up the wall
6. After examining our dog, the veterinarian said He looks healthy and strong
7. The toddlers both wailed We want ice cream
8. The judge announced to the swimmers Take your places
9. Upon receiving the award, the actor said I'd like to thank my friends and family
10. These are my favorite chips said Becky.
11. This test is too hard moaned the class.
12. When their relay team came in first place, the runners shouted, Hooray
13. Where shall we go on vacation this year Dad asked.
14. As we walked past the machinery, the noise was deafening. Cover your ears said Mom.
15. Fire yelled the chef as his pan ignited.
16. I love basketball my little brother stated.

Capitalization/Punctuation

Directions: Rewrite the paragraphs below, adding punctuation where it is needed. Capitalize the first word of each sentence and all other words that should be capitalized.

most countries have laws that control advertising in norway no ads at all are allowed on radio or TV in the united states ads for alcoholic drinks, except beer and wine, are not permitted on radio or TV england has a law against advertising cigarettes on TV what do you think about these laws should they be even stricter

_____
_____
_____
_____

my cousin jeff is starting college this fall he wants to be a medical doctor, so he's going to central university the mayor of our town went there mayor stevens told jeff all about the university our town is so small that everyone knows what everyone else is doing is your town like that

_____
_____
_____
_____

my grandparents took a long vacation last year grandma really likes to go to the atlantic ocean and watch the dolphins my grandfather likes to fish in the ocean my aunt went with them last summer they all had a party on the fourth of july

_____
_____
_____
_____

Capitalization

Directions: Write **C** if capital letters are used correctly or **X** if they are used incorrectly.

____ 1. Who will win the election for Mayor in November?

____ 2. Tom Johnson used to be a police officer.

____ 3. He announced on monday that he wants to be mayor.

____ 4. My father said he would vote for Tom.

____ 5. Mom and my sister Judy haven't decided yet.

____ 6. They will vote at our school.

____ 7. Every Fall and Spring they put up voting booths there.

____ 8. I hope the new mayor will do something about our river.

____ 9. That River is full of chemicals.

____ 10. I'm glad our water doesn't come from Raven River.

____ 11. In late Summer, the river actually stinks.

____ 12. Is every river in our State so dirty?

____ 13. Scientists check the water every so often.

____ 14. Some professors from the college even examined it.

____ 15. That is getting to be a very educated River!

Directions: Write sentences that include:

16. A person's title that should be capitalized.

_____

17. The name of a place that should be capitalized.

_____

18. The name of a time (day, month, holiday) that should be capitalized.

_____

"Who" Clauses

A **clause** is a group of words with a subject and a verb. When the subject of two sentences is the same person or people, the sentences can sometimes be combined with a "who" clause.

Examples:
Mindy likes animals. Mindy feeds the squirrels.
Mindy, **who likes animals**, feeds the squirrels.

A "who" clause is set off from the rest of the sentence with commas.

Directions: Combine the pairs of sentences, using "who" clauses.

1. Teddy was late to school. Teddy was sorry later.

   _____

2. Our principal is retiring. Our principal will be 65 this year.

   _____

3. Michael won the contest. Michael will receive an award.

   _____

4. Charlene lives next door. Charlene has three cats.

   _____

5. Burt drew that picture. Burt takes art lessons.

   _____

6. Marta was elected class president. Marta gave a speech.

   _____

7. Amy broke her arm. Amy has to wear a cast for 6 weeks.

   _____

8. Dr. Bank fixed my tooth. He said it would feel better soon.

   _____

"Which" Clauses

When the subject of two sentences is the same thing or things, the sentences can sometimes be combined with a "which" clause.

Examples:
The guppy was first called "the millions fish." The guppy was later named after Reverend Robert Guppy in 1866.
The guppy, **which was first called "the millions fish,"** was later named after Reverend Robert Guppy in 1866.

A "which" clause is set off from the rest of the sentence with commas.

Directions: Combine the pairs of sentences using "which" clauses.

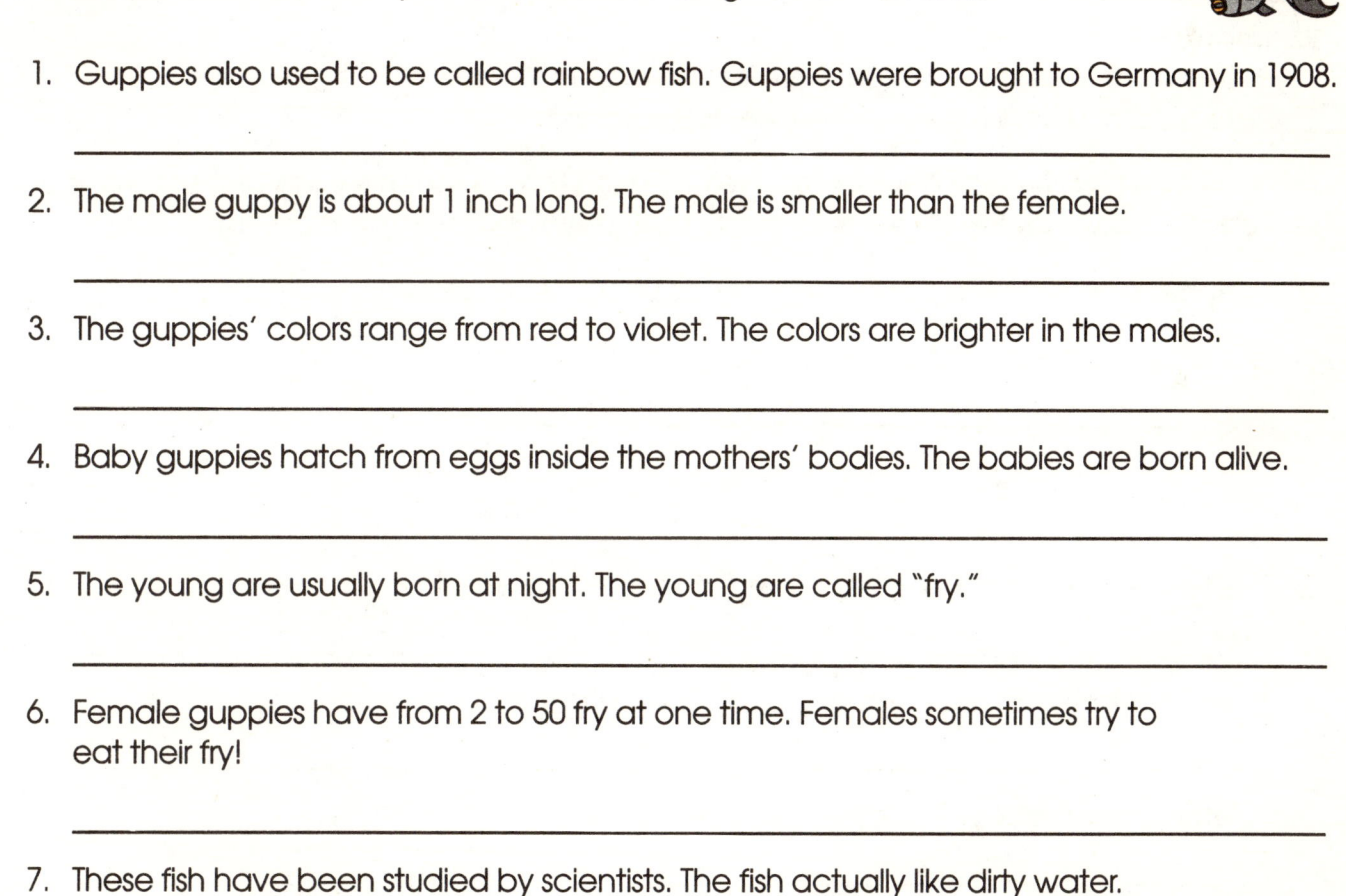

1. Guppies also used to be called rainbow fish. Guppies were brought to Germany in 1908.
   _____

2. The male guppy is about 1 inch long. The male is smaller than the female.
   _____

3. The guppies' colors range from red to violet. The colors are brighter in the males.
   _____

4. Baby guppies hatch from eggs inside the mothers' bodies. The babies are born alive.
   _____

5. The young are usually born at night. The young are called "fry."
   _____

6. Female guppies have from 2 to 50 fry at one time. Females sometimes try to eat their fry!
   _____

7. These fish have been studied by scientists. The fish actually like dirty water.
   _____

8. Wild guppies eat mosquito eggs. Wild guppies help control the mosquito population.
   _____

English   Total Basic Skills Grade 5

"That" Clauses

When the subject of two sentences is the same thing or things, the sentences can sometimes be combined with a "that" clause. We use **that** instead of **which** when the clause is very important in the sentence.

Examples:
　　The store is near our house. The store was closed.
　　The store **that is near our house** was closed.

The words "**that is near our house**" are very important in the combined sentence. They tell the reader which store was closed.
A "that" clause is not set off from the rest of the sentence with commas.

Examples:
　　Pete's store is near our house. Pete's store was closed.
　　Pete's store, which is near our house, was closed.

The words "**which is near our house**" are not important to the meaning of the combined sentence. The words **Pete's store** already told us which store was closed.

Directions: Combine the pairs of sentences using "that" clauses.

1. The dog lives next door. The dog chased me.

   _____

2. The bus was taking us to the game. The bus had a flat tire.

   _____

3. The fence is around the school. The fence is painted yellow.

   _____

4. The notebook had my homework in it. The notebook is lost.

   _____

5. A letter came today. The letter was from Mary.

   _____

6. The lamp was fixed yesterday. The lamp doesn't work today.

   _____

7. The lake is by our cabin. The lake is filled with fish.

   _____

Total Basic Skills Grade 5　　　　　　　　　English

"That" and "Which" Clauses

Directions: Combine the pairs of sentences using either a "that" or a "which" clause.

1. The TV show was on at 8:00 last night. The TV show was funny.

   _____

2. *The Snappy Show* was on at 8:00 last night. *The Snappy Show* was funny.

   _____

3. The Main Bank is on the corner. The Main Bank is closed today.

   _____

4. The bank is on the corner. The bank is closed today.

   _____

5. The bus takes Dad to work. The bus broke down.

   _____

6. The Broad Street bus takes Dad to work. The Broad Street bus broke down.

   _____

Combining Sentences

Not every pair of sentences can be combined with "who," "which" or "that" clauses. These sentences can be combined in other ways, either with a conjunction or by renaming the subject.

Examples:
　　Tim couldn't go to sleep. Todd was sleeping soundly.
　　Tim couldn't go to sleep, **but** Todd was sleeping soundly.

　　The zoo keeper fed the baby ape. A crowd gathered to watch.
　　When the zoo keeper fed the baby ape, a crowd gathered to watch.

Directions: Combine each pair of sentences using "who," "which" or "that" clauses, by using a conjunction or by renaming the subject.

1. The box slipped off the truck. The box was filled with bottles.

   _____

2. Carolyn is our scout leader. Carolyn taught us a new game.

   _____

3. The girl is 8 years old. The girl called the emergency number when her grandmother fell.

   _____

4. The meatloaf is ready to eat. The salad isn't made yet.

   _____

5. The rain poured down. The rain canceled our picnic.

   _____

6. The sixth grade class went on a field trip. The school was much quieter.

   _____

Total Basic Skills Grade 5　　　　158　　　　English

"Who's" and "Whose"

Who's is a contraction for **who is**.

Whose is a possessive pronoun.

Examples:
   Who's going to come?
   Whose shirt is this?

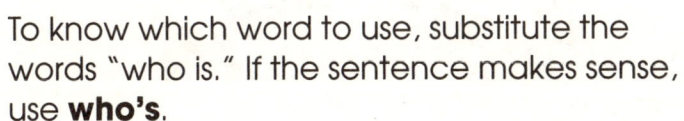

To know which word to use, substitute the words "who is." If the sentence makes sense, use **who's**.

Directions: Write the correct words to complete these sentences.

_____ 1. Do you know who's/whose invited to the party?

_____ 2. I don't even know who's/whose house it will be at.

_____ 3. Who's/Whose towel is on the floor?

_____ 4. Who's/Whose going to drive us?

_____ 5. Who's/Whose ice cream is melting?

_____ 6. I'm the person who's/whose gloves are lost.

_____ 7. Who's/Whose in your group?

_____ 8. Who's/Whose group is first?

_____ 9. Can you tell who's/whose at the door?

_____ 10. Who's/Whose friend are you?

_____ 11. Who's/Whose cooking tonight?

_____ 12. Who's/Whose cooking do you like best?

"Their," "There" and "They're"

Their is a possessive pronoun meaning "belonging to them."

There is an adverb that indicates place.

They're is a contraction for **they are**.

Examples:
Ron and Sue took **their** dog to the park.
They like to go **there** on Sunday afternoon.
They're probably going back next Sunday, too.

Directions: Write the correct words to complete these sentences.

_____ 1. All the students should bring their/there/they're books to class.

_____ 2. I've never been to France, but I hope to travel their/there/they're someday.

_____ 3. We studied how dolphins care for their/there/they're young.

_____ 4. My parents are going on vacation next week, and their/there/they're taking my sister.

_____ 5. Their/There/They're was a lot of food at the party.

_____ 6. My favorite baseball team lost their/there/they're star pitcher this year.

_____ 7. Those peaches look good, but their/there/they're not ripe yet.

_____ 8. The book is right their/there/they're on the table.

SUPER! Fantastic! Awesome! Excellent! Cool! GREAT JOB! Wow! TOTALLY!

"Teach" and "Learn"

Teach is a verb meaning "to explain something." Teach is an irregular verb. Its past tense is **taught**.

Learn is a verb meaning "to gain information."

Examples:
Carrie will **teach** me how to play the piano.
Yesterday she **taught** me "Chopsticks."

I will **learn** a new song every week.
Yesterday I **learned** to play "Chopsticks."

Directions: Write the correct words to complete these sentences.

_____ 1. My brother taught/learned me how to ice skate.

_____ 2. With his help, I taught/learned in three days.

_____ 3. First, I tried to teach/learn skating from a book.

_____ 4. I couldn't teach/learn that way.

_____ 5. You have to try it before you can really teach/learn how to do it.

_____ 6. Now I'm going to teach/learn my cousin.

_____ 7. My cousin already taught/learned how to roller skate.

_____ 8. I shouldn't have any trouble teaching/learning her how to ice skate.

_____ 9. Who taught/learned you how to skate?

_____ 10. My brother taught/learned Mom how to skate, too.

_____ 11. My mother took longer to teach/learn it than I did.

_____ 12. Who will he teach/learn next?

_____ 13. Do you know anyone who wants to teach/learn how to ice skate?

_____ 14. My brother will teach/learn you for free.

_____ 15. You should teach/learn how to ice skate in the wintertime, though. The ice is a little thin in the summer!

"Lie" and "Lay"

Lie is a verb meaning "to rest." Lie is an intransitive verb that doesn't need a direct object.

Lay is a verb meaning "to place or put something down." Lay is a transitive verb that requires a direct object.

Examples:
> **Lie** here for a while. (**Lie** has no direct object; **here** is an adverb.)
> **Lay** the book here. (**Lay** has a direct object: **book**.)

Lie and lay are especially tricky because they are both irregular verbs. Notice the past tense of lie is lay!

Present tense	ing form	Past tense	Past participle
lie	lying	lay	has/have/had lain
lay	laying	laid	has/have/had laid

Examples:
> I **lie** here today.
> I **lay** here yesterday.
> I **was lying** there for three hours.
> I **lay** the baby in her bed.
> I will be **laying** her down in a minute.
> I **laid** her in her bed last night, too.

Directions: Write the correct words to complete these sentences.

_____ 1. Shelly lies/lays a blanket on the grass.

_____ 2. Then she lies/lays down in the sun.

_____ 3. Her dog lies/lays there with her.

_____ 4. Yesterday, Shelly lay/laid in the sun for an hour.

_____ 5. The workers are lying/laying bricks for a house.

_____ 6. Yesterday, they lay/laid a ton of them.

_____ 7. They lie/lay one brick on top of the other.

_____ 8. The bricks just lie/lay in a pile until the workers are ready for them.

_____ 9. At lunchtime, some workers lie/lay down for a nap.

_____ 10. Would you like to lie/lay bricks?

_____ 11. Last year, my uncle lay/laid bricks for his new house.

_____ 12. He was so tired every day that he lay/laid down as soon as he finished.

"Rise" and "Raise"

Rise is a verb meaning "to get up" or "to go up." Rise is an intransitive verb that doesn't need a direct object.

Raise is a verb meaning "to lift" or "to grow." Raise is a transitive verb that requires a direct object.

Examples:
The curtain **rises**.
The girl **raises** her hand.

Raise is a regular verb. Rise is irregular.

Present tense	**Past tense**	**Past participle**
rise	rose	has/have/had risen
raise	raised	has/have/had raised

Examples:
The sun **rose** this morning.
The boy **raised** the window higher.

Directions: Write the correct words to complete these sentences.

_____ 1. This bread dough rises/raises in an hour.

_____ 2. The landlord will rise/raise the rent.

_____ 3. The balloon rose/raised into the sky.

_____ 4. My sister rose/raised the seat on my bike.

_____ 5. The baby rose/raised the spoon to his mouth.

_____ 6. The eagle rose/raised out of sight.

_____ 7. The farmer rises/raises pigs.

_____ 8. The scouts rose/raised the flag.

_____ 9. When the fog rose/raised, we could see better.

_____ 10. The price of ice cream rose/raised again.

_____ 11. The king rose/raised the glass to his lips.

_____ 12. Rise/Raise the picture on that wall higher.

English   163   Total Basic Skills Grade 5

"All Right," "All Ready" and "Already"

All right means "well enough" or "very well." Sometimes **all right** is incorrectly spelled. **Alright** is not a word.

Example:
    Correct: We'll be all right when the rain stops.
    Incorrect: Are you feeling **alright** today?

All ready is an adjective meaning "completely ready."

Already is an adverb meaning "before this time" or "by this time."

Examples:
    Are you **all ready** to go?
    He was **already** there when I arrived.

Directions: Write the correct words to complete these sentences.

_____ 1. The children are all ready/already for the picnic.

_____ 2. Ted was all ready/already late for the show.

_____ 3. Is your sister going to be all right/alright?

_____ 4. I was all ready/already tired before the race began.

_____ 5. Joan has all ready/already left for the dance.

_____ 6. Will you be all right/alright by yourself?

_____ 7. We are all ready/already for our talent show.

_____ 8. I all ready/already read that book.

_____ 9. I want to be all ready/already when they get here.

_____ 10. Dad was sick, but he's all right/alright now.

_____ 11. The dinner is all ready/already to eat.

_____ 12. Cathy all ready/already wrote her report.

WRITING

Writing: Topic Sentences

The topic sentence in a paragraph usually comes first. Sometimes, however, the topic sentence can come at the end or even in the middle of a paragraph. When looking for the topic sentence, try to find the one that tells the main idea of a paragraph.

Directions: Read the following paragraphs and underline the topic sentence in each.

The maple tree sheds its leaves every year. The oak and elm trees shed their leaves, too. Every autumn, the leaves on these trees begin changing color. Then, as the leaves gradually begin to die, they fall from the trees. Trees that shed their leaves annually are called deciduous trees.

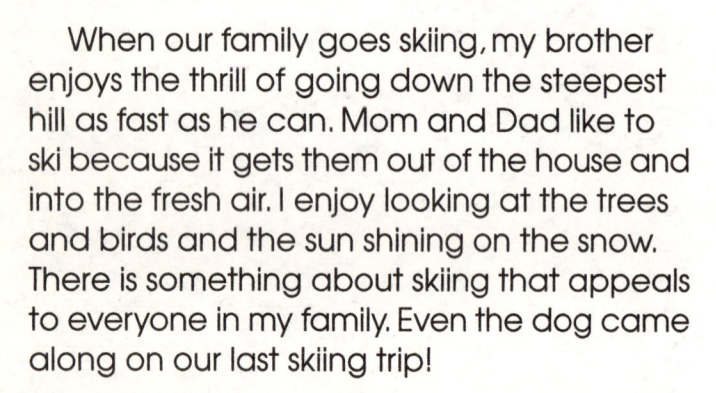

When our family goes skiing, my brother enjoys the thrill of going down the steepest hill as fast as he can. Mom and Dad like to ski because it gets them out of the house and into the fresh air. I enjoy looking at the trees and birds and the sun shining on the snow. There is something about skiing that appeals to everyone in my family. Even the dog came along on our last skiing trip!

If you are outdoors at night and there is traffic around, you should always wear bright clothing so that cars can see you. White is a good color to wear at night. If you are riding a bicycle, be sure it has plenty of reflectors, and if possible, headlamps as well. Be especially careful when crossing the street, because sometimes drivers cannot see you in the glare of their headlights. Being outdoors at night can be dangerous, and it is best to be prepared!

Writing: Supporting Sentences

A **paragraph** is a group of sentences that tell about one topic. The **topic sentence** in a paragraph usually comes first and tells the main idea of the paragraph. **Supporting sentences** follow the topic sentence and provide details about the topic.

Directions: Write at least three supporting sentences for each topic sentence below.

Example: Topic Sentence: Carly had an accident on her bike.
Supporting Sentences: She was on her way to the store to buy some bread. A car came weaving down the road and scared her. She rode her bike off the road so the car wouldn't hit her. Now, her knee is scraped, but she's all right.

1. I've been thinking of ways I could make some more money after school.

_____
_____
_____

2. In my opinion, cats (dogs, fish, etc.) make the best pets.

_____
_____
_____

3. My life would be better if I had a(n) (younger sister, younger brother, older sister, older brother).

_____
_____
_____

4. I'd like to live next door to a (swimming pool, video store, movie theater, etc.).

_____
_____
_____

Writing: Building Paragraphs

Directions: Read the groups of topic sentences and questions below. On another sheet of paper, write supporting sentences that answer the questions. Use your imagination! Write the supporting sentences in order, and copy them on this page after the topic sentence.

1. On her way home from school, Mariko made a difficult decision.

   Questions: What was Mariko's decision? Why did she decide that? Why was the decision hard to make?

   _____
   _____
   _____
   _____

2. Suddenly, Conrad thought of a way to clear up all the confusion.

   Questions: What was the confusion about? How was Conrad involved in it? What did he do to clear it up?

   _____
   _____
   _____
   _____

3. Bethany used to feel awkward at the school social activities.

   Questions: Why did Bethany feel awkward before? How does she feel now? What happened to change the way she feels?

   _____
   _____
   _____
   _____

Writing: Sequencing

When writing paragraphs, it is important to write events in the correct order. Think about what happens first, next, later and last.

Directions: The following sentences tell about Chandra's day, but they are all mixed up. Read each sentence and number them in the order in which they happened.

____ She arrived at school and went to her locker to get her books.

____ After dinner, she did the dishes, then read a book for a while.

____ Chandra brushed her teeth and put on her pajamas.

____ She rode the bus home, then she fixed herself a snack.

____ She ate breakfast and went out to wait for the bus.

____ Chandra woke up and picked out her clothes for school.

____ She met her friend Sarah on the way to the cafeteria.

____ She worked on homework and watched TV until her mom called her for dinner.

Directions: Write a short paragraph about what you did today. Use words like **first**, **next**, **then**, **later** and **finally** to indicate the order in which you did things.

_____
_____
_____
_____
_____
_____
_____
_____
_____
_____

Sequencing

Sequencing means to place events in order from beginning to end or first to last.

Example:
  To send a letter, you must:
  Get paper, pencil or pen, an envelope and a stamp.
  Write the letter.
  Fold the letter and put it in the envelope.
  Address the envelope correctly.
  Put a stamp on the envelope.
  Put the envelope in the mailbox or take
    it to the Post Office.

Directions: Write the sequence for making a peanut butter and jelly sandwich.

_____
_____
_____
_____
_____
_____
_____

Directions: After you finish, try making the sandwich **exactly** the way you wrote the steps. Did you leave out any steps? Which ones?

_____
_____
_____

Does a particular section you wrote require a better explanation? Clarify your explanation by adding missing information.

_____
_____
_____

Author's Purpose

Authors write to fulfill one of three purposes: to **inform**, to **entertain** or to **persuade**.

Authors who write to inform are providing facts for the reader in an informational context.

Examples: Encyclopedia entries and newspaper articles

Authors who write to entertain are hoping to provide enjoyment for the reader.

Examples: Funny stories and comics

Authors who write to persuade are trying to convince the reader to believe as they believe.

Examples: Editorials and opinion essays

Directions: Read each paragraph. Write **inform**, **entertain** or **persuade** on the line to show the author's purpose.

1. The whooping crane is a migratory bird. At one time, this endangered bird was almost extinct. These large white cranes are characterized by red faces and trumpeting calls. Through protection of both the birds and their habitats, the whooping crane is slowly increasing in number.

   _____

2. It is extremely important that all citizens place bird feeders in their yards and keep them full for the winter. Birds that spend the winter in this area are in danger of starving due to lack of food. It is every citizen's responsibility to ensure the survival of the birds.

   _____

3. Imagine being able to hibernate like a bear each winter! Wouldn't it be great to eat to your heart's content all fall? Then, sometime in late November, inform your teacher that you will not be attending school for the next few months because you'll be resting and living off your fat? Now, that would be the life!

   _____

4. Bears, woodchucks and chipmunks are not the only animals that hibernate. The queen bumblebee also hibernates in winter. All the other bees die before winter arrives. The queen hibernates under leaves in a small hole. She is cold-blooded and therefore is able to survive slightly frozen.

   _____

Writing

Author's Purpose

Directions: Write a paragraph of your own for each purpose. The paragraph can be about any topic.

1. to inform

   _____
   _____
   _____
   _____

2. to persuade

   _____
   _____
   _____
   _____

3. to entertain

   _____
   _____
   _____
   _____

Directions: Reread your paragraphs. Do they make sense? Check for grammar, spelling and punctuation errors and make corrections where needed.

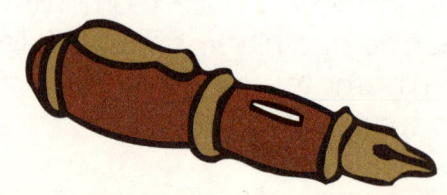

Descriptive Sentences

Descriptive sentences give readers a vivid image and enable them to imagine a scene clearly.

Example:
Nondescriptive sentence: There were grapes in the bowl.
Descriptive sentence: The plump purple grapes in the bowl looked tantalizing.

Directions: Rewrite these sentences using descriptive language.

1. The dog walked in its pen.

   _____

2. The turkey was almost done.

   _____

3. I became upset when my computer wouldn't work.

   _____

4. Jared and Michelle went to the ice-cream parlor.

   _____

5. The telephone kept ringing.

   _____

6. I wrote a story.

   _____

7. The movie was excellent.

   _____

8. Dominique was upset that her friend was ill.

   _____

Writing: Descriptive Details

A writer creates pictures in a reader's mind by telling him/her how something looks, sounds, feels, smells or tastes. For example, compare **A** and **B** below. Notice how the description in **B** makes you imagine how the heavy door and the cobweb would feel and how the broken glass would look and sound as someone walked on it.

A. I walked into the house.

B. I pushed open the heavy wooden door of the old house. A cobweb brushed my face, and broken glass, sparkling like ice, crushed under my feet.

Directions: Write one or two sentences about each topic below. Add details that will help your reader see, hear, feel, smell or taste what you are describing.

1. Your favorite dinner cooking

   _____

   _____

2. Old furniture

   _____

   _____

3. Wind blowing in the trees

   _____

   _____

4. A tired stranger

   _____

   _____

5. Wearing wet clothes

   _____

   _____

6. A strange noise somewhere in the house

   _____

   _____

Writing: Descriptive Details

Directions: For each topic sentence below, write three or four supporting sentences. Include details about how things look, sound, smell, taste or feel. Don't forget to use adjectives, adverbs, similes and metaphors.

Example: After my dog had his bath, I couldn't believe how much better he looked. His fur, which used to be all matted and dirty, was as clean as new snow. He still felt a little damp when I scratched behind his ears. The smell from rolling in our garbage was gone, too. He smelled like apples now because of the shampoo.

1. My little cousin's birthday party was almost over.

   _____
   _____
   _____

2. I always keep my grandpa company while he bakes bread.

   _____
   _____
   _____

3. By the end of our day at the beach, I was a mess.

   _____
   _____
   _____

4. Early morning is the best time to go for a bike ride.

   _____
   _____
   _____

Personal Narratives

A **personal narrative** tells about a person's own experiences.

Directions: Read the example of a personal narrative. Write your answers in complete sentences.

My Worst Year

When I look back on that year, I can hardly believe that one person could have such terrible luck for a whole year. But then again, I should have realized that if things could begin to go wrong in January, it didn't bode well for the rest of the year.

It was the night of January 26. One of my best friends was celebrating her birthday at the local roller-skating rink, and I had been invited. The evening began well enough with pizza and laughs. I admit I have never been a cracker jack roller skater, but I could hold my own. After a few minutes of skating, I decided to exit the rink for a cold soda.

Unfortunately, I did not notice the trailing ribbons of carpet which wrapped around the wheel of my skate, yanking my left leg from under me. My leg was broken. It wasn't just broken in one place but in four places! At the hospital, the doctor set the bone and put a cast on my leg. Three months later, I felt like a new person.

Sadly, the happiness wasn't meant to last. Five short months after the final cast was removed, I fell and broke the same leg again. Not only did it rebreak but it broke in the same four places! We found out later that it hadn't healed correctly. Three months later, it was early December and the end of a year I did not wish to repeat.

1. List the sequence of events in this personal narrative.

___

2. From reading the personal narrative, what do you think were the author's feelings toward the events that occurred?

___

Personal Narratives

A **narrative** is a spoken or written account of an actual event. A **personal narrative** tells about your own experience. It can be written about any event in your life and may be serious or comical.

When writing a personal narrative, remember to use correct sentence structure and punctuation. Include important dates, sights, sounds, smells, tastes and feelings to give your reader a clear picture of the event.

Directions: Write a personal narrative about an event in your life that was funny.

_____
_____
_____
_____
_____
_____
_____
_____
_____
_____
_____
_____
_____
_____
_____
_____

Complete the Story

Directions: Read the beginning of this story. Then complete the story with your own ideas.

It was a beautiful summer day in June when my family and I set off on vacation. We were headed for Portsmouth, New Hampshire. There we planned to go on a whale-watching ship and perhaps spy a humpback whale or two. However, there were many miles between our home and Portsmouth.

We camped at many lovely parks along the way to New Hampshire. We stayed in the Adirondack Mountains for a few days and then visited the White Mountains of Vermont before crossing into New Hampshire.

My family enjoys tent camping. My dad says you can't really get a taste of the great outdoors in a pop-up camper or RV. I love sitting by the fire at night, gazing at the stars and listening to the animal noises.

The trip was going well, and everyone was enjoying our vacation. We made it to Portsmouth and were looking forward to the whale-watching adventure. We arrived at the dock a few minutes early. The ocean looked rough, but we had taken seasickness medication. We thought we were prepared for any kind of weather.

_____
_____
_____
_____
_____
_____
_____
_____
_____
_____

Writing Fiction

Directions: Use descriptive writing to complete each story. Write at least five sentences.

1. It was a cold, wintry morning in January. Snow had fallen steadily for 4 days. I was staring out my bedroom window when I saw the bedraggled dog staggering through the snow.

2. Mindy was home Saturday studying for a big science test. Report cards were due next Friday, and the test on Monday would be on the report card. Mindy needed to do well on the test to get an A in Science. The phone rang. It was her best friend, Jenny.

3. Martin works every weekend delivering newspapers. He wakes up at 5:30 A.M. and begins his route at 6:00 A.M. He delivers 150 newspapers on his bike. He enjoys his weekend job because he is working toward a goal.

Writing: Point of View

People often have different opinions about the same thing. This is because each of us has a different "point of view." **Point of view** is the attitude someone has about a particular topic as a result of his or her personal experience or knowledge.

Directions: Read the topic sentence below about the outcome of a basketball game. Then write two short paragraphs, one from the point of view of a player for the Reds and one from the point of view of a player for the Cowboys. Be sure to give each person's opinion of the outcome of the game.

Topic Sentence: In the last second of the basketball game between the Reds and the Cowboys, the Reds scored and won the game.

Terry, a player for the Reds . . . _____

_____

_____

Chris, a player for the Cowboys . . . _____

_____

_____

Directions: Here's a different situation. Read the topic sentence, and then write three short paragraphs from the points of view of Katie, her dad and her brother.

Topic Sentence: Katie's dog had chewed up another one of her father's shoes.

Katie . . . _____

_____

Katie's father . . . _____

_____

Katie's brother Mark, who would rather have a cat . . . _____

_____

Name _____

Friendly Letters

A **friendly letter** has these parts: return address, date, greeting, body, closing and signature.

Directions: Read this letter. Then label the parts of the letter.

_____ ⟶ 222 West Middle Street
Boise, Idaho 33444
May 17, 1999 ⟵ _____

Dear Blaine, ⟵ _____

_____ ⟶ Hello! I know I haven't written in several weeks, but I've been very busy with school and baseball practice. How have you been? How is the weather in Boston? It is finally getting warm in Boise.

As I mentioned, I am playing baseball this year. My team is called the Rockets, and we are really good. We have a terrific coach. We practice two nights a week and play games on the weekends. Are you playing baseball?

I can hardly wait to visit you this summer. I can't believe I'll be flying on an airplane and staying with you and your family for 2 weeks! There is probably a lot to do in Boston. When you write, tell me some ideas you have for the 2 weeks.

_____ ⟶ Your friend,

_____ ⟶ Mason

Envelopes should follow this format:

Mason Fitch
222 West Middle Street
Boise, ID 33444

Blaine Morgan
111 E. 9th Street, Apt 22B
Boston, MA 00011

Writing

181

Total Basic Skills Grade 5

Friendly Letters

Directions: Write a friendly letter. Then address the envelope.

Writing: Supporting Your Opinion

Directions: Decide what your opinion is on each topic below. Then write a paragraph supporting your opinion. Begin with a topic sentence that tells the reader what you think. Add details in the next three or four sentences that show why you are right.

Example: Whether kids should listen to music while they do homework

Kids do a better job on their homework if they listen to music. The music makes the time more enjoyable. It also drowns out the sounds of the rest of the family. If things are too quiet while kids do homework, every little sound distracts them.

1. Whether young people should have a choice about going to school, no matter how old they are

   _____
   _____
   _____

2. Whether all parents should give their children the same amount of money for an allowance

   _____
   _____
   _____

3. Whether you should tell someone if you doubt he/she is telling the truth

   _____
   _____
   _____

Writing From a Prompt: An Opinion Essay

Directions: Write an opinion essay in response to the prompt.

Writing Prompt: Think about rainforests. What is the importance of preserving the rainforests of the world? What problems could arise if there were no longer any rainforest areas? What problems could arise for humans due to the preservation of rainforests? How do rainforests affect you?

_____

_____

_____

_____

_____

_____

_____

_____

_____

_____

Directions: When you finish writing, reread your essay. Use this checklist to help make corrections.

- [ ] I have used correct spelling, grammar and punctuation.
- [ ] I have no sentence fragments.
- [ ] My essay makes sense.
- [ ] I wrote complete sentences.
- [ ] I have no run-on sentences.
- [ ] I answered the prompt.

Writing a Summary

A **summary** is a short description of what a selection or book is about.

Directions: Read the following selection and the example summary.

Fads of the 1950s

A fad is a practice or an object that becomes very popular for a period of time. Recent popular fads include yo-yos and Beanie Babies®. In the 1950s, there were many different fads, including coonskin caps, hula hoops and 3-D movies.

Coonskin caps were made popular by the weekly television show about Davy Crockett, which began in December of 1954. Not only did Davy's hat itself become popular but anything with Davy Crockett on it was in hot demand.

Also popular were hula hoops. They were produced by the Wham-O company in 1958. The company had seen similar toys in Australia. Hula hoops were priced at $1.98, and over 30 million hoops were sold within 6 months.

Another fad was the 3-D movie. When television sets began to appear in every American home, the movie industry began to suffer financially. Movie companies rushed to produce 3-D movies, and movie-goers once more flocked to theaters. The first 3-D movie was shown in Los Angeles on November 26, 1952. People loved the special Polaroid® glasses and scenes in the movie that seemed to jump out at them. As with the hula hoop and Davy Crockett, people soon tired of 3-D movies, and they became old news as they were replaced by new fads.

Summary

Over the years, many fads have become popular with the American public. During the 1950s, three popular fads were the hula hoop, Davy Crockett and 3-D movies. Davy Crockett's coonskin cap became a fad with the beginning of the weekly television show. Hula hoops were sold by the millions, and 3-D movies were enjoyed by people everywhere. However, like all fads, interest in these items soon died out.

Writing a Summary

Directions: Read the following selection. Using page 309 as a guide, write a summary of the selection.

Man's First Flights

In the first few years of the 20th century, the majority of people strongly believed that man could not and would not ever be able to fly. There were a few daring individuals who worked to prove the public wrong.

On December 8, 1903, Samuel Langley attempted to fly his version of an airplane from the roof of a houseboat on the Potomac River. Langley happened to be the secretary of the Smithsonian Institution, so his flight was covered not only by news reporters but also by government officials. Unfortunately, his trip met with sudden disaster when his aircraft did a nose dive into the river.

Nine days later, brothers Orville and Wilbur Wright attempted a flight. They had assembled their aircraft at their home in Dayton, Ohio, and shipped it to Kitty Hawk, North Carolina. On December 17, the Wright brothers made several flights, the longest one lasting an incredible 59 seconds. Since the Wright brothers had kept their flight attempts secret, their miraculous flight was only reported by two newspapers in the United States.

_____

_____

_____

_____

_____

_____

_____

Comparing and Contrasting

When writing comparison/contrast essays, it is helpful to write one paragraph which contains all the similarities and another paragraph which contains all the differences.

Directions: Write an essay in response to the prompt.

Writing Prompt: Think of your brother, sister or a friend. What similarities are there between you and this person? What differences are there?

_____
_____
_____
_____
_____
_____
_____
_____
_____
_____
_____
_____
_____

Directions: When you finish writing, reread your essay. Use this checklist to help make corrections.

☐ My essay makes sense.

☐ I listed at least two similarities and two differences.

☐ My sentences are correctly written.

☐ I used correct spelling, grammar and punctuation.

Writing

187

Total Basic Skills Grade 5

Advantages and Disadvantages

As in the comparison/contrast essay, it is easiest to put all of the advantages in one paragraph and the disadvantages in another paragraph.

Directions: Write an essay in response to the prompt.

Writing Prompt: Think about what a society would be like if all people had the same skin tone, hair color, eye color, height and weight. What would the benefits of living in such a society be? Would there be any disadvantages? What would they be?

_____
_____
_____
_____
_____
_____
_____
_____
_____
_____
_____
_____
_____

Directions: When you finish writing, reread your essay. Use this checklist to help make corrections.

☐ My essay makes sense.

☐ I used correct spelling, grammar and punctuation.

☐ I answered the writing prompt.

☐ I have varied sentence length.

Newswriting

Newswriting is a style of writing used by newspaper reporters and other journalists who write for periodicals. **Periodicals** are newspapers, magazines and newsletters that are published regularly.

Magazine and newspaper writers organize their ideas and their writing around what is called "the five W's and the H" — who, what, when, where, why and how. As they conduct research and interview people for articles, journalists keep these questions in mind.

Directions: Read a newspaper article of your choice. Use the information you read to answer the questions.

Who
Who is involved? _____
Who is affected? _____
Who is responsible? _____

What
What is the event or subject? _____
What exactly has happened? _____
_____

When
When did this happen? _____

Where
Where did it happen? _____
_____

Why
Why did it happen? _____
Why will readers care? _____
_____

How
How did it happen? _____
_____

Newswriting: Inverted Pyramid Style

Newspaper reporters organize their news stories in what is called the **inverted pyramid** style. The inverted pyramid places the most important facts at the beginning of the story—called the lead (LEED)—and the least important facts at the end.

There are two practical reasons for this approach:

1) If the story must be shortened by an editor, he or she simply cuts paragraphs from the end of the story rather than rewriting the entire story.

2) Because newspapers contain so much information, few people read every word of every newspaper story. Instead, many readers skim headlines and opening paragraphs. The inverted pyramid style of writing enables readers to quickly get the basics of what the story is about without reading the entire story.

Directions: Read the news story. Then answer the questions.

> Cleveland—Ohio State University student John Cook is within one 36-hole match of joining some of amateur golf's top performers. The 21-year-old Muirfield Village Golf Club representative will try for his second straight U.S. Amateur championship Sunday against one of his California golf buddies, Mark O'Meara, over the 6,837-yard Canterbury Golf Club course. Starting times are 8 a.m. and 12:30 p.m.
>
> "Winning the U.S. Amateur once is a great thrill," said Cook after Saturday's breezy 5-3 semifinal decision over Alabama's Cecil Ingram III. "But winning the second time is something people don't very often do."

1. Who is the story about? _____

2. The "dateline" at the beginning of a news article tells where the event happened and where the reporter wrote the story. Where was the story about John Cook written?
_____

3. What is Cook trying to accomplish? _____
_____

4. Who did Cook beat on Saturday? _____

5. Which of the above paragraphs could be cut by an editor? _____

Writing: Just the Facts

Some forms of writing, such as reports and essays, contain opinions that are supported by the writer. In other kinds of writing, however, it is important to stick to the facts. Newspaper reporters, for example, must use only facts when they write their stories.

Directions: Read the following newspaper story about a fire, and underline the sentences or parts of sentences that are opinions. Then rewrite the story in your own words, giving only the facts.

   At around 10:30 p.m. last night, a fire broke out in a house at 413 Wilshire Boulevard. The house is in a very nice neighborhood, surrounded by beautiful trees. The family of four who lives in the house was alerted by smoke alarms, and they all exited the house safely, although they must have been very frightened. Firefighters arrived on the scene at approximately 10:45 p.m., and it took them over 3 hours to extinguish the blaze. The firefighters were very courageous. The cause of the fire has not yet been determined, although faulty electric wiring is suspected. People should have their electric wiring checked regularly. The family is staying with relatives until repairs to their home can be made, and they are probably very anxious to move back into their house.

_____
_____
_____
_____
_____
_____
_____
_____
_____
_____
_____
_____

Writing   Total Basic Skills Grade 5

Writing: You're the Reporter

Directions: Now, write your own short newspaper story about an interesting event that occurred at your school or in your neighborhood. Find out who and what the story is about, where and when it happened, and why and how it happened. Take some notes, interview some of the people involved and write your story. Give your story a title, and remember to stick to the facts! In the box, draw a picture (or "photo") to go with your story.

Writing: Personification

Sometimes writers use descriptions like: The fire engine **screamed** as it rushed down the street. The sun **crawled** slowly across the sky. We know that fire engines do not really scream, and the sun does not really crawl. Writers use descriptions like these to make their writing more interesting and vivid. When a writer gives an object or animal human qualities, it is called **personification**.

Directions: For each object below, write a sentence using personification. The first one has been done for you.

1. the barn door

   The old, rusty barn door groaned loudly when I pushed it open.

2. the rain

3. the pickup truck

4. the radiator

5. the leaves

6. the television

7. the kite

8. the river

Similes

A **simile** is a comparison of two things that have something in common but are really very different. The words **like** and **as** are used in similes.

Examples:
   The baby was **as** happy **as** a lark.
   She is **like** a ray of sunshine to my tired eyes.

Directions: Choose a word from the box to complete each comparison. The first one has been done for you.

| tack | grass | fish | mule | ox | rail | hornet | monkey |

1. as stubborn as a __mule__
2. as strong as an _____
3. swims like a _____
4. as sharp as a _____
5. as thin as a _____
6. as mad as a _____
7. climbs like a _____
8. as green as _____

Directions: Use your own words to complete these similes.

9. as _____ as a tack
10. _____ like a bird
11. as hungry as a _____
12. as white as _____
13. as light as a _____
14. as _____ as honey
15. _____ like a snake
16. as cold as _____

Directions: Use your own similes to complete these sentences.

17. Our new puppy sounded _____.
18. The clouds were _____.
19. Our new car is _____.
20. The watermelon tasted _____.

Total Basic Skills Grade 5   Writing

Writing: Common Similes

There are many similes that are used often in the English language. For example, "as frightened as a mouse" is a very common simile. Can you think of others?

Directions: Match the first part of each common simile to the second part. The first one has been done for you.

as slippery as	a mule
as smart as	a statue
as sly as	a rock
as still as	a bee
as quick as	an eel
as slow as	a pancake
as busy as	a whip
as cold as	a turtle
as flat as	a fox
as stubborn as	lightning
as hungry as	ice
as hard as	a bear

Directions: Write sentences using these common similes.

1. eats like a bird

    _____

2. fits like a glove

    _____

3. sits there like a bump on a log

    _____

4. like a bull in a china shop

    _____

5. works like a charm

    _____

Metaphors

A **metaphor** makes a direct comparison between two unlike things. A noun must be used in the comparison. The words **like** and **as** are not used.

Examples:
 Correct: The exuberant puppy was a **bundle of energy**.
 Incorrect: The dog is **happy**. (**Happy** is an adjective.)

Directions: Circle the two objects being compared.

1. The old truck was a heap of rusty metal.
2. The moon was a silver dollar in the sky.
3. Their vacation was a nightmare.
4. That wasp is a flying menace.
5. The prairie was a carpet of green.
6. The flowers were jewels on stems.
7. This winter, our pond is glass.
8. The clouds were marshmallows.

Directions: Complete the metaphor in each sentence.

9. The ruby was _____.

10. The hospital is _____.

11. The car was _____.

12. This morning when I awoke, I was _____.

13. When my brother is grumpy, he is _____.

14. Her fingers on the piano keys were _____.

How to Write a Book Report

Writing a book report should not be a chore. Instead, consider it an opportunity to share the good news about a book you have enjoyed. Simply writing, "I really liked this book. You will, too!" is not enough. You need to explain what makes the book worth reading.

Like other essays, book reports have three parts. An essay is a short report that presents the personal views of the writer. The three parts of an essay (and a book report) are introduction, body and conclusion.

The **introduction** to a book report should be a full paragraph that will capture the interest of your readers. The **body** paragraphs contain the main substance of your report. Include a brief overview of the plot of your book, along with supporting details that make it interesting. In the **conclusion**, summarize the central ideas of your report. Sum up why you would or would not recommend it to others.

Directions: Answer these questions about writing book reports.

1. Which of these introductory sentences is more interesting?

   ☐ Richie, a 12-year-old runaway, cries himself to sleep every night in the bowling alley where he lives.

   ☐ Many children run away from home, and this book is about one of them, a boy named Richie.

2. In a report on a fiction book about runaways, where would these sentences go?

   "Richie's mother is dead. He and his father don't get along."

   ☐ introduction
   ☐ conclusion

3. In the same report, where would these sentences go?

   "Author Clark Howard has written a sad and exciting book about runaways that shows how terrible the life of a runaway can be. I strongly recommend the book to people of all ages."

   ☐ body
   ☐ conclusion

Writing 197 Total Basic Skills Grade 5

Name _____

Book Report: A Book I Devoured

Directions: Follow the writing prompts to write a short book report on a book you truly enjoyed.

Recently, I read a book I could not put down.

Its title is _____

One reason I "devoured" this book was _____

_____

_____

If I could be one of the characters, I'd be _____ because _____

_____

_____

_____

_____

My favorite part of the story was when _____

_____

_____

_____

_____

_____

_____

_____

_____

_____

Library Research

Directions: Read about doing research in a library. Then answer the questions.

Step 1: Look in a general encyclopedia, such as *Encyclopedia Americana* or *World Book*, for background information on your topic. Use the index volume to locate the main article and all related articles. Look at the suggested cross-references that direct you to other sources. Also, check for a bibliography at the end of the article for clues to other sources. A **bibliography** lists all the books and magazines used to write the article.

Step 2: Use a special encyclopedia for more specific information or for definitions of special terms. The *Encyclopedia of Education*, *International Encyclopedia of the Social Sciences* and the *Encyclopedia of Bioethics* are examples of special encyclopedias.

Step 3: Look for a general book on your topic using the subject headings in the library catalog. Be sure to note the copyright date (date published) on all books you select. For current topics such as medical research or computers, you will want to use only the most recently published and up-to-date sources.

Step 4: Use *Facts on File* to pinpoint specific facts or statistics related to your topic. *Facts on File* is a weekly summary of national and international news.

Step 5: An index helps you locate magazine articles on your topic. To find the most current information, try the *Reader's Guide to Periodical Literature*. The *Guide* lists articles by subject published during a particular month, the magazines containing the articles and the date and page numbers of the articles.

1. Name two general encyclopedias. _____

2. Name three special encyclopedias. _____

3. Which reference book contains a weekly summary of national and international news?

Library Research

Directions: Read the remaining steps for doing library research. Then answer the questions.

Step 6: Newspaper indexes will direct you to newspaper articles related to your topic. See *The New York Times Index* for national and international coverage of a topic or event. If you are researching a local subject or event, ask the librarian if indexes for the local newspapers are available.

Step 7: Ask the librarian if the library keeps "clip files" of articles on particular topics. Clip files contain articles librarians have cut out and saved in folders. Consulting a clip file can sometimes save time because the librarian has already done the research and filed it together in one place!

Step 8: If your research topic is a person—for example, President Bill Clinton—a good source is *Current Biography*. This reference contains long articles about people in the news. Another source is *Biography Index*, which will direct you to articles in magazines and newspapers.

Step 9: If you need to locate statistics—for example, how many students play a certain school sport—check the *World Almanac and Book of Facts* or *Statistical Abstract of the United States*. The *Abstract* contains government statistics on education, politics and many other subjects.

Step 10: For detailed instructions about writing your paper, check one of these references: *Elements of Style* by Strunk and White or *A Manual for Writers of Term Papers, Theses, and Dissertations* by Kate Turabian.

1. What index should you consult if you're researching an article about water pollution in your town?

   _____

2. What is a "clip file"? _____

   _____

   _____

3. What are two sources of information on people in the news?

   _____

   _____

Fiction, Nonfiction and Biographies

Fiction books are stories that are not based on facts or real events. They are based on the imagination of the author.

Examples: picture books and novels

Nonfiction books are about facts or events that actually occurred.

Examples: reference books and history books

Biographies are written about a person's life. They are based on true events. Biographies have been written about Presidents and First Ladies, as well as other people.

Directions: Use your library to answer the following questions.

1. What are the titles and authors of three fiction books? _____

_____

_____

2. What are the titles and authors of three nonfiction books? _____

_____

_____

3. What are the call numbers of the three nonfiction books you listed? _____

_____

Directions: Use the library catalog to locate two biographies of each of the people listed. Write the titles, authors and call numbers.

4. Abraham Lincoln _____

5. George Washington Carver _____

6. John F. Kennedy _____

7. Princess Diana _____

8. Pocahontas _____

Reports: Choosing a Topic

Directions: Read about how to write a report. Then answer the questions.

A report is a written paper based on the writer's research. It is logically organized and, if it is a good report, presents information in an interesting way. Reports can focus on many different topics. A social studies report may provide information about a city or state. A science report may explain why the oceans are polluted.

If possible, choose a topic you're interested in. Sometimes a teacher assigns a general topic to the whole class, such as the solar system. This is a very broad topic, so you must first narrow it to a smaller topic about which you can write an interesting four- or five-page report. For example, your report could be on "The Sun, the Center of the Solar System" or "Jupiter, the Jumbo Planet."

A narrower topic gives your paper a better focus. Be careful not to make your topic too narrow, because then you may not be able to find much information about it for your report.

The inverted pyramid on the right shows how to narrow your topic from the general, at the top of the pyramid, to the specific, at the bottom.

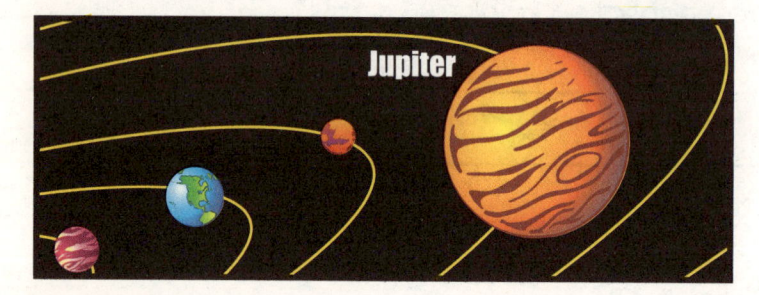

The solar system

Planets in the solar system

Jupiter, the jumbo planet

Directions: Select a topic for a paper you will write. You may choose one of these topics or select one of your own. Then answer the questions.

| American wars | Games | Presidents | States |
| Famous American women | Solar system | Sports heroes | Ecology |

1. What is a report? _____

_____

2. Which general topic did you choose? _____

3. What specific topic will you write about? _____

_____

Reports: Doing Research

Directions: Review the information on pages 199 and 200 about doing library research. Then read about how to do research for a report and answer the questions.

Before starting your report, locate the most likely places to find relevant information for your research. Ask the librarian for help if necessary. A good report will be based on at least three or four sources, so it's important to find references that provide varied information.

Is the topic a standard one, such as a report on the skeletal system? A general encyclopedia, such as *World Book*, is a good place to begin your research. Remember to use the encyclopedia's index to find related entries. For related entries on the skeletal system, you could check the index for entries on bones, health and the musculo-skeletal system. The index entry will show which encyclopedia number and pages to read to find information related to each entry topic.

Does your report require current statistics and/or facts? *Facts on File* and *Editorial Research Reports* are two sources for statistics. Ask the librarian to direct you to more specialized reference sources, such as *The People's Almanac* or *The New Grove Dictionary of Music and Musicians* which are related specifically to your topic.

For current magazine articles, see the *Reader's Guide to Periodical Literature*, which lists the names and page numbers of magazine articles related to a variety of topics. If you need geographical information about a country, check an atlas such as the *Rand McNally Contemporary World Atlas*.

1. How many reference sources should you consult before writing your report? _____

2. What are two references that provide statistics and facts? _____
_____

3. Where will you find a listing of magazine articles? _____
_____

4. Where should you look for geographical information? _____
_____

5. If you're stumped or don't know where to begin, who can help? _____
_____

Writing

Reports: Taking Notes

Directions: Read about taking notes for your report. Use the "index card" below to write a sample note from one of your reference sources.

When gathering information for a report, it is necessary to take notes. You'll need to take notes when you read encyclopedia entries, books and magazine or newspaper articles related to your topic.

Before you begin gathering information for a report, organize your thoughts around the who, what, when, where, why and how questions of your topic. This organized approach will help direct you to the references that best answer these questions. It will also help you select and write in your notes only useful information.

There are different ways of taking notes. Some people use notebook paper. If you write on notebook paper, put a heading on each page. Write only notes related to each heading on specific pages. Otherwise, your notes will be disorganized, and it will be difficult to begin writing your paper.

Many people prefer to put their notes on index cards. Index cards can be easily sorted and organized when you begin writing your report and are helpful when preparing an outline. If you use index cards for your notes, put one fact on each card.

Take several notes from each reference source you use. Having too many notes is better than not having enough information when you start to write your report.

_____

_____

_____

_____

_____

_____

_____

_____

_____

_____

Encyclopedia Skills: Taking Notes

A **biography** is a written report of a person's life. It is based on facts and actual events. To prepare to write a biographical essay, you could look up information about the person in an encyclopedia.

Directions: Select one of the people listed below. Read about that person in an encyclopedia. Take notes to prepare for writing a biographical essay. Then use your notes to answer the questions.

Babe Ruth
Mikhail Baryshnikov
Golda Meir
Dolly Madison
Pearl S. Buck

Billie Jean King
Willie Mays
Woodrow Wilson
Charles Darwin
Marie Curie

My Notes:

1. Where and when was he/she born? _____

2. If deceased, when did the person die? _____

3. When and why did he/she first become famous? _____
_____
_____

4. What are some important points about this person's career?
_____
_____
_____
_____
_____
_____
_____

Writing   Total Basic Skills Grade 5

Reports: Making an Outline

An outline will help you organize your ideas before you begin writing your report.

    Title
- I. First Main Idea
    - A. A supporting idea or fact
    - B. Another supporting idea or fact
        1. An example or related fact
        2. An example or related fact
- II. Second Main Idea
    - A. A supporting idea or fact
    - B. Another supporting idea or fact
- III. Third Main Idea
    - A. A supporting idea or fact
    - B. Another supporting idea or fact

Directions: Use information from your notes to write an outline for your report. Follow the above format, but expand your outline to include as many main ideas, facts and examples as necessary.

_____
_____
_____
_____
_____
_____
_____
_____
_____

Reports: Writing the Paper

Directions: Read more about writing a report. Then write your report.

Before you begin, be certain you clearly understand what is expected. How long should your report be? Must it be typed? Can it be written in pen? Should it be double-spaced?

Begin the first draft of your report with a general introduction of your topic. In the introduction, briefly mention the main points you will write about. One paragraph is usually enough to introduce your paper.

Next, comes the body of your report. Start a new paragraph for each main point. Include information that supports that point. If you are writing a long report, you may need to write a new paragraph for each supporting idea and/or each example. Follow your outline to be certain you cover all points. Depending on the number of words required to cover your topic, the body of the report will be anywhere from three or four paragraphs to several pages long.

In one or two concluding paragraphs, briefly summarize the main points you wrote about in the body of the report and state any conclusions you have drawn as a result of your research.

Once you finish the first draft, you will need to edit and rewrite your report to make it read smoothly and correct errors. You may need to rewrite your report more than once to make it the best it can be.

If possible, put the report aside for a day or two before you rewrite it so you can look at it with fresh eyes and a clear mind. Professional writers often write several drafts, so don't be discouraged about rewrites! Rewriting and editing are the keys to good writing—keys that every writer, no matter how old or experienced, relies on.

Directions: Circle the words in the puzzle related to writing a report.

```
K K N K T O P I C D T B
L D O B T T O D P T D O
I N T R O D U C T I O N
E N E R G D E E O O O N
D W S R G E Y C P C X R
S A F E A T T E I E Y O
R W A Q U B W P C D G F
L I C O N C L U S I O N
O U T L I N E U T T E D
R E S E A R C H R E S E
```

topic
facts
outline
introduction
body
conclusion
notes
research
edit

Editing

To **edit** means to revise and correct written work. Learning how to edit your work will help you become a better writer. First, you should write a rough draft of your paper, then edit it to make it better. Remember these things when writing your rough draft:

▶ **Do not overcrowd your page.** Leave space between every line and at the sides of your pages to make notes and changes.

▶ **Write so you can read it.** Don't be sloppy just because you're only writing a rough draft.

▶ **Number your pages.** This will help you keep everything in order.

▶ **Write on only one side of the page.** This gives you plenty of space if you want to make changes or add information between paragraphs.

▶ **Use the same size notebook paper for all drafts.** If all pages are the same size, you're less likely to lose any.

Before turning in your report or paper, ask yourself these questions:

▶ **Have I followed my outline?**

▶ **Have I told the who, what, when, where, why and how?**

▶ **Have I provided too much information?** (Good writers are concise. Don't repeat yourself after you have made a point.)

▶ **Do I still have unanswered questions?** (If you have questions, you can bet your readers will also. Add the missing information.)

It is always a good idea to let a day or so pass before rereading your paper and making final corrections. That way you will see what you actually wrote, instead of what you **think** you wrote.

When you edit your work, look for:

▶ **Correct grammar.**

▶ **Correct spelling.** Use the dictionary if you are not 100 percent sure.

▶ **Correct punctuation.**

▶ **Complete sentences.** Each should contain a complete thought.

Directions: Answer these questions about editing by writing **T** for true or **F** for false.

___ 1. When you are editing, you should look for correct grammar and spelling.

___ 2. Editors do not look for complete sentences.

___ 3. Editors do not have to read each word of a story.

___ 4. It is best to use both sides of a sheet of paper when writing the rough draft of your report.

___ 5. It does not matter how neat your first draft is.

___ 6. Editors make sure that sentences are punctuated correctly.

Name _____

Editing

Editors and proofreaders use certain marks to note the changes that need to be made. In addition to circling spelling errors and fixing capitalization mistakes, editors and proofreaders also use the following marks to indicate other mistakes that need to be corrected.

the	Delete.	∧	Insert a comma.
a nt	Remove the space.	∨	Insert an apostrophe.
In#this	Insert a space.	∨	Insert quotation marks.
is∧	Insert a word.	⊙	Insert a period.

Directions: Use editing marks to correct the errors in these sentences. Then write the sentences correctly on the lines.

1. Mr. Ramsey was a man who liked to do nothing
_____

2. Lili a young hawaiian girl, liked to swim in the sea.
_____

3. Youngsters who play baseballalways have a favorite player.
_____

4. Too many people said, That movie was terrible."
_____

5. I didn't wantto go to the movie with sally
_____

6. Prince charles always wants to play polo
_____

7. The little boy's name was albert leonard longfellow
_____

Writing

Total Basic Skills Grade 5

Editing

Directions: Use editing marks to show the changes that need to be made in the following sentences.

1. billy bob branstool was was the biggest bully at our school

2. mr. Smith told my mother that i was not a good student

3. I heard your mom say, "give your mother a kiss.

4. david and justin liked reading about dinosaurs especially tyrannosaurus rex.

5. milton said to to mabel "maybe we can play tomorrow."

6. lisa and Phil knew the answers to the questions but they would not raise hands

7. too many people were going to see the movie so we decided to go get pizza instead

8. tillie's aunt teresa was coming to visit for the month of may

9. we lived in a small town called sophia, north carolina, for 20 days before we decided to move away.

10. little people do not always live under bridges but sometimes little fish do.

11. i was reading the book called, *haunting at midnight.*

12. kevin and i decided that we would be detective bob and detective joe.

13. there were thirteen questions on the test. kevin missed all but the first one

14. thirty of us were going on a fieldtrip when suddenly the teachertold the bus driver to turn around.

Editing

not is	Flip the words around; transpose.
wan l ut	Flip letters around; transpose.
¶That was when Peter began talking.	Indent the paragraph or start a new paragraph.
with you. The movie we went to see was good.	Move text down to line below.
There were no people there. Jason thought we should go.	Move text up to line above.

Directions: Use editing marks to edit this story.

The Fallen Log

There was once a log on the floor of a very damp and eerie forest two men came upon the log and sat down for a rest. these two men, leroy and larry, did not know that someone could hear every word they said. "I'm so tired, moaned larry, as he began unlacing his heavy hikingboots. "and my feet hurt, too."

"Quit complaining" friend his said. We've got miles to walk before we'll find the cave with the hidden treasure. besides, if you think you're tired at look feet my. with that he kicked off his tennis shoe and discovered a very red big toe. "i think i won't be able to go any farther.

"Sh-h-h, already!" the two men heard a voice. "enough about feet, enough!" Larry and Leroy began loking around them. theycouldn't see anyone, though. "I'm in hree the voice said hoarsely.

Editing

Directions: Use editing marks to edit the continuing story of Larry and Leroy.

Larry and Leroy

larry and leroy jumped up from the log as soon as they realized that they were sitting on something that had a voice. "Hey, that was fast, said the voice. "How did you figure out where i was?"

By this time larry and leroy felt a little silly. Theycertainly didn't want to talk to a log. they looked at each other and then back at the log again. together they turned around and started walking down the path that had brought them to this point in the forest. "Hey were are you going?" the voice called.

"Well, i-i-i don't know," Larry replied, wondering if he sould be answering a log. "Who are you?"

"I'm a tiny elf who has been lostin this tree foryears," said the voice.

"Sure you are," replied larr. with that he and lroy began running for their lives.

Editing

Directions: Draw a line from the editing mark on the left to its meaning on the right.

co(pm)lain

Close up a word

The two boys came to class.
The girls, though,

Insert an apostrophe

¶This is the best pie ever.

Insert a comma

this

Delete a word

copy⌒editor

Transpose words

We went (zoo) to the.

Transpose letters

There#were two of us in the house.

Insert a space

Once upon a time‸there were

Capitalize

leonardo da vinci

Move text down to line below

T/homas was the best.

Change letter to lower-case

The two girls came to class. The two boys never came back until the principal left.

Start a new paragraph

Now I will end the story⊙

Move text up to line above

My mother the best lady I know
         ‸was

Insert a period

This is my mothers hat.

Insert a word

Proofreading

Proofreading or "proofing" means to carefully look over what has been written, checking for spelling, grammar, punctuation and other errors. At a newspaper, this is the job of a copyeditor. All good writers carefully proofread and correct their own work before turning it in to a copyeditor—or a teacher.

Here are three common proofreading marks:

Correct spelling ~~dot~~ dog

Replace with lower-case letter A̸

Replace with upper-case letter a̲

Directions: Carefully read the following paragraphs. Use proofreading marks to mark errors in the second paragraph. Correct all errors. The first sentence has been done for you.

A six-~~alurm~~ alarm fire at 2121 w̲indsor Terrace on the northeast side awoke apartment /Residents at 3 A.M. yesterday morning.

Elven people were in the biulding. No one was hurt in the blase, which caused $200,000 of property damage.

Proporty manager Jim smith credits a perfectly Functioning smoke alurm system for waking residents so they could get out safely. A springkler system were also in plase. "There was No panick," Smith said proudly. "Everone was calm and Orderly."

Proofreading

Directions: Proofread the news article. Mark and correct the 20 errors in capitalization and spelling.

Be Wise When Buying a Car

Each year, about five percent of the U.S. popalation buys a new car, acording to J.D. Link and Associates, a New York-based auto industry reserch company.

"A new car is the second most expenseve purchase most people Ever make," says Link. "it's amazing how litle reserch people do before they enter the car showroom."

Link says reseerch is the most impotant Thing a new car buyer can do to pertect himself or herself. That way, he or she wil get the Best car at the best price.

"the salesman is not trying to get You the best deal," says Link. "he's trying to get himself the best deal. Bee smart! Read up on new cars in magazines like *Car and Driver* and *motortrend* before you talk to a saleman!"

Editing: Check Your Proofreading Skills

Directions: Read about the things you should remember when you are revising your writing. Then follow the instructions to revise the paper below.

After you have finished writing your rough draft, you should reread it later to determine what changes you need to make to ensure it's the best possible paper you are capable of writing.

Check yourself by asking the following questions:
- **Does my paper stick to the topic?**
- **Have I left out any important details?**
- **Can I make the writing more lively?**
- **Have I made errors in spelling, punctuation or capitalization?**
- **Is there any information that should be left out?**

Directions: Revise the following story by making changes to correct spelling, punctuation and capitalization; add details; and cross out words or sentences that do not stick to the topic.

Hunting for Treasure

No one really believes me when I tell them that I'm a tresure hunter. But, really, i am. It isn't just any treasure that I like to hunt, though. I like treasures related to coins. Usually when I go treasure huting I go alone. I always wear my blue coat.

One day my good friend Jesse wanted to come with me. Why would you want to do that?" I said. "Because I like coins, too," he replied. What Jesse did not know was that the Coins that I dig to find are not the coins that just anyone collects. The coins i like are special. They are coins that have been buried in dirt for years!

Ancient Egypt

Have you ever wished you could visit Egypt for a first-hand look at the pyramids and ancient mummies? For most people, learning about Egypt is the closest they will come to visiting these ancient sites.

Directions: Test your knowledge about Egypt by writing as many of the answers as you can.

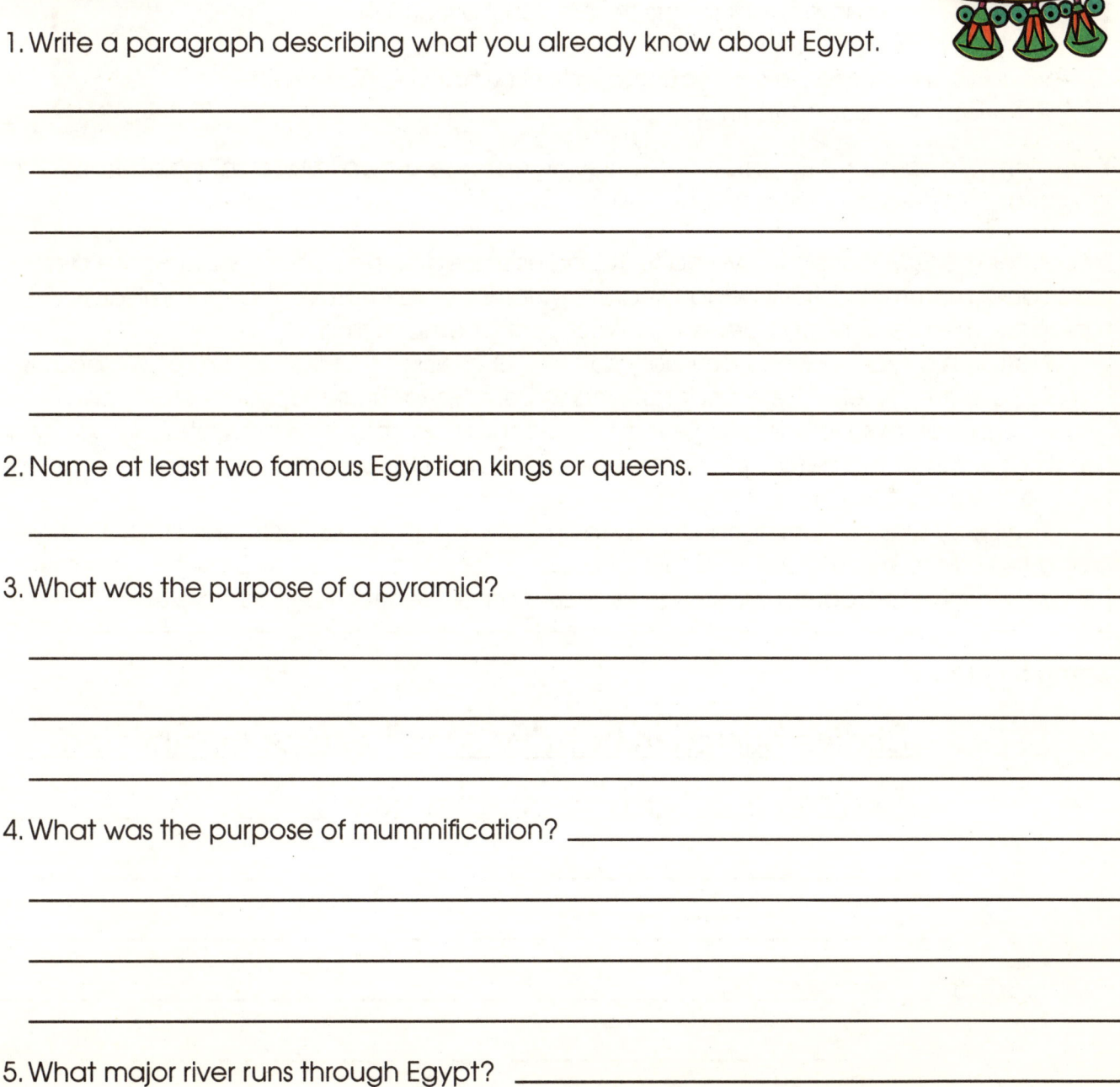

1. Write a paragraph describing what you already know about Egypt.

   _____
   _____
   _____
   _____
   _____
   _____
   _____

2. Name at least two famous Egyptian kings or queens. _____
   _____

3. What was the purpose of a pyramid? _____
   _____
   _____
   _____

4. What was the purpose of mummification? _____
   _____
   _____
   _____

5. What major river runs through Egypt? _____

Taking Notes: Egyptian Mummies

Taking notes is the process of writing important points to remember, such as taking notes from material prepared by your teacher or from what is discussed in class or from an article you read. Taking notes is useful when preparing for a test or when writing a report. When taking notes, follow these steps:

1. Read the article carefully.
2. Select one or two important points from each paragraph.
3. Write your notes in your own words.
4. Reread your notes to be sure you understand what you have written.
5. Abbreviate words to save time.

Directions: Read about Egyptian mummies. Select one or two important points from each paragraph. Write your notes in your own words.

> After the Egyptians discovered that bodies buried in the hot, dry sand of the desert became mummified, they began searching for ways to improve the mummification process. The use of natron became a vital part of embalming.
>
> Natron is a type of white powdery salt found in oases throughout Egypt. An oasis is a place in the desert where underground water rises to the surface. This water contains many types of salts, including table salt. It also contained natron. As the water evaporated in the hot sun of the desert, the salts were left behind. Natron was then collected for use in the mummification process.
>
> The body was dried in natron for up to 40 days. The natron caused the body to shrink and the skin to become leathery. For thousands of years, natron was a vital ingredient in preserving the bodies of kings, queens and other wealthy Egyptian citizens.

Sample notes:

Paragraph 1 _Bodies buried in hot dry sand became mummified._
Natron is vital for embalming.

Paragraph 2 _____

Paragraph 3 _____

Outlining

Outlining is a way to organize information before you write an essay or informational paragraph. Outlining helps you understand the information you read.

This sample form will help you get started. When outlining, you can add more main points, more smaller points and/or more examples.

    Title
I. First Main Idea
   A. A smaller idea
      1. An example
      2. An example
   B. Another smaller idea
II. Second Main Idea
   A. A smaller idea
   B. Another smaller idea
      1. An example
      2. An example
III. Third Main Idea
   A. A smaller idea
   B. A smaller idea

Directions: Read about building pyramids. Then complete the outline on the next page.

> The process of building pyramids began as a way to honor a king or queen. Since the Egyptians believed in an afterlife, they thought it only fitting for their kings and queens to have elaborate burial tombs filled with treasures to enjoy in the afterlife. Thus, the idea of the pyramid was born.
>
> At first pyramids were not built as they are known today. In the early stages of the Egyptian dynasty, kings were entombed in a *mastaba*. Mastabas were tombs made of mud-dried bricks. They formed a rectangular tomb with angled sides and a flat roof.
>
> Later, as the Egyptian kingdom became more powerful, kings felt they needed grander tombs. The step pyramid was developed. These pyramids were made of stone rather than mud and were much taller. A large mastaba was built on the ground. Then, four more mastabas (each smaller than the previous) were stacked on top.
>
> Finally, the pyramids took the shape that is familiar today. They were constructed with a flat bottom and four slanting sides which ascended to a final point. One of the tallest is over 400 feet high. These pyramids were also built of stone and were finished with an exterior of white limestone.

Outlining: Egyptian Pyramids

Directions: Complete the outline. Then answer the question.

_____
(title)

I. Mastabas
 A. _____
 B. _____
 C. _____

II. Step pyramids
 A. _____
 B. _____
 C. _____

III. Pyramids
 A. _____
 B. _____
 C. _____

What do you find is the most interesting aspect about the pyramids of ancient Egypt? Why?

_____
_____
_____
_____
_____
_____

Summarizing

A **summary** includes the main points from an article, book or speech.

Example:

Tomb robbing was an important business in ancient Egypt. Often entire families participated in the plunder of tombs. These robbers may have been laborers, officials, tomb architects or guards, but they all probably had one thing in common. They were involved in the building or designing of the tomb or they wouldn't have had the knowledge necessary to successfully rob the burial sites. Not only did tomb robbing ensure a rich life for the robbers but it also enabled them to be buried with many riches themselves.

Summary:

Tomb robbing occurred in ancient Egypt. The robbers stole riches to use in their present lives or in their burials. Tomb robbers usually had some part in the building or design of the tomb. This allowed them to find the burial rooms where the treasures were stored.

Directions: Read about life in ancient Egypt. Then write a three- to five-sentence summary.

Egyptologists have learned much from the pyramids and mummies of ancient Egypt from the items left by grave robbers.

Women of ancient Egypt wore makeup to enhance their features. Dark colored minerals called *kohl* were used as eyeliner and eye shadow. Men also wore eyeliner. Women used another mineral called *ocher* on their cheeks and lips to redden them. Henna, a plant which produces an orange dye, tinted the fingernails, the palms of their hands and the soles of their feet.

Perfume was also important in ancient Egypt. Small cones made of wax were worn on top of the head. These cones contained perfume oils. The sun slowly melted the wax, and the perfume would scent the hair, head and shoulders.

_____

_____

_____

_____

_____

Summarizing: King Tut

Directions: Read about King Tut. Then write a five- to seven-sentence summary.

King Tutankhamen (TO-TAN-KO-MEN) became king of Egypt when he was only nine years old. Known today as "King Tut," he died in 1355 B.C. when he was 18. Because King Tut died so young, not much is known about what he did while he was king.

After his death, Tut's body was "mummified" and buried in a pyramid in the Valley of the Kings in Egypt. Many other kings of ancient Egypt were buried there also.

In 1922, King Tut became famous when an Englishman named Howard Carter discovered and explored his tomb. The king's mummy, wearing a gold mask decorated with precious stones, was found intact. Amazingly, all King Tut's riches were still in his tomb. His was the only one in the Valley of the Kings that had not been discovered and robbed.

The King's tomb contained four rooms. One contained his mummy. The other rooms were filled with beautiful furniture, including King Tut's throne. Also found in Tut's tomb were more than 3,000 objects, like clothes, jewelry, wine, food—and a trumpet that could still be played. Obviously, King Tut planned to live royally in the next world!

MATH

Place Value

The place value of a digit or numeral is shown by where it is in the number. In the number 1,234, 1 has the place value of thousands, 2 is hundreds, 3 is tens and 4 is ones.

Example: 1,250,000,000

Read: One billion, two hundred fifty million

Write: 1,250,000,000

Billions	Millions	Thousands	Ones
h t o	h t o	h t o	h t o
1,	2 5 0,	0 0 0,	0 0 0

Directions: Read the words. Then write the numbers.

twenty million, three hundred four thousand _____

five thousand, four hundred twenty-three _____

one hundred fifty billion, eight million,
one thousand, five hundred _____

sixty billion, seven hundred million,
one hundred thousand, three hundred twelve _____

four hundred million, fifteen thousand,
seven hundred one _____

six hundred ninety-nine million, four thousand,
nine hundred forty-two _____

Here's a game to play with a partner.

Write a ten-digit number using each digit, 0 to 9, only once. Do not show the number to your partner. Give clues like: "There is a five in the hundreds place." The clues can be given in any order. See if your partner can write the same number you have written.

Total Basic Skills Grade 5   Math

Place Value

Directions: Draw a line to connect each number to its correct written form.

1. 791,000 — Seven hundred ninety-one thousand
2. 350,000 — Three hundred fifty thousand
3. 17,500,000 — Seventeen million, five hundred thousand
4. 3,500,000 — Three million, five hundred thousand
5. 70,910 — Seventy thousand, nine hundred ten
6. 35,500,000 — Thirty-five million, five hundred thousand
7. 17,000,500,000 — Seventeen billion, five hundred thousand

Directions: Look carefully at this number: 2,071,463,548. Write the numeral for each of the following places.

8. __6__ ten thousands
9. __1__ millions
10. __5__ hundreds
11. __2__ billions
12. __4__ hundred thousands
13. __7__ ten millions
14. __3__ one thousands
15. _____ hundred millions

Name: Jasmine

Addition

Addition is "putting together" two or more numbers to find the sum.

Directions: Add. Fill the backpacks with the right answers.

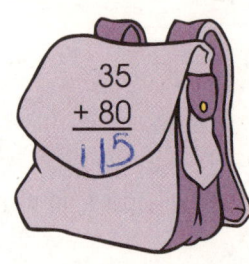

38 + 92 = 130	71 + 48 = 119	43 + 62 = 105	56 + 14 = 70	87 + 13 = 100
24 + 39 = 63	15 + 67 = 82	83 + 47 = 130	35 + 80 = 115	17 + 64 = 81
95 + 25 = 120	54 + 19 = 73	61 + 77 = 138	42 + 89 = 131	37 + 97 = 134
62 + 39 = 101	18 + 43 = 61	27 + 94 = 121	11 + 89 = 100	48 + 58 = 106

Total Basic Skills Grade 5 — 226 — Math

Addition

Teachers of an Earth Science class planned to take 50 students on an overnight hiking and camping experience. After planning the menu, they went to the grocery store for supplies.

Breakfast	**Lunch**	**Dinner**	**Snacks**
bacon	hot dogs/buns	pasta	crackers
eggs	apples	sauce	marshmallows
bread	chips	garlic bread	chocolate bars
cereal	juice	salad	cocoa mix
juice	granola bars	cookies	
$34.50	$ 52.15	$ 47.25	$ 23.40

Directions: Answer the questions. Write the total amount spent on food for the trip.

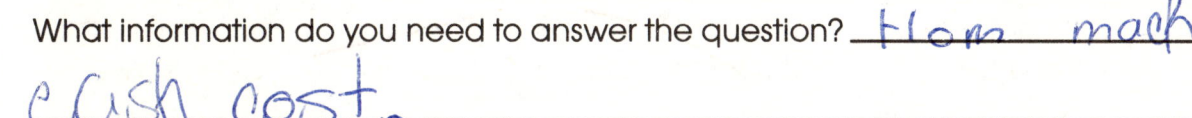

What information do you need to answer the question? _How much does each cost._

What is the total? _____

Directions: Add.

```
  462      918      527      386      295
+ 574    + 359    + 582    + 745    + 764


  397      524      906      750      891
+ 448    + 725    + 337    + 643    + 419


1,568    3,214    5,147    7,259    9,317
+2,341  +2,896   +4,285   +2,451   +3,583
```

Addition

Directions: Add.

1. Tourists travel to national parks to see the many animals which live there. Park Rangers estimate 384 buffalo, 282 grizzly bears and 426 deer are in the park. What is the total number of buffalo, bears and deer estimated in the park?

   _____

2. Last August, 2,248 visitors drove motor homes into the campgrounds for overnight camping. 647 set up campsites with tents. How many campsites were there altogether in August?

   _____

3. During a 3-week camping trip, Tom and his family hiked 42 miles, took a 126-mile long canoeing trip and drove their car 853 miles. How many miles did they travel in all?

   _____

4. Old Faithful is a geyser which spouts water high into the air. 10,000 gallons of water burst into the air regularly. Two other geysers spout 2,400 gallons of water during each eruption. What is the amount of water thrust into the air during one cycle?

   _____

5. Yellowstone National Park covers approximately 2,221,772 acres of land. Close by, the Grand Tetons cover approximately 310,350 acres. How many acres of land are there in these two parks?

   _____

6. Hiking trails cover 486 miles, motor routes around the north rim total 376 miles, and another 322 miles of road allow visitors to follow a loop around the southern part of the park. How many miles of trails and roadways are there?

   _____

Addition

Bob the butcher is popular with the dogs in town. He was making a delivery this morning when he noticed he was being followed by two dogs. Bob tried to climb a ladder to escape from the dogs. Solve the following addition problems and shade in the answers on the ladder. If all the numbers are shaded when the problems have been solved, Bob made it up the ladder. Some answers may not be on the ladder.

1.   986,145
        621,332
    + 200,008

2.   1,873,402
       925,666
    +   4,689

3.   506,328
       886,510
    + 342,225

4.   43,015
     2,811,604
    + 987,053

5.   18,443
       300,604
    + 999,999

6.   8,075
        14,608
    +   33,914

7.   9,162
        7,804
    + 755,122

8.   88,714
       213,653
    + 5,441,298

9.   3,244,662
     1,986,114
    + 521,387

10.   4,581
       22,983
    + 5,618,775

11.   818,623
         926
    + 3,260,004

12.   80,436
        9,159
    + 3,028,761

Ladder answers:
- 1,319,046
- 2,803,757
- 5,743,665
- 3,118,356
- 56,597
- 4,079,553
- 1,807,485
- 2,943,230
- 18,344,666
- 1,735,063
- 5,752,163
- 896,316
- 3,841,672
- 5,646,339

Does Bob make it? _____

Subtraction

Subtraction is "taking away" one number from another to find the difference between the two numbers.

Directions: Subtract.

```
  76        93        68        49        88        54
- 23      - 14      - 25      - 17      - 39      - 25
```

Brent saved $75.00 of the money he earned delivering the local newspaper in his neighborhood. He wanted to buy a new bicycle that cost $139.00. How much more would he need to save in order to buy the bike?

_____

```
  38        74        67        92        43        85
- 29      - 25      - 49      - 35      - 26      - 37
```

When Brent finally went to buy the bicycle, he saw a light and basket for the bike. He decided to buy them both. The light was $5.95 and the basket was $10.50. He gave the clerk a twenty dollar bill his grandmother had given him for his birthday. How much change did he get back?

_____

Subtraction

When working with larger numbers, it is important to keep the numbers lined up according to place value.

Subtract.

```
  398        543        491
- 149      - 287      - 311
```

```
  786      1,825      4,172
- 597      - 495    - 2,785
```

```
 8,391    63,852    24,107    52,900
-5,492   -34,765   -19,350   -43,081
```

Eagle Peak is the highest mountain peak at Yellowstone National Park. It is 11,353 feet high. The next highest point at the park is Mount Washburn. It is 10,243 feet tall. How much higher is Eagle Peak?

_____

The highest mountain peak in North America is Mount McKinley, which stretches 20,320 feet toward the sky. Two other mountain ranges in North America have peaks at 10,302 feet and 8,194 feet. What is the greatest difference between the peaks?

_____

Checking Subtraction

You can check your subtraction by using addition.

Example: 34,436   Check: 22,172
            − 12,264   + 12,264
              22,172   34,436

Directions: Subtract. Then check your answers by adding.

15,326 − 11,532	Check:	28,615 − 25,329	Check:
96,521 − 47,378	Check:	46,496 − 35,877	Check:
77,911 − 63,783	Check:	156,901 −112,732	Check:
395,638 −187,569	Check:	67,002 − 53,195	Check:
16,075 −15,896	Check:	39,678 −19,769	Check:
84,654 − 49,997	Check:	12,335 −10,697	Check:

During the summer, 158,941 people visited Yellowstone National Park. During the fall, there were 52,397 visitors. How many more visitors went to the park during the summer than the fall?

Total Basic Skills Grade 5   Math

Addition and Subtraction

Directions: Check the answers. Write **T** if the answer is true and **F** if it is false.

Example:
```
  48,973       Check:      35,856
- 35,856         F        +13,118
  13,118                   48,974
```

```
  18,264    Check:              458,342    Check:
+ 17,893    _____              - 297,652   _____
  36,157                         160,680
```

```
  39,854    Check:              631,928    Check:
+ 52,713    _____              - 457,615   _____
  92,577                         174,313
```

```
  14,389    Check:              554,974    Check:
+ 93,587    _____              - 376,585   _____
 107,976                         178,389
```

```
  87,321    Check:              109,568    Check:
- 62,348    _____              +  97,373   _____
  24,973                         206,941
```

Directions: Read the story problem. Write the equation and check the answer.

A camper hikes 53,741 feet out into the wilderness. On his return trip he takes a shortcut, walking 36,752 feet back to his cabin. The shortcut saves him 16,998 feet of hiking. True or False?

Math   233   Total Basic Skills Grade 5

Addition and Subtraction

Directions: Add or subtract to find the answers.

Eastland School hosted a field day. Students could sign up for a variety of events. 175 students signed up for individual races. Twenty two-person teams competed in the mile relay and 36 kids took part in the high jump. How many students participated in the activities?

_____

Westmore School brought 42 students and 7 adults to the field day event. Northern School brought 84 students and 15 adults. There was a total of 300 students and 45 adults at the event. How many were from other schools?

_____

The Booster Club sponsored a concession stand during the day. Last year, they made $1,000 at the same event. This year they hoped to earn at least $1,250. They actually raised $1,842. How much more did they make than they had anticipated?

_____

Each school was awarded a trophy for participating in the field day's activities. The Booster Club planned to purchase three plaques as awards, but they only wanted to spend $150. The first place trophy they selected was $68. The second place award was $59. How much would they be able to spend on the third place award if they stay within their budgeted amount?

_____

The Booster Club decided to spend $1,000 to purchase several items for the school with the money they had earned. Study the list of items suggested and decide which combination of items they could purchase.

A. Swing set $425 _____

B. Sliding board $263 _____

C. Scoreboard $515 _____

D. Team uniforms $180 _____

Rounding

Rounding a number means to express it to the nearest ten, hundred, thousand and so on. When rounding a number to the nearest ten, if the number has five or more ones, round up. Round down if the number has four or fewer ones.

Examples:

Round to the nearest ten: 84 → 80   86 → 90

Round to the nearest hundred: 187 → 200   120 → 100

Round to the nearest thousand: 981 → 1,000   5,480 → 5,000

Directions: Round these numbers to the nearest ten.

87 → _____   53 → _____   48 → _____   32 → _____   76 → _____

Directions: Round these numbers to the nearest hundred.

168 → _____   243 → _____   591 → _____   743 → _____   493 → _____

Directions: Round these numbers to the nearest thousand.

895 → _____   3,492 → _____   7,521 → _____   14,904 → _____   62,387 → _____

| City Populations ||
City	Population
Cleveland	492,801
Seattle	520,947
Omaha	345,033
Kansas City	443,878
Atlanta	396,052
Austin	514,013

Directions: Use the city population chart to answer the questions.

Which cities have a population of about 500,000?
_____

Which city has a population of about 350,000?
_____

How many cities have a population of about 400,000? _____

Which ones? _____

_____

Math   Total Basic Skills Grade 5

Estimating

To **estimate** means to give an approximate rather than an exact answer. Rounding each number first makes it easy to estimate an answer.

Example:

$$\begin{array}{r}93\\+48\end{array} \rightarrow \begin{array}{r}90\\+50\\\hline 140\end{array} \qquad \begin{array}{r}321\\+597\end{array} \rightarrow \begin{array}{r}300\\+600\\\hline 900\end{array} \qquad \begin{array}{r}1,859\\-997\end{array} \rightarrow \begin{array}{r}2,000\\-1,000\\\hline 1,000\end{array}$$

Directions: Estimate the sums and differences by rounding the numbers first.

68 + 34 →	12 + 98 →	89 + 23 →
638 − 395 →	281 − 69 →	271 − 126 →
1,532 − 998 →	8,312 − 4,789 →	6,341 + 9,286 →

Bonnie has $50 to purchase tennis shoes, a tennis racquet and tennis balls. Does she have enough money?

_____

$23.00
$16.00
$3.00

Rounding and Estimating

Rounding numbers and estimating answers is an easy way of finding the approximate answer without writing out the problem or using a calculator.

Directions: Circle the correct answer.

Round to the nearest **ten**:

73 → 70 / 80   48 → 40 / 50   65 → 60 / 70

85 → 80 / 90   92 → 90 / 100   37 → 30 / 40

Round to the nearest **hundred**:

139 → 100 / 200   782 → 700 / 800   390 → 300 / 400

640 → 600 / 700   525 → 500 / 600   457 → 400 / 500

Round to the nearest **thousand**:

1,375 → 1,000 / 2,000   21,800 → 21,000 / 22,000   36,240 → 36,000 / 37,000

Sam wanted to buy a new computer. He knew he only had about $1,200 to spend. Which of the following ones could he afford to buy?

$1,165 $1,279 $1,249

If Sam spent $39 on software for his new computer, $265 for a printer and $38 for a cordless mouse, about how much money did he need?

_____

Prime Numbers

Example: 3 is a prime number 3 ÷ 1 = 3 and 3 ÷ 3 = 1
Any other divisor will result in a mixed number or fraction.

A prime number is a positive whole number which can be divided evenly only by itself or one.

An easy way to test a number to see if it is prime is to divide by 2 and 3. If the number can be divided by 2 or 3 without a remainder, it is not a prime number. (Exceptions, 2 and 3.)

Example:

11 cannot be divided evenly by 2 or 3. It can only be divided by 1 and 11. It is a prime number.

Directions: Write the first 15 prime numbers. Test by dividing by 2 and by 3.

Prime Numbers:

_____ _____ _____ _____ _____

_____ _____ _____ _____ _____

_____ _____ _____ _____ _____

How many prime numbers are there between 0 and 100? _____

Prime Numbers

Directions: Circle the prime numbers.

71	3	82	20	43	69
128	97	23	111	75	51
13	44	137	68	171	83
61	21	77	101	34	16
2	39	92	17	52	29
19	156	63	99	27	147
121	25	88	12	87	55
57	7	139	91	9	37
67	183	5	59	11	95

Multiples

A **multiple** is the product of a specific number and any other number. When you multiply two numbers, the answer is called the **product**.

Example:

The multiples of 2 are 2 (2 x 1), 4 (2 x 2), 6, 8, 10, 12, and so on.

The **least common multiple** (LCM) of two or more numbers is the smallest number other than 0 that is a multiple of each number.

Example:

Multiples of 3 are 3, 6, 9, 12, 15, 18, 21, 24, etc.
Multiples of 6 are 6, 12, 18, 24, 30, 36, 42, etc.
Multiples that 3 and 6 have in common are 6, 12, 18, 24.
The LCM of 3 and 6 is 6.

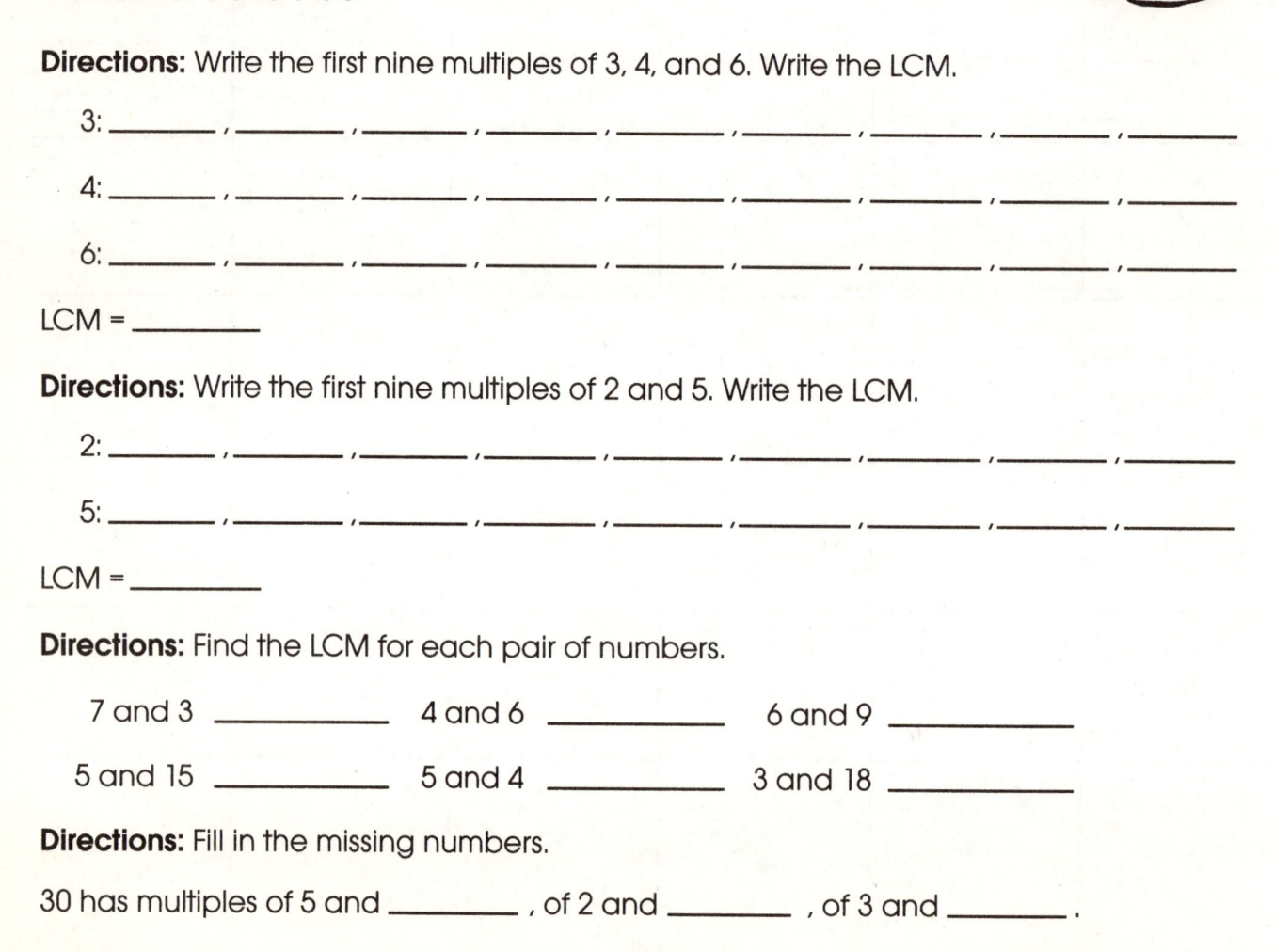

Directions: Write the first nine multiples of 3, 4, and 6. Write the LCM.

3: _____ , _____ , _____ , _____ , _____ , _____ , _____ , _____ , _____

4: _____ , _____ , _____ , _____ , _____ , _____ , _____ , _____ , _____

6: _____ , _____ , _____ , _____ , _____ , _____ , _____ , _____ , _____

LCM = _____

Directions: Write the first nine multiples of 2 and 5. Write the LCM.

2: _____ , _____ , _____ , _____ , _____ , _____ , _____ , _____ , _____

5: _____ , _____ , _____ , _____ , _____ , _____ , _____ , _____ , _____

LCM = _____

Directions: Find the LCM for each pair of numbers.

7 and 3 _____   4 and 6 _____   6 and 9 _____

5 and 15 _____   5 and 4 _____   3 and 18 _____

Directions: Fill in the missing numbers.

30 has multiples of 5 and _____ , of 2 and _____ , of 3 and _____ .

Factors

Factors are the numbers multiplied together to give a product. The **greatest common factor** (GCF) is the largest number for a set of numbers that divides evenly into each number in the set.

Example:

The factors of 12 are 3 x 4, 2 x 6 and 1 x 12.
We can write the factors like this: 3, 4, 2, 6, 12, 1.
The factors of 8 are 2, 4, 8, 1.
The common factors of 12 and 8 are 2 and 4 and 1.
The GCF of 12 and 8 is 4.

Directions: Write the factors of each pair of numbers. Then write the common factors and the GCF.

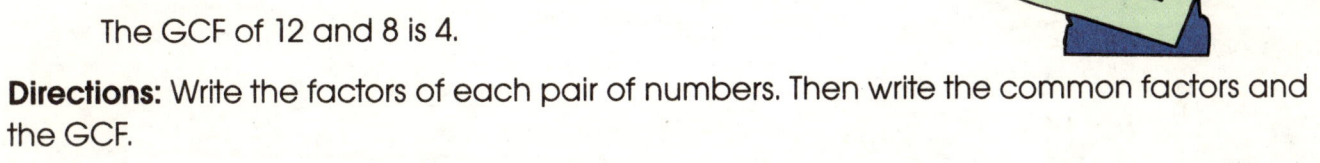

12: _____ , _____ , _____ , _____ , _____ , _____

15: _____ , _____ , _____ , _____

The common factors of 12 and 15 are _____ , _____ .

The GCF is _____ .

20: _____ , _____ , _____ , _____ , _____ , _____

10: _____ , _____ , _____ , _____

The common factors of 10 and 20 are _____ , _____ , _____ , _____ .

The GCF is _____ .

32: _____ , _____ , _____ , _____ , _____ , _____

24: _____ , _____ , _____ , _____ , _____ , _____ , _____ , _____

The common factors of 24 and 32 are _____ , _____ , _____ , _____ .

The GCF is _____ .

Directions: Write the GCF for the following pairs of numbers.

28 and 20 _____   42 and 12 _____

36 and 12 _____   20 and 5 _____

Factor Trees

A **factor tree** shows the prime factors of a number. A prime number, such as 7, has for its factors only itself and 1.

Example:

30
6 x 5
3 2 5

30 = 3 x 2 x 5.

3, 2, and 5 are prime numbers.

Directions: Fill in the numbers in the factor trees.

Tree 1: 18 = 6 x ☐, then ☐ ☐ ☐

Tree 2: 30 = 15 x ☐, then ☐ ☐ ☐

Tree 3: 45 = ☐ x ☐, then ☐ ☐ ☐

Tree 4: 20 = ☐ x ☐, then ☐ ☐ ☐

Tree 5: 18 = 9 x ☐, then ☐ ☐ ☐

Tree 6: 28 = 4 x ☐, then ☐ ☐ ☐

Total Basic Skills Grade 5

Math

Factor Trees

Directions: Fill in the numbers in the factor trees. The first one has been done for you.

Tree 1 (completed):
- 13,720
- 140 × 98
- 10 × 14 × 7
- 5 × 2 × 7 × 1

Tree 2 (blank top levels):
- ☐
- ☐ × ☐
- ☐ × ☐ × ☐
- 1 × 2 × 2 × 3

Tree 3 (blank top levels):
- ☐
- ☐ × ☐
- ☐ × ☐ × ☐
- 3 × 5 × 1 × 3

Greatest Common Factor

Directions: Write the greatest common factor for each set of numbers.

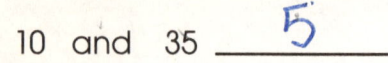

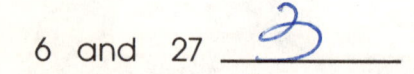

10 and 35 ___5___

2 and 10 ___2___

42 and 63 ___21___

16 and 40 ___8___

25 and 55 ___5___

12 and 20 ___4___

14 and 28 ___14___

8 and 20 ___4___

6 and 27 ___3___

15 and 35 ___5___

18 and 48 ___6___

Least Common Multiple

Directions: Write the least common multiple for each pair of numbers.

12 and 7 __84__

2 and 4 _____

22 and 4 _____

6 and 10 _____

3 and 7 _____

6 and 8 _____

5 and 10 _____

8 and 12 _____

9 and 15 _____

7 and 5 _____

3 and 8 _____

9 and 4 _____

Multiplication

Multiplication is a process of quick addition of a number a certain number of times.

Example: 3 x 15 = 45   is the same as adding   15 + 15 + 15 = 45
                              15 three times.

Directions: Multiply.

32	48	26	19	63
x 3	x 7	x 5	x 6	x 2

251	523	915	431	275
x 4	x 8	x 3	x 7	x 3

412	643	526	742
x 21	x 17	x 22	x 35

256	874	372	951
x 74	x 15	x 45	x 34

Cathy is on the cross country team. She runs 3 miles every day except on her birthday. How many miles does she run each year?

_____

Multiplication

Be certain to keep the proper place value when multiplying by tens and hundreds.

Examples:

```
   143         250
 x 262       x 150
   286         000
   858        1250
   286         250
 37,466      37,500
```

Directions: Multiply.

701	621	348	597
x 308	x 538	x 200	x 424

537	416	682	180
x 189	x 727	x 472	x 340

878	267	893	907
x 638	x 196	x 214	x 428

An airplane flies 720 trips a year between the cities of Chicago and Columbus. Each trip is 375 miles. How many miles does the airplane fly each year?

_____

Division

Division is the reverse of multiplication. It is the process of dividing a number into equal groups of smaller numbers.

Directions: Divide.

Greg had 936 marbles to share with his two brothers. If the boys divided them evenly, how many will each one get? _____

The marbles Greg kept were four different colors: blue, green, red and orange. He had the same number of each color. He divided them into two groups. One group had only orange marbles. The rest of the marbles were in the other group. How many marbles did he have in each group? orange _____ others _____

The **dividend** is the number to be divided by another number. In the problem 28 ÷ 7 = 4, 28 is the dividend.

The **divisor** is the number by which another number is divided. In the problem 28 ÷ 7 = 4, 7 is the divisor.

The **quotient** is the answer in a division problem. In the problem 28 ÷ 7 = 4, 4 is the quotient.

The **remainder** is the number left over in the quotient of a division problem. In the problem 29 ÷ 7 = 4 r1, 1 is the remainder.

Directions: Write the answers.

In the problem 25 ÷ 8 = 3 r1 . . .

What is the divisor? _____ What is the remainder? _____

What is the quotient? _____ What is the dividend? _____

Directions: Divide.

9)2,025   6)2,508   3)225   5)400   2)1,156

Division

The remainder in a division problem must always be less than the divisor.

Example:

```
         244 r 23
    26 ) 6,367
         52
         116
         104
          127
          104
           23
```

Directions: Divide.

53) 1,220   37) 1,528   83) 6,270   26) 3,618

14) 389   29) 2,645   60) 8,010   57) 5,406

35) 2,546   43) 492   83) 4,608   19) 185

The Oregon Trail is 2,197 miles long. How long would it take a covered wagon traveling 20 miles a day to complete the trip?

_____

Checking Division

Answers in division problems can be checked by multiplying.

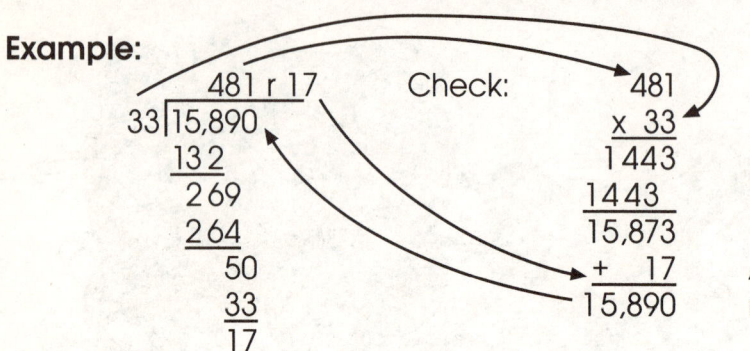

Example:

```
      481 r 17        Check:      481
33)15,890                       x  33
   13 2                          1443
    2 69                        1443
    2 64                       15,873
      50                       +   17
      33                       15,890     Add the
      17                                  remainder
```

Directions: Divide and check your answers.

61)2,736 Check:	73)86,143 Check:
59)9,390 Check:	43)77,141 Check:
33)82,050 Check:	93)84,039 Check:

Denny has a baseball card collection. He has 13,789 cards. He wants to put the cards in a scrapbook that holds 15 cards on a page. How many pages does Denny need in his scrapbook? _____

Multiplication and Division

Directions: Multiply or divide to find the answers.

Brianne's summer job is mowing lawns for three of her neighbors. Each lawn takes about 1 hour to mow and needs to be done once every week. At the end of the summer, she will have earned a total of $630. She collected the same amount of money from each job. How much did each neighbor pay for her summer lawn service?
_____

If the mowing season lasts for 14 weeks, how much will Brianne earn for each job each week? _____

If she had worked for two more weeks, how much would she have earned? _____

Brianne agreed to shovel snow from the driveways and sidewalks for the same three neighbors. They agreed to pay her the same rate. However, it only snowed seven times that winter. How much did she earn shoveling snow? _____

What was her total income for both jobs? _____

Directions: Multiply or divide.

12) 7,476   23) 21,620   40) 32,600

32 x 45 = _____   28 x 15 = _____   73 x 14 = _____   92 x 30 = _____

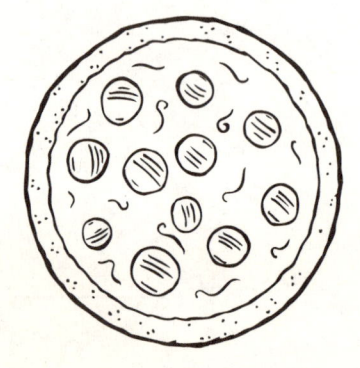

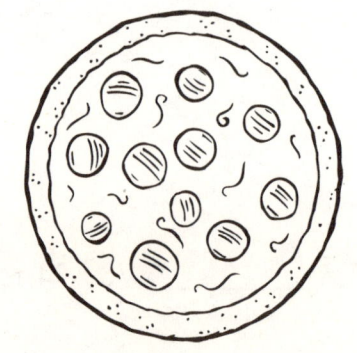

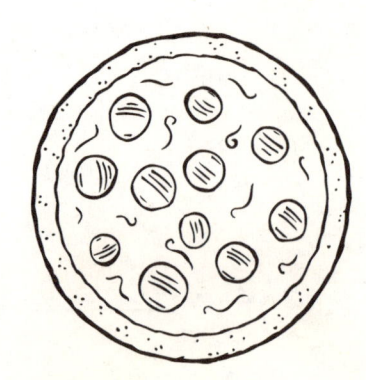

Adding and Subtracting Like Fractions

A **fraction** is a number that names part of a whole. Examples of fractions are $\frac{1}{2}$ and $\frac{1}{3}$.
Like fractions have the same **denominator**, or bottom number. Examples of like fractions are $\frac{1}{4}$ and $\frac{3}{4}$.

To add or subtract fractions, the denominators must be the same. Add or subtract only the **numerators**, the numbers above the line in fractions.

Example:

numerators
denominators $\frac{5}{8} - \frac{1}{8} = \frac{4}{8}$

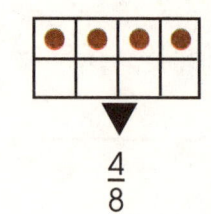

Directions: Add or subtract these fractions.

$\frac{6}{12} - \frac{3}{12} = \frac{3}{12}$	$\frac{4}{9} + \frac{1}{9} = \frac{5}{9}$	$\frac{1}{3} + \frac{1}{3} = \frac{2}{3}$	$\frac{5}{11} + \frac{4}{11} = \frac{9}{11}$
$\frac{3}{5} - \frac{1}{5} = \frac{4}{5}$	$\frac{5}{6} - \frac{2}{6} = \frac{3}{6} = \frac{1}{2}$	$\frac{3}{4} - \frac{2}{4} = \frac{5}{4} = 1\frac{1}{4}$	$\frac{5}{10} + \frac{3}{10} = \frac{8}{10}$
$\frac{3}{8} + \frac{2}{8} = \frac{5}{8}$	$\frac{1}{7} + \frac{4}{7} =$	$\frac{2}{20} + \frac{15}{20} =$	$\frac{11}{15} - \frac{9}{15} =$

Directions: Color the part of each pizza that equals the given fraction.

$\frac{2}{4}$ + $\frac{1}{4}$ =

Adding and Subtracting Unlike Fractions

Unlike fractions have different denominators. Examples of unlike fractions are $\frac{1}{4}$ and $\frac{2}{5}$. To add or subtract fractions, the denominators must be the same.

Example:

Step 1: Make the denominators the same by finding the least common denominator. The LCD of a pair of fractions is the same as the least common multiple (LCM) of their denominators.

$$\frac{1}{3} + \frac{1}{4} =$$

Multiples of 3 are 3, 6, 9, **12**, 15.
Multiples of 4 are 4, 8, **12**, 16.
LCM (and LCD) = 12

Step 2: Multiply by a number that will give the LCD. The numerator and denominator must be multiplied by the same number.

A. $\frac{1}{3} \times \frac{4}{4} = \frac{4}{12}$ B. $\frac{1}{4} \times \frac{3}{3} = \frac{3}{12}$

Step 3: Add the fractions. $\frac{1}{3} + \frac{1}{4} = \frac{4}{12} + \frac{3}{12} = \frac{7}{12}$

Directions: Follow the above steps to add or subtract unlike fractions. Write the LCM.

$\frac{2}{4} + \frac{3}{8} =$ LCM = _____	$\frac{3}{6} + \frac{1}{3} =$ LCM = _____	$\frac{4}{5} - \frac{1}{4} =$ LCM = _____
$\frac{2}{3} + \frac{2}{9} =$ LCM = _____	$\frac{4}{7} - \frac{2}{14} =$ LCM = _____	$\frac{7}{12} - \frac{2}{4} =$ LCM = _____

The basketball team ordered two pizzas. They left $\frac{1}{3}$ of one and $\frac{1}{4}$ of the other. How much pizza was left?

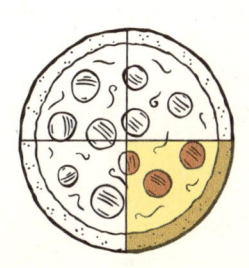

_____

Math

Total Basic Skills Grade 5

Name _____

Reducing Fractions

A fraction is in lowest terms when the GCF of both the numerator and denominator is 1. These fractions are in lowest possible terms: $\frac{2}{3}$, $\frac{5}{8}$ and $\frac{99}{100}$.

Example: Write $\frac{4}{8}$ in lowest terms.

Step 1: Write the factors of 4 and 8.

Factors of 4 are **4**, 2, 1.

Factors of 8 are 1, 8, 2, **4**.

Step 2: Find the GCF: 4.

Step 3: Divide both the numerator and denominator by 4.

$$\frac{4}{8} \div \frac{4}{4} = \frac{1}{2}$$

Directions: Write each fraction in lowest terms.

$\frac{6}{8}$ = _____ lowest terms $\frac{9}{12}$ = _____ lowest terms

factors of 6: 6, 1, 2, 3   factors of 9: ____, ____, ____   ____ GCF

factors of 8: 8, 1, 2, 4   factors of 12: ____, ____, ____, ____, ____, ____   ____ GCF

$\frac{2}{6}$ =	$\frac{10}{15}$ =	$\frac{8}{32}$ =	$\frac{4}{10}$ =
$\frac{12}{18}$ =	$\frac{6}{8}$ =	$\frac{4}{6}$ =	$\frac{3}{9}$ =

Directions: Color the pizzas to show that $\frac{4}{6}$ in lowest terms is $\frac{2}{3}$.

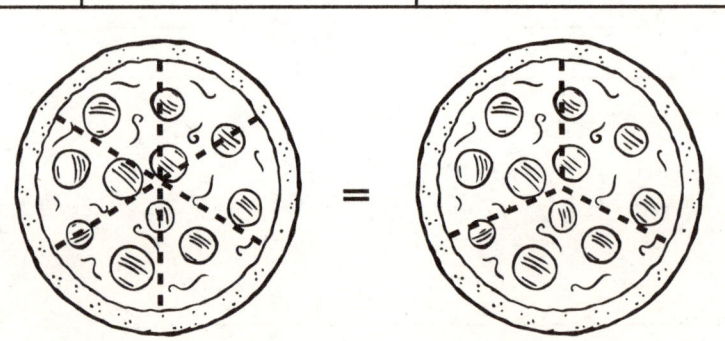

Total Basic Skills Grade 5   254   Math

Improper Fractions

An **improper fraction** has a numerator that is greater than its denominator. An example of an improper fraction is $\frac{7}{6}$. An improper fraction should be reduced to its lowest terms.

Example: $\frac{5}{4}$ is an improper fraction because its numerator is greater than its denominator.

   Step 1: Divide the numerator by the denominator: $5 \div 4 = 1$, r1

   Step 2: Write the remainder as a fraction: $\frac{1}{4}$

$\frac{5}{4} = 1\frac{1}{4}$ $1\frac{1}{4}$ is a mixed number—a whole number and a fraction.

Directions: Follow the steps above to change the improper fractions to mixed numbers.

$\frac{9}{8} =$	$\frac{11}{5} =$	$\frac{5}{3} =$	$\frac{7}{6} =$	$\frac{8}{7} =$	$\frac{4}{3} =$
$\frac{21}{5} =$	$\frac{9}{4} =$	$\frac{3}{2} =$	$\frac{9}{6} =$	$\frac{25}{4} =$	$\frac{8}{3} =$

Sara had 29 duplicate stamps in her stamp collection. She decided to give them to four of her friends. If she gave each of them the same number of stamps, how many duplicates will she have left? _____

Name the improper fraction in this problem. _____

What step must you do next to solve the problem? _____

_____

Write your answer as a mixed number. _____

How many stamps could she give each of her friends? _____

Mixed Numbers

A **mixed number** is a whole number and a fraction together. An example of a mixed number is $2\frac{3}{4}$. A mixed number can be changed to an improper fraction.

Example: $2\frac{3}{4}$

Step 1: Multiply the denominator by the whole number: 4 x 2 = 8

Step 2: Add the numerator: 8 + 3 = 11

Step 3: Write the sum over the denominator: $\frac{11}{4}$

Directions: Follow the steps above to change the mixed numbers to improper fractions.

$3\frac{2}{3}$ =	$6\frac{1}{5}$ =	$4\frac{7}{8}$ =	$2\frac{1}{2}$ =
$1\frac{4}{5}$ =	$5\frac{3}{4}$ =	$7\frac{1}{8}$ =	$9\frac{1}{9}$ =
$8\frac{1}{2}$ =	$7\frac{1}{6}$ =	$5\frac{3}{5}$ =	$9\frac{3}{8}$ =
$12\frac{1}{5}$ =	$25\frac{1}{2}$ =	$10\frac{2}{3}$ =	$14\frac{3}{8}$ =

Adding Mixed Numbers

To add mixed numbers, first find the least common denominator.

Always reduce the answer to lowest terms.

Example:

$$5\tfrac{1}{4} \rightarrow 5\tfrac{3}{12}$$
$$+6\tfrac{1}{3} \rightarrow +6\tfrac{4}{12}$$
$$\overline{11\tfrac{7}{12}}$$

Directions: Add. Reduce the answers to lowest terms.

$$8\tfrac{1}{2} \qquad 5\tfrac{1}{4} \qquad 9\tfrac{3}{10} \qquad 8\tfrac{1}{5}$$
$$+7\tfrac{1}{4} \qquad +2\tfrac{3}{8} \qquad +7\tfrac{1}{5} \qquad +6\tfrac{7}{10}$$

$$4\tfrac{4}{5} \qquad 3\tfrac{1}{2} \qquad 4\tfrac{1}{2} \qquad 6\tfrac{1}{12}$$
$$+3\tfrac{3}{10} \qquad +7\tfrac{1}{4} \qquad +1\tfrac{1}{3} \qquad +3\tfrac{3}{4}$$

$$5\tfrac{1}{3} \qquad 6\tfrac{1}{3} \qquad 2\tfrac{2}{7} \qquad 3\tfrac{1}{2}$$
$$+2\tfrac{3}{9} \qquad +2\tfrac{2}{5} \qquad +4\tfrac{1}{14} \qquad +3\tfrac{1}{4}$$

The boys picked $3\tfrac{1}{2}$ baskets of apples. The girls picked $5\tfrac{1}{2}$ baskets. How many baskets of apples did the boys and girls pick in all? _____

Math   257   Total Basic Skills Grade 5

Subtracting Mixed Numbers

To subtract mixed numbers, first find the least common denominator. Reduce the answer to its lowest terms.

Directions: Subtract. Reduce to lowest terms.

Example:

$$6\frac{5}{8} \rightarrow 6\frac{10}{16}$$
$$-3\frac{4}{16} \rightarrow -3\frac{4}{16}$$
$$3\frac{6}{16} = 3\frac{3}{8}$$

$$2\frac{3}{7} \qquad 7\frac{2}{3} \qquad 6\frac{3}{4} \qquad 9\frac{5}{12}$$
$$-1\frac{1}{14} \qquad -5\frac{1}{8} \qquad -2\frac{3}{12} \qquad -5\frac{9}{24}$$

$$5\frac{1}{2} \qquad 7\frac{3}{8} \qquad 8\frac{3}{8} \qquad 11\frac{5}{6}$$
$$-3\frac{1}{3} \qquad -5\frac{1}{6} \qquad -6\frac{5}{12} \qquad -7\frac{1}{12}$$

$$9\frac{3}{5} \qquad 4\frac{4}{5} \qquad 9\frac{2}{3} \qquad 14\frac{3}{8}$$
$$-7\frac{1}{15} \qquad -2\frac{1}{4} \qquad -4\frac{1}{6} \qquad -9\frac{3}{16}$$

The Rodriguez Farm has $9\frac{1}{2}$ acres of corn. The Johnson Farm has $7\frac{1}{3}$ acres of corn. How many more acres of corn does the Rodriguez Farm have? _____

Comparing Fractions

Directions: Use the symbol > (greater than), < (less than) or = (equal to) to show the relationship between each pair of fractions.

$\frac{1}{2}$ > $\frac{1}{3}$ $\frac{2}{5}$ < $\frac{3}{7}$ $\frac{3}{8}$ < $\frac{2}{4}$

$\frac{3}{4}$ > $\frac{6}{8}$ $\frac{2}{3}$ = $\frac{4}{5}$ $\frac{3}{9}$ > $\frac{1}{3}$

$\frac{3}{12}$ < $\frac{1}{4}$ $\frac{2}{14}$ < $\frac{1}{7}$ $\frac{5}{15}$ < $\frac{2}{3}$

If Kelly gave $\frac{1}{3}$ of a pizza to Holly and $\frac{1}{5}$ to Diane, how much did she have left?

_____

Holly decided to share $\frac{1}{2}$ of her share of the pizza with Deb. How much did each of them actually get?

_____

Ordering Fractions

When putting fractions in order from smallest to largest or largest to smallest, it helps to find a common denominator first.

Example:

$\frac{1}{3}, \frac{1}{2}$ changed to $\frac{2}{6}, \frac{3}{6}$

Directions: Put the following fractions in order from least to largest value.

Least　　　　　　　　　　　　　　　Largest

$\frac{1}{2}$　　$\frac{2}{7}$　　$\frac{4}{5}$　　$\frac{1}{3}$　　_____ _____ _____ _____

$\frac{3}{12}$　　$\frac{3}{6}$　　$\frac{1}{3}$　　$\frac{3}{4}$　　_____ _____ _____ _____

$\frac{2}{5}$　　$\frac{4}{15}$　　$\frac{3}{5}$　　$\frac{5}{15}$　　_____ _____ _____ _____

$3\frac{4}{5}$　　$3\frac{2}{5}$　　$\frac{9}{5}$　　$3\frac{1}{5}$　　_____ _____ _____ _____

$9\frac{1}{3}$　　$9\frac{2}{3}$　　$9\frac{9}{12}$　　$8\frac{2}{3}$　　_____ _____ _____ _____

$5\frac{8}{12}$　　$5\frac{5}{12}$　　$5\frac{4}{24}$　　$5\frac{3}{6}$　　_____ _____ _____ _____

$4\frac{3}{5}$　　$5\frac{7}{15}$　　$6\frac{2}{5}$　　$5\frac{1}{5}$　　_____ _____ _____ _____

Four dogs were selected as finalists at a dog show. They were judged in four separate categories. One received a perfect score in each area. The dog with a score closest to four is the winner. Their scores are listed below. Which dog won the contest? _____

Dog A　$3\frac{4}{5}$　　　Dog B　$3\frac{2}{3}$　　　Dog C　$3\frac{5}{15}$　　　Dog D　$3\frac{9}{12}$

Multiplying Fractions

To multiply fractions, follow these steps:

$\frac{1}{2} \times \frac{3}{4} =$ **Step 1:** Multiply the numerators. $1 \times 3 = 3$
                  Step 2: Multiply the denominators. $2 \times 4 = 8$

When multiplying a fraction by a whole number, first change the whole number to a fraction.

Example:

$\frac{1}{2} \times 8 = \frac{1}{2} \times \frac{8}{1} = \frac{8}{2} = 4$ reduced to lowest terms

Directions: Multiply. Reduce your answers to lowest terms.

$\frac{3}{4} \times \frac{1}{6} =$	$\frac{1}{2} \times \frac{5}{8} =$	$\frac{2}{3} \times \frac{1}{6} =$	$\frac{2}{3} \times \frac{1}{2} =$
$\frac{5}{6} \times 4 =$	$\frac{3}{8} \times \frac{1}{16} =$	$\frac{1}{5} \times 5 =$	$\frac{7}{8} \times \frac{3}{4} =$
$\frac{7}{11} \times \frac{1}{3} =$	$\frac{2}{9} \times \frac{9}{4} =$	$\frac{1}{3} \times \frac{1}{3} \times \frac{1}{3} =$	$\frac{1}{8} \times \frac{1}{4} \times \frac{1}{2} =$

Jennifer has 10 pets. Two-fifths of the pets are cats, one-half are fish and one-tenth are dogs. How many of each pet does she have?

_____

_____

_____

Multiplying Mixed Numbers

Multiply mixed numbers by first changing them to improper fractions. Always reduce your answers to lowest terms.

Example:

$$2\frac{1}{3} \times 1\frac{1}{8} = \frac{7}{3} \times \frac{9}{8} = \frac{63}{24} = 2\frac{15}{24} = 2\frac{5}{8}$$

Directions: Multiply. Reduce to lowest terms.

$4\frac{1}{4} \times 2\frac{1}{5} =$	$1\frac{1}{3} \times 3\frac{1}{4} =$	$1\frac{1}{9} \times 3\frac{3}{5} =$
$1\frac{6}{7} \times 4\frac{1}{2} =$	$2\frac{3}{4} \times 2\frac{3}{5} =$	$4\frac{2}{3} \times 3\frac{1}{7} =$
$6\frac{2}{5} \times 2\frac{1}{8} =$	$3\frac{1}{7} \times 4\frac{5}{8} =$	$7\frac{3}{8} \times 2\frac{1}{9} =$

Sunnyside Farm has two barns with 25 stalls in each barn. Cows use $\frac{3}{5}$ of the stalls, and horses use the rest.

How many stalls are for cows? _____

How many are for horses? _____

(Hint: First, find how many total stalls are in the two barns.)

Dividing Fractions

To divide fractions, follow these steps:

$$\frac{3}{4} \div \frac{1}{4} =$$

Step 1: "Invert" the divisor. That means to turn it upside down.

$$\frac{3}{4} \div \frac{4}{1}$$

Step 2: Multiply the two fractions:

$$\frac{3}{4} \times \frac{4}{1} = \frac{12}{4}$$

Step 3: Reduce the fraction to lowest terms by dividing the denominator into the numerator.

$$12 \div 4 = 3$$
$$\frac{3}{4} \div \frac{1}{4} = 3$$

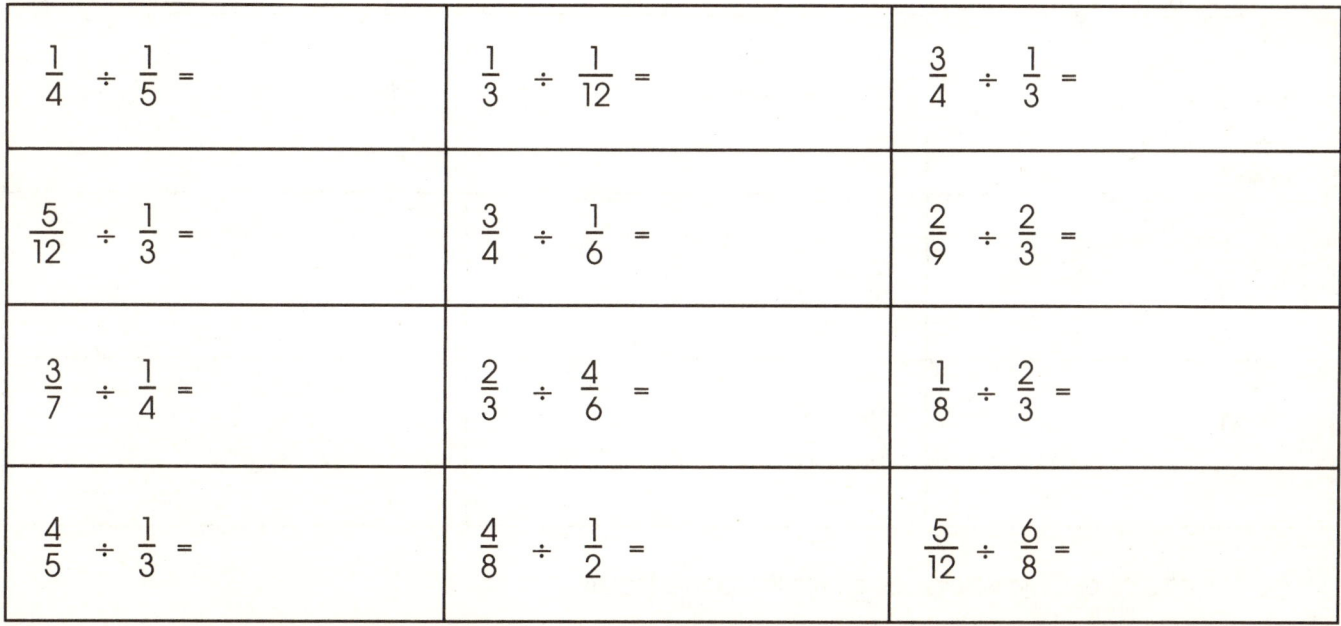

Directions: Follow the above steps to divide fractions.

$\frac{1}{4} \div \frac{1}{5} =$	$\frac{1}{3} \div \frac{1}{12} =$	$\frac{3}{4} \div \frac{1}{3} =$
$\frac{5}{12} \div \frac{1}{3} =$	$\frac{3}{4} \div \frac{1}{6} =$	$\frac{2}{9} \div \frac{2}{3} =$
$\frac{3}{7} \div \frac{1}{4} =$	$\frac{2}{3} \div \frac{4}{6} =$	$\frac{1}{8} \div \frac{2}{3} =$
$\frac{4}{5} \div \frac{1}{3} =$	$\frac{4}{8} \div \frac{1}{2} =$	$\frac{5}{12} \div \frac{6}{8} =$

Dividing Whole Numbers by Fractions

Follow these steps to divide a whole number by a fraction:

$$8 \div \frac{1}{4} =$$

Step 1: Write the whole number as a fraction:

$$\frac{8}{1} \div \frac{1}{4} =$$

Step 2: Invert the divisor.

$$\frac{8}{1} \div \frac{4}{1} =$$

Step 3: Multiply the two fractions:

$$\frac{8}{1} \times \frac{4}{1} = \frac{32}{1}$$

Step 4: Reduce the fraction to lowest terms by dividing the denominator into the numerator: $32 \div 1 = 32$

Directions: Follow the above steps to divide a whole number by a fraction.

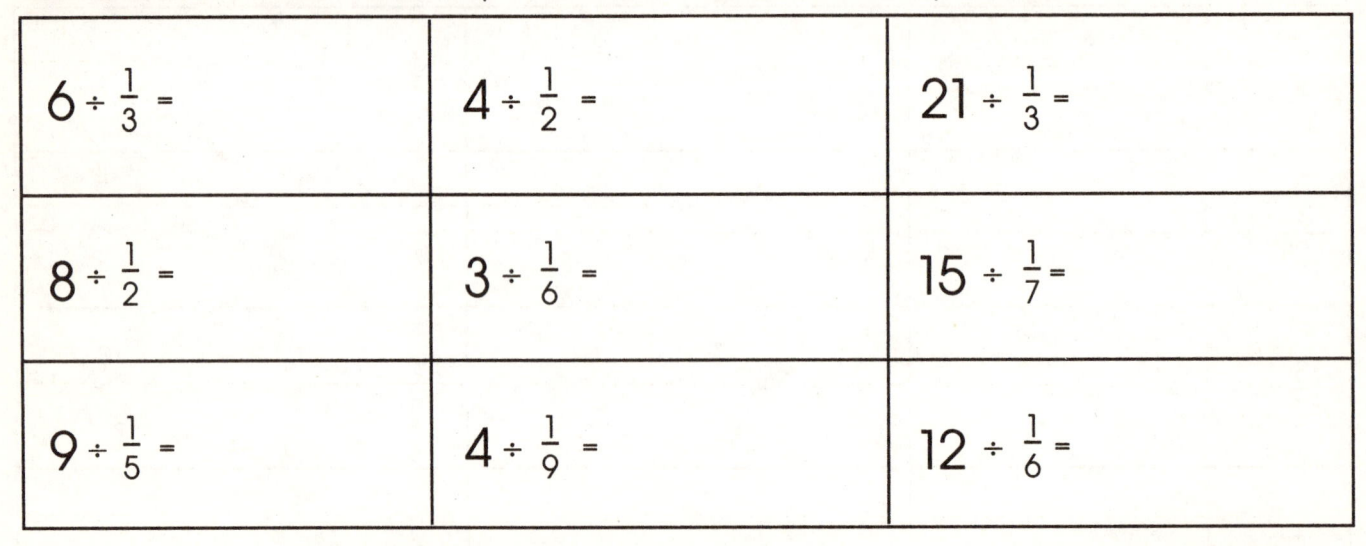

$6 \div \frac{1}{3} =$	$4 \div \frac{1}{2} =$	$21 \div \frac{1}{3} =$
$8 \div \frac{1}{2} =$	$3 \div \frac{1}{6} =$	$15 \div \frac{1}{7} =$
$9 \div \frac{1}{5} =$	$4 \div \frac{1}{9} =$	$12 \div \frac{1}{6} =$

Three-fourths of a bag of popcorn fits into one bowl.
How many bowls do you need if you have six bags of popcorn? _____

Decimals

A **decimal** is a number with one or more places to the right of a decimal point.

Examples: 6.5 and 2.25

Fractions with denominators of 10 or 100 can be written as decimals.

Examples:

$\frac{7}{10} = 0.7$

$\frac{0}{\text{ones}} . \frac{7}{\text{tenths}} \frac{0}{\text{hundredths}}$

$1\frac{52}{100} = 1.52$

$\frac{1}{\text{ones}} . \frac{5}{\text{tenths}} \frac{2}{\text{hundredths}}$

1/2   0.50

Directions: Write the fractions as decimals.

$\frac{1}{2} = \frac{}{10} = 0.\underline{}$

$\frac{2}{5} = \frac{}{10} = 0.\underline{}$

$\frac{1}{5} = \frac{}{10} = 0.\underline{}$

$\frac{3}{5} = \frac{}{10} = 0.\underline{}$

$\frac{63}{100} =$	$2\frac{8}{10} =$	$38\frac{4}{100} =$	$6\frac{13}{100} =$
$\frac{1}{4} =$	$\frac{2}{5} =$	$\frac{1}{50} =$	$\frac{100}{200} =$
$5\frac{2}{100} =$	$\frac{4}{25} =$	$15\frac{3}{5} =$	$\frac{3}{100} =$

265

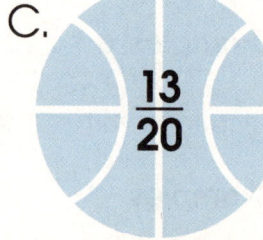

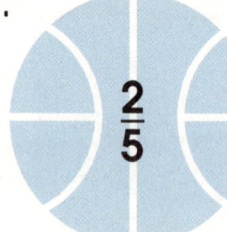

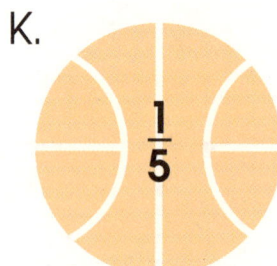

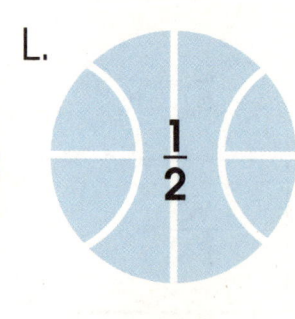

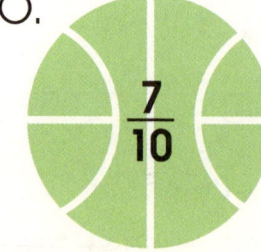

Decimals and Fractions

Directions: Write the letter of the fraction that is equal to the decimal.

0.25 = _____

0.5 = _____

0.7 = _____

0.8 = _____

0.37 = _____

0.2 = _____

0.65 = _____

0.75 = _____

0.6 = _____

0.12 = _____

0.33 = _____

0.95 = _____

0.24 = _____

0.3 = _____

0.4 = _____

A. $\dfrac{33}{100}$ B. $\dfrac{3}{4}$ C. $\dfrac{13}{20}$

D. $\dfrac{3}{5}$ E. $\dfrac{3}{25}$ F. $\dfrac{19}{20}$

G. $\dfrac{1}{4}$ H. $\dfrac{2}{5}$ I. $\dfrac{3}{10}$

J. $\dfrac{37}{100}$ K. $\dfrac{1}{5}$ L. $\dfrac{1}{2}$

M. $\dfrac{6}{25}$ N. $\dfrac{4}{5}$ O. $\dfrac{7}{10}$

Adding and Subtracting Decimals

Add and subtract with decimals the same way you do with whole numbers. Keep the decimal points lined up so that you work with hundreths, then tenths, then ones, and so on.

Directions: Add or subtract. Remember to keep the decimal point in the proper place.

```
    0.5           0.35          47.5          85.7
  + 0.8         + 0.25        - 32.7        -  9.8
```

```
   13.90          9.53          72.8          6.43
 +  4.23        - 8.16        - 63.9        + 4.58
```

```
  638.07        811.060       521.09
 - 19.34       + 78.430      - 148.75
```

```
  916.635       287.768       467.05
 +172.136      - 63.951      - 398.19
```

Sean ran a 1-mile race in 5.58 minutes. Carlos ran it in 6.38 minutes. How much less time did Sean need?

_____

Math   267   Total Basic Skills Grade 5

Multiplying Decimals

Multiply with decimals the same way you do with whole numbers. The decimal point moves in multiplication. Count the number of decimal places in the problem and use the same number of decimal places in your answer.

Example:

```
   3.5
 x 1.5
 ─────
  1 7 5
 3 5
 ─────
 5.2 5
```

Directions: Multiply.

    2.5   67.4   83.7   13.35
x .9   x 2.3   x 9.8   x 3.06

   9.06   28.97   33.41   28.7
x 2.38   x 5.16   x .93   x 11.9

The jet flies 1.5 times faster than the plane with a propeller. The propeller plane flies 165.7 miles per hour. How fast does the jet fly?

_____

Dividing With Decimals

When the dividend has a decimal, place the decimal point for the answer directly above the decimal point in the dividend. The first one has been done for you.

```
      12.5
   ┌──────
 3 │ 37.5
   − 3
   ─────
     07
    − 6
    ────
     15
    −15
    ────
      0
```

4 ⟌ 34.4   2 ⟌ 31.6   3 ⟌ 131.4

5 ⟌ 187.5   7 ⟌ 181.3   6 ⟌ 340.8   9 ⟌ 294.3

3 ⟌ 135.6   5 ⟌ 264.5   2 ⟌ 134.6   8 ⟌ 754.4

5 ⟌ 35.25   7 ⟌ 79.45   9 ⟌ 28.71   36 ⟌ 199.44

Dividing Decimals by Decimals

When the divisor has a decimal point you must eliminate it before dividing. You can do this by moving the decimal point to the right to create a whole number. You must also move the decimal point the same number of spaces to the right in the dividend.

Sometimes you need to add zeros to do this.

Example:

0.25 ⟌ 85.50   changes to

```
       342
   25 ⟌ 8550
      - 75
        105
      - 100
          50
          50
           0
```

Directions: Divide.

0.3 ⟌ 27.9   0.6 ⟌ 42.6   0.9 ⟌ 81.9   0.7 ⟌ 83.3

0.4 ⟌ 23.2   0.7 ⟌ 56.7   1.2 ⟌ 10.8   2.2 ⟌ 138.6

12.6 ⟌ 5,670   4.7 ⟌ 564   8.6 ⟌ 842.8   3.7 ⟌ 2,009.1

5.9 ⟌ 1,917.5   4.3 ⟌ 1,376   2.9 ⟌ 922.2   2.7 ⟌ 5613.3

Geometry

Geometry is the branch of mathematics that has to do with points, lines and shapes.

Directions: Write the word from the box that is described below.

| triangle | square | cube | angle |
| line | ray | segment | rectangle |

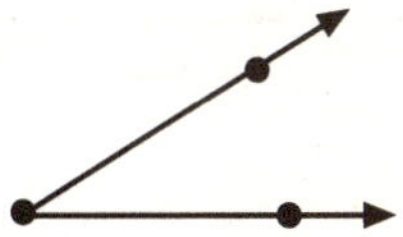

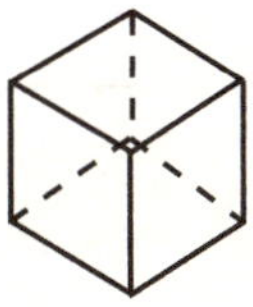

a collection of points on a straight path
that goes on and on in opposite directions   _____

a figure with three sides and three corners   _____

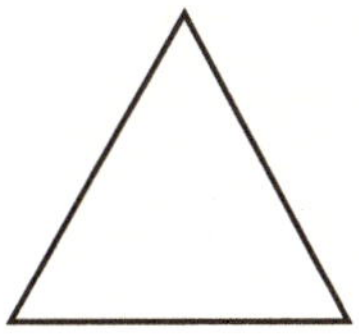

a figure with four equal sides
and four corners   _____

part of a line that has one end point
and goes on and on in one direction   _____

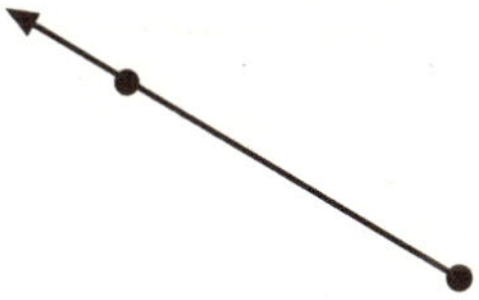

part of a line having two end points   _____

a space figure with six square faces   _____

two rays with a common end point   _____

a figure with four corners and four sides   _____

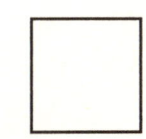

Geometry

Review the definitions on the previous page before completing the problems below.

Directions: Identify the labeled section of each of the following diagrams.

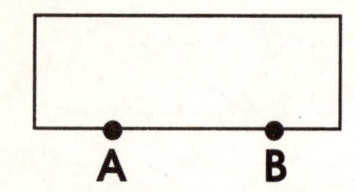

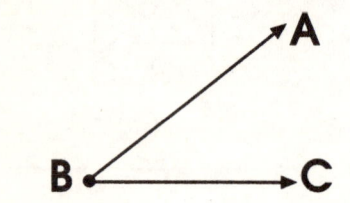

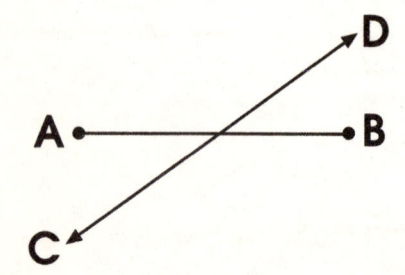

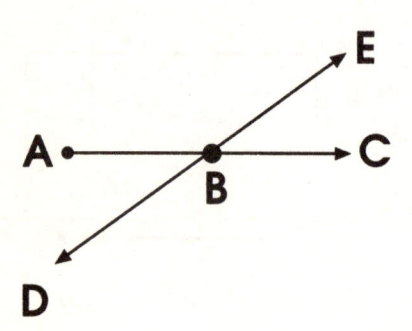

AB = _____

ABC = _____

AB = _____

CD = _____

AC = _____

AB = _____

EBC = _____

BC = _____

Similar, Congruent and Symmetrical Figures

Similar figures have the same shape but have varying sizes.

Figures that are **congruent** have identical shapes but different orientations. That means they face in different directions.

Symmetrical figures can be divided equally into two identical parts.

Directions: Cross out the shape that does not belong in each group. Label the two remaining shapes as similiar, congruent or symmetrical.

Perimeter and Area

The **perimeter** (P) of a figure is the distance around it. To find the perimeter, add the lengths of the sides.

The **area** (A) of a figure is the number of units in a figure. Find the area by multiplying the length of a figure by its width.

Example:

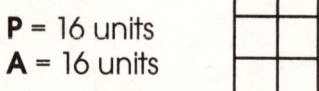

P = 16 units
A = 16 units

Directions: Find the perimeter and area of each figure.

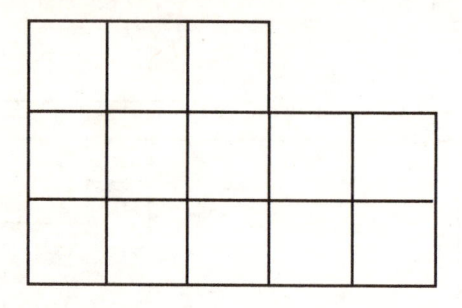

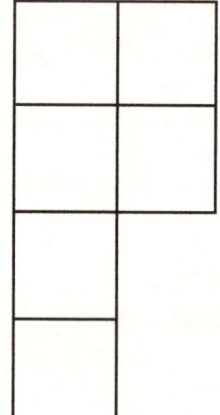

P = _____
A = _____

P = _____
A = _____

9 Yards
9 Yards

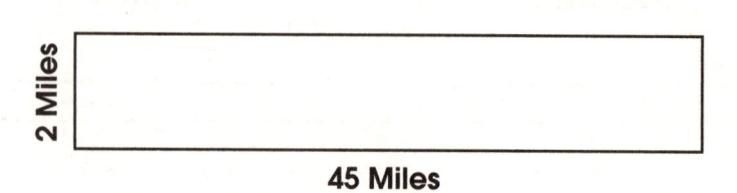

P = _____
A = _____

2 Miles
45 Miles

P = _____
A = _____

Total Basic Skills Grade 5   Math

Volume

The formula for finding the volume of a box is length times width times height **(L x W x H)**. The answer is given in cubic units.

Directions: Solve the problems.

Example:

Height 8 ft.
Length 8 ft.
Width   8 ft.   **L x W x H = volume**
8' x 8' x 8' = 512 cubic ft. or 512 ft.³

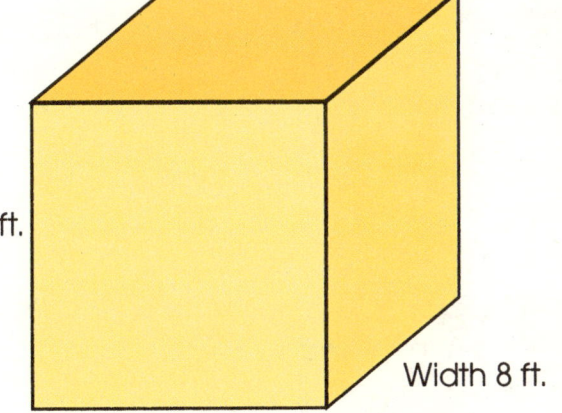

Height 8 ft.
Width 8 ft.
Length 8 ft.

4 ft.
12 ft.
6 ft.
V = _____

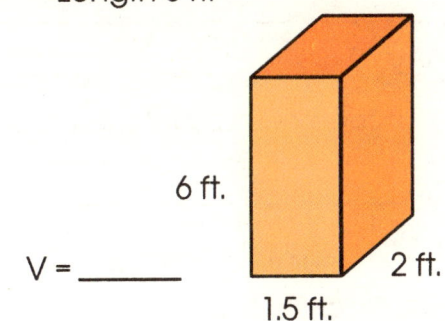

6 ft.
1.5 ft.
2 ft.
V = _____

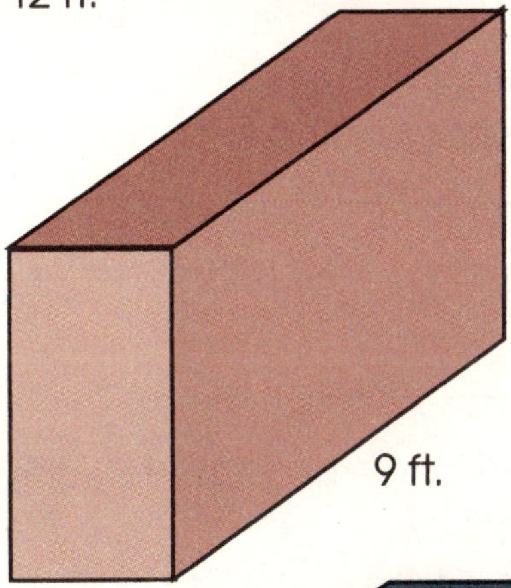

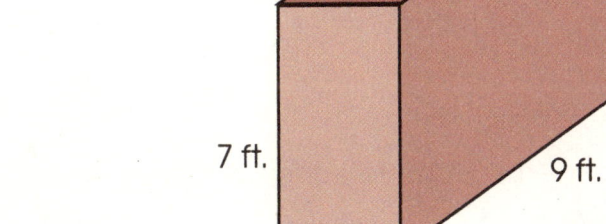

7 ft.
3 ft.
9 ft.
V = _____

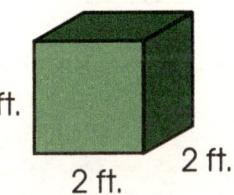

2 ft.
2 ft.
2 ft.
V = _____

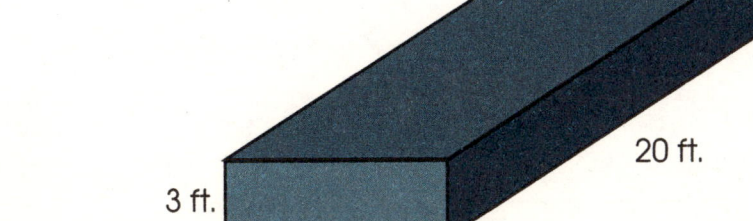

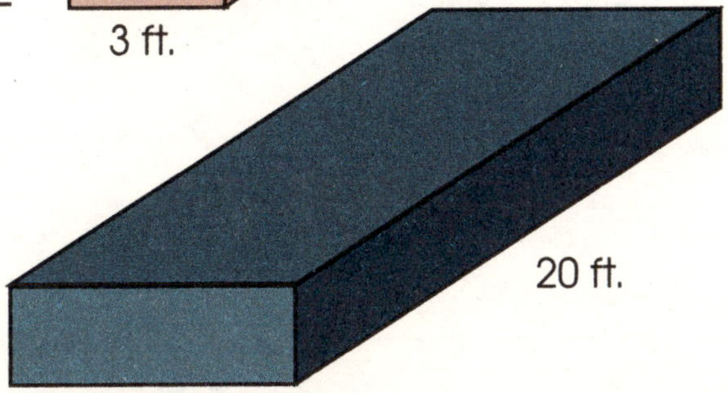

3 ft.
6 ft.
20 ft.
V = _____

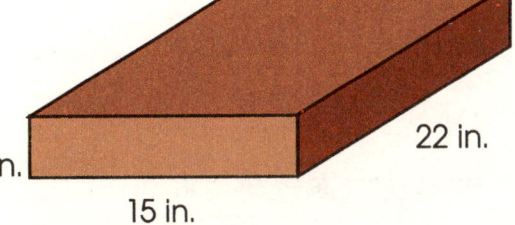

5 in.
15 in.
22 in.
V = _____ in.³   V = _____ ft.³

Perimeter and Area

Directions: Use the formulas for finding perimeter and area to solve these problems.

Julie's family moved to a new house. Her parents said she could have the largest bedroom. Julie knew she would need to find the area of each room to find which one was largest.

One rectangular bedroom is 7 feet wide and 12 feet long. Another is 11 feet long and 9 feet wide. The third bedroom is a square. It is 9 feet wide and 9 feet long. Which one should she select to have the largest room?

_____

The new home also has a swimming pool in the backyard. It is 32 feet long and 18 feet wide. What is the perimeter of the pool?

_____

Julie's mother wants to plant flowers on each side of the new house. She will need three plants for every foot of space. The house is 75 feet across the front and back and 37.5 feet along each side. Find the perimeter of the house.

_____

How many plants should she buy? _____

The family decided to buy new carpeting for several rooms. Complete the necessary information to determine how much carpeting to buy.

Den: 12 ft. x 14 ft. = _____ sq. ft.

Master Bedroom: 20 ft. x _____ = 360 sq. ft.

Family Room: _____ x 25 ft. = 375 sq. ft.

Total square feet of carpeting: _____

Perimeter, Area and Volume

Directions: Find the perimeter and area.

1. Length = 8 ft.
   Width = 11 ft.
   P = _____ A = _____

2. Length = 12 ft.
   Width = 10 ft.
   P = _____ A = _____

3. Length = 121 ft.
   Width = 16 ft.
   P = _____ A = _____

4. Length = 72 in.
   Width = 5 ft.
   P = _____ A = _____

Directions: Find the perimeter, area and volume.

5. Length = 7 ft.
   Width = 12 ft.
   Height = 10 ft.
   P = _____
   A = _____
   V = _____

6. Length = 48 in.
   Width = 7 ft.
   Height = 12 in.
   P = _____
   A = _____
   V = _____

7. Length = 12 in.
   Width = 15 in.
   Height = 20 in.
   P = _____
   A = _____
   V = _____

8. Length = 22 ft.
   Width = 40 ft.
   Height = 10 ft.
   P = _____
   A = _____
   V = _____

Circumference

Circumference is the distance around a circle. The **diameter** is a line segment that passes through the center of a circle and has both end points on the circle.

To find the circumference of any circle, multiply 3.14 times the diameter. The number 3.14 represents **pi** (pronounced *pie*) and is often written by this Greek symbol, π.

The formula for circumference is $C = \pi \times d$

    C = circumference

    d = diameter

    π = 3.14

Example:

    Circle A
    d = 2 in.
    C = 3.14 x 2 in.
    C = 6.28 in.

Directions: Find the circumference of each circle.

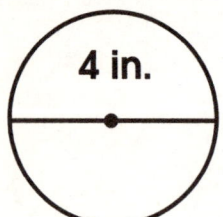

4 in.

C = _____

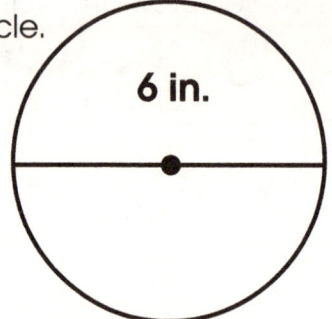

6 in.

C = _____

d = 10 in.
C = _____

d = 14 in.
C = _____

d = 3 yd.
C = _____

d = 4 ft.
C = _____

d = 8 ft.
C = _____

d = 12 ft.
C = _____

Circumference

The **radius** of a circle is the distance from the center of the circle to its outside edge. The diameter equals two times the radius.

Find the circumference by multiplying π (3.14) times the diameter or by multiplying π (3.14) times 2r (2 times the radius).

C = π x d or C = π x 2r

Directions: Write the missing radius, diameter or circumference.

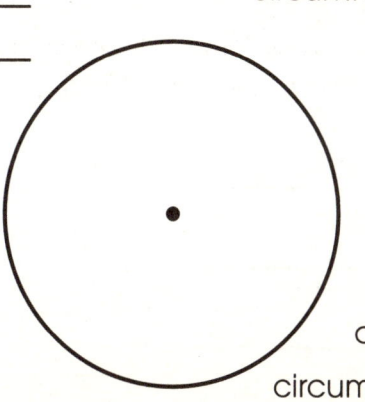

radius ___3___
diameter _____
circumference _____

radius _____
diameter ___14___
circumference _____

radius _____
diameter ___12___
circumference _____

radius ___2___
diameter _____
circumference _____

radius _____
diameter ___8___
circumference _____

radius ___5___
diameter _____
circumference _____

Diameter, Radius and Circumference

C = π x d or C = π x 2r

Directions: Write the missing radius, diameter or circumference.

Katie was asked to draw a circle on the playground for a game during recess. If the radius of the circle needed to be 14 inches, how long is the diameter? _____

What is the circumference? _____

A friend told her that more kids could play the game if they enlarged the circle. She had a friend help her. They made the diameter of the circle 45 inches long.

What is the radius? _____

What is the circumference? _____

Jamie was creating an art project. He wanted part of it to be a sphere. He measured 24 inches for the diameter.

What would the radius of the sphere be? _____

Find the circumference. _____

Unfortunately, Jamie discovered that he didn't have enough material to create a sphere that large, so he cut the dimensions in half. What are the new dimensions for his sphere?

Radius _____

Diameter _____

Circumference _____

Triangle Angles

A **triangle** is a figure with three corners and three sides. Every triangle contains three angles. The sum of the angles is always 180°, regardless of the size or shape of the triangle.

If you know two of the angles, you can add them together, then subtract the total from 180 to find the number of degrees in the third angle.

Directions: Find the number of degrees in the third angle of each triangle.

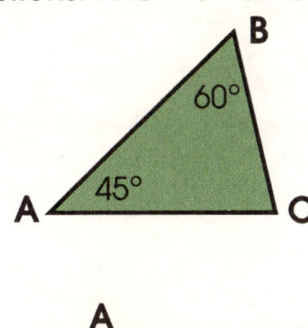

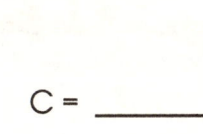

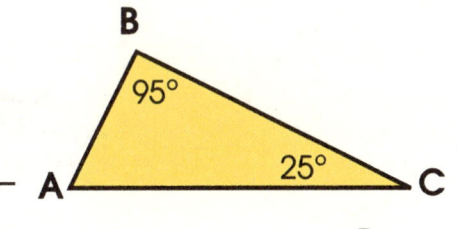

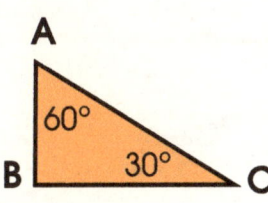

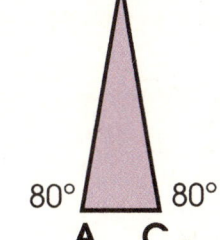

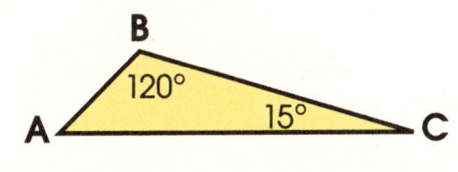

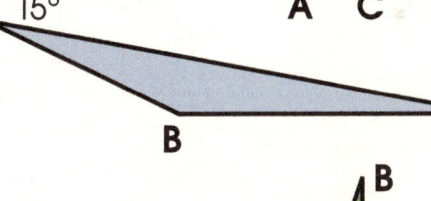

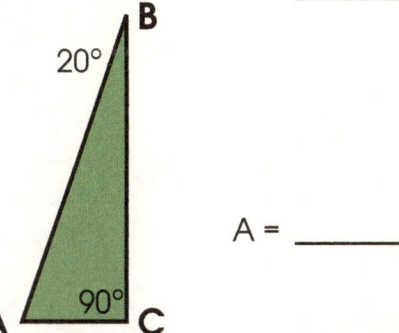

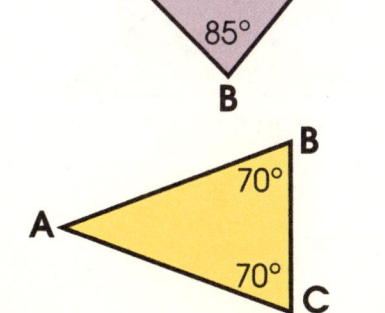

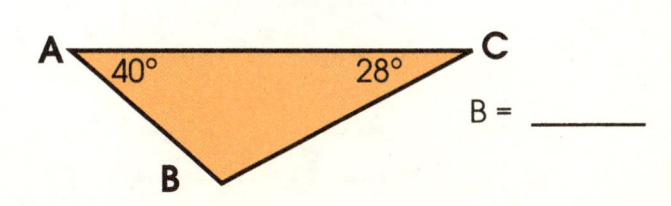

C = _____

A = _____

B = _____

B = _____

A = _____

B = _____

C = _____

A = _____

A = _____

B = _____

Area of a Triangle

The area of a triangle is found by multiplying $\frac{1}{2}$ times the base times the height.
$A = \frac{1}{2} \times b \times h$

Example:

$\overline{CD}$ is the height.   4 in.

$\overline{AB}$ is the base.   8 in.

Area = $\frac{1}{2} \times 4 \times 8 = \frac{32}{2}$ = 16 sq. in.

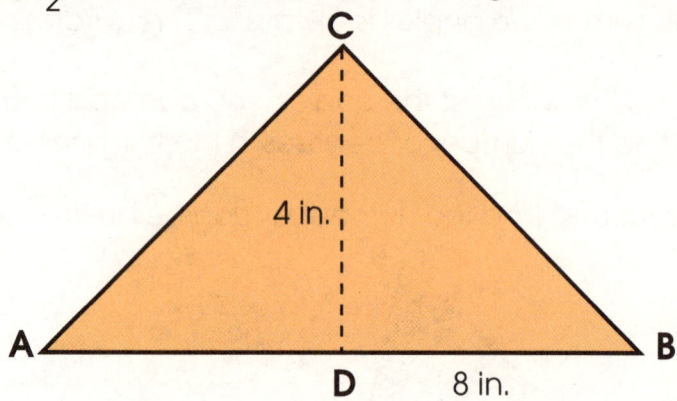

Directions: Find the area of each triangle.

4 in.
2 in.

A = _____

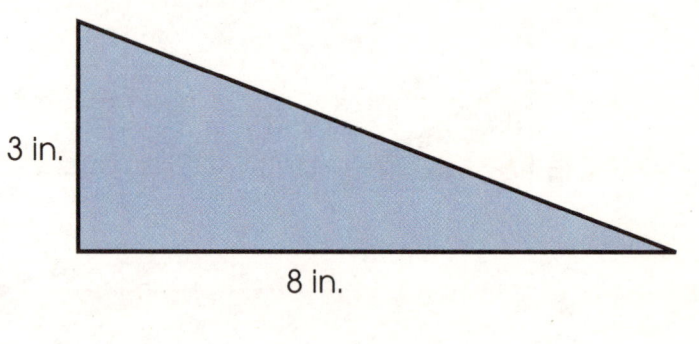

3 in.
8 in.

A = _____

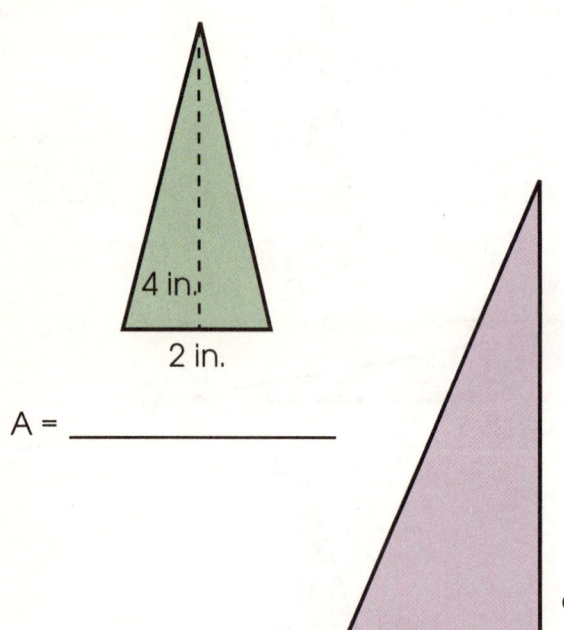

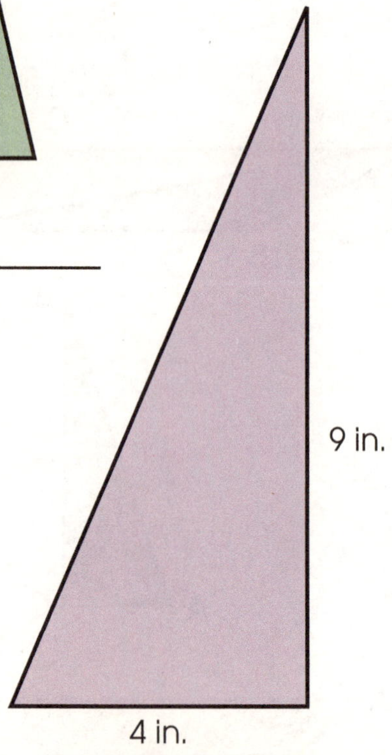

9 in.
4 in.

A = _____

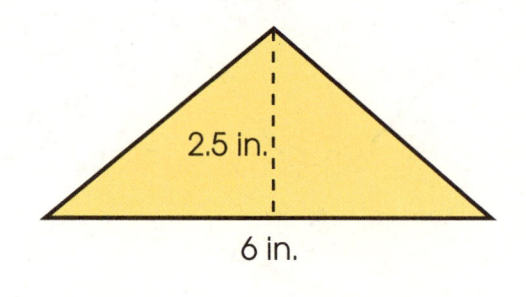

2.5 in.
6 in.

A = _____

Total Basic Skills Grade 5   Math

Space Figures

Space figures are figures whose points are in more than one plane. Cubes and cylinders are space figures.

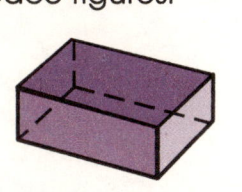

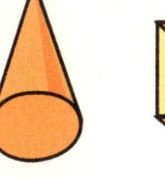

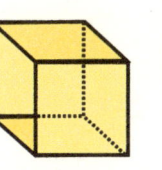

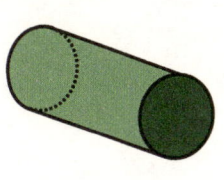

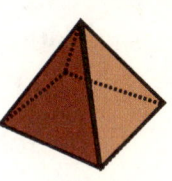

rectangular prism **cone** **cube** **cylinder** **sphere** **pyramid**

A **prism** has two identical, parallel bases.

All of the faces on a **rectangular prism** are rectangles.

A **cube** is a prism with six identical, square faces.

A **pyramid** is a space figure whose base is a polygon and whose faces are triangles with a common vertex—the point where two rays meet.

A **cylinder** has a curved surface and two parallel bases that are identical circles.

A **cone** has one circular, flat face and one vertex.

A **sphere** has no flat surface. All points are an equal distance from the center.

Directions: Circle the name of the figure you see in each of these familiar objects

basketball	cone	sphere	cylinder
trash can	cone	sphere	cylinder
lunch box	cube	rectangular prism	pyramid
teepee	cone	pyramid	cylinder

Math

283

Total Basic Skills Grade 5

Length

Inches, **feet**, **yards** and **miles** are used to measure length in the United States.

   12 inches = 1 foot (ft.)
   3 feet = 1 yard (yd.)
   36 inches = 1 yard
   1,760 yards = 1 mile (mi.)

Directions: Circle the best unit to measure each object. The first one has been done for you.

the length of a 🐱   (inches)   feet   yards   miles

the height of a 🏠   inches   feet   yards   miles

the length of a 🦗   inches   feet   yards   miles

distance to the ☀️   inches   feet   yards   miles

the height of a 🌳   inches   feet   yards   miles

the length of a ⬚ field   inches   feet   yards   miles

Length: Metric

Millimeters, **centimeters**, **meters** and **kilometers** are used to measure length in the metric system.

    1 meter = 39.37 inches
    1 kilometer = about $\frac{5}{8}$ mile
    10 millimeters = 1 centimeter (cm)
    100 centimeters = 1 meter (m)
    1,000 meters = 1 kilometer (km)

Directions: Circle the best unit to measure each object. The first one has been done for you.

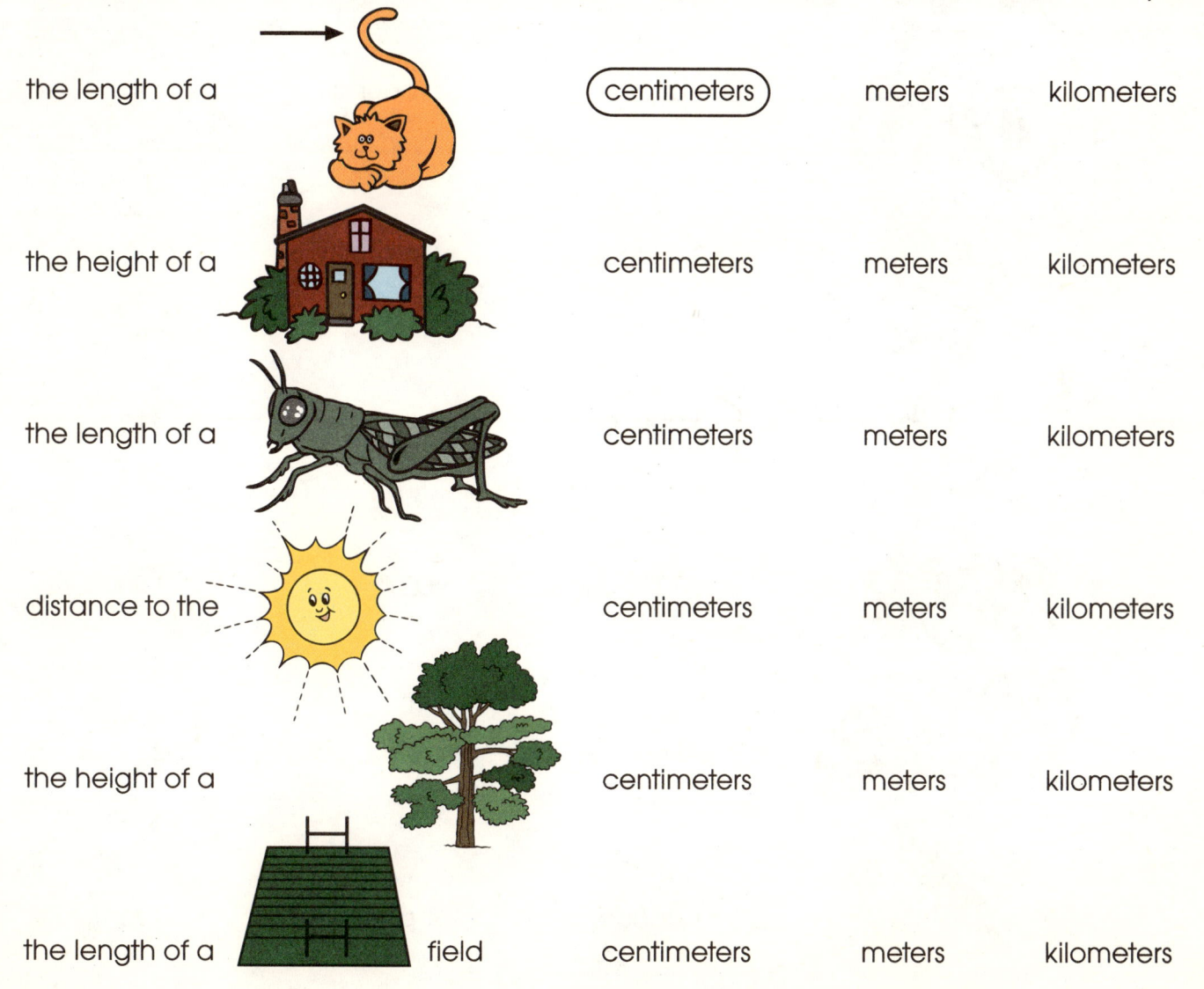

the length of a		(centimeters)	meters	kilometers
the height of a		centimeters	meters	kilometers
the length of a		centimeters	meters	kilometers
distance to the		centimeters	meters	kilometers
the height of a		centimeters	meters	kilometers
the length of a	field	centimeters	meters	kilometers

Math   285   Total Basic Skills Grade 5

Weight

Ounces, pounds and **tons** are used to measure weight in the United States.

16 ounces = 1 pound (lb.)
2,000 pounds = 1 ton (tn.)

Directions: Circle the most reasonable estimate for the weight of each object. The first one has been done for you.

 dog	10 ounces	(10 pounds)	10 tons
 bicycle	6 ounces	(6 pounds)	6 tons
 elephant	2 ounces	2 pounds	(2 tons)
 bird	(3 ounces)	3 pounds	3 tons
 car	1,800 ounces	(1,800 pounds)	1,800 tons
 truck	20 ounces	20 pounds	(20 tons)
 pencil	(1 ounce)	1 pound	1 ton

Weight: Metric

Grams and **kilograms** are units of weight in the metric system. A paper clip weighs about 1 gram. A kitten weighs about 1 kilogram.

1 kilogram (kg) = about 2.2 pounds

1,000 grams (g) = 1 kilogram

Directions: Circle the best unit to weigh each object.

Object	Answer	Object	Answer
dog	(kilogram) / gram	flower	kilogram / (gram)
bicycle	(kilogram) / gram	truck	(kilogram) / gram
leaf	kilogram / (gram)	elephant	(kilogram) / gram
car	(kilogram) / gram	pencil	kilogram / (gram)
bird	kilogram / (gram)	weightlifter	(kilogram) / gram

Capacity

The **fluid ounce**, **cup**, **pint**, **quart** and **gallon** are used to measure capacity in the United States.

1 cup    1 pint    1 quart    1 half gallon    1 gallon

8 fluid ounces (fl. oz.) = 1 cup (c.)
2 cups = 1 pint (pt.)
2 pints = 1 quart (qt.)
2 quarts = 1 half gallon ($\frac{1}{2}$ gal.)
4 quarts = 1 gallon (gal.)

Directions: Convert the units of capacity.

13 gal. = _____ qt.   10 pt. = _____ c.   12 c. = _____ pt.

4 gal. = _____ qt.   16 qt. = _____ gal.   5 c. = _____ pt.

36 pt. = _____ gal.   12 qt. = _____ pt.   6 gal. = _____ pt.

16 c. = _____ qt.   32 oz. = _____ c.   16 oz. = _____ pt.

Total Basic Skills Grade 5   288   Math

Capacity: Metric

Milliliters and liters are units of capacity in the metric system. A can of soda contains about 350 milliliters of liquid. A large plastic bottle contains 1 liter of liquid. A liter is about a quart.

1,000 milliliters (mL) = 1 liter (L)

Directions: Circle the best unit to measure each liquid.

milliliters
liters

milliliters
liters

milliliters
liters

milliliters
liters

milliliters
liters

milliliters
liters

milliliters
liters

milliliters
liters

milliliters
liters

milliliters
liters

Comparing Measurements

Directions: Use the symbols greater than (>), less than (<) or equal to (=) to complete each statement.

10 inches _____ 10 centimeters

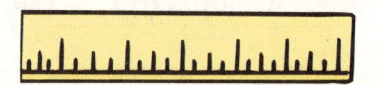

40 feet _____ 120 yards

25 grams _____ 25 kilograms

16 quarts _____ 4 gallons

2 liters _____ 2 milliliters

16 yards _____ 6 meters

3 miles _____ 3 kilometers

20 centimeters _____ 20 meters

85 kilograms _____ 8 grams

2 liters _____ 1 gallon

Temperature: Fahrenheit

Degrees Fahrenheit (°F) is a unit for measuring temperature.

Directions: Write the temperature in degrees Fahrenheit (°F).

Example:

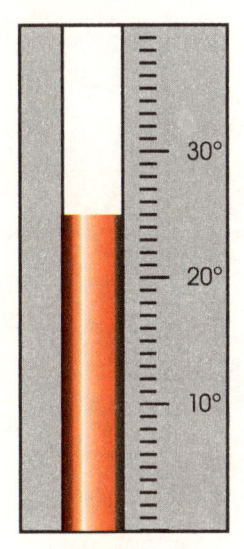

__25°F__

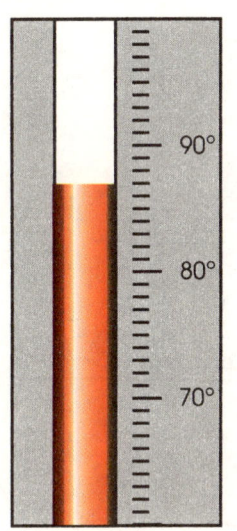

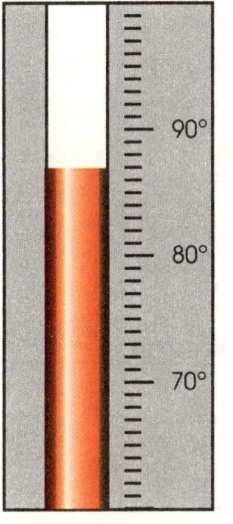

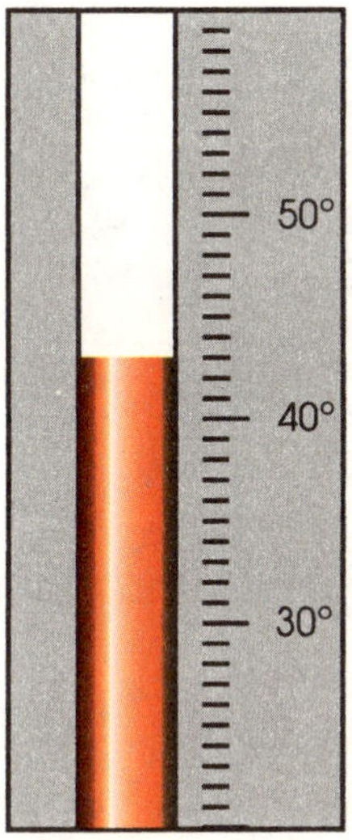

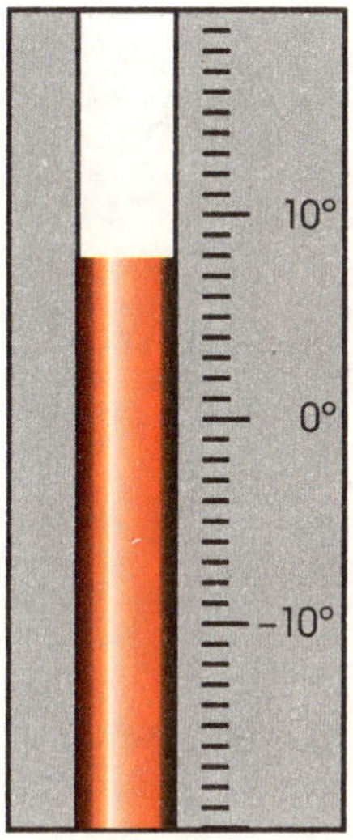

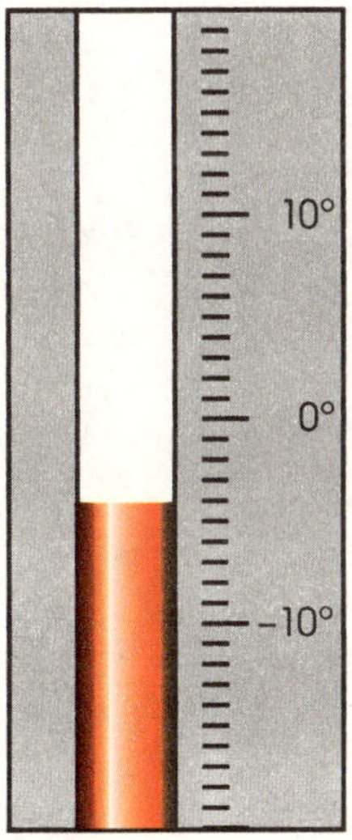

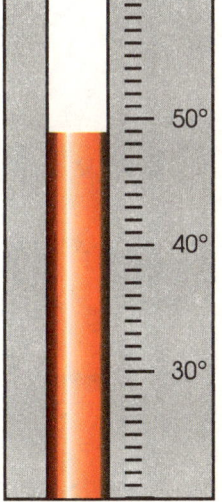

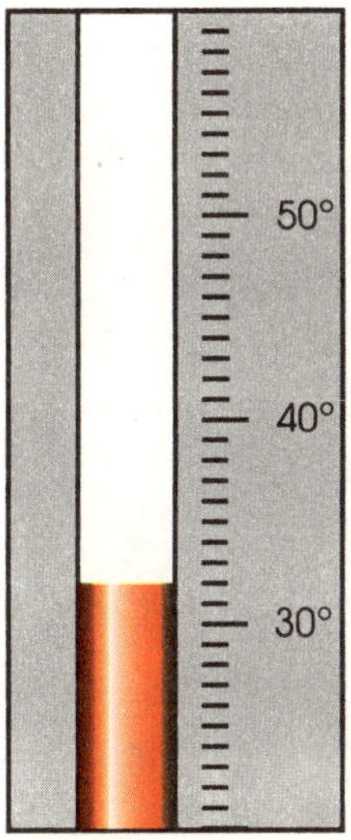

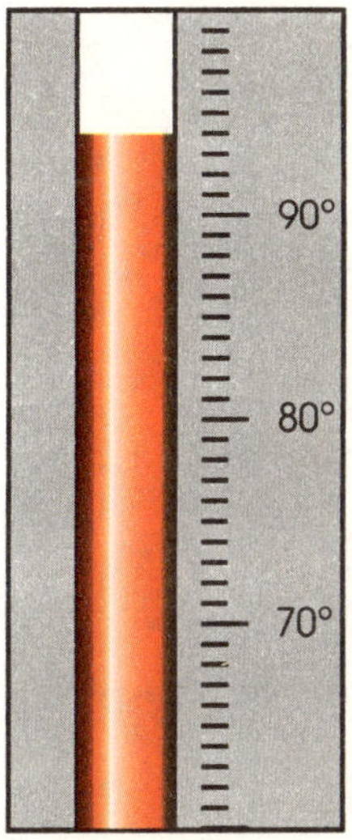

Temperature: Celsius

Degrees Celsius (°C) is a unit for measuring temperature in the metric system.

Directions: Write the temperature in degrees Celsius (°C).

Example:

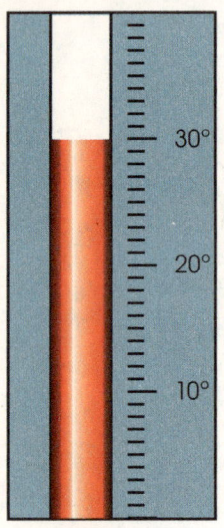

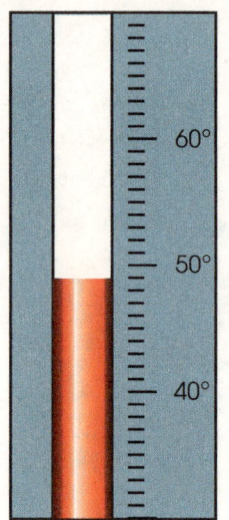

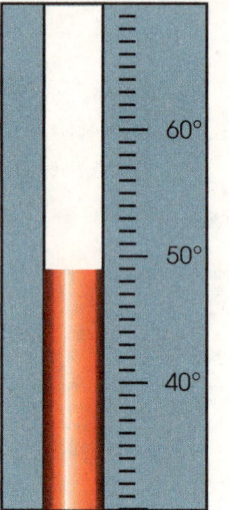

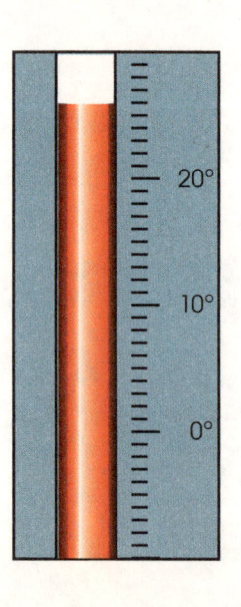

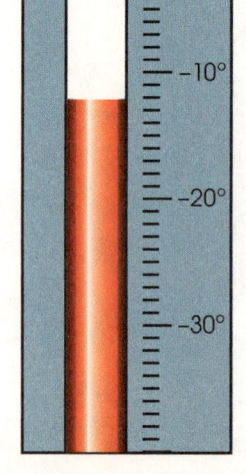

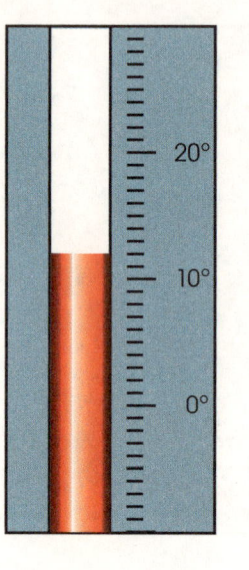

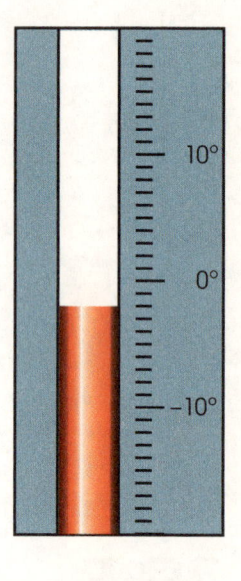

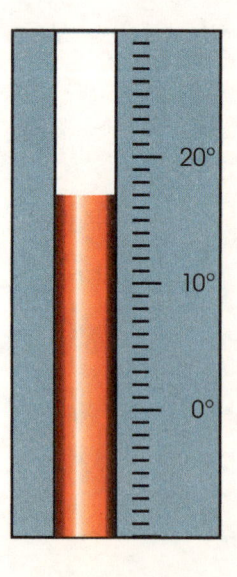

30°C

Review

Directions: Write the best unit to measure each item: inch, foot, yard, mile, ounce, pound, ton, fluid ounce, cup, pint, quart or gallon.

distance from New York to Chicago _____

weight of a goldfish _____

height of a building _____

water in a large fish tank _____

glass of milk _____

weight of a whale _____

length of a pencil _____

distance from first base to second base _____

distance traveled by a space shuttle _____

length of a soccer field _____

amount of paint needed to cover a house _____

material needed to make a dress _____

Ratio

A **ratio** is a comparison of two quantities.

Ratios can be written three ways: 2 to 3 or 2 : 3 or $\frac{2}{3}$. Each ratio is read: two to three.

Example:

The ratio of triangles to circles is 2 to 3.

The ratio of circles to triangles is 3 to 2.

Directions: Write the ratio that compares these items.

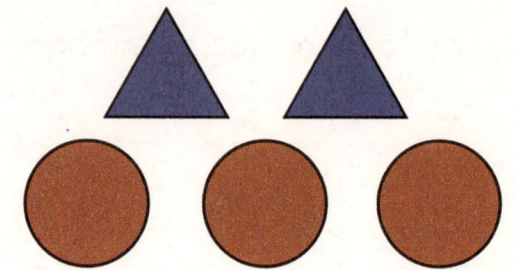

ratio of tulips to cacti _____

ratio of cubes to triangles _____

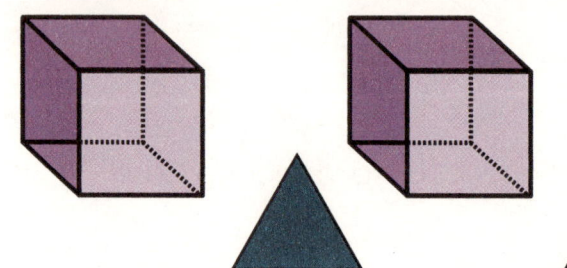

ratio of pens to pencils _____

Percent

Percent is a ratio meaning "per hundred." It is written with a % sign. 20% means 20 percent or 20 per hundred.

Example:

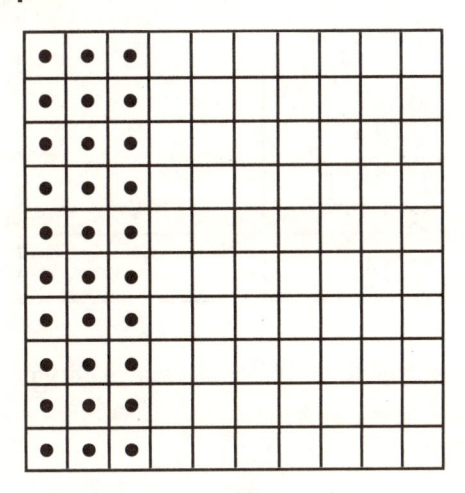

ratio = $\frac{30}{100}$

percent = 30%

ratio = _____

percent = _____

Directions: Write the percent for each ratio.

$\frac{7}{100}$ =	$\frac{38}{100}$ =
$\frac{63}{100}$ =	$\frac{3}{100}$ =
$\frac{40}{100}$ =	$\frac{1}{5}$ =

The school received 100 books for the Book Fair. It sold 43 books.

What is the percent of books sold to books received? _____

Probability

Probability is the ratio of favorable outcomes to possible outcomes of an experiment.

Vehicle	Number Sold
4 door	26
2 door	18
Sport	7
Van	12
Wagon	7
Compact	5
Total	75

Example:

This table records vehicle sales for 1 month. What is the probability of a person buying a van?

number of vans sold = 12   total number of cars = 75

The probability that a person will choose a van is 12 in 75 or $\frac{12}{75}$.

Directions: Look at the chart of flowers sold in a month. What is the probability that a person will buy each?

Roses _____

Tulips _____

Violets _____

Orchids _____

Flowers	Number Sold
Roses	48
Tulips	10
Violets	11
Orchids	7
Total	76

How would probability help a flower store owner keep the correct quantity of each flower in the store?

_____

_____

_____

Using Calculators to Find Percent

A **calculator** is a machine that rapidly does addition, subtraction, multiplication, division and other mathematical functions.

Example:

Carlos got 7 hits in 20 "at bats."

$$\frac{7}{20} = \frac{35}{100} = 35\%$$

To use a calculator:

Step 1: Press 7.

Step 2: Press the ÷ symbol.

Step 3: Press 20.

Step 4: Press the = symbol.

Step 5: 0.35 appears.
0.35 = 35%.

Directions: Use a calculator to find the percent of hits to the number of "at bats" for each baseball player. Round your answer to two digits. If your calculator displays the answer 0.753, round it to 0.75 or 75%.

Player	Hits	At Bats	Percent
Carlos	7	20	35%
Troy	3	12	_____
Sasha	4	14	_____
Dan	8	18	_____
Jaye	5	16	_____
Keesha	9	17	_____
Martin	11	16	_____
Robi	6	21	_____
Devan	4	15	_____

Who is most likely to get a hit? _____

Finding Percents

Find percent by dividing the number you have by the number possible.

Example:

15 out of 20 possible: $\frac{0.75}{20 \overline{)15.00}}$ = 75%
    −140
     100
     100

Annie has been keeping track of the scores she earned on each spelling test during the grading period.

Directions: Find out each percentage grade she earned. The first one has been done for you.

Week	Number Correct		Total Number of Words	Score in Percent
1	14	(out of)	20	70%
2	16		20	_____
3	18		20	_____
4	12		15	_____
5	16		16	_____
6	17		18	_____
Review Test	51		60	_____

If Susan scored 5% higher than Annie on the review test, how many words did she get right? _____

Carrie scored 10% lower than Susan on the review test. How many words did she spell correctly? _____

Of the 24 students in Annie's class, 25% had the same score as Annie. Only 10% had a higher score. What percent had a lower score? _____

Is that answer possible? _____

Why? _____

Locating Points on a Grid

To locate points on a grid, read the first coordinate and follow it to the second coordinate.

Example: C, 3

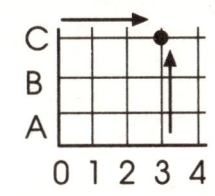

Directions: Maya is new in town. Help her learn the way around her new neighborhood. Place the following locations on the grid below.

Location	Coordinates
Grocery	C, 10
Home	B, 2
School	A, 12
Playground	B, 13
Library	D, 6
Bank	G, 1
Post Office	E, 7
Ice-Cream Shop	D, 3

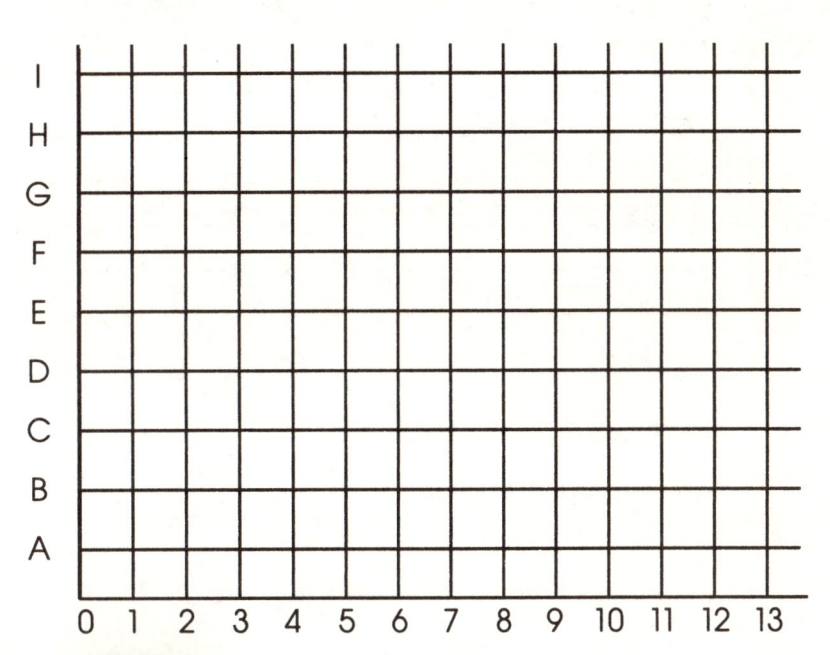

Is her home closer to the bank or the grocery? _____

Does she pass the playground on her way to school? _____

If she needs to stop at the library after school, will she be closer to home or farther away? _____

Math   299   Total Basic Skills Grade 5

Graphs

A **graph** is a drawing that shows information about changes in numbers.

Directions: Use the graph to answer the questions.

Line Graph   **Temperatures for 1 Year**

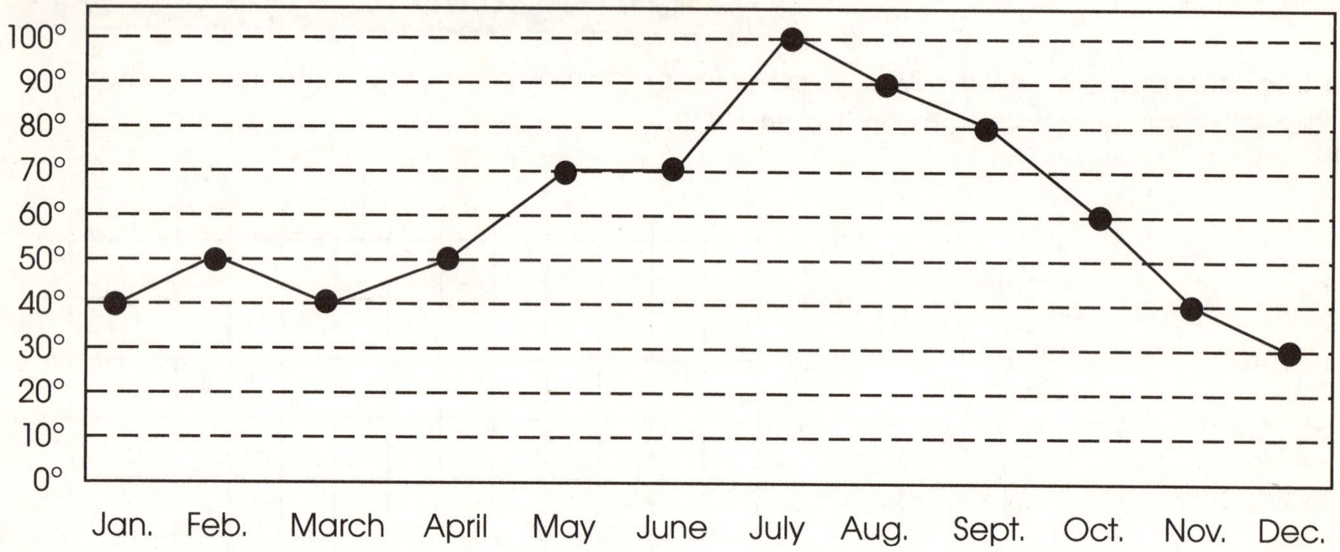

Which month was the coldest? _____

Which month was the warmest? _____

Which three months were 40 degrees? _____

How much warmer was it in May than October? _____

Bar Graph

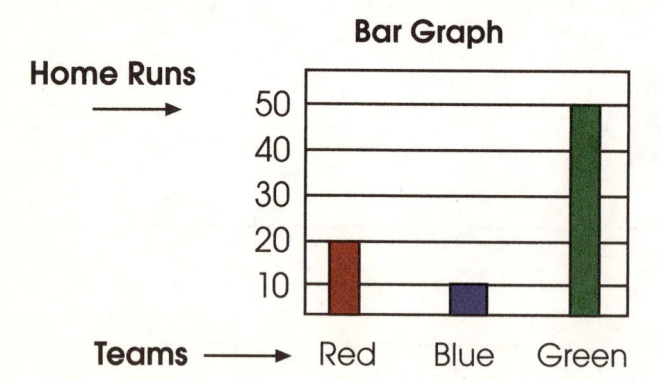

Home Runs →

Teams → Red   Blue   Green

How many home runs did the Green team hit? _____

How many more home runs did the Green team hit than the Red team and Blue team combined? _____

Graphs

Directions: Read each graph and follow the directions.

List the names of the students from the shortest to the tallest.

1. _____   4. _____
2. _____   5. _____
3. _____   6. _____

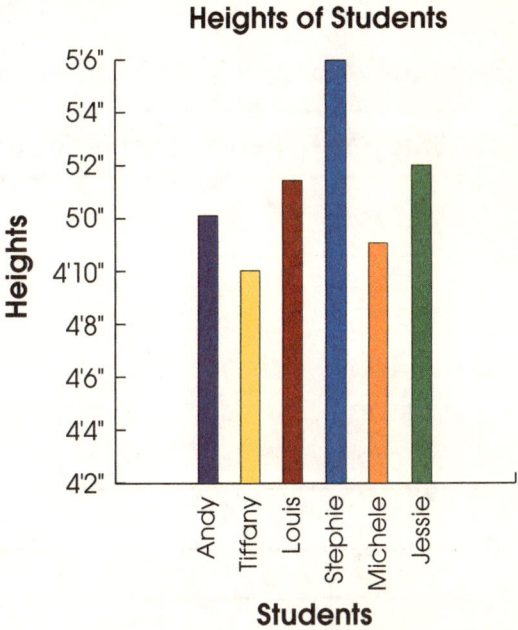

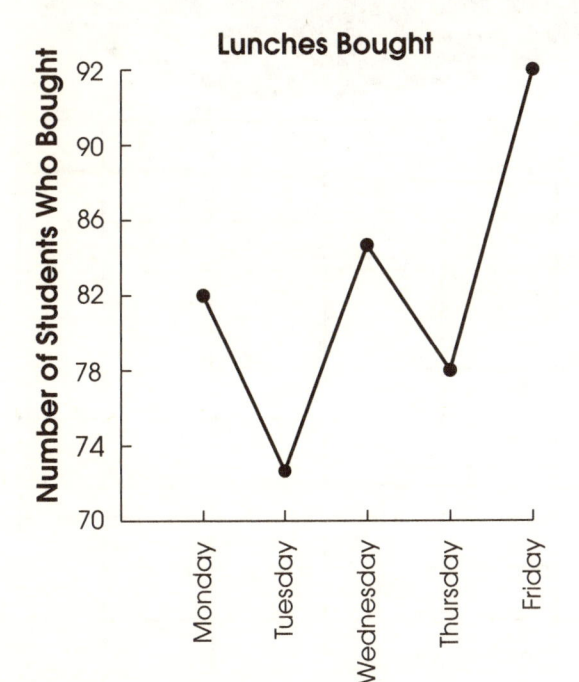

Heights of Students

List how many lunches the students bought each day, from the day the most were bought to the least.

1. _____   4. _____
2. _____   5. _____
3. _____

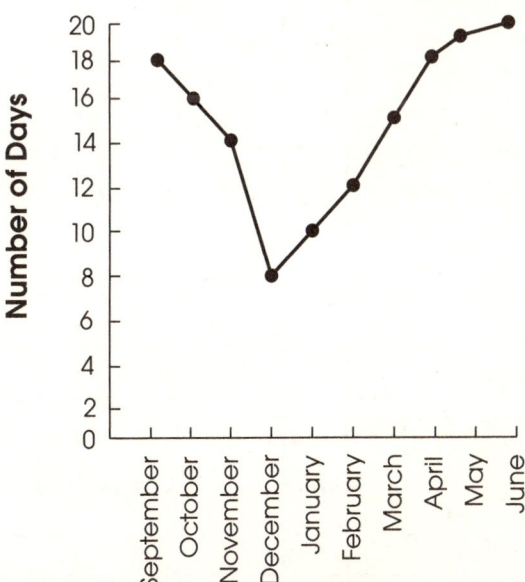

List the months in the order of the most number of outside recesses to the least number.

1. _____   6. _____
2. _____   7. _____
3. _____   8. _____
4. _____   9. _____
5. _____   10. _____

Math   301   Total Basic Skills Grade 5

Graphs

Directions: Complete the graph using the information in the table.

Student	Books read in February
Sue	20
Joe	8
Peter	12
Cindy	16
Dean	15
Carol	8

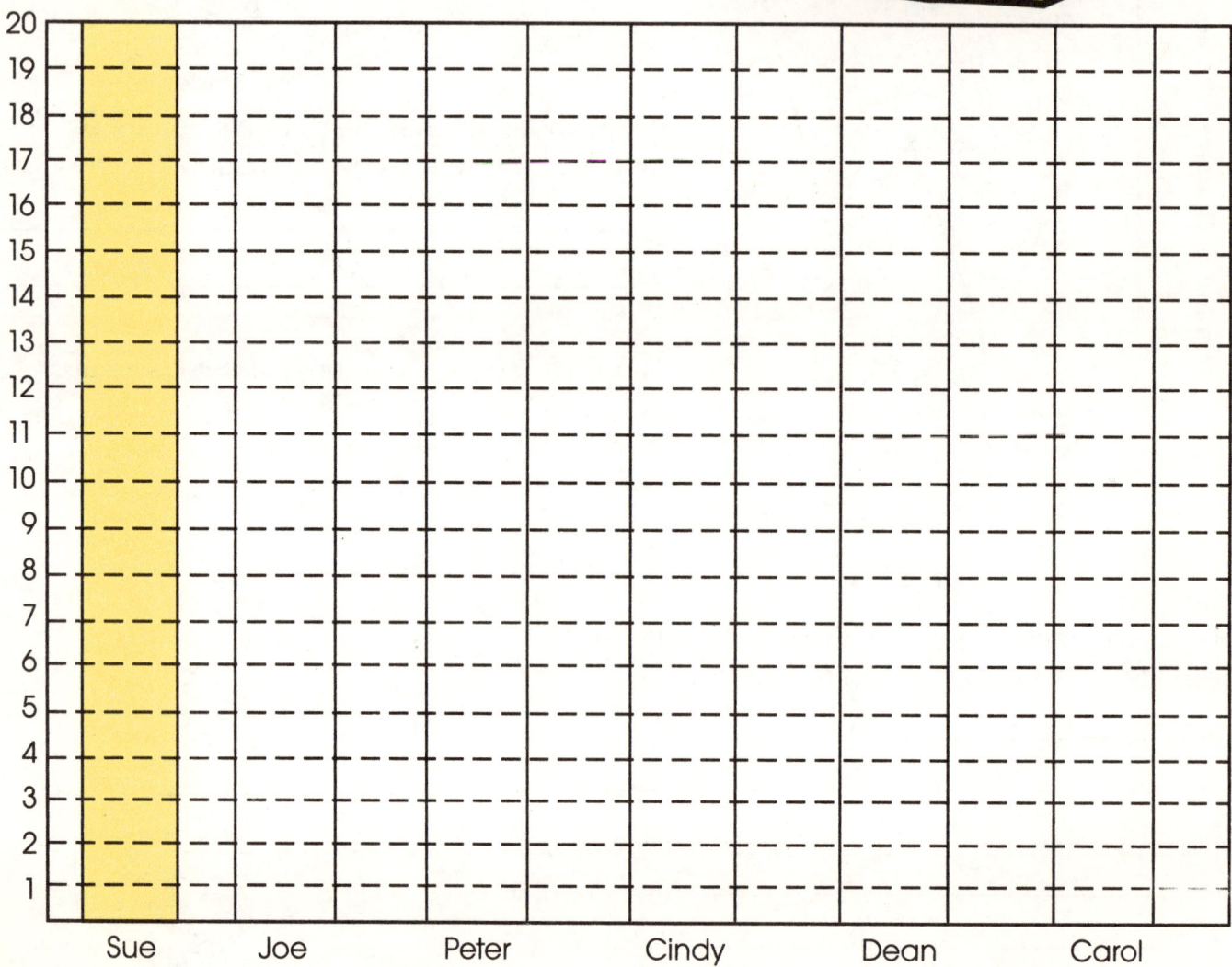

GRADE 5

Page 6

Spelling: Digraphs

A **digraph** is two consonants pronounced as one sound.
Examples: **sh** as in **shell**, **ch** as in **chew**, **th** as in **thin**
Directions: Write **sh**, **ch** or **th** to complete each word below.

1. **th** reaten
2. **ch** ill
3. **sh** ock
4. **sh** iver
5. **th** aw
6. **ch** allenge
7. **peri sh**
8. **sh** ield
9. **ch** art
10. **th** rive

Directions: Complete these sentences with a word, or form of the word, from the list above.

1. A trip to the South Pole would really be a (ch) __challenge__.
2. The ice there never (th) __thaws__ because the temperature averages –50°C.
3. How can any living thing (th) __thrive__ or even live when it's so cold?
4. With 6 months of total darkness and those icy temperatures, any plants would soon (sh) __perish__.
5. Even the thought of that numbing cold makes me (sh) __shiver__.
6. The cold and darkness (th) __threaten__ the lives of explorers.
7. The explorers take along maps and (ch) __charts__ to help them find their way.
8. Special clothing helps protect and (sh) __shield__ them from the cold.
9. Still, the weather must be a (sh) __shock__ at first.
10. Did someone leave a door open? Suddenly I feel a (ch) __chill__.

Page 7

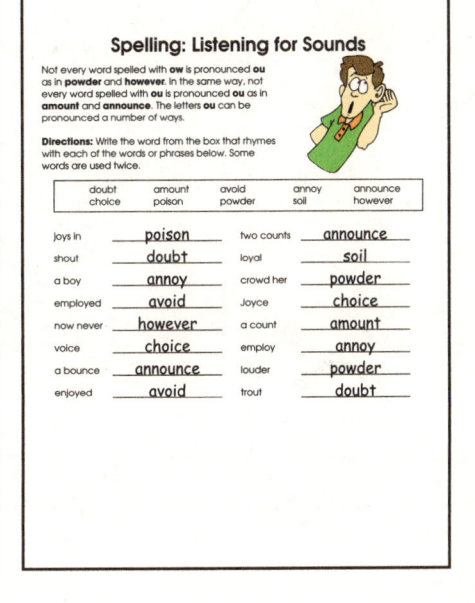

Spelling: Listening for Sounds

Not every word spelled with **ow** is pronounced **ou** as in **powder** and **however**. In the same way, not every word spelled with **ou** is pronounced **ou** as in **amount** and **announce**. The letters **ou** can be pronounced a number of ways.

Directions: Write the word from the box that rhymes with each of the words or phrases below. Some words are used twice.

doubt	amount	avoid	annoy	announce
choice	poison	powder	soil	however

joys in	__poison__	two counts	__announce__
shout	__doubt__	loyal	__soil__
a boy	__annoy__	crowd her	__powder__
employed	__avoid__	Joyce	__choice__
now never	__however__	a count	__amount__
voice	__choice__	employ	__annoy__
a bounce	__announce__	louder	__powder__
enjoyed	__avoid__	trout	__doubt__

Page 8

Spelling: The j and ch Sounds

The **j** sound can be spelled with a **j** as in **jump**, with a **g** before **e** or **i** as in **agent** and **giant**, or with **ge** at the end of a word as in **page**.
The **ch** sound is often spelled with the letters **ch** but can also be spelled with a **t** before **u**, as in **nature**.

Directions: Use words from the box to complete the exercises below.

| statue | imagination | jealous | future | arrangements |
| furniture | stranger | project | justice | capture |

1. Say each word and then write it in the correct row, depending on whether it has the **j** or **ch** sound.

j: __imagination__ __stranger__ __jealous__
   __project__ __justice__ __arrangements__
ch: __statue__ __furniture__ __future__ __capture__

2. Write a word from the box that belongs to the same word family as each word below.

imagine __imagination__   arranging __arrangements__
strangely __stranger__   furnish __furniture__
just __justice__   jealousy __jealous__

Directions: Complete each sentence with a word containing the given sound.

1. What is your group's (j) __project__ this week?
2. There is a (ch) __statue__ of George Washington in front of our school.
3. She used her (j) __imagination__ to solve the problem.
4. My sister keeps rearranging the (ch) __furniture__ in our room.

Page 9

Spelling: Words With Silent Letters

Some letters in words are not pronounced, such as the **s** in **island**, the **t** in **listen**, the **k** in **knee**, the **h** in **hour** and the **w** in **write**.

Directions: Use words from the box to complete the exercises below.

| wrinkled | honest | aisle | knife | wrist |
| rhyme | exhaust | glisten | knowledge | wrestle |

1. Write each word beside its silent letter. Two words have two silent letters—write them twice.

s __aisle__
t __glisten__ __wrestle__
h __rhyme__ __honest__ __exhaust__
w __wrinkle__ __wrist__ __wrestle__ __knowledge__
k __knife__ __knowledge__

2. Write in the missing letter or letters for each word.

w res **t** le   ex **h** aust   **k** nife   glis **t** en   ai **s** le
k nowledge   **w** rinkle   r **h** yme   **h** onest   **w** rist

Directions: Complete each sentence with a word that has the given silent letter. Use each word only once.

1. He always tells the truth. He's very (h) __honest__.
2. I like (s) __aisle__ seats in airplanes.
3. I need a sharper (k) __knife__ to cut this bread.
4. I think a long hike might (h) __exhaust__ me.
5. Did you sleep in that shirt? It is so (w) __wrinkled__.
6. The snow seemed to (t) __glisten__ in the sunlight.
7. To play tennis, you need a strong (w) __wrist__.

Page 10

Spelling: Syllables

A **syllable** is a part of a word with only one vowel sound. Some words have only one syllable, like **cat**, **leaf** and **ship**. Some words have two or more syllables. **Be-lief** and **trac-tor** have two syllables, **to-ge-ther** and **ex-cel-lent** have three syllables and **con-ver-sa-tion** has four syllables. Some words can have six or more syllables! The word **ex-tra-ter-res-tri-al**, for example, has six syllables.

Directions: Follow the instructions below.

1. Count the syllables in each word below, and write the number of syllables on the line.

a. badger __2__   f. grease __1__
b. location __3__   g. relationship __4__
c. award __2__   h. communication __5__
d. national __3__   i. government __3__
e. necessary __4__   j. Braille __1__

2. Write four words with four syllables each in the blanks.

a. __Answers will vary.__   c. _____
b. _____   d. _____

3. Write one word with five syllables and one with six syllables. If you need help, use a dictionary.

Five syllables: __Answers will vary.__
Six syllables: _____

Answer Key   303   Total Basic Skills Grade 5

Page 11

Writing: Sounding Out Syllables

Directions: Use words from the box to complete the exercises below.

| decision | division | pressure | addition | ancient |
| subtraction | confusion | multiplication | social | correction |

1. Write each word in the row showing the correct number of syllables.
   - Two: **pressure**, **social**, **ancient**
   - Three: **decision**, **division**, **addition**, **subtraction**, **confusion**, **correction**
   - Five: **multiplication**

2. Write in the missing syllables for each word.
   - **so**cial, sub**trac**tion, mul**ti**pli**ca**tion, pres**sure**
   - di**vi**sion, an**cient**, deci**sion**, ad**di**tion
   - **con**fusion, cor**rec**tion

3. Beside each word below, write a word with the same number of syllables. Use each word from the box only once. **Answers may include:**
   - daily — **pressure**; challenging — **addition**
   - syllable — **decision**; election — **correction**
   - decreasing — **subtraction**; threaten — **ancient**
   - advantage — **division**; shivering — **confusion**
   - title — **social**; experimenting — **multiplication**

Page 12

Writing: Word Families

A **word family** is a group of words based on the same word. For example, **playful**, **playground** and **playing** are all based on the word **play**.

Directions: Use words from the box to complete the exercises below.

| decision | division | pressure | addition | create |
| subtraction | confusion | multiplication | social | correction |

1. Write the word that belongs to the same word family as each word below.
   - correctly — **correction**; confused — **confusion**
   - divide — **division**; subtracting — **subtraction**
   - pressing — **pressure**; society — **social**
   - multiply — **multiplication**; decide — **decision**
   - added — **addition**; creativity — **create**

2. Complete each sentence by writing the correct form of the given word.
   - **Example:** Have you (decide) _decided_ what to do? Did you make a (decide) _decision_ yet?
   - I am (add) **adding** the numbers right now. Would you check my (add) **addition**?
   - This problem has me (confuse) **confused**. Can you clear up my (confuse) **confusion**?
   - This is a (press) **pressing** problem. We feel (press) **pressure** to solve it right away.
   - Is he (divide) **dividing** by the right number? Will you help him with his (divide) **division**?
   - Try to answer (correct) **correctly**. Then you won't have to make any (correct) **corrections** on your paper later on.

Page 13

Writing: Word Families

Directions: Write the word that belongs to the same word family as each word below.

| doubt | amount | avoid | annoy | announce |
| choice | poison | powder | soil | however |

- avoidance — **avoid**; annoyance — **annoy**
- doubtful — **doubt**; soiled — **soil**
- announcement — **announce**; poisonous — **poison**
- choose — **choice**; amounted — **amount**
- powdery — **powder**; whenever — **however**

Directions: Complete each sentence by writing the correct form of the given word.

Example: Are you (doubt) _doubting_ my word? You never (doubt) _doubted_ it before.

1. The teacher is (announce) **announcing** the next test. Did you hear what he (announce) **announced**?
2. This stream was (poison) **poisoned** by a chemical from a factory nearby.
3. Is the chemical (poison) **poisoning** any other water supply? How many (poison) **poisons** does the factory produce?
4. My cat always (annoy) **annoys** our dog.
5. Last night, Camie (annoy) **annoyed** Lucas for hours.
6. I think Carrie is (avoid) **avoiding** me. Yesterday, she (avoid) **avoided** walking home with me.

Page 14

Spelling: Double Consonants

When adding endings such as **ng** and **ed** to verbs, use the following rule: Double the final consonant of verbs that have short vowel sounds and end with only one consonant. For example, **rip** becomes **ripped** and **beg** becomes **begging**. However, do not double the final consonant in words that end in double consonants. For example, **rock** ends with two consonants, **ck**. So even though it has a short vowel sound, **rock** becomes **rocked**.

Directions: Add **ed** to the verbs below. Remember, when a verb ends with **e**, drop the **e** before adding an ending (**taste, tasting**). The first one has been done for you.

- top — **topped**; rip — **ripped**
- pet — **petted**; punch — **punched**
- sob — **sobbed**; rinse — **rinsed**
- brag — **bragged**; stock — **stocked**
- scrub — **scrubbed**; lack — **lacked**
- flip — **flipped**; dent — **dented**

Directions: Add **ing** to the verbs below. The first one has been done for you.

- flap — **flapping**; snack — **snacking**
- scrub — **scrubbing**; flip — **flipping**
- stock — **stocking**; rinse — **rinsing**
- dent — **denting**; brag — **bragging**
- pet — **petting**; lack — **lacking**
- sob — **sobbing**; punch — **punching**

Page 15

Writing: Verb Forms

Directions: In the following story, some of the verbs are missing. Write the proper form of the verbs shown, adding **ed** or **ing** when necessary.

Yesterday, I was (brag) **bragging** to my brother about how much I (help) **helped** our mother around the house. I had (scrub) **scrubbed** the kitchen floor, (wipe) **wiped** off all the counters and (rinse) **rinsed** out the sink. I was (pour) **pouring** the dirty water out of the bucket when our mother came in. She looked around the kitchen and (smile) **smiled**. "Who did all this work?" she (ask) **asked**.

I was (get) **getting** ready to tell her what I had done when my brother (interrupt) **interrupted** me. "We both did! We've been (work) **working** very hard!" he said. "He's not (tell) **telling** the truth!" I said to Mom. "I did everything!" My brother (glare) **glared** at me.

"Is that true?" asked Mom. My brother (look) **looked** at the floor and (nod) **nodded**. He was (think) **thinking** about all the trouble he would get into. Instead, Mom smiled again. "Well, that's okay," she said. "The rest of the house needs to be (clean) **cleaned**, too. You can get (start) **started** right away!"

Page 16

Spelling: Math Plurals

To make most nouns plural, add **s**. When a noun ends with **s, ss, sh, ch** or **x**, add **es**: bus—buses, cross—crosses, brush—brushes, church—churches, box—boxes. When a noun ends with a consonant and **y**, change the **y** to **i** and add **es**: berry—berries. For some words, instead of adding **s** or **es**, the spelling of the word changes: man—men, mouse—mice.

Directions: Write the correct plural or singular form of the words in these math problems. Write whether the problem requires addition (**A**), subtraction (**S**), multiplication (**M**) or division (**D**). The first one has been done for you.

1. 3 (box) **boxes** − 2 (box) **boxes** = 1 box **S**
2. 2 (supply) **supplies** + 5 (supply) **supplies** = 7 supplies **A**
3. 4 (copy) **copies** x 2 (copy) **copies** = 8 copies **M**
4. 6 (class) **classes** ÷ 2 (class) **classes** = 3 classes **D**
5. 5 (factory) **factories** − 3 (factory) **factories** = 2 factories **S**
6. 3 (daisy) **daisies** x 3 (daisy) **daisies** = 9 daisies **M**
7. 8 (sandwich) **sandwiches** + 4 (sandwich) **sandwiches** = 12 sandwiches **A**
8. 3 (child) **children** − 1 (child) **child** = 2 children **S**
9. 10 (brush) **brushes** ÷ 5 (brush) **brushes** = 2 brushes **D**
10. 4 (goose) **geese** + 1 (goose) **goose** = 5 geese **A**
11. 3 (mouse) **mice** + 1 (mouse) **mouse** = 4 mice **A**

Page 17

Spelling: More Plurals

Remember, in some words, an f changes to a v to make the plural form.

Examples: life — lives   wife — wives   knife — knives   leaf — leaves

Directions: Complete these sentences by writing the correct plural form of the given word. Also, circle the spelling errors and write the words correctly on the lines to the right.

1. The (leaf) __leaves__ are dry and (rinkled).
2. The (knife) __knives__ (glisened) in the sun.
3. I think the (child) __children__ in this school are (honist).
4. The (supply) __supplies__ were stacked in the (isle).
5. (mouse) __Mice__ (rimes) with twice.
6. Some people feel (exausted) all their (life) __lives__.
7. The (class) __classes__ were trying to gain more (knowlege) about Olympic athletes.
8. The kittens were (wresling) in the (bush) __bushes__.
9. Jamie nearly broke his (rist) trying to carry all those (box) __boxes__.
10. Some kings had several (wife) __wives__ who (new) about each other.
11. (Daisy) __Daisies__ are (knot) expensive.
12. (Right) your name on both (copy) __copies__.
13. We watched the (monkey) __monkeys__ play on the swings for (ours).
14. Do you like (strawberry) __strawberries__ (hole) or sliced?

wrinkled
glistened
honest
aisle
rhymes
exhausted
knowledge
wrestling
wrist
knew
not
Write
hours
whole

Page 18

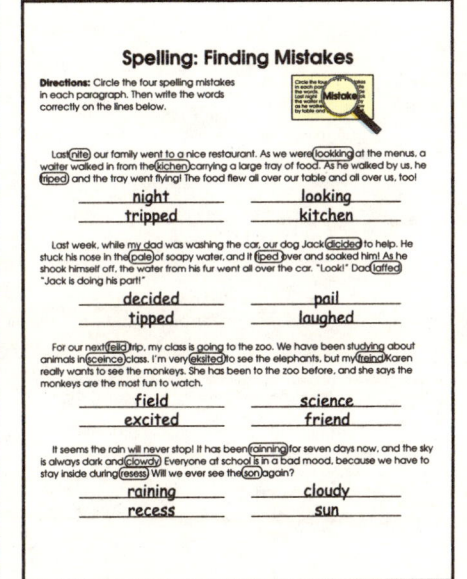

Spelling: Finding Mistakes

Directions: Circle the four spelling mistakes in each paragraph. Then write the words correctly on the lines below.

Last (nite) our family went to a nice restaurant. As we were (lookking) at the menus, a waiter walked in from the (kichen) carrying a large tray of food. As he walked by us, he (triped) and the tray went flying! The food flew all over our table and all over us, too!

night   looking
tripped   kitchen

Last week, while my dad was washing the car, our dog Jack (dicided) to help. He stuck his nose in the (pale) of soapy water, and it (tiped) over and soaked him! As he shook himself off, the water flew all over the car. "Look!" Dad (laffed). "Jack is doing his part!"

decided   pail
tipped   laughed

For our next (feld) trip, my class is going to the zoo. We have been studying about animals in (sceince) class. I'm very (eksited) to see the elephants, but my (freind) Karen really wants to see the monkeys. She has been to the zoo before, and she says the monkeys are the most fun to watch.

field   science
excited   friend

It seems the rain will never stop! It has been (rainning) for seven days now, and the sky is always dark and (clowdy). Everyone at school is in a bad mood, because we have to stay inside during (resess). Will we ever see the (son) again?

raining   cloudy
recess   sun

Page 19

Spelling: Proofreading Practice

Directions: Circle the six spelling and pronoun mistakes in each paragraph. Write the words correctly on the lines below.

Jenna always (braged) about being ready to meet (any) challenge or reach any (gole). When it was time for our class to (elekt) (it's) new officers, Jenna said we should (voat) for her to be president.

bragged   challenge   goal
elect   its   vote

Simon wanted to be (ours) president, too. He tried to (coaks) everyone to vote for (his) He even (lowned) kids money to get their votes! Well, Jenna may have too much (pryde) in herself, but I like her in (spit) of that. At least she didn't try to buy our votes!

our   coax   him
loaned   pride   spite

(Its) true that Jenna tried other ways to get us to vote for (hers). She (scrubed) the chalkboards even though it was my (dayly) job for that week. One day, I saw her (rinseing) out the paintbrushes when it was Peter's turn to do it. Then she made sure we knew about her good deeds so we would (praze) her.

It's   her   scrubbed
daily   rinsing   praise

We held the election, but I was (shaked) when the teacher (releesed) the results. Simon won! I wondered if he (cheeted) somehow. I feel like our class was (robed). Now Simon is the one who's (braging) about how great he is. I wish he knew the (titel) of president doesn't mean anything if no one wants to be around you!

shocked   released   cheated
robbed   bragging   title

Page 20

Adding Suffixes

A **suffix** is a syllable at the end of a word that changes its meaning. The suffixes **ant** and **ent** mean a person or thing that does something.

Examples:
A person who occupies a place is an **occupant**.
A person who obeys is **obedient**.

A **root word** is the common stem that gives related words their basic meanings.

When a word ends in silent **e**, keep the **e** before adding a suffix beginning with a consonant. Drop the **e** before adding a suffix beginning with a vowel.

Examples:
announce + ment = **announcement**
announce + ing = **announcing**

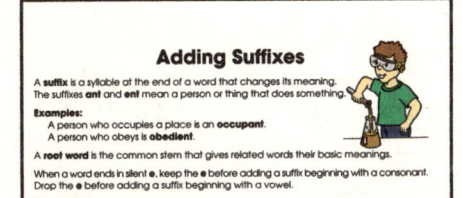

Announce is the root word in this example.

Directions: Combine each root word and suffix to make a new word. The first one has been done for you.

Root word	Suffix	New word
observe	ant	observant
contest	ant	contestant
please	ant	pleasant
preside	ent	president
differ	ent	different

Directions: Use the meanings in parentheses to complete the sentences with one of the above new words. The first one has been done for you.

1. To be a good scientist, you must be very __observant__. (pay careful attention)
2. Her perfume has a strong but very __pleasant__ smell. (nice)
3. Because the bridge was out, we had to find a __different__ route home. (not the same)
4. The game show __contestant__ jumped up and down when she won the grand prize. (person who competes)
5. Next week we will elect a new student council __president__. (highest officer)

Page 21

Adding Prefixes

A **prefix** is a syllable at the beginning of a word that changes its meaning. The prefixes **il, im, in** and **ir** all mean not.

Examples:
Illogical means not logical or practical.
Impossible means not possible.
Invisible means not visible.
Irrelevant means not relevant or practical.

Directions: Divide each word into its prefix and root word. The first one has been done for you.

	Prefix	Root Word
illogical	il	logical
impatient	im	patient
immature	im	mature
incomplete	in	complete
insincere	in	sincere
irresponsible	ir	responsible
irregular	ir	regular

Directions: Use the meanings in parentheses to complete the sentences with one of the above words.

1. I had to turn in my assignment __incomplete__ because I was sick last night. (not finished)
2. It was __illogical__ for Jimmy to give me his keys because he can't get into his house without them. (not practical)
3. Sue and Joel were __irresponsible__ to leave their bikes out in the rain. (not doing the right thing)
4. I sometimes get __impatient__ waiting for my ride to school. (restless)
5. The boys sounded __insincere__ when they said they were sorry. (not honest)
6. These towels didn't cost much because they are __irregular__. (not straight or even)

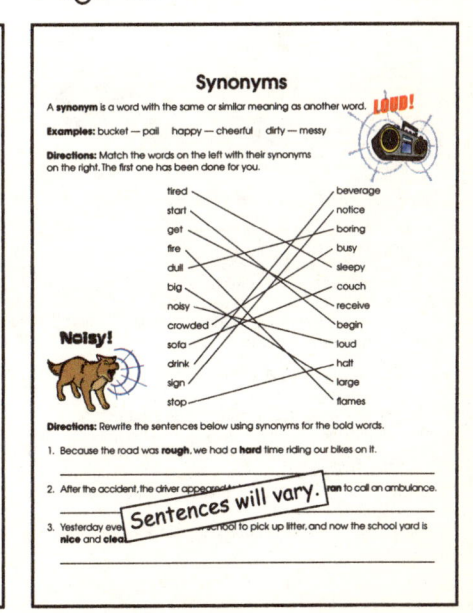

Page 22

Synonyms

A **synonym** is a word with the same or similar meaning as another word.

Examples: bucket — pail   happy — cheerful   dirty — messy

Directions: Match the words on the left with their synonyms on the right. The first one has been done for you.

tired — beverage
start — notice
get — boring
fire — busy
dull — sleepy
big — couch
noisy — receive
crowded — begin
sofa — loud
drink — hot
sign — large
stop — flames

Directions: Rewrite the sentences below using synonyms for the bold words.

1. Because the road was **rough**, we had a **hard** time riding our bikes on it.

Sentences will vary.

2. After the accident, the driver appeared ____ ran to call an ambulance.

3. Yesterday ev____ school to pick up litter, and now the school yard is **nice** and **clea**____

Page 23

Synonyms

Directions: Circle a word or a phrase in each sentence that is a synonym for a word in the box. Write the synonym on the line.

| challenged | shocked | thaw | chart | thrive |
| perish | chill | shivering | frighten | shield |

Example: The writing was in an (old) code. — ancient

1. A fish out of water will quickly (die). — perish
2. The ice carving is beginning to (melt). — thaw
3. I was (amazed) when I saw how he looked. — shocked
4. The puppy was (trembling) with excitement. — shivering
5. Ferns need moisture to (grow well). — thrive
6. Are you trying to (scare) me? — frighten
7. Let the salad (get cold) in the refrigerator. — chill
8. She tried to (protect) him from the truth. — shield
9. He made a (list) of different kinds of birds. — chart
10. They (dared) us to enter the contest. — challenged

Directions: Write your own sentences using five words from the box. If you're not sure what a word means, look it up in a dictionary.

Sentences will vary.

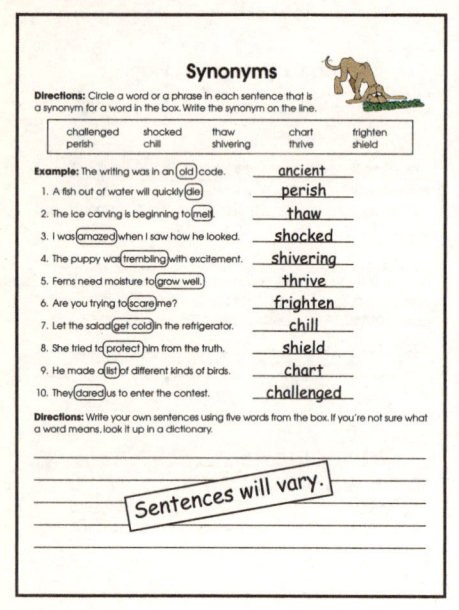

Page 24

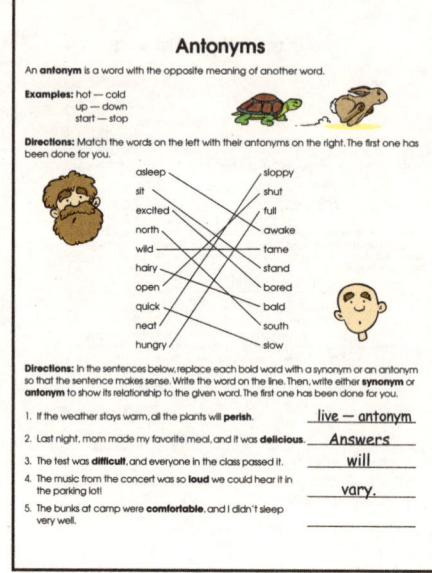

Antonyms

An **antonym** is a word with the opposite meaning of another word.

Examples:
hot — cold
up — down
start — stop

Directions: Match the words on the left with their antonyms on the right. The first one has been done for you.

asleep — awake
sit — stand
excited — bored
north — south
wild — tame
hairy — bald
open — shut
quick — slow
neat — sloppy
hungry — full

Directions: In the sentences below, replace each bold word with a synonym or an antonym so that the sentence makes sense. Write the word on the line. Then, write either **synonym** or **antonym** to show its relationship to the given word. The first one has been done for you.

1. If the weather stays warm, all the plants will **perish**. — live — antonym
2. Last night, mom made my favorite meal, and it was **delicious**.
3. The test was **difficult**, and everyone in the class passed it.
4. The music from the concert was so **loud** we could hear it in the parking lot!
5. The bunks at camp were **comfortable**, and I didn't sleep very well.

Answers will vary.

Page 25

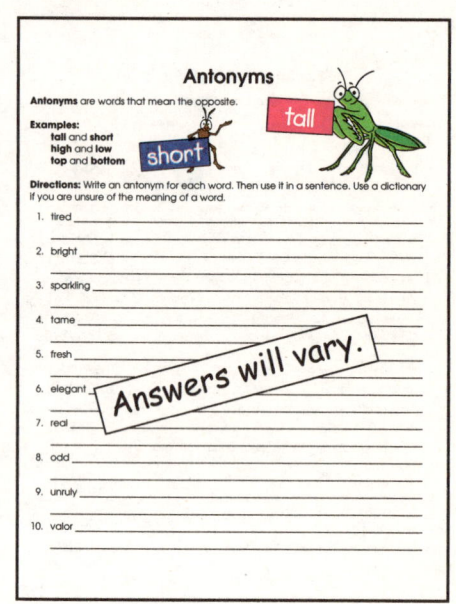

Antonyms

Antonyms are words that mean the opposite.

Examples:
tall and **short**
high and **low**
top and **bottom**

Directions: Write an antonym for each word. Then use it in a sentence. Use a dictionary if you are unsure of the meaning of a word.

1. tired
2. bright
3. sparkling
4. tame
5. fresh
6. elegant
7. real
8. odd
9. unruly
10. valor

Answers will vary.

Page 26

Homophones

Homophones are words that sound alike but have different spellings and meanings. The words **no** and **know** are homophones. They sound alike, but their spellings and meanings are very different.

Directions: Use words from the box to complete the exercises below.

| hour | wring | knot | whole | knew |
| wrap | knight | piece | write |

1. Write each word beside its homophone.
   peace — piece   new — knew   ring — wring
   hole — whole   rap — wrap   night — knight
   not — knot   right — write   our — hour

2. Write three words that have a silent k. — knight, knot, knew
3. Write one word that has a silent h. — hour

Directions: Circle the misused homophones in each sentence. Then rewrite the sentences, using the correct homophones.

1. By the time (knight) fell, I (new) she was (knot) coming.
   By the time night fell, I knew she was not coming.
2. I would never have any (piece) until (new) the (hole) story.
   I would never have any peace until I knew the whole story.
3. He spent an (our) (righting) down what had happened.
   He spent an hour writing down what had happened.
4. I could see (write) through the (whole) in the (night's) armor.
   I could see right through the hole in the knight's armor.

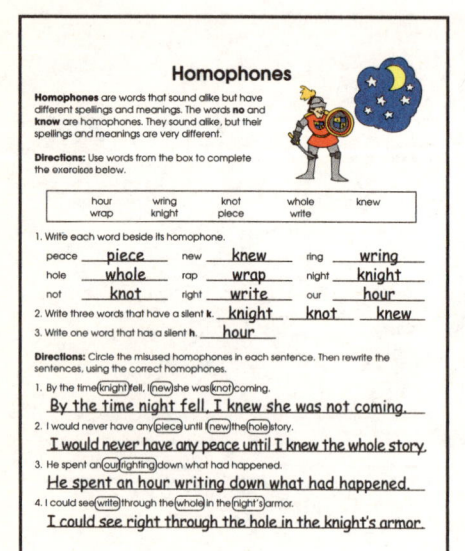

Page 27

Homophones

Directions: Complete the story below by writing the correct homophones for the words in parentheses.

Last Saturday, I went to (meat) __meet__ my friend, Andrea, at the mall.

When I got there, I noticed she looked a little (pail) __pale__.

"What's wrong?" I asked her.

She (side) __sighed__. "I'm (knot) __not__ feeling so (grate) __great__," she said. "I don't (no) __know__ what's wrong with me."

"Maybe you (knead) __need__ to take some aspirin," I said. "Let's go to the drugstore. It's this (weigh) __way__."

As we were walking, we passed a (flour) __flower__ shop, and I bought (sum) __some__ roses for my mother. Then we found the drugstore, and Andrea bought some aspirin and took (too) __two__ of them. An (our) __hour__ later, she felt much better.

That (knight) __night__, I gave the roses to my mother. "You shouldn't (waist) __waste__ your money on (presence) __presents__ for me!" she said, but she was smiling. I (new) __knew__ she was pleased.

"That's okay, Mom, I wanted to buy them for you," I said. "But now I'm broke. How about a (lone) __loan__?"

Page 28

Similes

A **simile** uses the words **like** or **as** to compare two things.

Examples:
The snow glittered **like** diamonds.
He was **as** slow **as** a turtle.

Directions: Circle the two objects being compared in each sentence.

1. The (kittens) were like (gymnasts) performing tricks.
2. My old (computer) is as slow as (molasses).
3. When the lights went out in the (basement), it was as dark as (night).
4. The (sun) was like a (fire) heating up the earth.
5. The young (girl) was as graceful as a (ballerina).
6. The (puppy) cried like a (baby) all night.
7. He (flies) that airplane like a (daredevil).
8. The (girl) was as pretty as a (picture).
9. The (snow) on the mountain tops was like (whipped cream).
10. The (tiger's eyes) were like (emeralds).

Directions: Complete the simile in each sentence.

11. My cat is as _____ as _____.
12. He was as _____ as _____.
13. Melissa's eyes shone _____.
14. The pa_____ as _____.
15. The ope_____ as _____ as _____.
16. My friend _____ as _____.

Answers will vary.

Page 29

Metaphors

A **metaphor** is a direct comparison between two things. The words **like** or **as** are not used in a metaphor.

Example: The **sun** is a **yellow ball** in the sky.

Directions: Underline the metaphor in each sentence. Write the two objects being compared on the line.

1. As it bounded toward me, the dog was a quivering furball of excitement.
   dog/furball of excitement
2. The snow we skied on was mashed potatoes.
   snow/mashed potatoes
3. John is a mountain goat when it comes to rock climbing.
   John/mountain goat
4. The light is a beacon shining into the dark basement.
   light/beacon
5. The famished child was a wolf, eating for the first time in days.
   famished child/wolf
6. The man's arm was a tireless lever as he fought to win the wrestling contest.
   man's arm/tireless lever
7. The flowers were colorful circles against the green of the yard.
   flowers/colorful circles

Page 30

Using a Dictionary

Directions: Read about dictionaries. Then answer the questions.

Dictionaries are books that give definitions of words. Dictionaries list words in alphabetical order. **Guide words** at the top of each page show the first and last words listed on the page. All other words on the page are listed in alphabetical order between the guide words. This helps you locate the word you want quickly and easily.

In addition to definitions, dictionaries also show the following: how to pronounce, or say, each word; the individual syllables found in each word; the part of speech for each word; and the plural form or verb forms if the base word changes.

Some dictionaries provide considerably more information. For example, *The Tormont Webster's Illustrated Encyclopedic Dictionary* includes many color illustrations of terms, a pronunciation key on every other page and two pages of introductory information on how to use the dictionary effectively.

Other highlights of the *Tormont Webster* are **historic labels** that tell the history of words no longer in common use; **geographic labels** that tell in what part of the world uncommon words are used; **stylistic labels** that tell whether a word is formal, informal, humorous or a slang term; and **field labels** that tell what field of knowledge—such as medicine—the word is used in.

1. Where are guide words found? at the top of each page
2. What is the purpose of guide words? They show the first and last words listed on the page.
3. Which label tells if a word is a slang term? stylistic
4. Which label tells the history of a word? historic
5. Which type of information is not provided for each word in the dictionary?
   ☐ definition
   ☐ part of speech
   ☑ picture

Page 31

Using a Dictionary

Directions: Use the dictionary entry below to answer the questions.

ad·he·sive (ad-hē'-siv) adj. 1. Tending to adhere; sticky. 2. Gummed so as to adhere. n. 3. An adhesive substance such as paste or glue. **ad·he·sive·ly** adv. **ad·he·sive·ness** n.

1. Based on the first definition of **adhesive**, what do you think **adhere** means?
   to stick to something
2. Which definition of **adhesive** is used in this sentence? The tape was so adhesive that we couldn't peel it loose. tending to adhere, sticky
3. Which part of speech is **adhesive** used as in this sentence? We put a strong adhesive on the package to keep it sealed. noun
4. How many syllables does **adhesive** have? three
5. Is **adhesive** used as a noun or an adjective in this sentence? The adhesive we chose to use was not very gummy. noun
6. **Adhesive** and variations of the word can be used as what parts of speech? noun, adjective, adverb

Directions: Write sentences using these words.

7. adhesiveness
8. adhesively
9. adhere

Answers will vary.

Page 32

Using the Dictionary

Guide words are the words that appear at the top of dictionary pages. They show the first and last words on each page.

Directions: Read the guide words on each dictionary page below. Then look around for objects whose names come between the guide words. Write the names of the objects, and then number them in alphabetical order.

babble	buzz	magic	myself
cabin	cycle	pea	puzzle
dairy	dwarf	scar	sword
feast	future	tack	truth

Answers will vary.

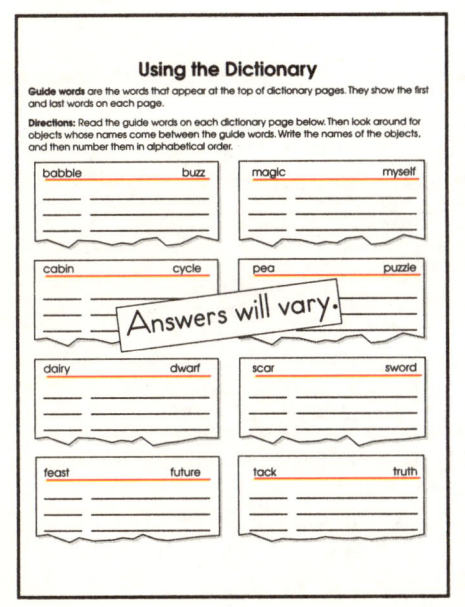

Page 33

Learning New Words

Directions: Write a word from the box to complete each sentence. Use a dictionary to look up words you are unsure of.

bouquet	unconscious	inspire	disability
inherit	hovering	assault	enclosure
commotion	criticize		

1. He was knocked unconscious by the blow to his head.
2. Megan never let her disability stand in the way of accomplishing what she wanted.
3. The teacher burst into the noisy room and demanded to know what all the commotion was about.
4. He offered her a bouquet of flowers as a truce after their argument.
5. The zoo was in the process of building a new enclosure for the elephants.
6. The mother was hovering over her sick child.
7. The movie was meant to inspire people to do good deeds.
8. My friend will eventually inherit a fortune from his grandmother.
9. Not many people enjoy having someone criticize their work.
10. The female leopard led the assault on the herd of zebras.

Page 34

Using a Thesaurus

A **thesaurus** is a type of reference book that lists words in alphabetical order followed by their synonyms and antonyms. **Synonyms** are words that mean the same. **Antonyms** are words that mean the opposite.

A thesaurus is an excellent tool for finding "just the right word." It is also a valuable resource for finding a variety of synonyms and/or antonyms to make your writing livelier.

Each main entry in a thesaurus consists of a word followed by the word's part of speech, its definition, an example, a list of related words and other information.

Here is a typical entry in a thesaurus, with an explanation of terms below:

SLOW
ADJ SYN deliberate, dilatory, laggard, leisurely, unhasty, unhurried REL lateness, limited, measured, slowish, steady, unhurrying, slow-footed, plodding, pokey, straggling, snail-like IDIOM as slow as molasses in January; as slow as a turtle CON blitz, quick, rapid, swift ANT fast

ADJ means adjective
CON means contrasted words
SYN means synonym
ANT means antonym
REL means related words
Idiom means a common phrase that is not literal

Directions: Use the thesaurus entry to answer the questions.

1. What is the antonym listed for **slow**? fast
2. How many contrasting words are listed for **slow**? 4
3. How many synonyms are listed for **slow**? 6
4. What is **slow** compared to in the two idioms listed? molasses, turtle
5. What is the last related word listed for **slow**? snail-like

---

Answer Key   307   Total Basic Skills Grade 5

Page 35

Using a Thesaurus

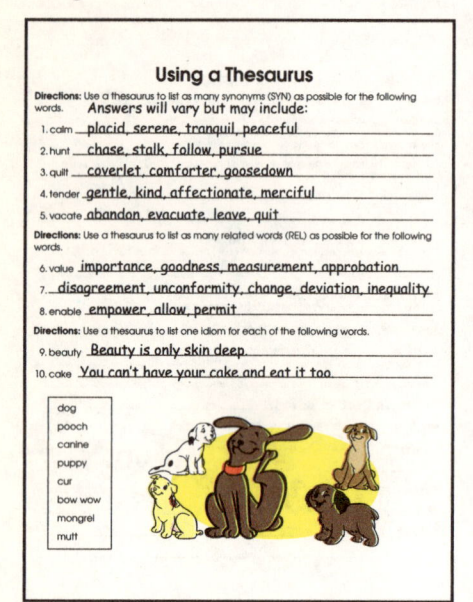

Directions: Use a thesaurus to list as many synonyms (SYN) as possible for the following words. *Answers will vary but may include:*

1. calm — placid, serene, tranquil, peaceful
2. hunt — chase, stalk, follow, pursue
3. quilt — coverlet, comforter, goosedown
4. tender — gentle, kind, affectionate, merciful
5. vacate — abandon, evacuate, leave, quit

Directions: Use a thesaurus to list as many related words (REL) as possible for the following words.

6. value — importance, goodness, measurement, approbation
7. disagreement — unconformity, change, deviation, inequality
8. enable — empower, allow, permit

Directions: Use a thesaurus to list one idiom for each of the following words.

9. beauty — Beauty is only skin deep.
10. cake — You can't have your cake and eat it too.

dog
pooch
canine
puppy
cur
bow wow
mongrel
mutt

Page 36

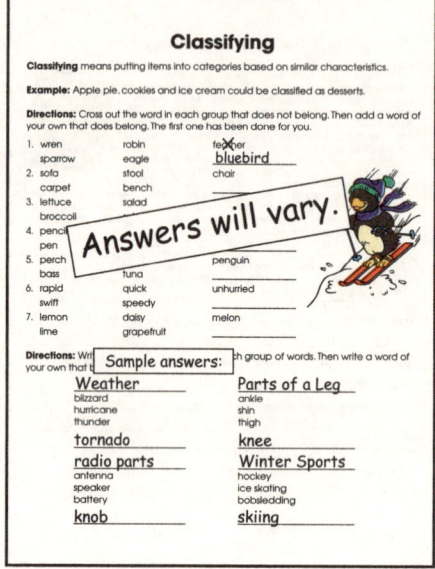

Classifying

Classifying means putting items into categories based on similar characteristics.

Example: Apple pie, cookies and ice cream could be classified as desserts.

Directions: Cross out the word in each group that does not belong. Then add a word of your own that does belong. The first one has been done for you.

1. wren, sparrow, ~~eagle~~, robin — bluebird
2. sofa, stool, ~~carpet~~, bench — chair
3. lettuce, ~~broccoli~~, salad — (Answers will vary.)
4. pencil, pen, ~~perch~~ — penguin
5. bass, tuna — (Answers will vary.)
6. rapid, quick, unhurried, speedy
7. lemon, daisy, melon, lime, grapefruit

Directions: Write ... each group of words. Then write a word of your own that ... *Sample answers:*

Weather
blizzard
hurricane
thunder
tornado

radio parts
antenna
speaker
battery
knob

Parts of a Leg
ankle
shin
thigh
knee

Winter Sports
hockey
ice skating
bobsledding
skiing

Page 37

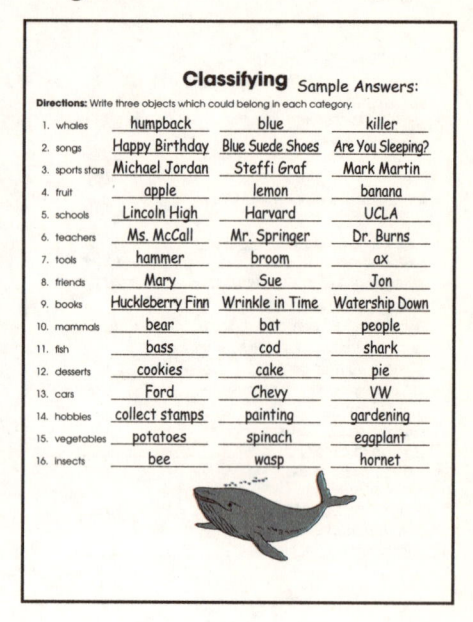

Classifying *Sample Answers:*

Directions: Write three objects which could belong in each category.

1. whales	humpback	blue	killer
2. songs	Happy Birthday	Blue Suede Shoes	Are You Sleeping?
3. sports stars	Michael Jordan	Steffi Graf	Mark Martin
4. fruit	apple	lemon	banana
5. schools	Lincoln High	Harvard	UCLA
6. teachers	Ms. McCall	Mr. Springer	Dr. Burns
7. tools	hammer	broom	ax
8. friends	Mary	Sue	Jon
9. books	Huckleberry Finn	Wrinkle in Time	Watership Down
10. mammals	bear	bat	people
11. fish	bass	cod	shark
12. desserts	cookies	cake	pie
13. cars	Ford	Chevy	VW
14. hobbies	collect stamps	painting	gardening
15. vegetables	potatoes	spinach	eggplant
16. insects	bee	wasp	hornet

Page 38

Analogies

An **analogy** is a way of comparing objects to show how they relate.

Example: Nose is to smell as tongue is to taste.

Directions: Write the correct word on the blank to fill in the missing part of each analogy. The first one has been done for you.

1. **Scissors** are to paper as saw is to wood. — fold, (scissors), thin
2. Man is to boy as woman is to **girl**. — mother, (girl), lady
3. **Attic** is to cellar as sky is to ground. — down, (attic), up
4. Rag is to dust as **broom** is to sweep. — floor, straw, (broom)
5. Freezer is to cold as stove is to **hot**. — cook, (hot), recipe
6. Car is to **garage** as book is to bookshelf. — ride, gas, (garage)
7. Window is to **glass** as car is to metal. — (glass), clear, house
8. Eyes are to seeing as feet are to **walking**. — legs, (walking), shoes
9. Gas is to car as **electricity** is to lamp. — (electricity), plug, cord
10. Refrigerator is to food as **closet** is to clothes. — fold, material, (closet)
11. Floor is to down as ceiling is to **up**. — high, over, (up)
12. Pillow is to soft as rock is to **hard**. — dirt, (hard), hurt
13. Carpenter is to house as poet is to **verse**. — (verse), novel, writing
14. Lamp is to light as clock is to **time**. — (time), hands, numbers
15. **Palm** is to hand as sole is to foot. — wrist, finger, (palm)

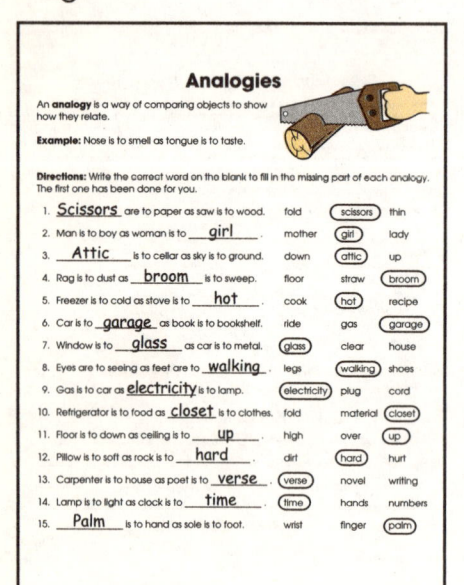

Page 39

Answers will vary. Examples given.

Analogies

Directions: Write your own words on the blanks to complete each analogy. The first one has been done for you.

1. Fuse is to firecracker as wick is to **candle**.
2. Wheel is to steering as **brake** is to stopping.
3. Scissors are to **cut** as needles are to sew.
4. Water is to skiing as rink is to **skating**.
5. Steam shovel is to dig as tractor is to **plow**.
6. Stick is to hockey as **bat** is to baseball.
7. Watch is to television as **listen** is to radio.
8. **Geese** are to goose as children are to child.
9. Multiply is to multiplication as **subtract** is to subtraction.
10. Milk is to cow as egg is to **hen**.
11. Yellow is to banana as **red** is to tomato.
12. **Fast** is to slow as day is to night.
13. Pine is to tree as **daisy** is to flower.
14. Zipper is to jacket as **button** is to shirt.
15. Museum is to painting as library is to **book**.
16. Petal is to flower as branch is to **tree**.
17. Cow is to barn as car is to **garage**.
18. Dresser is to bedroom as **stove** is to kitchen.
19. Teacher is to **student** as doctor is to patient.
20. Ice is to cold as fire is to **hot**.

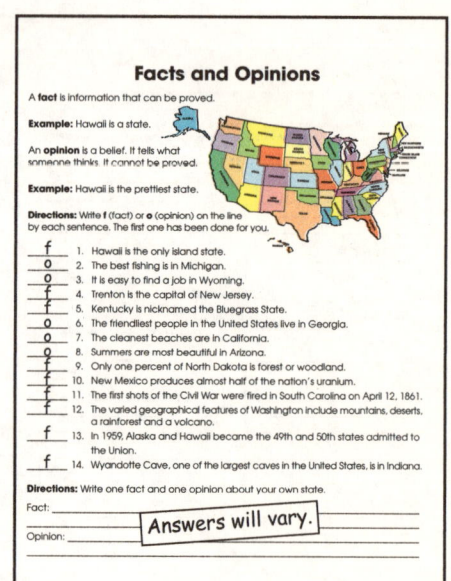

Page 40

Facts and Opinions

A **fact** is information that can be proved.

Example: Hawaii is a state.

An **opinion** is a belief. It tells what someone thinks. It cannot be proved.

Example: Hawaii is the prettiest state.

Directions: Write f (fact) or o (opinion) on the line by each sentence. The first one has been done for you.

- f 1. Hawaii is the only island state.
- o 2. The best fishing is in Michigan.
- o 3. It is easy to find a job in Wyoming.
- f 4. Trenton is the capital of New Jersey.
- f 5. Kentucky is nicknamed the Bluegrass State.
- o 6. The friendliest people in the United States live in Georgia.
- o 7. The cleanest beaches are in California.
- o 8. Summers are most beautiful in Arizona.
- f 9. Only one percent of North Dakota is forest or woodland.
- f 10. New Mexico produces almost half of the nation's uranium.
- f 11. The first shots of the Civil War were fired in South Carolina on April 12, 1861.
- f 12. The varied geographical features of Washington include mountains, deserts, a rainforest and a volcano.
- f 13. In 1959, Alaska and Hawaii became the 49th and 50th states admitted to the Union.
- f 14. Wyandotte Cave, one of the largest caves in the United States, is in Indiana.

Directions: Write one fact and one opinion about your own state.

Fact: *Answers will vary.*
Opinion:

Total Basic Skills Grade 5 — 308 — Answer Key

Page 41

Facts and Opinions

A **fact** is a statement based on truth. It can be proven. **Opinions** are the beliefs of an individual that may or may not be true.

Examples:
  Fact: Alaska is a state.
  Opinion: Alaska is the most magnificent state.

Directions: Write F if the statement is a fact. Write O if the statement is an opinion.

1. O The Grand Canyon is the most scenic site in the United States.
2. F Dinosaurs roamed Earth millions of years ago.
3. F Scientists have discovered how to clone sheep.
4. O All people should attend this fair.
5. O Purebreds are the best dogs to own because they are intelligent.
6. O Nobody likes being bald.
7. O Students should be required to get straight A's to participate in extracurricular activities.
8. F Reading is an important skill that is vital in many careers.
9. O Snakes do not make good pets.
10. F Many books have been written about animals.
11. F Thomas Edison invented the lightbulb.
12. O Most people like to read science fiction.
13. F Insects have three body parts.

Page 42

Cause and Effect

A **cause** is an event or reason which has an effect on something else.
Example:
  The heavy rains produced flooding in Chicago.
  Heavy rains were the **cause** of the flooding in Chicago.

An **effect** is an event that results from a cause.
Example:
  Flooding in Chicago was due to the heavy rains.
  Flooding was the **effect** caused by the heavy rains.

Directions: Read the paragraphs. Complete the charts by writing the missing cause (reason) or effect (result).

Club-footed toads are small toads that live in the rainforests of Central and South America. Because they give off a poisonous substance on their skins, other animals cannot eat them.

Cause: Effect:
They give off a poisonous substance.   Other animals cannot eat them.

Civets (siv its) are weasel-like animals. The best known of the civets is the mongoose, which eats rats and snakes. For this reason, it is welcome around homes in its native India.

Cause: Effect:
It eats rats and snakes,   It is welcome around homes in its native India.

Bluebirds can be found in most areas of the United States. Like other members of the thrush family of birds, young bluebirds have speckled breasts. This makes them difficult to see and helps them hide from their enemies. The Pilgrims called them "blue robins" because they are much like the English robin. They are the same size and have the same red breast and friendly song as the English robin.

Cause: Effect:
Young bluebirds have speckled breasts.   It helps them hide from enemies.
They are much like English robins.   The Pilgrims called them "blue robins."

Page 43

Main Idea

The **main idea** is the most important idea, or main point, in a sentence, paragraph or story.

Directions: Read the paragraphs below. For each paragraph, underline the sentence that tells the main idea.

Sometimes people think they have to choose between exercise and fun. For many people, it is more fun to watch television than to run 5 miles. Yet, if you don't exercise, your body gets soft and out of shape. You move more slowly. You may even think more slowly. But why do something that isn't fun? Well, there are many ways to exercise and have fun.

One family solved the exercise problem by using their TV. They hooked up the television to an electric generator. The generator was operated by an exercise bike. Anyone who wanted to watch TV had to ride the bike. The room with their television in it must have been quite a sight!

Think of the times when you are just "hanging out" with your friends. You go outside and jump rope, play ball, run races, and so on. Soon you are all laughing and having a good time. Many group activities can provide you with exercise and be fun, too.

Maybe there aren't enough kids around after school for group games. Perhaps you are by yourself. Then what? You can get plenty of exercise just by walking, biking or even dancing. In the morning, walk the long way to the bus. Ride your bike to and from school. Practice the newest dance by yourself. Before you know it, you will be the fittest dancer of all your friends!

Directions: Write other ideas you have for combining fun and exercise below.

Answers will vary.

Page 44

Reading Skills: Skimming

Skimming an article means to read quickly, looking for headings and key words to give an overall idea of the content of an article or to find a particular fact. When skimming for answers, read the questions first. Then look for specific words that will help locate the answers.

Directions: Skim the paragraph to answer this question.

1. What "marvel" is the paragraph about? Grand Canyon

In America, there is so much magnificent scenery. Perhaps the most stunning sight of all is the Grand Canyon. This canyon is in northern Arizona. It is the deepest, widest canyon on Earth. The Grand Canyon is 217 miles long, 4 to 18 miles wide and, in some places, more than a mile deep. The rocks at the bottom of the steep walls are at least 500 million years old. Most of the rocks are sandstone, limestone and shale. By studying these rocks, scientists know that this part of the world was once under the sea.

Directions: Skim the paragraph again to find the answers to these questions.

1. How deep are the lowest points in the Grand Canyon?
   more than a mile
2. How old are the rocks at the bottom of the Grand Canyon?
   at least 500 million years old
3. What kinds of rocks would you find in the Grand Canyon?
   sandstone, limestone, shale
4. What do these rocks tell us?
   This part of the world was once under the sea.

Page 45

Reading Skills: Maps

Directions: Use this map to answer the questions.

1. What state borders Louisiana to the north?
   Arkansas
2. What is the state capital of Louisiana?
   Baton Rouge
3. What cities are located near Lake Pontchartrain?
   New Orleans and Baton Rouge
4. In which direction would you be traveling if you drove from Monroe to Alexandria?
   Southwest
5. About how far is it from Alexandria to Lake Charles?
   About 125 miles
6. Besides Arkansas, name one other state that borders Louisiana.
   Texas/Mississippi

Page 46

Following Directions: Continents

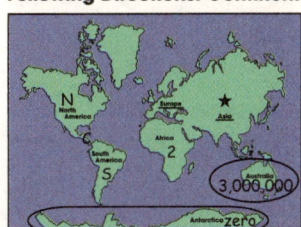

Directions: Read the facts about the seven continents and follow the directions.

1. Asia is the largest continent. It has the largest land mass and the largest population. Draw a star on Asia.
2. Africa is the second largest continent. Write a **2** on Africa.
3. Australia is the smallest continent in area: 3 million square miles, compared to 17 million square miles for Asia. Write **3,000,000** on Australia.
4. Australia is not a very crowded continent, but it does not rank lowest in population. That honor goes to Antarctica, which has no permanent population at all! This ice-covered continent is too cold for life. Write **zero** on Antarctica.
5. Australia and Antarctica are the only continents entirely separated by water. Draw circles around Australia and Antarctica.
6. North America and South America are joined together by a narrow strip of land. It is called Central America. Write an **N** on North America, an **S** on South America and a **C** on Central America.
7. Asia and Europe are joined together over such a great distance that they are sometimes called one continent. The name given to it is Eurasia. Draw lines under the names of the two continents in Eurasia.

Answer Key   309   Total Basic Skills Grade 5

GRADE 5

Page 47

Reading a Recipe
Directions: Read the recipe. Then answer the questions.

Graham Cracker Smoothies
Graham crackers
Icing:
2 T. peanut butter
2 T. butter
2 c. powdered sugar
milk

Break graham crackers in half. Mix peanut butter, butter and powdered sugar with a spoon. Add enough milk to make creamy icing. Stir vigorously until no lumps remain. Spread on graham cracker half and top with another graham cracker half, sandwich style. Enjoy! The smoothie icing will keep in the refrigerator for two days.

1. What do these abbreviations stand for?
   T. __tablespoon__
   c. __cup__

2. Number the steps in the correct order.
   _4_ Spread icing on graham crackers.
   _3_ Add milk and stir until creamy.
   _1_ Break graham crackers in half.
   _5_ Eat and enjoy.
   _2_ Mix the peanut butter, butter and powdered sugar together.

3. Why is it important to follow the correct sequence when cooking?
   __to be certain it turns out correctly__

Page 48

Reading Skills: Labels
Labels provide information about products.
Directions: Read the label on the medicine bottle. Answer the questions.

Remember: Children should never take medicines without their parents' knowledge and consent.

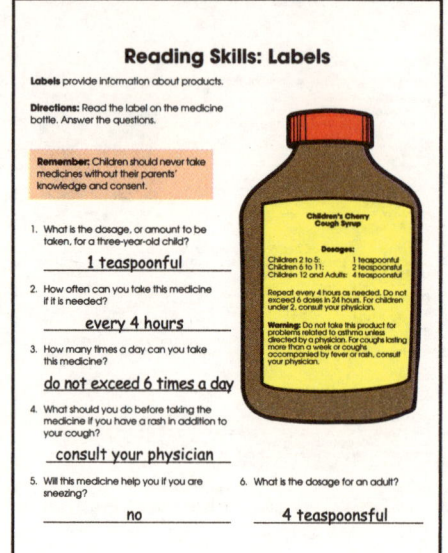

1. What is the dosage, or amount to be taken, for a three-year-old child?
   __1 teaspoonful__

2. How often can you take this medicine if it is needed?
   __every 4 hours__

3. How many times a day can you take this medicine?
   __do not exceed 6 times a day__

4. What should you do before taking the medicine if you have a rash in addition to your cough?
   __consult your physician__

5. Will this medicine help you if you are sneezing?
   __no__

6. What is the dosage for an adult?
   __4 teaspoonsful__

Page 49

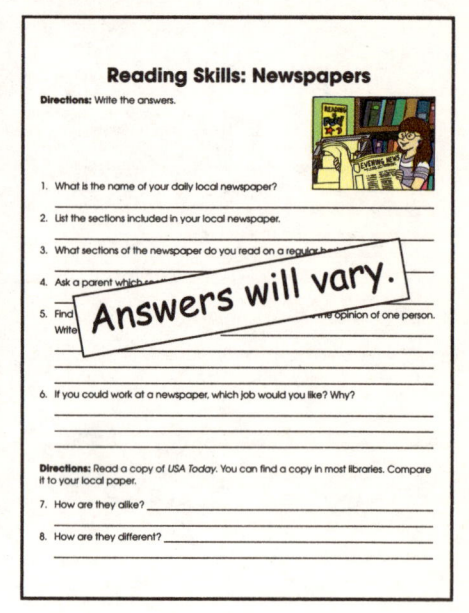

Reading Skills: Newspapers
Directions: Write the answers.

1. What is the name of your daily local newspaper?
2. List the sections included in your local newspaper.
3. What sections of the newspaper do you read on a regular basis?
4. Ask a parent which sections...
5. Find...

Answers will vary.

6. If you could work at a newspaper, which job would you like? Why?

Directions: Read a copy of *USA Today*. You can find a copy in most libraries. Compare it to your local paper.

7. How are they alike?
8. How are they different?

Page 50

Reading Skills: Schedules
A **schedule** lists events or programs by time, date and place or channel.
Example:

Packer Preseason Games
August 14	7 P.M.	NY Jets at Green Bay
August 23	7 P.M.	Denver Broncos at Madison
August 28	3 P.M.	Saints at New Orleans
September 2	Noon	Miami Dolphins at Green Bay

Directions: Use this newspaper television schedule to answer the questions.

Evening
6:00 8 Let's Talk! Guest: Animal expert Jim Porter
       3 Cartoons
       5 News
       9 News
7:00   3 Farm Report
       5 Movie. *A Laugh a Minute* (1955) James Rayburn. Comedy about a boy who wants to join the circus.
       8 Spin for Dollars!
       9 Cooking with Cathy. Tonight: Chicken with mushrooms
7:30   3 Double Trouble (comedy). The twins disrupt the high school dance.
       5 Wall Street Today: Stock Market Report
8:00   3 NBA Basketball. Teams to be announced.
       5 News Special. "Saving Our Waterways: Pollution in the Mississippi."
       9 Movie. *At Day's End* (1981). Michael Collier, Julie Romer. Drama set in World War II.

1. What two stations have the news at 6:00? __8 and 9__
2. What time would you turn on the television to watch a funny movie? __7:00 P.M.__
   What channel? __5__
3. What could you watch if you are a sports fan? __NBA Basketball__
   What time and channel is it on? __8:00 P.M. Channel 3__
4. Which show title sounds like it could be a game show? __Spin for Dollars!__
5. What show might you want to watch if you are interested in the environment?
   __"Saving Our Waterways: Pollution in the Mississippi"__
   What time and channel is it on? __8:00 P.M. Channel 8__

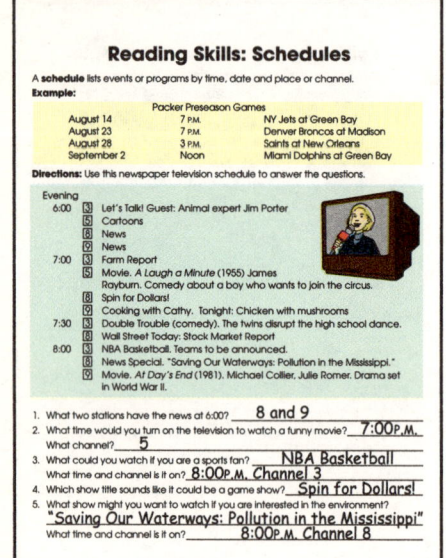

Page 51

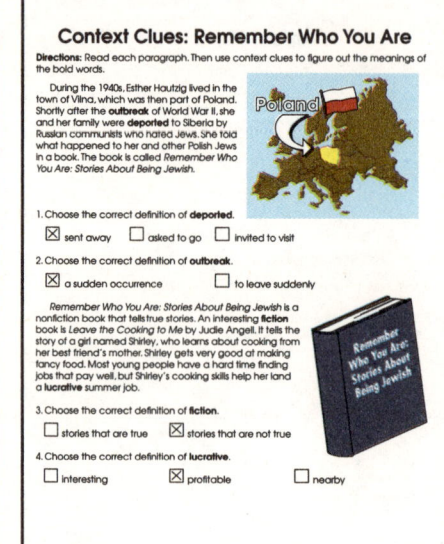

Context Clues: Remember Who You Are
Directions: Read each paragraph. Then use context clues to figure out the meanings of the bold words.

During the 1940s, Esther Hautzig lived in the town of Vilna, which was then part of Poland. Shortly after the **outbreak** of World War II, she and her family were **deported** to Siberia by Russian communists who hated Jews. She told what happened to her and other Polish Jews in a book. The book is called *Remember Who You Are: Stories About Being Jewish*.

1. Choose the correct definition of **deported**.
   ☒ sent away   ☐ asked to go   ☐ invited to visit

2. Choose the correct definition of **outbreak**.
   ☒ a sudden occurrence   ☐ to leave suddenly

Remember Who You Are: Stories About Being Jewish is a nonfiction book that tells true stories. An interesting **fiction** book is *Leave the Cooking to Me* by Judie Angell. It tells the story of a girl named Shirley, who learns about cooking from her best friend's mother. Most young people have a hard time finding jobs that pay well, but Shirley's cooking skills help her land a **lucrative** summer job.

3. Choose the correct definition of **fiction**.
   ☐ stories that are true   ☒ stories that are not true

4. Choose the correct definition of **lucrative**.
   ☐ interesting   ☒ profitable   ☐ nearby

Page 52

Context Clues: Kids' Books Are Big Business
Between 1978 and 1988, the number of children's books published in the United States doubled. The publishing industry, which prints, promotes and sells books, does not usually move this fast. Why? Because if publishers print too many books that don't sell, they lose money. They like to wait, if they can, to see what the "public demand" is for certain types of books. Then they accept manuscripts from writers who have written the types of books the public seems to want. More than 4,600 children's books were published in 1988, because publishers thought they could sell that many titles. Many copies of each title were printed and sold to bookstores and libraries. The publishers made good profits and, since then, the number of children's books published each year has continued to grow.

The title of a recent new book for children is *The Wild Horses of Sweetbriar* by Natalie Kinsey-Warnock. It is the story of a girl and a band of wild horses that lived on an island off the coast of Massachusetts in 1903. The story sounds very exciting! Wild horses can be quite dangerous. The plot of *The Wild Horses of Sweetbriar* is probably filled with danger and suspense.

Directions: Answer these questions about how interest in writing, reading and selling children's books has grown.

1. Use context clues to choose the correct definition of **industry**.
   ☐ booksellers   ☐ writers   ☒ entire business

2. If 4,600 books were sold in 1988, how many books were sold in 1978? __2,300__

3. The number of children's books published in the United States doubled between 1978 and 1988.   (Fact)   Opinion

4. *The Wild Horses of Sweetbriar* is the story of a girl and a band of wild horses that lived on an island in 1903.   (Fact)   Opinion

5. The story sounds very exciting!   Fact   (Opinion)

6. The plot of *The Wild Horses of Sweetbriar* is probably filled with danger and suspense.   Fact   (Opinion)

Total Basic Skills Grade 5 — 310 — Answer Key

Page 54

Using Prior Knowledge: Music

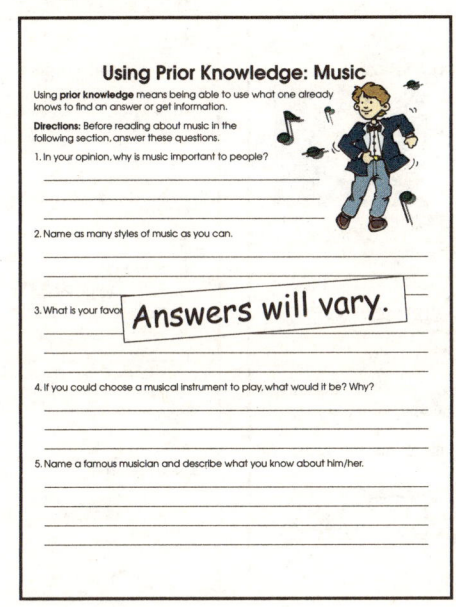

Using **prior knowledge** means being able to use what one already knows to find an answer or get information.

Directions: Before reading about music in the following section, answer these questions.

1. In your opinion, why is music important to people?
2. Name as many styles of music as you can.
3. What is your favorite style of music? Why?
4. If you could choose a musical instrument to play, what would it be? Why?
5. Name a famous musician and describe what you know about him/her.

Answers will vary.

Page 55

Main Idea: Where Did Songs Come From?

Historians say the earliest music was probably connected to religion. Long ago, people believed the world was controlled by a variety of gods. Singing was among the first things humans did to show respect to the gods.

Singing is still an important part of most religions. Buddhists (bood-ists), Christians and Jews all use chants and/or songs in their religious ceremonies. If you have ever sung a song—religious or otherwise—you know that singing is fun. The feeling of joy that comes from singing must also have made ancient people feel happy.

Another time people sang was when they worked. Egyptian slaves sang as they carried the heavy stones to build the pyramids. Soldiers sang as they marched into battle. Farmers sang one song as they planted and another when they harvested. Singing made the work less burdensome. People used the tunes to pace themselves. Sometimes they followed instructions through songs. For example, "Yo-oh, heave ho!/Yo-oh, heave ho!" was sung when sailors pulled on a ship's ropes to lift the sails. **Heave** means "to lift," and that is what they did as they sang the song. The song helped sailors work together and pull at the same time. This made the task easier.

Directions: Answer these questions about music.

1. Circle the main idea:

   Singing is fun, and that is why early people liked it so much.

   Singing began as a way to show respect to the gods and is still an important part of most religious ceremonies.

   (Traditionally, singing has been important as a part of religious ceremonies and as inspiration to workers.)

Sample answers:

2. Besides religious ceremonies, what other activity fostered singing? **working, marching into battle, planting, harvesting**
3. When did farmers sing two different songs? **planting and harvesting**
4. How did singing "Yo-oh, heave ho!" help sailors work? **The song helped them work together to pull the ropes at the same time.**

Page 56

Comprehension: Facts About Folk Music

Folk music literally means music "of the folks," and it belongs to everyone. The names of the musicians who composed most folk music have long been forgotten. Even so, folk music has remained popular because it tells about the lives of people. Usually, the tune is simple, and even though folk songs often have many verses, the words are easy to remember. Do you know the words to "She'll Be Comin' 'Round the Mountain"?

Although no one ever says who "she" is, the verses tell you that she will be "riding six white horses" and that "we'll go out to greet her." The song also describes what will be eaten when she comes (chicken and dumplings) and what those singing will be wearing (red pajamas).

"Clementine" is a song that came out of the California gold rush in the mid-1800s. It tells the story of a woman who was "lost and gone forever" when she was killed. ("In a cavern, in a canyon, excavating for a mine/Met a miner '49er and his daughter, Clementine.")

Another famous folk song is "Swing Low, Sweet Chariot." This song was sung by slaves in the United States and today is sung by people of all races. The words "Swing low, sweet chariot, coming for to carry me home . . ." describe the soul being united with God after death. Like other folk songs that sprang from slaves, "Swing Low, Sweet Chariot" is simple, moving and powerful.

Directions: Answer these questions about folk music.

1. What is the purpose of folk music? **It tells about people's lives.**
2. What food is sung about in "She'll Be Comin' 'Round the Mountain"? **chicken and dumplings**
3. Where did Clementine live?
   ☐ Florida ☐ Mississippi ☒ California
4. Where in the United States do you think "Swing Low, Sweet Chariot" was first sung?
   ☐ the North ☐ the West ☒ the South

Page 57

Recalling Details: Woodwinds

There are four kinds of woodwind instruments in modern bands. They are flutes, oboes, clarinets and bassoons. They are called "woodwind" instruments for two sensible reasons. In the beginning, they were all made of wood. Also, the musician's breath, or "wind," was required to play them.

Although they are all woodwinds, these instruments look different and are played differently. To play an oboe, the musician blows through a mouthpiece on the front of the instrument. The mouthpiece, called a reed, is made of two flat pieces of a kind of wood called cane. Clarinet players also blow into a reed mouthpiece. The clarinet has only one reed in its mouthpiece.

To play the flute, the musician blows across a hole near one end of the instrument. The way the breath is aimed helps to make the flute's different sounds. The bassoon is the largest woodwind instrument. Bassoon players blow through a mouthpiece that goes through a short metal pipe before it goes into the body of the bassoon. It makes a very different sound from the clarinet or the oboe.

Woodwind instruments also have keys—but not the kind of keys that open locks. These keys are more like levers that the musician pushes up and down. The levers cover holes. When the musician pushes down on a lever, it closes that hole. When he/she lifts his/her finger, it opens the hole. Different sounds are produced by controlling the amount of breath, or "wind," that goes through the holes.

Directions: Answer these questions about woodwind instruments.

1. What instruments are in the woodwind section? **oboe, clarinet, flute, bassoon**
2. Why are some instruments called woodwinds? **In the beginning, they were all made of wood. They require "breath" to play them.**
3. How is a flute different from the other woodwinds? **It does not have a mouthpiece**
4. What happens when a musician pushes down on a woodwind key? **It covers a hole in the instrument.**
5. How would a woodwind musician open the holes on his/her instrument? **lift his/her finger**

Page 58

Comprehension: Harp Happenings

If you have ever heard a harpist play, you know what a lovely sound a harp makes. Music experts say the harp is among the oldest of instruments. It probably was invented several thousand years ago in or near Egypt.

The first harps are believed to have been made by stretching a string tightly between an empty tortoise shell and a curved pole. The empty shell magnified the sound the string made when it was plucked. More strings were added later so that more sounds could be made. Over the centuries, the shape of the harp gradually was changed into that of the large, graceful instruments we recognize today.

Here is how a harpist plays a harp. First, he/she leans the harp against his/her right shoulder. Then, the harpist puts his/her hands on either side of the harp and plucks its strings with both hands.

A harp has seven pedals on the bottom back. The audience usually cannot see these pedals. Most people are surprised to learn about them. The pedals are connected to the strings. Stepping on a particular pedal causes certain strings to tighten. The tightening and loosening of the strings makes different sounds; so does the way the strings are plucked with the hands.

At first glance, harps look like simple instruments. Actually, they are rather complicated and difficult to keep in tune. A harpist often spends as long as half an hour before a performance tuning his/her harp's strings so it produces the correct sounds.

Directions: Answer these questions about harps.

1. When were harps invented? **several thousand years ago**
2. Where were harps invented? **in or near Egypt**
3. What is a person called who plays the harp? **harpist**
4. The harpist leans the harp against his/her
   ☒ right shoulder. ☐ left shoulder. ☐ left knee.
5. How many pedals does a harp have?
   ☐ five ☐ six ☒ seven
6. Harps are easy to play.
   ☐ yes ☒ no

Answer Key   311   Total Basic Skills Grade 5

Page 59

Comprehension: Brass Shows Class

1. Who invented the sousaphone? **John Phillip**
2. What were the first horns made from? **hollowed-out animal**
3. Where was John Phillip Sousa born? **Washington, D.C.**
4. When did John Phillip Sousa die? **1932**
5. Why did Sousa invent the sousaphone? **It was easier to carry than a tuba.**
6. What types of instruments make up a modern brass band? **tubas, trombones and trumpets**

Page 60

Comprehension: Violins

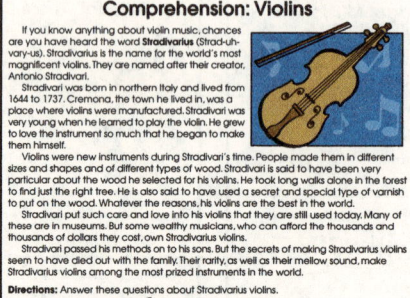

1. Where did Stradivari live? **Cremona**
2. Why did he begin making violins? **because he loved them so much**
3. Why are Stradivarius violins special? **He used special wood and varnish.**
4. Where can Stradivarius violins be found today? **museums and some wealthy musicians**
5. How did Stradivari select the wood for his violins? **He took long walks alone in the forest to find just the right tree.**
6. Who else knew Stradivari's secrets for making such superior violins? **his sons**

Page 61

Using Prior Knowledge: Art

Answers will vary.

Page 62

Main Idea: Creating Art

1. Circle the main idea:
   - (Through the ages, artists have created paintings that reflect the culture, history and politics of the times, as well as their own inner visions.)
2. Why is an artist living in the Rocky Mountains less likely to paint city scenes? **Artists usually portray something that is part of their lives.**
3. In addition to what they see with their eyes, what do some artists' paintings also show? **their inner feelings or visions**

Page 63

Comprehension: Leonardo da Vinci

1. How old was da Vinci when he died? **67**
2. Name two of da Vinci's inventions. **parachute and helicopter**
3. Name two famous paintings by da Vinci. **Mona Lisa, The Last Supper**
4. In which Paris museum does *Mona Lisa* hang? ☐ Lourre ☐ Loure ☒ Louvre

Page 64

Context Clues: Leonardo da Vinci

1. ☐ unhappy ☐ happy ☒ puzzled
2. ☒ sad ☐ unfriendly ☐ hostile
3. ☐ rightly ☐ correctly ☒ wrongly
4. ☐ dull ☒ not ordinary ☐ ordinary
5. ☐ the picture frame ☒ parts of the picture
6. ☒ great mental abilities ☐ great physical abilities
   ☐ improper way to do things ☐ proper way to do things
7. ☐ friends ☒ people who grieve ☐ people who smile

Page 65

Comprehension: Michelangelo

Another famous painter of the late 14th and early 15th centuries was Michelangelo Buonarroti. Michelangelo, who lived from 1475 to 1564, was also an Italian. Like da Vinci, his genius was apparent at a young age. When he was 13, the ruler of his hometown of Florence, Lorenzo Medici (Muh-dee-chee), befriended Michelangelo and asked him to live in the palace. There Michelangelo studied sculpture and met many artists.

By the time he was 18, Michelangelo was a respected sculptor. He created one of his most famous religious sculptures, the *Pieta* (pee-ay-tah), when he was only 21. Then the Medici family abruptly fell from power and Michelangelo had to leave Florence.

Still, his work was well known and he was able to make a living. In 1503, Pope Julius II called Michelangelo to Rome. He wanted Michelangelo to paint the tomb where he would someday be buried. Michelangelo preferred sculpting to painting, but no one turned down the pope! Before Michelangelo finished his painting, however, the pope ordered Michelangelo to begin painting the ceiling of the Sistine Chapel inside the Vatican. (The Vatican is the palace and surrounding area where the pope lives in Rome.)

Michelangelo was very angry! He did not like to paint. He wanted to create sculptures. But no one turns down the pope. After much complaining, Michelangelo began work on what would be his most famous project.

Directions: Answer these questions about Michelangelo.

1. How old was Michelangelo when he died? **89**
2. What was the first project Pope Julius II asked Michelangelo to paint? **his tomb**
3. What is the Vatican? **palace and grounds where the Pope lives**
4. What was the second project the pope asked Michelangelo to do?
   ☐ paint his tomb's ceiling   ☒ paint the Sistine Chapel's ceiling

Page 66

Comprehension: Rembrandt

Most art critics agree that Rembrandt (Rem-brant) was one of the greatest painters of all time. This Dutch artist, who lived from 1606 to 1669, painted some of the world's finest portraits.

Rembrandt, whose full name was Rembrandt van Rijn, was born in Holland to a wealthy family. He was sent to a fine university, but he did not like his studies. He only wanted to paint. He sketched the faces of people around him. During his lifetime, Rembrandt painted 11 portraits of his father and nearly as many of his mother. From the beginning, the faces of old people fascinated him.

When he was 25, Rembrandt went to paint in Amsterdam, a large city in Holland where he lived for the rest of his life. There he married a wealthy woman named Saskia, whom he loved deeply. She died from a disease called tuberculosis (ta-bur-ku-lo-sis) after only 8 years, leaving behind a young son named Titus (Ty-tuss).

Rembrandt was heartbroken over his wife's death. He began to spend all his time painting. But instead of painting what his customers wanted, he painted exactly the way he wanted. Unsold pictures filled his house. They were wonderful paintings, but they were not the type of portraits people wanted. Rembrandt could not pay his debts. He and his son were thrown into the streets. The creditors took his home, his possessions and his paintings. One of the finest painters on Earth was treated like a criminal.

Directions: Answer these questions about Rembrandt.

1. How old was Rembrandt when he died? **63**
2. In what city did he spend most of his life? **Amsterdam**
3. How many children did Rembrandt have? **one**
4. Rembrandt's wife was named
   ☐ Sasha.   ☒ Saskia.   ☐ Saksia.
5. These filled his house after his wife's death.
   ☐ friends   ☐ customers   ☒ unsold paintings

Page 67

Using Prior Knowledge: Big Cats

Directions: Before reading about big cats in the following section, answer these questions.

1. Name at least four big wild cats.

2. Compare and contrast a house cat with a wild cat.

3. What impact *Answers will vary.* on big cats?

4. Do you have a cat? What are the special qualities of this pet? Write about your cat's name and its personality traits. If you don't have a cat, write about a cat you would like to have.

Page 68

Comprehension: Jaguars

The jaguar is a large cat, standing up to 2 feet tall at the shoulder. Its body can reach 73 inches long, and the tail can be another 30 inches long. The jaguar is characterized by its yellowish-red coat covered with black spots. The spots themselves are made up of a central spot surrounded by a circle of spots.

Jaguars are not known to attack humans, but some ranchers claim that jaguars attack their cattle. This claim has given jaguars a bad reputation.

The jaguar can be found in southern North America, but is most populous in Central and South America. Jaguars are capable climbers and swimmers, and they eat a wide range of animals. Female jaguars have between one and four cubs after a gestation of 93 to 105 days. Cubs stay with the mother for 2 years. Jaguars are known to have a life expectancy of at least 22 years.

Directions: Use context clues for these definitions.

1. populous:
2. reputation: *Answers will vary.*
3. gestation:

Directions: Answer these questions about jaguars.

4. Describe the spots on a jaguar's coat.
   a central spot surrounded by a circle of spots

5. Why would it be to a jaguar's advantage to have spots on its coat?
   Answers will vary.

Page 69

Comprehension: Leopards

The leopard is a talented nocturnal hunter and can see very well in the dark. Because of its excellent climbing ability, the leopard is able to stalk and kill monkeys and baboons. Leopards are also known to consume mice, porcupines and fruit.

Although the true leopard is characterized by a light beige coat with black spots, some leopards can be entirely black. These leopards are called black panthers. Many people refer to other cat species as leopards. Cheetahs are sometimes referred to as hunting leopards. The clouded leopard lives in southeastern Asia and has a grayish spotted coat. The snow leopard, which has a white coat, lives in Central Asia. A leopard's spots help to camouflage (cam-o-flaj) it as it hunts.

True leopards can grow to over 6 feet long, not including their 3-foot-long tail. Leopards can be found in Africa and Asia.

Directions: Use context clues for these definitions.

1. consume:
2. ability: *Answers will vary.*
3. nocturnal:

Directions: Answer these questions about leopards.

4. List three differences between the leopard and the jaguar.
   1. **Leopards live in Africa and Asia, while jaguars live in Central and South America.**
   2. **Leopards are light beige with black spots; jaguars are yellowish-red with black spots.**
   3. **Leopards have black spots; jaguars have a central spot surrounded by a circle of spots.**

5. What makes a leopard able to hunt monkeys and baboons?
   It has excellent climbing ability.

Page 70

Comprehension: Lynxes

Lynxes are strange-looking cats with very long legs and large paws. Their bodies are a mere 51 inches in length, and they have short little tails. Most lynxes have a clump of hair that extends past the tip of their ears.

Lynxes not only are known to chase down their prey, but also to leap on them from a perch above the ground. They eat small mammals and birds, as well as an occasional deer.

There are four types of lynxes. Bobcats can be found in all areas of the United States except the Midwest. The Spanish lynx is an endangered species. The Eurasian lynx, also known as the northern lynx, and the Canadian lynx are two other kinds of lynxes.

Directions: Use context clues for these definitions.

1. prey:
2. perch: *Answers will vary.*

Directions: Answer these questions about lynxes.

3. What are the four types of lynxes? **bobcats, Spanish lynx, Eurasian lynx, Canadian lynx**

4. Use the following words in a sentence of your own.
   mammal
   endangered *Answers will vary.*

5. Do you believe it is important to classify animals as "endangered" to protect a species that is low in population? Explain your answer.
   Answers will vary.

Answer Key   313   Total Basic Skills Grade 5

Page 71

Comprehension: Pumas

1. What is a muzzle? *Answers will vary.*
2. As the population increases in North America, predict what might happen to pumas. *Answers will vary.*
3. What are two other popular names for the puma? cougar, mountain lion
4. What other cat besides the puma is blamed for killing cattle? jaguar
5. Reviewing the sizes of cats discussed so far, write their names in order, from smallest to largest.
   1) lynx
   2) puma
   3) leopard
   4) jaguar

Page 72

Comprehension: Tigers

Directions: Use context clues for these definitions.
1. rare:
2. solitary: *Answers will vary.*
3. extinction:

Directions: Answer these questions about tigers.
4. Why have tigers been hunted almost to extinction? Their body parts are used in Chinese medicine and recipes.
5. Name the three types of tigers. Siberian, Bengal and Sumatran

Page 73

Comprehension: Lions

1. What are the differences between male and female lions? Male lions have a mane of hair and are larger in size.
2. Why would living on a savanna make the lion an "easy target"?

Directions: Use cont— *Answers will vary.*
3. pride:
4. territory:
5. savanna:
6. capable:

Page 74

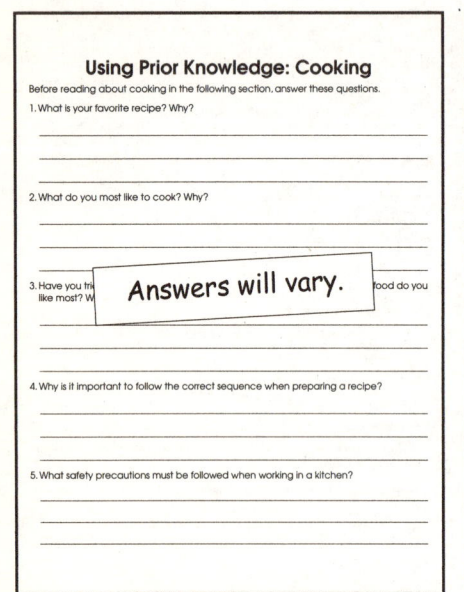

Using Prior Knowledge: Cooking

1. What is your favorite recipe? Why?
2. What do you most like to cook? Why?
3. Have you tr— *Answers will vary.* —food do you like most? W
4. Why is it important to follow the correct sequence when preparing a recipe?
5. What safety precautions must be followed when working in a kitchen?

Page 75

Following Directions: Chunky Tomato and Green Onion Sauce

1. What is the last thing the cook does to prepare the tomatoes before cooking them? chops them
2. What kind of oil does the cook heat in the heavy skillet? corn oil
3. How long should the garlic be cooked? about 1 minute
4. What does the cook do to the tomatoes right before removing the seeds? peels them
5. Is the sauce served hot or cold? hot

Page 76

Comprehension: Cooking With Care

1. Why do fewer people cook nowadays? They are too busy
2. Why are family meals important? They bring everyone together
3. What do homemade cookies do besides satisfy a child's sweet tooth? Someone cared enough to spend his/her time making them.
4. Real estate agents often advise home sellers holding open houses to
   ☐ clean the garage. ☒ bake cookies or bread.
5. The smell of baking at open houses may encourage buyers to
   ☐ bake cookies. ☒ buy the house. ☐ bake bread.

Total Basic Skills Grade 5 — Answer Key

Page 77

Sequencing: Chocolate Chunk Cookies

These chocolate chunk cookies require only five ingredients. Before you combine them, preheat the oven to 350 degrees. Preheating the oven to the correct temperature is always step number one in baking.

Now, into a large mixing bowl, empty an 18 1/4-ounce package of chocolate fudge cake mix (any brand). Add a 10-ounce package of semi-sweet chocolate, broken into small pieces, two 5 1/8-ounce packages of chocolate fudge pudding mix (any brand) and 1 1/2 cups chopped walnuts.

Use a large wooden spoon to combine the ingredients. When they are well-mixed, add 1 1/2 cups mayonnaise and stir thoroughly. Shape the dough into small balls and place the balls 2 inches apart on an ungreased cookie sheet. Bake 12 minutes. Cool and eat!

Directions: Number in correct order the steps for making chocolate chunk cookies.

6 Place 1 1/2 cups of mayonnaise in the bowl.
8 Shape dough into small balls and place them on a cookie sheet.
2 Empty the package of chocolate fudge cake mix into the bowl.
9 Bake the dough for 12 minutes.
4 Place two 5 1/8-ounce packages of chocolate fudge pudding in the bowl.
5 Put 1 1/2 cups chopped walnuts in the bowl.
1 Preheat the oven to 350 degrees.
3 Place the 10-ounce package of semi-sweet chocolate pieces in the bowl.
7 Stir everything thoroughly.

Page 78

Comprehension: Eating High-Fiber Foods

Have you heard your parents or other adults talk about "high-fiber" diets? Foods that are high in fiber, like oats and other grains, are believed to be very healthy. Here's why: The fiber adds bulk to the food the body digests and helps keep the large intestines working properly. Corn, apples, celery, nuts and other chewy foods also contain fiber that helps keep the body's systems for digesting and eliminating food working properly.

Researchers at the University of Minnesota have found another good reason to eat high-fiber food, especially at breakfast. Because fiber is bulky, it absorbs a lot of liquid in the stomach. As it absorbs the liquid, it swells. This "fools" the stomach into thinking it's full. As a result, when lunchtime comes, those who have eaten a high-fiber breakfast are not as hungry. They eat less food at lunch. Without much effort on their parts, dieters eating a high-fiber breakfast can lose weight.

The university researchers say a person could lose 10 pounds in a year just by eating a high-fiber breakfast! This is good news for people who are only slightly overweight and want an easy method for losing that extra 10 pounds.

Directions: Answer these questions about eating high-fiber foods.

1. Why is fiber healthy? **It adds bulk and helps the large intestine work properly.**
2. How does fiber "fool" the stomach? **It absorbs liquid and swells.**
3. How does "fooling" the stomach help people lose weight? **People feel full and aren't as hungry.**
4. How many pounds could a dieter eating a high-fiber breakfast lose in a year?
   ☐ 20 pounds ☐ 30 pounds ☒ 10 pounds
5. The university that did the research is in which state?
   ☐ Michigan ☒ Minnesota ☐ Montana

Page 79

Main Idea: New Corn

I will clothe myself in spring clothing
And visit the slopes of the eastern hill.
By the mountain stream, a mist hovers,
Hovers a moment and then scatters.
Then comes a wind blowing from the south
That brushes the fields of new corn.

Directions: Answer these questions about this ancient poem, which is translated from Chinese.

1. Circle the main idea:
   The poet will dress comfortably and go to where the corn grows so he/she can enjoy the beauty of nature.
   The poet will dress comfortably and visit the slopes of the eastern hill, where he/she will plant corn.
2. From which direction does the wind blow? **the south**
3. Where does the mist hover? **by the mountain stream**
4. What do you think the poet means by "spring clothing"? **Answers will vary.**

Page 80

Comprehension: The French Eat Differently

Many people believe that French people are very different from Americans. This is certainly true where eating habits are concerned! According to a report by the World Health Organization, each year the French people eat four times more butter than Americans. The French also eat twice as much cheese! In addition, they eat more vegetables, potatoes, grain and fish.

Yet, despite the fact that they eat larger amounts of these foods, the French take in about the same number of calories each day as Americans. (French and American men consume about 2,500 calories daily. French and American women take in about 1,600 calories daily.)

How can this be? If the French are eating more of certain types of foods, shouldn't this add up to more calories? And why are so few French people overweight compared to Americans? The answer—Americans consume 18 times more refined sugar than the French and drink twice as much whole milk!

Although many Americans believe French eat each meal with grand and gooey desserts, this just isn't so. Except for special occasions, dessert in a typical French home consists of fresh fruit or cheese. Many French families, on the other hand, like to end their meals with a bowl or two of ice cream or another sweet treat.

It's believed that this difference in the kind of calories consumed—rather than in the total number of calories taken in—is what causes many Americans to be chubby and most French people to be thin.

Directions: Answer these questions about the eating habits of French and American people.

1. How many calories does the average French man eat each day? **2,500**
2. How much whole milk does the average French person drink compared to the average American? **half as much**
3. How much more refined sugar do Americans eat than the French?
   ☐ 2 times more ☒ 18 times more ☐ 15 times more
4. What do French families usually eat for dessert?
   ☐ refined sugar ☐ ice cream ☒ fruit and cheese

Page 81

Comprehension: Chinese Cabbage

Many Americans enjoy Chinese food. In big cities, like New York and Chicago, many Chinese restaurants deliver their food in boxes to homes. It's just like ordering a pizza! Then the people who ordered the "take-out" food simply open it, put it on their plates and eat it while it's hot.

Because it tastes so good, many people are curious about the ingredients in Chinese food. Siu choy and choy sum are two types of Chinese cabbage that many people enjoy eating. Siu choy grows to be 2 to 3 feet! Of course, it is chopped into small pieces before it is cooked and served. Its leaves are light green and soft. It is not crunchy like American cabbage. Siu choy is used in soups and stews. Sometimes it is pickled with vinegar and other ingredients and served as a side dish to other courses.

Choy sum looks and tastes different from siu choy. Choy sum grows to be only 8 to 10 inches. It is a flowering cabbage that grows small yellow flowers. The flowers are "edible," which means they can be eaten. Its leaves are long and bright green. After its leaves are boiled for 4 minutes, the choy sum is often served as a salad. Oil and oyster sauce are mixed together and poured over choy sum as a salad dressing.

Directions: Answer these questions about Chinese cabbage.

1. Which Chinese cabbage grows small yellow flowers? **choy sum**
2. Which Chinese cabbage is served as a salad? **choy sum**
3. Is siu choy crunchy? **no**
4. What ingredients are in the salad dressing used on choy sum? **oil and oyster sauce**
5. To what size does siu choy grow? **2 to 3 feet**
6. Name two main dishes in which siu choy is used. **soups and stews**

Page 82

Recognizing Details: The Coldest Continent

Directions: Read the information about Antarctica. Then answer the questions.

Antarctica lies at the South Pole and is the coldest continent. It is without sunlight for months at a time. Even when the sun does shine, its angle is so slanted that the land receives little warmth. Temperatures often drop to 100 degrees below zero, and a fierce wind blows almost endlessly. Most of the land is covered by snow heaped thousands of feet deep. The snow is so heavy and tightly packed that it forms a great ice cap covering more than 95 percent of the continent.

Considering the conditions, it is no wonder there are no towns or cities in Antarctica. There is no permanent population at all, only small scientific research stations. Many teams of explorers and scientists have braved the freezing cold since Antarctica was sighted in 1820. Some have died in their effort, but a great deal of information has been learned about the continent.

From fossils, pieces of coal and bone samples, we know that Antarctica was not always an ice-covered land. Scientists believe that 200 million years ago it was connected to southern Africa, South America, Australia and India. Forests grew in warm swamps, and insects and reptiles thrived there. Today, there are animals that live in and around the waters that border the continent. In fact, the waters surrounding Antarctica contain more life than oceans in warmer areas of the world.

1. Where is Antarctica? **at the South Pole**
2. How much of the continent is covered by an ice cap? **more than 95%**
3. When was Antarctica first sighted by explorers? **1820**
4. What clues indicate that Antarctica was not always an ice-covered land? **fossils, pieces of coal, bone samples**
5. Is Antarctica another name for the North Pole? Yes ☒No

Answer Key 315 Total Basic Skills Grade 5

Page 83

Reading Comprehension: The Arctic Circle

Directions: Read the article about the Arctic Circle. Then answer the questions.

On the other side of the globe from Antarctica, at the northernmost part of the Earth, is another icy land. This is the Arctic Circle. It includes the North Pole itself and the northern fringes of three continents—Europe, Asia and North America, including the state of Alaska—as well as Greenland and other islands.

The seasons are opposite at the two ends of the Earth. When it is summer in Antarctica, it is winter in the Arctic Circle. In both places, there are very long periods of sunlight in summer and very long nights in the winter. On the poles themselves, there are six full months of sunlight and six full months of darkness each year.

Compared to Antarctica, the summers are surprisingly mild in some areas of the Arctic Circle. Much of the snow cover may melt, and temperatures often reach 50 degrees in July. Antarctica is covered by water—frozen water, of course—so nothing can grow there. Plant growth is limited in the polar regions not only by the cold, but also by wind, lack of water and the long winter darkness.

In the far north, willow trees grow but only become a few inches high! The annual rings, the circles within the trunk of a tree that show its age and how fast it grows, are so narrow in those trees that you need a microscope to see them.

A permanently frozen layer of soil, called "permafrost," keeps roots from growing deep enough into the ground to anchor a plant. Even if a plant could survive the cold temperatures, it could not grow roots deep enough or strong enough to allow the plant to get very big.

1. What three continents have land included in the Arctic Circle?
   Europe   **Asia**   **North America**

2. Is the Arctic Circle generally warmer or colder than Antarctica?
   warmer

3. What is "permafrost"? **a permanently frozen layer of soil**

4. Many tall pine trees grow in the Arctic Circle. Yes (**No**)

Page 84

Main Idea: The Polar Trail

Directions: Read the article about explorers to Antarctica.

A recorded sighting of Antarctica, the last continent to be discovered, was not made until the early nineteenth century. Since then, many brave explorers and adventurers have sailed south to conquer the icy land. Their achievements once gained as much world attention as those of the first astronauts.

Long before the continent was first spotted, the ancient Greeks suspected there was a continent at the bottom of the Earth. Over the centuries, legends of the undiscovered land spread. Some of the world's greatest seamen tried to find it, including Captain James Cook in 1772.

Cook was the first to sail all the way to the solid field of ice that surrounds Antarctica every winter. In fact, he sailed all the way around the continent but never saw it. Cook went farther south than anyone had ever gone. His record lasted 50 years.

Forty years after Cook, a new kind of seamen sailed the icy waters. They were hunters of seals and whales. Sailing through unknown waters in search of seals and whales, these men became explorers as well as hunters. The first person known to sight Antarctica was an American hunter, 21-year-old Nathaniel Brown Palmer in 1820.

Directions: Draw an **X** on the blank for the correct answer.

1. The main idea is:
   ___ Antarctica was not sighted until the early nineteenth century.
   X Many brave explorers and adventurers have sailed south to conquer the icy land.

2. The first person to sail to the ice field that surrounds Antarctica was:
   ___ Nathaniel Brown Palmer
   X Captain James Cook
   ___ Neal Armstrong

3. His record for sailing the farthest south stood for:
   ___ 40 years
   X 50 years
   ___ 500 years

4. The first person known to sight Antarctica was:
   ___ an unknown ancient Greek
   ___ Captain James Cook
   X Nathaniel Brown Palmer

5. His profession was:
   X hunter
   ___ ship captain
   ___ explorer

Page 85

Reading Skills: Research

To learn more about the explorers to Antarctica, reference sources like encyclopedias, CD-ROMs, the Internet and history books are excellent sources for finding more information.

Directions: Use reference sources to learn more about Captain James Cook and Captain James Clark Ross. Write an informational paragraph about each man.

1. Captain James Cook

2. Captain James Clark Ross

Answers will vary.

3. What dangers did both these men and their teams face in their attempts to reach the South Pole?

Page 86

Recognizing Details: The Frozen Continent

Directions: Read the information about explorers. Then answer the questions.

By the mid-1800s, most of the seals of Antarctica had been killed. The seal hunters no longer sailed the icy waters. The next group of explorers who took an interest in Antarctica were scientists. Of these, the man who took the most daring chances and made the most amazing discoveries was British Captain James Clark Ross.

Ross first made a name for himself sailing to the north. In 1831, he discovered the North Magnetic Pole—one of two places on Earth toward which a compass needle points. In 1840, Ross set out to find the South Magnetic Pole. He made many marvelous discoveries, including the Ross Sea, a great open sea beyond the ice packs that stopped other explorers, and the Ross Ice Shelf, a great floating sheet of ice bigger than all of France!

The next man to make his mark exploring Antarctica was British explorer Robert Falcon Scott. Scott set out in 1902 to find the South Pole. He and his team suffered greatly, but they were able to make it a third of the way to the pole. Back in England, Scott was a great hero. In 1910, he again attempted to become the first man to reach the South Pole. But this time he had competition: an explorer from Norway, Roald Amundsen, was also leading a team to the South Pole.

It was a brutal race. Both teams faced many hardships, but they pressed on. Finally, on December 14, 1911, Amundsen became the first man to reach the South Pole. Scott arrived on January 17, 1912. He was bitterly disappointed at not being first. The trip back was even more horrible. None of the five men in the Scott expedition survived.

1. After the seal hunters, who were the next group of explorers interested in Antarctica?
   scientists

2. What great discovery did James Ross make before ever sailing to Antarctica?
   He discovered the North Magnetic Pole.

3. What were two other great discoveries made by James Ross?
   Ross Sea   **Ross Ice Shelf**

4. How close did Scott and his team come to the South Pole in 1902?
   one-third of the way

5. Who was the first person to reach the South Pole? **Roald Amundsen**

Page 87

Reading Comprehension: Polar Bears

Directions: Read the information about polar bears. Then answer the questions by circling **Yes** or **No**.

Some animals are able to survive the cold weather and difficult conditions of the snow and ice fields in the Arctic polar regions. One of the best known is the polar bear.

Polar bears live on the land and the sea. They may drift hundreds of miles from land on huge sheets of floating ice. They use their great paws to paddle the ice along. Polar bears are excellent swimmers, too. They can cross great distances of open water. While in the water, they feed mostly on fish and seals.

On land, these huge animals, which measure 10 feet long and weigh about 1,000 pounds, can run 25 miles an hour. Surprisingly, polar bears live as plant-eaters rather than hunters while on land. Unlike many kinds of bears, polar bears do not hibernate. They are active the whole year.

Baby polar bears are born during the winter. At birth, they are pink and almost hairless. These helpless cubs weigh only two pounds—less than one-third the size of most human infants. The mother bears raise their young in dens dug in snowbanks. By the time they are 10 weeks old, polar bear cubs are about the size of puppies and have enough white fur to protect them in the open air. The mothers give their cubs swimming, hunting and fishing lessons. By the time autumn comes, the cubs are left to survive on their own.

1. Polar bears can live on the land and the sea. (**Yes**) No
2. Polar bears are excellent swimmers. (**Yes**) No
3. Polar bears hibernate in the winter. Yes (**No**)
4. A newborn polar bear weighs more than a newborn human baby. Yes (**No**)
5. Mother polar bears raise their babies in caves. Yes (**No**)
6. Father polar bears give the cubs swimming lessons. Yes (**No**)

Page 88

Context Clues: Seals

Directions: Read the information about seals. Use context clues to determine the meaning of the bold words. Check the correct answers.

Seals are **aquatic** mammals that also live on land at times. Some seals stay in the sea for weeks or months at a time, even sleeping in the water. When seals go on land, they usually choose **secluded** spots to avoid people and other animals.

The 31 different kinds of seals belong to a group of animals often called pinnipeds meaning "fin-footed." Their fins, or flippers, make them very good swimmers and divers. Their nostrils close tightly when they dive. They have been known to stay **submerged** for as long as a half-hour at a time!

Seals are warm-blooded animals that can adjust to various temperatures. They live in both **temperate** and cold climates. Besides their fur to keep them warm, seals have a thick layer of fat, called blubber, to protect them against the cold. It is harder for seals to cool themselves in hot weather than to warm themselves in cold weather. They can sometimes become so overheated that they die.

1. Based on other words in the sentence, what is the correct definition of **aquatic**?
   ___ living on the land
   ✓ living on or in the sea
   ___ living in large groups

2. Based on other words in the sentence, what is the correct definition of **submerged**?
   ✓ under the water
   ___ on top of the water
   ___ in groups

3. Based on other words in the sentence, what is the correct definition of **secluded**?
   ___ rocky
   ✓ private or hidden
   ___ near other animals

4. Based on other words in the sentence, what is the correct definition of **temperate**?
   ___ rainy
   ___ measured on a thermometer
   ✓ warm

Total Basic Skills Grade 5 — Answer Key

Page 89

Reading Comprehension: Walruses

Directions: Read the information about walruses. Then answer the questions.

A walrus is actually a type of seal that lives only in the Arctic Circle. It has two huge upper teeth, or tusks, which it uses to pull itself out of the water or to move over the rocks on land. It also uses its tusks to dig clams, one of its favorite foods, from the bottom of the sea. On an adult male walrus, the tusks may be three and a half feet long!

A walrus has an unusual face. Besides its long tusks, it has a big, bushy mustache made up of hundreds of movable, stiff bristles. These bristles also help the walrus push food into its mouth. Except for small wrinkles in the skin, a walrus has no outer ears.

Like a seal, the walrus uses its flippers to help it swim. Its front flippers serve as paddles, and while swimming, it swings the back of its huge body from side to side. A walrus looks awkward using its flippers to walk on land, but don't be fooled! A walrus can run as fast as a man.

Baby walruses are born in the early spring. They stay with their mothers until they are two years old. There is a good reason for this—they must grow little tusks, at least three or four inches long, before they can catch their own food from the bottom of the sea. Until then, they must stay close to their mothers to eat. A young walrus that is tired from swimming will climb onto its mother's back for a ride, holding onto her with its front flippers.

1. The walrus is a type of seal found only ___in the Arctic Circle___.
2. List two ways the walrus uses its tusks.   ___to pull itself out of water___   ___to dig clams___
3. A walrus cannot move quickly on land.   Yes   (No)
4. A walrus has a large, bushy mustache.   (Yes)   No
5. A baby walrus stays very close to its mother until it is two years old.   (Yes)   No
6. Baby walruses are born late in fall.   Yes   (No)

Page 90

Main Idea: Penguins

Directions: Read the information about penguins.

People are amused by the funny, duck-like waddle of penguins and by their appearance because they seem to be wearing little tuxedos. Penguins are among the best-liked animals on Earth, but are also a most misunderstood animal. People may have more wrong ideas about penguins than any other animal.

For example, many people are surprised to learn that penguins are really birds, not mammals. Penguins do not fly, but they do have feathers, and only birds have feathers. Also, like other birds, penguins build nests and their young hatch from eggs. Because of their unusual looks, though, you would never confuse them with any other bird!

Penguins are also thought of as symbols of the polar regions, but penguins do not live north of the equator, so you would not find a penguin on the North Pole. Penguins don't live at the South Pole, either. Only two of the seventeen **species** of penguins spend all of their lives on the frozen continent of Antarctica. You would be just as likely to see a penguin living on an island in a warm climate as in a cold area.

Directions: Draw an **X** on the blank for the correct answer.

1. The main idea is:
   ___ Penguins are among the best-liked animals on earth.
   _X_ The penguin is a much misunderstood animal.

2. Penguins live
   ___ only at the North Pole.
   ___ only at the South Pole.
   _X_ only south of the equator.

3. Based on the other words in the sentence, what is the correct definition of the word **species**?
   ___ number
   ___ bird
   _X_ a distinct kind

Directions: List three ways penguins are like other birds.
___have feathers, lay eggs, build nests___

Page 92

Nouns

A **noun** is a word that names a person, place or thing.

Examples:
 person — friend
 place — home
 thing — desk

Nouns are used many ways in sentences. They can be the subjects of sentences.
Example: Noun as subject: Your high-topped **sneakers** look great with that outfit.

Nouns can be direct objects of a sentence. The **direct object** follows the verb and completes its meaning. It answers the question **who** or **what**.
Example: Noun as direct object: Shelly's family bought a new **car**.

Nouns can be indirect objects. An **indirect object** comes between the verb and the direct object and tells **to whom** or **for whom** something was done.
Example: Noun as indirect object: She gave **Tina** a big hug.

Directions: Underline all the nouns. Write **S** above the noun if it is a subject, **DO** if it is a direct object or **IO** if it is an indirect object. The first one has been done for you.

1. Do <u>alligators</u>(S) eat <u>people</u>(DO)?
2. <u>James</u>(S) hit a <u>home run</u>(DO), and our <u>team</u>(S) won the <u>game</u>(DO).
3. The famous <u>actor</u>(S) gave <u>Susan</u>(IO) his <u>autograph</u>(DO).
4. <u>Eric</u>(S) loaned <u>Keith</u>(IO) his <u>bicycle</u>(DO).
5. The kindergarten <u>children</u>(S) painted cute <u>pictures</u>(DO).
6. <u>Robin</u>(S) sold <u>David</u>(IO) some chocolate chip <u>cookies</u>(DO).
7. The <u>neighbors</u>(S) planned a going-away <u>party</u>(DO) and bought a <u>gift</u>(DO).
8. The <u>party</u>(S) and <u>gift</u>(S) surprised <u>Kurt</u>(IO) and his <u>family</u>(DO).
9. My scout <u>leader</u>(S) told our <u>group</u>(IO) a funny <u>joke</u>(DO).
10. <u>Karen</u>(S) made her little <u>sister</u>(IO) a clown <u>costume</u>(DO).

Page 93

Proper and Common Nouns

Proper nouns name specific people, places or things.
Examples: Washington, D.C., Thomas Jefferson, Red Sea
Common nouns name nonspecific people, places or things.
Examples: man, fortress, dog

Directions: Underline the proper nouns and circle the common nouns in each sentence.

1. My friend <u>Josephine</u>, loves to go to the (docks) to watch the (boats) sail into the (harbor).
2. <u>Josephine</u> is especially interested in the (boat) named <u>Maiden Voyage</u>.
3. This (boat) is painted red with yellow (stripes) and has several large (masts).
4. Its (sails) are white and billow in the (wind).
5. At <u>Misty Harbor</u>, many (boats) are always sailing in and out.
6. The (crew) on the (boats) rush from (bow) to (stern) working diligently to keep the (sailboats) moving.
7. <u>Josephine</u> has been invited aboard <u>Maiden Voyage</u> by its (captain).
8. <u>Captain Ferdinand</u> knew of her (interest) in (sailboats) so he offered a (tour).
9. <u>Josephine</u> was amazed at the (gear) aboard the (boat) and the (skills) of the (crew).
10. It is <u>Josephine's</u> (dream) to sail the <u>Atlantic Ocean</u> on a (boat) similar to <u>Maiden Voyage</u>.
11. Her (mother) is not sure of this dangerous (dream) and urges <u>Josephine</u> to consider safer (dreams).
12. <u>Josephine</u> thinks of early (explorers) like <u>Christopher Columbus</u>, <u>Amerigo Vespucci</u> and <u>Leif Ericson</u>.
13. She (thinks) these (men) must have been brave to set out into the unknown (waters) of the (world).
14. Their (boats) were often small and provided little (protection) from major ocean (storms).
15. <u>Josephine</u> believes that if early (explorers) could challenge the rough ocean (waters), she could, too.

Page 94

Abstract and Concrete Nouns

Concrete nouns name something that can be touched or seen.
Abstract nouns name an idea, a thought or a feeling which cannot be touched or seen.

Examples:
 concrete nouns: house, puppy, chair
 abstract nouns: love, happiness, fear

Directions: Write **concrete** or **abstract** in the blank after each noun.

1. loyalty ___abstract___
2. light bulb ___concrete___
3. quarter ___concrete___
4. hope ___abstract___
5. satellite ___concrete___
6. ability ___abstract___
7. patio ___concrete___
8. door ___concrete___
9. allegiance ___abstract___
10. Cuba ___concrete___
11. Michael Jordan ___concrete___
12. friendship ___abstract___
13. telephone ___concrete___
14. computer ___concrete___

Directions: Write eight nouns for each category. Answers will vary, but may include:

Concrete	Abstract
1. glass	1. love
2. battle	2. faith
3. apple	3. loneliness
4. pig	4. fear
5. ruler	5. anger
6. hand	6. joy
7. page	7. pride
8. paper	8. shyness

Answer Key   317   Total Basic Skills Grade 5

Page 95

Verbs

A **verb** tells what something does or that something exists.

Examples:
Tim **has shared** his apples with us.
Those apples **were** delicious.
I hope Tim **is bringing** more apples tomorrow.
Tim **picked** the apples himself.

Directions: Underline the verbs.

1. Gene moved here from Philadelphia.
2. Now he is living in a house on my street.
3. His house is three houses away from mine.
4. I have lived in this house all my life.
5. I hope Gene will like this town.
6. I am helping Gene with his room.
7. He has a lot of stuff!
8. We are painting his walls green.
9. He picked the color himself.
10. I wonder what his parents will say.

Directions: Write verbs to complete these sentences.

11–15. *Answers will vary.*

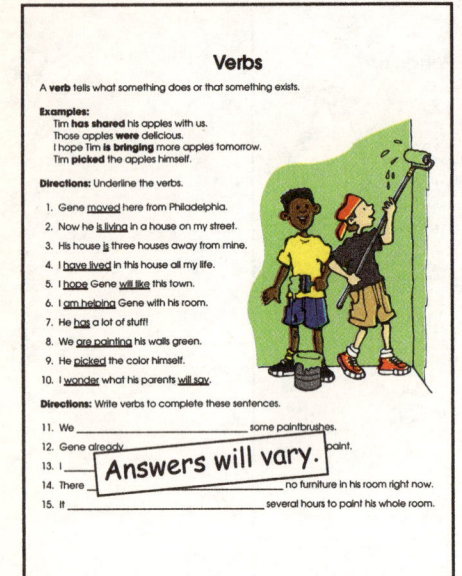

Page 96

Verbs

A **verb** is the action word in a sentence. It tells what the subject does (**build, laugh, express, fasten**) or that it exists (**is, are, was, were**).

Examples: Randy **raked** the leaves into a pile.
I **was** late to school today.

Answers may include:

Directions: In the following sentences, write verbs that make sense.

1. The quarterback **threw** the ball to the receiver.
2. My mother **baked** some cookies yesterday.
3. John **sold** newspapers to make extra money.
4. The teacher **wrote** the instructions on the board.
5. Last summer, our family **took** a trip to Florida to visit relatives.

Sometimes, a verb can be two or more words. Verbs used to "support" other verbs are called **helping verbs**.

Examples: We **were** listening to music in my room.
Chris **has been** studying for over 2 hours.

Directions: In the following sentences, write helping verbs along with the correct form of the given verbs. The first one has been done for you.

1. Michelle (write) **is writing** a letter to her grandmother right now.
2. My brother (have) **is having** trouble with his math homework.
3. When we arrived, the movie (start) **had started** already.
4. My aunt (live) **has lived** in the same house for 30 years.
5. Our football team (go) **is going** to win the national championship this year.
6. My sister (talk) **has been talking** on the phone all afternoon!
7. I couldn't sleep last night because the wind (blow) **was blowing** so hard.
8. Last week, Pat was sick, but now he (feel) **is feeling** much better.
9. Tomorrow, our class (have) **will have** a bake sale.
10. Mr. Smith (collect) **has collected** stamps for 20 years.

Page 97

Verb Tenses

Verbs have different forms to show whether something already happened, is happening right now or will happen.

Examples:
Present tense: I walk.
Past tense: I walked.
Future tense: I will walk.

Directions: Write **PAST** if the verb is past tense, **PRES** for present tense or **FUT** for future tense. The first one has been done for you.

PRES 1. My sister Sara works at the grocery store.
PAST 2. Last year, she worked in an office.
PRES 3. Sara is going to college, too.
FUT 4. She will be a dentist some day.
PRES 5. She says studying is difficult.
PAST 6. Sara hardly studied at all in high school.
FUT 7. I will be ready for college in a few years.
PAST 8. Last night, I read my history book for 2 hours.

Directions: Complete these sentences using verbs in the tenses listed. The first one has been done for you.

9. take: future tense — My friends and I **will take** a trip.
10. talk: past tense — We **talked** for a long time about where to go.
11. want: present tense — Pam **wants** to go to the lake.
12. want: past tense — Jake **wanted** to go with us.
13. say: past tense — His parents **said** no.
14. ride: future tense — We **will ride** our bikes.
15. pack: past tense — Susan and Jared already **packed** lunches for us.

Page 98

Writing: Verb Forms

Present-tense verbs tell what is happening right now. To form present-tense verbs, use the "plain" verbs or use **is** or **are** before the verb and add **ing** to the verb.

Examples: We **eat**. We **are eating**.
He **serves**. He **is serving**.

Directions: Complete each sentence with the correct verb form, telling what is happening right now. Read carefully, as some sentences already have **is** or **are**.

Examples: Scott is (loan) **loaning** Jenny his math book.
Jenny (study) **is studying** for a big math test.

1. The court is (release) **releasing** the prisoner early.
2. Jonah and Jill (write) **are writing** their notes in code.
3. Are you (vote) **voting** for Baxter?
4. The girls are (coax) **coaxing** the dog into the bathtub.
5. The leaves (begin) **are beginning** to fall from the trees.
6. My little brother (stay) **is staying** at his friend's house tonight.
7. Is she (hide) **hiding** behind the screen?

To tell what already happened, or in the **past tense**, add **ed** to many verbs or use **was** or **were** and add **ing** to the verb.

Example: I watched. I was watching.

Directions: Complete each sentence with the correct verb form. This time, tell what already happened.

Examples: We (walk) **walked** there yesterday.
They were (talk) **talking**.

1. The government was (decrease) **decreasing** our taxes.
2. Was anyone (cheat) **cheating** in this game?
3. We were (try) **trying** to set goals for the project.

Page 99

Writing: Future-Tense Verbs

Future-tense verbs tell about things that will happen in the future. To form future-tense verbs, use **will** before the verb.

Example: Tomorrow I **will walk** to school.

When you use **will**, you may also have to add a helping verb and the ending **ing**.

Example: Tomorrow I **will be walking** to school.

Directions: Imagine what the world will be like 100 years from now. Maybe you think robots will be doing our work for us, or that people will be living on the moon. What will our houses look like? What will school be like? Write a paragraph describing what you imagine. Be sure to use future-tense verbs.

Paragraphs will vary.

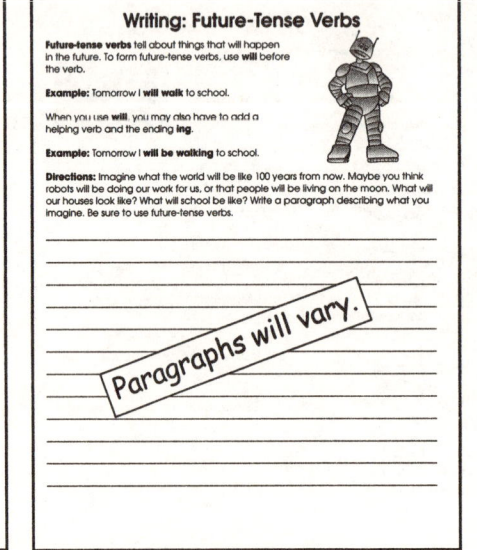

Page 100

Irregular Verbs

Irregular verbs change completely in the past tense. Unlike regular verbs, the past tense forms of irregular verbs are not formed by adding **ed**.

Examples:
Chung **eats** the cookies.
Chung **ate** them yesterday.
Chung **has eaten** them for weeks.

Present Tense	Past Tense	Past Participle
begin	began	has/have/had begun
speak	spoke	has/have/had spoken
drink	drank	has/have/had drunk
know	knew	has/have/had known
eat	ate	has/have/had eaten
wear	wore	has/have/had worn

Directions: Rewrite these sentences once using the past tense and again using the past participle of each verb.

1. Todd begins football practice this week.
   Todd began football practice this week.
   Todd has begun football practice this week.
2. She wears her hair in braids.
   She wore her hair in braids.
   She had worn her hair in braids.
3. I drink two glasses of milk.
   I drank two glasses of milk.
   I have drunk two glasses of milk.
4. The man is speaking to us.
   The man spoke to us.
   The man has spoken to us.
5. The dogs are eating.
   The dogs ate.
   The dogs have eaten.

Page 101

"Be" as a Helping Verb

A **helping verb** tells when the action of a sentence takes place. The helping verb **be** has several forms: **am, is, are, was, were** and **will**. These helping verbs can be used in all three tenses.

Examples:
Past tense: Ken **was** talking. We **were** eating.
Present tense: I **am** coming. Simon **is** walking. They **are** singing.
Future tense: I **will** work. The puppies **will** eat.

In the present and past tense, many verbs can be written with or without the helping verb **be**. When the verb is written with a form of **be**, add **ing**. **Was** and **is** are used with singular subjects. **Were** and **are** are used with plural subjects.

Examples:
Present tense: Angela **sings**. Angela **is singing**. The children **sing**. They **are singing**.
Past tense: I **studied**. I **was studying**. They **studied**. They **were studying**.

The helping verb **will** is always needed for the future tense, but the **ing** ending is not used with will. Will is both singular and plural.

Examples:
Future tense: I **will** eat. We **will** watch.

Directions: Underline the helping verbs.
1. Brian <u>is</u> helping me with this project.
2. We <u>are</u> working together on it.
3. Susan <u>was</u> painting the background yesterday.
4. Matt and Mike <u>were</u> cleaning up.
5. Tomorrow, we <u>will</u> present our project to the class.

Directions: Rewrite the verbs using a helping verb. The first one has been done for you.
6. Our neighborhood plans a garage sale. _is planning_
7. The sale starts tomorrow. _is starting_
8. My brother Doug and I think about things we sell. _are thinking/are selling_
9. My grandfather cleans out the garage. _is cleaning_
10. Doug and I help him. _are helping_

Page 102

"Be" as a Linking Verb

A **linking verb** links a noun or adjective in the predicate to the subject. Forms of the verb **be** are the most common linking verbs. Linking verbs can be used in all three tenses.

Examples:
Present: My father **is** a salesman.
Past: The store **was** very busy last night.
Future: Tomorrow **will be** my birthday.

In the first sentence, **is** links the subject (father) with a noun (salesman). In the second sentence, **was** links the subject (store) with an adjective (busy). In the third sentence, **will be** links the subject (tomorrow) with a noun (birthday).

Directions: Circle the linking verbs. Underline the two words that are linked by the verb. The first one has been done for you.

1. <u>Columbus</u> (is) the <u>capital</u> of Ohio.
2. By bedtime, <u>Nicole</u> (was) <u>bored</u>.
3. <u>Andy</u> (will be) the <u>captain</u> of our team.
4. <u>Tuesday</u> (is) the first <u>day</u> of the month.
5. I hate to say this, but <u>we</u> (are) <u>lost</u>.
6. Ask him if the <u>water</u> (is) <u>cold</u>.
7. By the time I finished my paper, <u>it</u> (was) <u>late</u>.
8. <u>Spaghetti</u> (is) my favorite <u>dinner</u>.
9. The <u>children</u> (were) <u>afraid</u> of the big truck.
10. <u>Karen</u> (will be) a good <u>president</u> of our class.
11. These <u>lessons</u> (are) <u>helpful</u>.
12. (Was) that <u>report</u> <u>due</u> today?

Page 103

Transitive and Intransitive Verbs

An **intransitive verb** can stand alone in the predicate because its meaning is complete. In the examples below, notice that each short sentence is a complete thought.

Examples: Intransitive verbs: The tree **grows**. The mouse **squeaked**. The deer **will run**.

A **transitive verb** needs a direct object to complete its meaning. The meaning of a sentence with a transitive verb is not complete without a direct object.

Examples: Transitive verbs: The mouse **wants** seeds. The deer **saw** the hunter. The tree **will lose** its leaves.

The direct object **seeds** tells what the mouse wants. **Leaves** tells what the tree will lose and **hunter** tells what the deer saw.

Both transitive and intransitive verbs can be in the past, present or future tense.

Directions: Underline the verb in each sentence. Write **I** if the sentence has an intransitive verb or **T** if it has a transitive verb.

_I_ 1. The snake <u>slid</u> quietly along the ground.
_T_ 2. The snake <u>scared</u> a rabbit.
_I_ 3. The rabbit <u>hopped</u> quickly back to its hole.
_I_ 4. Safe from the snake, the rabbit <u>shivered</u> with fear.
_T_ 5. In the meantime, the snake <u>caught</u> a frog.
_T_ 6. The frog <u>was watching</u> flies and <u>didn't see</u> the snake.

Directions: Complete these sentences with intransitive verbs.
7. Our friends _____
8. The movie _____

Answers will vary.

Directions: Complete _____ direct objects.
9. My family _____
10. The lightning _____

Page 104

Subjects and Predicates

The **subject** tells who or what a sentence is about. The **predicate** tells what the subject does, did or is doing. All complete sentences must have a subject and a predicate.

Examples:
Subject	Predicate
Hamsters	are common pets.
Pets	need special care.

Directions: Circle the subjects and underline the predicates.
1. (Many children) <u>keep hamsters as pets</u>.
2. (Mice) <u>are good pets, too</u>.
3. (Hamsters) <u>collect food in their cheeks</u>.
4. (My sister) <u>sneezes around furry animals</u>.
5. (My brother) <u>wants a dog instead of a hamster</u>.

Directions: Write subjects to complete these sentences.
6. _____ has two pet hamsters.
7. _____ got a new pet last week.
8. _____ _Answers will vary._ d his goldfish.

Directions: _____ these sentences.
9. Baby hamsters _____
10. Pet mice _____
11. I _____

Directions: Write **S** if the group of words is a sentence or **NS** if the group of words is not a sentence.
12. _NS_ A new cage for our hamster.
13. _NS_ Picked the cutest one.
14. _S_ We started out with two.
15. _NS_ Liking every one in the store.

Page 105

Which Noun Is the Subject?

A **noun** is a word that names a person, place or thing.

Examples: Andy, Mrs. Henderson, doctor, child, house, shirt, dog, freedom, country

Often a noun is the subject of a sentence. The **subject** tells who or what the sentence is about. In this sentence, the subject is **Sara**: Sara drank some punch. A sentence can have several nouns, but they are not all subjects.

Directions: Underline each noun in the sentences below. Then circle the noun that is the subject of the sentence.

Example: (Benny) caught a huge <u>fish</u> in a small <u>net</u>.
1. (Anna) bragged about her big <u>brother</u>.
2. The (car) has a <u>dent</u> in the <u>fender</u>.
3. Our (school) won the <u>city spirit award</u>.
4. The (cook) scrubbed the <u>pots</u> and <u>pans</u>.
5. The (quarter) flipped onto the <u>floor</u>.
6. My (sister) rinsed her <u>hair</u> in the <u>sink</u>.
7. Our (neighbor) has 12 <u>pets</u>.
8. The <u>cross country</u> (team) ran 5 <u>miles</u> at <u>practice</u>.
9. (Jo) walked to the <u>store</u> on the <u>corner</u>.
10. A (farmer) stocks this <u>pond</u> with <u>fish</u>.

Directions: Each sentence below has two subjects. Underline all the nouns, as you did above. Then circle both subjects.

Example: (Joe) and (Peter) walked to <u>school</u>.
1. (Apples) and (peaches) grow in different <u>seasons</u>.
2. The (chair) and (table) matched the other <u>furniture</u>.

Page 106

Subjects and Verbs

Directions: Underline the subject and verb in each sentence below. Write **S** over the subject and **V** over the verb. If the verb is two words, mark them both.

         S   V   V
Examples: <u>Dennis</u> <u>was drinking</u> some punch.
              S   V
The <u>punch</u> <u>was</u> too sweet.

  S   V
1. <u>Hayley</u> <u>brags</u> about her dog all the time.
        S   V
2. <u>Mrs. Thomas</u> <u>scrubbed</u> the dirt off her car.
       S   V
3. Then her <u>son</u> <u>rinsed</u> off the soap.
     S   V
4. The <u>teacher</u> <u>was flipping</u> through the cards.
      S   V
5. Jenny's <u>rabbit</u> <u>was</u> hungry and thirsty.
      S   V
6. Your science <u>report</u> <u>lacks</u> a little detail.
  S   V
7. <u>Chris</u> <u>is stocking</u> the shelves with cans of soup.
     S   V
8. The <u>accident</u> <u>caused</u> a huge dent in our car.

Just as sentences can have two subjects, they can also have two verbs.

         S   S   V   V
Example: <u>Jennifer</u> and <u>Amie</u> <u>fed</u> the dog and <u>gave</u> him clean water.

Directions: Underline all the subjects and verbs in these sentences. Write **S** over the subjects and **V** over the verbs.

  S   S   V   V
1. <u>Mom</u> and <u>Dad</u> <u>scrubbed</u> and <u>rinsed</u> the basement floor.
     S   V   V
2. The <u>men</u> <u>came</u> and <u>stocked</u> the lake with fish.
     S   V   V
3. <u>Someone</u> <u>broke</u> the window and <u>ran</u> away.
  S   V   V
4. <u>Carrie</u> <u>punched</u> a hole in the paper and <u>threaded</u> yarn through the hole.
  S   S   V   V
5. <u>Julie</u> and <u>Pat</u> <u>turned</u> their bikes around and <u>went</u> home.

Answer Key

Total Basic Skills Grade 5

GRADE 5

Page 107

Writing: Subjects and Verbs

Directions: Make each group of words below into a sentence by adding a subject, a verb, or a subject and a verb. Then write **S** over each subject and **V** over each verb.

Example: the dishes in the sink
 S   V
The dishes in the sink were dirty.

1. a leash for your pet
2. dented the table
3. a bowl of punch for the party
4. rinsed the soap
5. a lack of
6. bragging about his sister
7. the stock on the shelf
8. with a flip of the wrist

Answers will vary.

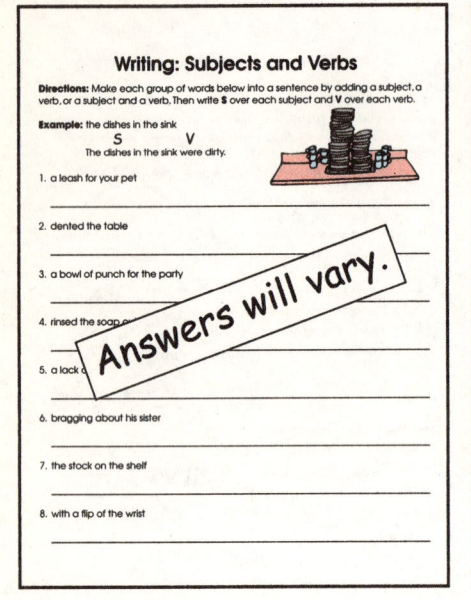

Page 108

Complete Sentences

A sentence which does not contain both a subject and a predicate is called a **fragment**.

Directions: Write **C** if the sentence is complete or **F** if it is a fragment.

1. C My mother and I hope to go to the mall this afternoon.
2. F To get shoes.
3. C We both need a new pair of tennis shoes.
4. F Maybe blue and white.
5. C Mom wants a pair of white shoes.
6. C That seems rather boring to me.
7. C There are many shoe stores in the mall.
8. F Sure to be a large selection.
9. C Tennis shoes are very expensive.
10. C My last pair cost $72.00!

Directions: Write the missing subject or predicate for these sentences.

11. _____ decided to go for hamburgers.
12. We _____
13. My parents _____
14. One day _____
15. My favorite subject in school _____
16. _____ went fishing on Sunday.

Answers will vary.

Page 109

Direct Objects

A **direct object** is a word or words that follow a transitive verb and complete its meaning. It answers the question **whom** or **what**. Direct objects are always nouns or pronouns.

Examples:
We built a **doghouse**. Doghouse is the direct object. It tells **what** we built.
I called **Mary**. Mary is the direct object. It tells **whom** I called.

Directions: Underline the direct objects.

1. Jean drew a <u>picture</u> of the doghouse.
2. Then we bought some <u>wood</u> at the store.
3. Erin measured each <u>board</u>.
4. Who will saw the <u>wood</u> into boards?
5. Chad hammered <u>nails</u> into the boards.
6. He accidentally hit his <u>thumb</u> with the hammer.
7. Kirsten found some <u>paint</u> in the basement.
8. Should we paint the <u>roof</u>?
9. Will you write Sparky's <u>name</u> above the door?
10. Spell his <u>name</u> correctly.

Directions: Write direct objects to complete these sentences.

11. Will Sparky like _____?
12. When we were finished, we put _____
13. We washed out _____
14. We threw away _____
15. Then, to celebrate, we ate _____

Answers will vary.

Page 110

Indirect Objects

An **indirect object** is a word or words that come between the verb and the direct object. An indirect object tells **to whom** or **for whom** something has been done. Indirect objects are always nouns or pronouns.

Examples:
She cooked **me** a great dinner. Me is the indirect object. It tells **for whom** something was cooked.
Give the **photographer** a smile. Photographer is the indirect object. It tells **to whom** the smile should be given.

Directions: Circle the indirect objects. Underline the direct objects.

1. Maria showed (me) her <u>drawing</u>.
2. The committee had given (her) an <u>award</u> for it.
3. The principal offered (Maria) a special <u>place</u> to put her drawing.
4. While babysitting, I read (Timmy) a <u>story</u>.
5. He told (me) the <u>end</u> of the story.
6. Then I fixed (him) some <u>hot chocolate</u>.
7. Timmy gave (me) a funny <u>look</u>.
8. Why didn't his mother tell (me)?
9. Hot chocolate gives (Timmy) a <u>rash</u>.
10. Will his mom still pay (me) three <u>dollars</u> for watching him?

Directions: Write indirect objects to complete these sentences.

11. I will write _____ a letter.
12. I'll give _____ part of my lunch.
13. Show _____ your model.
14. Did you send _____ a card?
15. Don't tell _____ my secret.

Answers will vary.

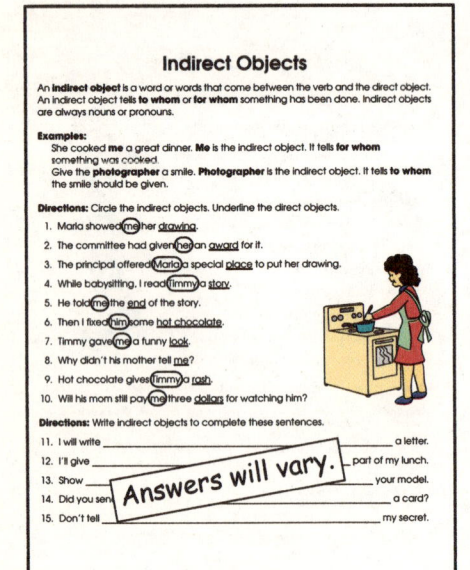

Page 111

Prepositions

A **preposition** is a word that comes before a noun or pronoun and shows the relationship of that noun or pronoun to other words in the sentence.

The **object of a preposition** is a noun or pronoun that follows a preposition and completes its meaning. A **prepositional phrase** includes a preposition and the object(s) of the preposition.

Examples:
The girl with red hair spoke first.
With is the preposition.
Hair is the object of the preposition.
With red hair is a prepositional phrase.

In addition to being subjects, direct and indirect objects and nouns and pronouns can also be objects of prepositions.

Prepositions					
across	behind	from	near	over	on
by	through	in	around	off	with
after	before	for	between	beyond	at	into

Directions: Underline the prepositional phrases in these sentences. Circle the prepositions. The first sentence has been done for you.

1. The name (of) our street is Redsail Court.
2. We have lived (in) our house (for) three years.
3. (In) our family, we eat a lot (of) hamburgers.
4. We like hamburgers (on) toasted buns (with) mustard.
5. Sometimes we eat (in) the living room (in) front (of) the TV.
6. (In) the summer, we have picnics (in) the backyard.
7. The ants crawl (into) our food and (into) our clothes.
8. (Behind) our house is a park (with) swings.
9. Kids (from) the neighborhood walk (through) our yard (to) the park.
10. Sometimes they cut (across) Mom's garden and stomp (on) her beans.
11. Mom says we need a tall fence (without) a gate.
12. (With) a fence (around) our yard, we could get a dog!

Page 112

Pronouns

A **pronoun** is a word used in place of a noun. Instead of repeating a noun again and again, use a pronoun.

Examples:
me	I	you	he	she	them us
my	your	him	her	they	it
	our	his	we	their	its

Each pronoun takes the place of a certain noun. If the noun is singular, the pronoun should be singular. If the noun is plural, the pronoun should be plural.

Examples: John told **his** parents **he** would be late.
The girls said **they** would ride **their** bikes.

Directions: In the sentences below, draw an arrow from each pronoun to the noun it replaces.

Example: Gail needs the salt. Please pass it to her.

1. The workers had faith they would finish the house in time.
2. Kathy fell and scraped her knees. She put bandages on them.
3. The teacher told the students he wanted to see their papers.

Directions: Cross out some nouns and write pronouns to replace them.

Example: Dan needed a book for ~~Dan's~~ his book report.

1. Brian doesn't care about the style of ~~Brian's~~ his clothes.
2. Joy dyed ~~Joy's~~ her jeans to make ~~the jeans~~ them dark blue.
3. Faith said ~~Faith~~ she was tired of sharing a bedroom with ~~Faith's~~ her two sisters. ~~Faith~~ She wanted a room of ~~Faith's~~ her own.
4. Bathe babies carefully so the soap doesn't get in ~~the babies'~~ their eyes and make ~~the babies~~ them cry.
5. When the children held up ~~the children's~~ their pictures, we could see the pride in ~~the children's~~ their eyes.

Total Basic Skills Grade 5   320   Answer Key

Page 113

Singular and Plural Pronouns

Directions: Rewrite the sentences so the pronouns match the nouns they replace in gender and number. Change the verb form if necessary. The first one has been done for you.

1. Canada geese are the best-known geese in North America. It was here when the first settlers came from Europe.
   Canada geese are the best-known geese in North America. They were here when the first settlers came from Europe.
2. A Canada goose has a white patch from their chin to a spot behind their eyes.
   A Canada goose has a white patch from its chin to a spot behind its eyes.
3. Canada geese can harm farmland when it grazes in fields.
   Canada geese can harm farmland when they graze in fields.
4. Geese have favorite fields where it likes to stop and eat.
   Geese have favorite fields where they like to stop and eat.
5. While most of the flock eats, some geese stand guard. He warns if there is any danger.
   While most of the flock eats, some geese stand guard. They warn if there is any danger.
6. Each guard gets their turn to eat, too.
   Each guard gets its turn to eat, too.
7. Female geese usually lay five or six eggs, but she may lay as many as eleven.
   Female geese usually lay five or six eggs, but they may lay as many as eleven.
8. While the female goose sits on the eggs, the male goose guards their mate.
   While the female goose sits on the eggs, the male goose guard his mate.

Page 114

Possessive Pronouns

A **possessive pronoun** shows ownership. A possessive pronoun can be used with the name of what is owned or by itself.

Examples:
This is **my** book. The book is **mine**.
This is **your** sandwich. It is **yours**.
This is **our** room. The room is **ours**.

The possessive pronouns are **my, your, our, his, her, their, its, mine, yours, ours, hers** and **theirs**. Possessive pronouns do not have apostrophes.

Directions: Complete the sentences with the correct possessive pronouns.

1. I entered **my** picture in the contest. That farm scene is **mine**.
2. Shelby entered **her** picture, too. Do you see **hers**?
3. Hal didn't finish **his** drawing. He left **his** at home.
4. Did you enter **your** clay pot? That looks like **yours**.
5. One picture has fallen off **its** stand.
6. Brian and Kendell worked together on a chalk drawing. That sketch by the doorway is **theirs**.
7. The judges have made **their** choices.
8. We both won! They picked both of **ours**!
9. Here come the judges with our ribbons in **their** hands.
10. Your ribbon is the same as **mine**.

Page 115

Writing: Possessive Pronouns

A **possessive pronoun** shows ownership. Instead of writing "That is Jill's book," write "That is her book" or "That is hers." Instead of "I lost my pencil," write "I lost mine." Use possessive pronouns to name what is possessed.

Examples: my (book)   our (car)   your (hat)   his (leg)
her (hair)   their (group)   its (team)

Use **mine, ours, yours, his, hers** and **theirs** when you do not name what is possessed. Notice that possessive pronouns don't use apostrophes.

Directions: Complete these sentences with the correct possessive pronoun.

Example: This book belongs to Jon. It is **his**.

1. I brought my lunch. Did you bring **yours**?
2. I can't do my homework. I wonder if Nancy figured out **hers**.
3. Jason saved his candy bar, but I ate **mine**.
4. Our team finished our project, but the other team didn't finish **theirs**.
5. They already have their assignment. When will we get **ours**?

It's easy to confuse the possessive pronoun **its** with the contraction for **it is**, which is spelled **it's**. The apostrophe in **it's** shows that the **i** in **is** has been left out.

Directions: Write **its** or **it's** in each sentence below.

Examples: The book has lost its cover. It's going to rain soon.

1. **It's** nearly time to go.
2. The horse hurt **its** leg.
3. Every nation has **its** share of problems.
4. What is **its** name?
5. I think **it's** too warm to snow.
6. The teacher said **it's** up to us.

Page 116

Indefinite Pronouns

Indefinite pronouns often end with **body, one** or **thing**.

Examples:
Everybody is going to be there.
No one wants to miss it.

Indefinite pronouns do not change form when used as subjects or objects. They are always singular.

Example:
Incorrect: Everyone must bring **their** own lunches.
Correct: All students must bring **their** own lunches.
Everyone must bring **his or her** own lunch.
Everyone must bring **a** lunch.

Directions: Write twelve indefinite pronouns by matching a word from column A with a word from column B.

Column A	Column B
any	thing
every	one
no	body
some	

1. anything
2. anyone
3. anybody
4. everything
5. everyone
6. everybody
7. nothing
8. no one
9. nobody
10. something
11. someone
12. somebody

Directions: Write all the indefinite pronouns that would make sense in the sentence below.
_____ can come.
13. Anyone, Anybody, Everyone, Everybody, No one, Nobody, Someone, Somebody

Directions: Rewrite this sentence correctly.
14. Everybody has their books.
   Everybody has his or her books.

Page 117

Interrogative and Relative Pronouns

An **interrogative pronoun** is used when asking a question. The interrogative pronouns are **who, what** and **which**. Use **who** when referring to people. Use **what** when referring to things. **Which** can be used to refer to people or things.

Directions: Circle the interrogative pronouns. Write whether the pronoun refers to people or things.

1. (Who) brought this salad for the picnic? people
2. (Which) car will we drive to the movies? things
3. (Which) girl asked the question? people
4. (What) time is it? things
5. (What) will we do with the leftover food? things
6. (Who) is going to the swim meet? people

Relative pronouns refer to the noun or pronoun which comes before them. The noun or pronoun to which it refers is called the **antecedent**. The relative pronouns are **who, whom, which** and **that**. **Who** and **whom** refer to people. **Which** refers to things or animals. **That** can refer to people, animals or things.

Directions: Circle the relative pronouns and underline the antecedents.

1. My <u>dog</u> (which) is very well-behaved, never barks.
2. The story was about a <u>girl</u> (who) wanted a horse of her own.
3. The <u>bookcase</u> (which) was full, toppled over during the night.
4. The <u>man</u> to (whom) I spoke gave me complicated directions.
5. The <u>book</u> (that) I wanted had already been checked out of the library.

Page 118

Gender and Number of Pronouns

Pronouns that identify males are **masculine gender**. The masculine pronouns are **he, his** and **him**. Pronouns that identify females are **feminine gender**. The feminine pronouns are **she, her** and **hers**. Pronouns that identify something that is neither male nor female are **neuter gender**. The neuter pronouns are **it** and **its**.

The plural pronouns **they** and **them** are used for masculine, feminine or neuter gender.

Examples:

Noun	Pronoun	Noun	Pronoun
boot	it	woman	she
man	he	John's	his
travelers	they	dog's	its

Directions: List four nouns that each pronoun could replace in a sentence. The first one has been done for you.

1. she — mother, doctor, girl, friend
2. he
3. it
4. they   *Answers will vary.*
5. hers
6. its

Singular pronouns take the place of singular nouns. Plural pronouns take the place of plural nouns. The singular pronouns are **I, me, mine, he, she, it, its, hers, his, him, her, you** and **yours**. The plural pronouns are **we, you, yours, they, theirs, ours, them** and **us**.

Directions: Write five sentences. Include a singular and a plural pronoun in each sentence.

1.
2.
3.   *Sentences will vary.*
4.
5.

Answer Key 321 Total Basic Skills Grade 5

Page 119

Writing: Pronouns

Sometimes, matching nouns and pronouns can be difficult.

Example: A teacher should always be fair to their students.

Teacher is singular, but **their** is plural, so they don't match. Still, we can't say "A teacher should always be fair to his students," because teachers are both men and women. "His or her students" sounds awkward. One easy way to handle this is to make **teacher** plural so it will match **their**.

Example: Teachers should always be fair to their students.

Directions: Correct the problems in the following sentences by crossing out the incorrect words and writing in the correct nouns and pronouns. (If you make the noun plural, make the verb plural, too.)

Examples: Ron's school won ~~their~~ **its** basketball game.

You can tell if ~~a cat is~~ **cats are** angry by watching their tails.

1. ~~A student~~ **Students** should try to praise their friends' strong points.
2. The group finished ~~their~~ **its** work on time in spite of the deadline.
3. ~~A parent~~ **Parents have** usually ~~has~~ a lot of faith in their children.
4. The company paid ~~their~~ **its** workers once a week.
5. The train made ~~their~~ **its** daily run from Chicago to Detroit.
6. ~~Each student~~ **Students** should have a title on their papers.

Directions: Complete these sentences with the correct pronouns.

1. Simon fell out of the tree and scraped **his** arm.
2. The citizens felt a deep pride in **their** community.
3. Heather and Sheila wear **their** hair in the same style.
4. I dyed some shirts, but **they** didn't turn out right.
5. The nurse showed the mother how to bathe **her** baby.
6. Our school made $75 from **its** carnival.

Page 120

Pronouns as Subjects

A **pronoun** is a word that takes the place of a noun. The pronouns **I, we, he, she, it, you** and **they** can be the subjects of a sentence.

Examples:
I left the house early.
You need to be more careful.
She dances well.

A pronoun must be singular if the noun it replaces is singular. A pronoun must be plural if the noun it replaces is plural. **He, she** and **it** are singular pronouns. **We** and **they** are plural pronouns. **You** is both singular and plural.

Examples:
Tina practiced playing the piano. **She** plays well.
Jim and I are studying Africa. **We** made a map of it.
The children clapped loudly. **They** liked the clown.

Directions: Write the correct pronouns.

1. Bobcats hunt at night. **They** are not seen during the day.
2. The mother bobcat usually has babies during February or March. **She** may have two litters a year.
3. The father bobcat stays away when the babies are first born. Later, **he** helps find food for them.
4. We have a new assignment. **It** is a project about bobcats.
5. My group gathered pictures of bobcats. **We** made a display.
6. Jennifer wrote our report. **She** used my notes.

Directions: Circle the pronouns that do not match the nouns they replace. Then write the correct pronouns on the lines.

7. Two boys saw a bobcat. (He) told us what happened. **They**
8. Then we saw a film. (They) showed bobcats climbing trees. **It**

Page 121

Pronouns as Direct Objects

The pronouns **me, you, him, her, it, us** and **them** can be used as direct objects.

Examples:
I heard Grant. Grant heard **me**.
We like the teacher. The teacher likes **us**.
He saw the dog. The dog saw **him**.

A pronoun used as a direct object must be plural if the noun is plural and singular if the noun is singular.

Directions: Write the correct pronouns.

1. Goldfish come from China. The Chinese used to eat **them** like trout.
2. The prettiest goldfish were kept as pets. The Chinese put **them** in small bowls and ponds.
3. My sister, brother and I have goldfish. Grandpa took **us** to the store to get them.
4. They come to the top when I am around. I think they like **me**.
5. My sister's fish was white. She kept **it** for 3 weeks.
6. She claimed the fish splashed **her** when she fed it.

Directions: Circle pronouns that do not match the nouns they replace. Rewrite the sentences using the correct pronouns. Change the verbs after the pronouns if necessary.

7. Goldfish often die because kids don't feed (it).
Goldfish often die because kids don't feed them.
8. Some goldfish live a long time because (it) is well cared for.
Some goldfish live a long time because they are well cared for.
9. A wild goldfish will eat anything (they) think looks good.
A wild goldfish will eat anything it thinks looks good.
10. Birds eat wild goldfish. (It) likes the young ones best.
Birds eat wild goldfish. They like the young ones best.

Page 122

Pronouns as Indirect Objects and Objects of Prepositions

The pronouns **me, you, him, her, it, us** and **them** can be used as indirect objects and objects of prepositions.

Examples:
Pronouns as indirect objects: Shawn showed **me** his new bike. The teacher gave **us** two more days to finish our reports.
Pronouns as objects of prepositions: It's your turn after **her**. I can't do it without **them**.

A pronoun used as an indirect object or an object of a preposition must be singular if the noun it replaces is singular and plural if the noun it replaces is plural.

Directions: Write the correct pronouns. Above the pronoun, write **S** if it is the subject, **DO** if it is the direct object, **IO** if it is the indirect object or **OP** if it is the object of a preposition.

1. Markos is coming to our party. I gave **him** (IO) the directions.
2. Janelle and Eldon used to be his friends. Is he still friends with **them** (OP)?
3. Kevin and I like each other, but **we** (S) are too young to go steady.
4. We listened closely while she told **us** (DO) what happened to **her** (OP).
5. My brother hurt his hand, but I took care of **it** (OP).
6. A piece of glass cut him when **he** (S) dropped **it** (DO).
7. When Annalisa won the race, the coach gave **her** (IO) a trophy.
8. We were hot and sweaty, but a breeze cooled **us** (DO) off.

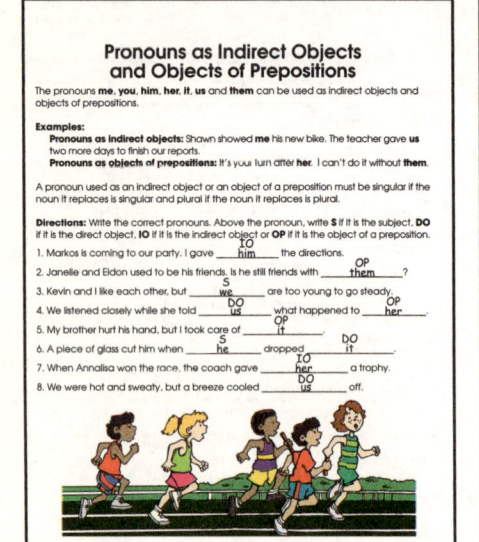

Page 123

Adjectives

An **adjective** describes a noun or pronoun. There are three types of adjectives. They are **positive, comparative** and **superlative**.

Examples:
Positive	Comparative	Superlative
big	bigger	biggest
beautiful	more beautiful	most beautiful
bright	less bright	least bright

Directions: Write the comparative and superlative forms of these adjectives.

	Positive	Comparative	Superlative
1.	happy	happier	happiest
2.	kind	kinder	kindest
3.	sad	sadder	saddest
4.	slow	slower	slowest
5.	low	lower	lowest
6.	delicious	more delicious	most delicious
7.	strong	stronger	strongest
8.	straight	straighter	straightest
9.	tall	taller	tallest
10.	humble	more humble	most humble
11.	hard	harder	hardest
12.	clear	clearer	clearest
13.	loud	louder	loudest
14.	clever	more clever	most clever

Page 124

Writing: Comparatives

Comparatives are forms of adjectives or adverbs used to compare different things. With adjectives, you usually add **er** to the end to make a comparative. If the adjective ends in **y**, drop the **y** and add **ier**.

Examples:
Adjective	Comparative
tall	taller
easy	easier

With adverbs, you usually add **more** before the word to make a comparative.

Examples:
Adverb	Comparative
quickly	more quickly
softly	more softly

Directions: Using the given adjective or adverb, write a sentence comparing the two nouns.

Example: clean   my room   my sister's room
My room is always cleaner than my sister's room.

1. cold   Alaska   Florida
colder
2. neatly   Maria   her brother
more neatly
3. easy   English   Math
easier
4. scary   book   movie
scarier
5. loudly   the drummer   the guitarist
more loudly
6. pretty   autumn   winter
prettier

Sentences will vary.

Total Basic Skills Grade 5 — 322 — Answer Key

Page 125

"Good" and "Bad"

When the adjectives **good** and **bad** are used to compare things, the entire word changes.

Examples:

	Comparative	Superlative
good	better	best
bad	worse	worst

Use the comparative form of an adjective to compare two people or objects. Use the superlative form to compare three or more people or objects.

Examples:
This is a **good** day.
Tomorrow will be **better** than today.
My birthday is the **best** day of the year.

This hamburger tastes **bad**.
Does it taste **worse** than the one your brother cooked?
It's the **worst** hamburger I have ever eaten.

Directions: Write the correct words in the blanks to complete these sentences.

1. worst — Our team just had its bad/worse/worst season ever.
2. bad — Not everything about our team was bad/worse/worst, though.
3. better — Our pitcher was good/better/best than last year.
4. best — Our catcher is the good/better/best in the league.
5. good — We had good/better/best uniforms, like we do every year.
6. better — I think we just needed good/better/best fielders.
7. better — Next season we'll do good/better/best than this one.
8. worse — We can't do bad/worse/worst than we did this year.
9. bad — I guess everyone has one bad/worse/worst year.
10. better — Now that ours is over, we'll get good/better/best.

Page 126

Demonstrative and Indefinite Adjectives

A **demonstrative adjective** identifies a particular person, place or thing. **This, these, that** and **those** are demonstrative adjectives.

Examples:
this pen — these earrings
that chair — those books

An **indefinite adjective** does not identify a particular person, place or thing but rather a group or number. **All, any, both, many, another, several, such, some, few** and **more** are indefinite adjectives.

Examples:
all teachers — any person
both girls — many flowers
another man — more marbles

Directions: Use each noun in a sentence with a demonstrative adjective.

1. dishes
2. clothes
3. cats
4. team
5. apples
6. stereo
7. mountains

Directions: [Use each noun in a sentence] with an indefinite adjective.

8. reporters
9. decisions
10. papers
11. pears
12. occupations
13. friends

Sentences will vary.

Page 127

Interrogative and Possessive Adjectives

An **interrogative adjective** is used when asking a question. The interrogative adjectives are **what** and **which**.

Examples:
What kind of haircut will you get?
Which dog snarled at you?

A **possessive adjective** shows ownership. The possessive adjectives are **our, your, her, his, its, my** and **their**.

Examples:
That is **my** dog.
He washed **his** jeans.
Our pictures turned out great.

Directions: Write six sentences containing interrogative adjectives and six sentences containing possessive adjectives.

Interrogative Adjectives
1.
2.
3.
4.
5.
6.

Possessive
1.
2.
3.
4.
5.
6.

Sentences will vary.

Page 128

Prepositional Phrases as Adjectives

An adjective can be one word or an entire prepositional phrase.

Examples:
The **new** boy **with red hair**
The **tall** man **in the raincoat**
The **white** house **with green shutters**

Directions: Underline the prepositional phrases used as adjectives.

1. The boy in the blue cap is the captain.
2. The house across the street is 100 years old.
3. Jo and Ty love cookies with nuts.
4. I lost the book with the green cover.
5. Do you know the girl in the front row?
6. I like the pony with the long tail.
7. The dog in that yard is not friendly.
8. The picture in this magazine looks like you.

Directions: Complete these sentences with prepositional phrases used as adjectives.

9. I'd like a hamburger
10. Did you read the book
11. The dog
12. The woman
13. I bought a
14. I'm wearing socks
15. I found a box

Answers will vary.

Page 129

Adverbs

Adverbs modify verbs. Adverbs tell **when, where** or **how**. Many, but not all adverbs, end in **ly**.

Adverbs of time answer the questions **how often** or **when**.

Examples:
The dog escapes its pen **frequently**.
Smart travelers **eventually** will learn to use travelers' checks.

Adverbs of place answer the question **where**.

Example: The police pushed bystanders **away** from the accident scene.

Adverbs of manner answer the questions **how** or **in what manner**.

Example: He **carefully** replaced the delicate vase.

Directions: Underline the verb in each sentence. Circle the adverb. Write the question each adverb answers on the line.

1. My grandmother walks (gingerly) to avoid falls.
   how or in what manner
2. The mice darted (everywhere) to escape the cat.
   where
3. He (decisively) moved the chess piece.
   how or in what manner
4. Our family (frequently) enjoys a night at the movies.
   how often or when
5. (Later) we will discuss the consequences of your behavior.
   when
6. The audience glanced (up) at the balcony where the noise originated.
   where
7. The bleachers are (already) built for the concert.
   when
8. My friend and I study (daily) for the upcoming exams.
   how often or when

Page 130

Prepositional Phrases as Adverbs

An adverb can be one word or an entire prepositional phrase.

Examples:
They'll be here **tomorrow**.
They always come **on time**.
Move it **down**.
Put it **under the picture**.
Drive **carefully**.
He drove **with care**.

Directions: Underline the adverb or prepositional phrase used as an adverb in each sentence. In the blank, write **how, when** or **where** to tell what the adverb or prepositional phrase explains.

1. Don't go swimming without a buddy. — how
2. Don't go swimming alone. — how
3. I wish you still lived here. — where
4. I wish you still lived on our street. — where
5. I will eat lunch soon. — when
6. I will eat lunch in a few minutes. — when
7. He will be here in a few hours. — when
8. He will be here later. — when
9. I'm going outside. — where
10. I'm going in the backyard. — where
11. She smiled happily. — how
12. She smiled with happiness. — how

Page 131

Writing: Adjectives and Adverbs

An **adjective** is a describing word. It describes nouns. Adjectives can tell:
- Which one or what kind — the dog's **floppy** ears, the **lost** child
- How many — **three** wagons, **four** drawers

An **adverb** is also a describing word. It describes verbs, adjectives or other adverbs. Adverbs can tell:
- How — ran **quickly**, talked **quietly**
- When — finished **promptly**, came **yesterday**
- Where — lived **there**, drove **backward**
- How often — sneezed **twice**, **always** wins

Directions: The adjectives and adverbs are bold in the sentences below. Above each, write **ADJ** for adjective or **ADV** for adverb. Then draw an arrow to the noun the adjective describes or to the verb the adverb describes.

Example: A girl in a **green** (ADJ) jacket **quickly** (ADV) released the birds into the sky.

1. An **old** (ADJ) mayor was elected **twice** (ADV).
2. He **carefully** (ADV) put the **tall** (ADJ) screen between our desks.
3. The **new** (ADJ) boy in our class moved **here** (ADV) from Phoenix.
4. Today, our **soccer** (ADJ) team **finally** (ADV) made its **first** (ADJ) goal.
5. The woman **gently** (ADV) coaxed the **frightened** (ADJ) kitten out of the tree.

Directions: Use adjectives and adverbs to answer the questions below.

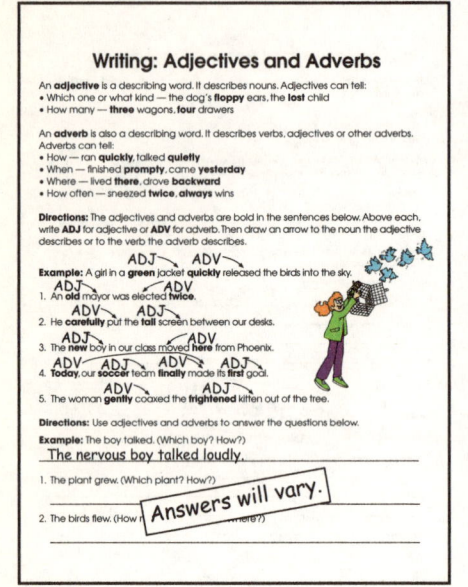

Example: The boy talked. (Which boy? How?)
The nervous boy talked loudly.

1. The plant grew. (Which plant? How?)
2. The birds flew. (How ... where?)

Answers will vary.

Page 132

Placement of Adjective and Adverb Phrases

Adjectives and adverbs, including prepositional phrases, should be placed as close as possible to the words they describe to avoid confusion.

Example:
Confusing: The boy under the pile of leaves looked for the ball.
(Is the boy or the ball under the pile of leaves?)
Clear: The boy looked under the pile of leaves for the ball.

Directions: Rewrite each sentence by moving the prepositional phrase closer to the word or words it describes. The first one has been done for you.

1. A bird at the pet store bit me in the mall.
   A bird at the pet store in the mall bit me.
2. The woman was looking for her dog in the large hat.
   The woman in the large hat was looking for her dog.
3. This yard would be great for a dog with a fence.
   This yard with a fence would be great for a dog.
4. The car hit the stop sign with the silver stripe.
   The car with the silver stripe hit the stop sign.
5. My cousin with a big bow gave me a present.
   My cousin gave me a present with a big bow.
6. The house was near some woods with a pond.
   The house with a pond was near some woods.
7. I'll be back to wash the dishes in a minute.
   I'll be back in a minute to wash the dishes.
8. We like to eat eggs in the morning with toast.
   We like to eat eggs with toast in the morning.
9. He bought a shirt at the new store with short sleeves.
   He bought a shirt with short sleeves at the new store.
10. We live in the house down the street with tall windows.
    We live in the house with tall windows down the street.

Page 133

Writing: Parts of Speech Story

Directions: Play the following game with a partner. In the story below, some of the words are missing. Without letting your partner see the story, ask him/her to provide a word for each blank. Each word should be a noun, verb, adjective or adverb, as shown. Then read the story aloud. It might not make sense, but it will make you laugh!

Last night, as I was _____ (verb + ing) through the _____ (noun), _____ (adjective) _____ (noun) fell from the _____ , head! "Yikes!" I shrieked. I _____ ... off, and it started _____ (noun). ... I tried to hit it with a _____ (noun), but it was _____ (adjective) _____ (adverb) managed to _____ (verb) it out of the house, where it quickly climbed the nearest _____ (noun).

Answers will vary.

Page 134

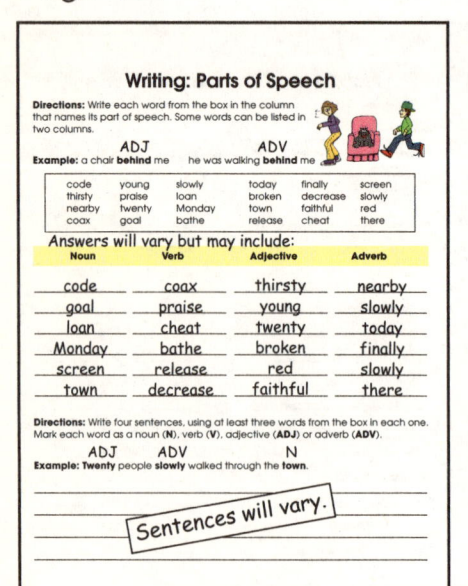

Writing: Parts of Speech

Directions: Write each word from the column that names its part of speech. Some words can be listed in two columns.

Example: a chair **behind** (ADJ) me   he was walking **behind** (ADV) me

code	young	slowly	finally
thirsty	praise	loan	decrease	slowly
nearby	twenty	Monday	faithful	red
coax	goal	bathe	release	cheat	there

Answers will vary but may include:

Noun	Verb	Adjective	Adverb
code	coax	thirsty	nearby
goal	praise	young	slowly
loan	cheat	twenty	today
Monday	bathe	broken	finally
screen	release	red	slowly
town	decrease	faithful	there

Directions: Write four sentences, using at least three words from the box in each one. Mark each word as a noun (**N**), verb (**V**), adjective (**ADJ**) or adverb (**ADV**).

Example: **Twenty** (ADJ) people **slowly** (ADV) walked through the **town** (N).

Sentences will vary.

Page 135

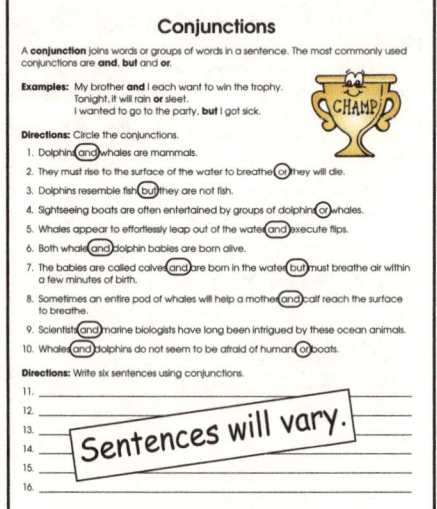

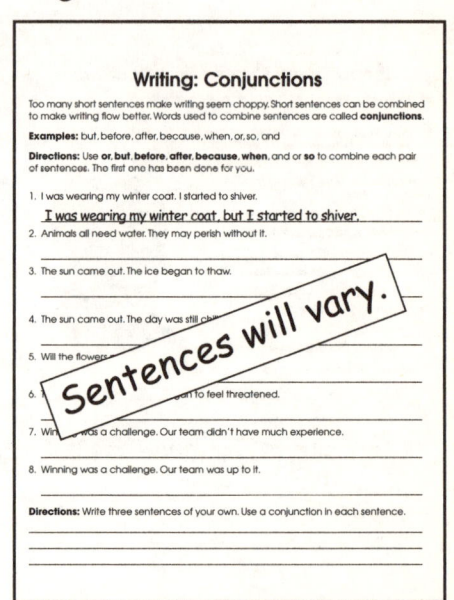

Conjunctions

A **conjunction** joins words or groups of words in a sentence. The most commonly used conjunctions are **and**, **but** and **or**.

Examples: My brother **and** I each want to win the trophy.
Tonight, it will rain **or** sleet.
I wanted to go to the party, **but** I got sick.

Directions: Circle the conjunctions.

1. Dolphins (and) whales are mammals.
2. They must rise to the surface of the water to breathe (or) they will die.
3. Dolphins resemble fish (but) they are not fish.
4. Sightseeing boats are often entertained by groups of dolphins (or) whales.
5. Whales appear to effortlessly leap out of the water (and) execute flips.
6. Both whale (and) dolphin babies are born alive.
7. The babies are called calves (and) are born in the water (but) must breathe air within a few minutes of birth.
8. Sometimes an entire pod of whales will help a mother (and) calf reach the surface to breathe.
9. Scientists (and) marine biologists have long been intrigued by these ocean animals.
10. Whales (and) dolphins do not seem to be afraid of humans (or) boats.

Directions: Write six sentences using conjunctions.

11–16. *Sentences will vary.*

Page 136

Writing: Conjunctions

Too many short sentences make writing seem choppy. Short sentences can be combined to make writing flow better. Words used to combine sentences are called **conjunctions**.

Examples: but, before, after, because, when, or, so, and

Directions: Use **or**, **but**, **before**, **after**, **because**, **when**, and **or so** to combine each pair of sentences. The first one has been done for you.

1. I was wearing my winter coat. I started to shiver.
   I was wearing my winter coat, but I started to shiver.
2. Animals all need water. They may perish without it.
3. The sun came out. The ice began to thaw.
4. The sun came out. The day was still ch...
5. Will the flowers...
6. ... can to feel threatened.
7. Win... was a challenge. Our team didn't have much experience.
8. Winning was a challenge. Our team was up to it.

Sentences will vary.

Directions: Write three sentences of your own. Use a conjunction in each sentence.

Page 137

Statements and Questions

A **statement** is a sentence that tells something. It ends with a period (.).
A **question** is a sentence that asks something. It ends with a question mark (?).
Examples:
  Statement: Shari is walking to school today.
  Question: Is Shari walking to school today?
In some questions, the subject comes between two parts of the verb. In the examples below, the subjects are underlined. The verbs and the rest of the predicates are bold.
Examples:
  Is Steve **coming with us**?
  Who will be there?
  Which one did you **select**?
To find the predicate, turn a question into a statement.
Example: Is Steve coming with us? Steve is coming with us.
Directions: Write **S** for statement or **Q** for question. Put a period after the statements and a question mark after the questions.

S 1. Today is the day for our field trip.
Q 2. How are we going to get there?
S 3. The bus will take us.
Q 4. Is there room for everyone?
Q 5. Who forgot to bring a lunch?
S 6. I'll save you a seat.

Directions: Circle the subjects and underline all parts of the predicates.

7. Do (you) like field trips?
8. Did (you) bring your coat?
9. Will (it) be cold there?
10. Do (you) see my gloves anywhere?
11. Is (anyone) sitting with you?
12. Does (the bus driver) have a map?
13. Are (all the roads) this bumpy?

Page 138

Statements and Questions

Directions: Write 10 statements and 10 questions.

Statements
1–10. _Sentences will vary._

Questions
1–10. _Sentences will vary._

Page 139

Commands, Requests and Exclamations

A **command** is a sentence that orders someone to do something. It ends with a period or an exclamation mark (!).
A **request** is a sentence that asks someone to do something. It ends with a period or a question mark (?).
An **exclamation** is a sentence that shows strong feeling. It ends with an exclamation mark (!).
Examples:
  Command: Stay in your seat.
  Request: Would you please pass the salt?
    Please pass the salt.
  Exclamation: Call the police!
In the first and last two sentences in the examples, the subject is not stated. The subject is understood to be **you**.
Directions: Write **C** if the sentence is a command, **R** if it is a request and **E** if it is an exclamation. Put the correct punctuation at the end of each sentence.

C 1. Look both ways before you cross the street.
R 2. Please go to the store and buy some bread for us.
E 3. The house is on fire!
R 4. Would you hand me the glue?
C 5. Don't step there.
C 6. Write your name at the top of the page.
R 7. Please close the door.
R 8. Would you answer the phone?
E 9. Watch out!
C 10. Take one card from each pile.

Page 140

Commands, Requests and Exclamations

Directions: Write six sentences for each type listed.

Command
1–6. _Sentences will vary._

Request
1–6. _Sentences will vary._

Exclamation
1–6. _Sentences will vary._

Page 141

Writing: Four Kinds of Sentences

There are four kinds of sentences used in writing. Different punctuation is used for different kinds of sentences.
A **statement** tells something. A period is used after statements.
Examples: I jogged five miles yesterday.
  We are going to have a spelling test on Friday.
A **question** asks something. A question mark is used after questions.
Examples: What are you wearing to the dance?
  Will it ever stop raining?
An **exclamation** shows strong feeling or excitement. An exclamation mark is used after exclamations.
Examples: Boy, am I tired!
  What a beautiful painting!
A **command** tells someone to do something. A period or an exclamation mark is used after a command, depending on how strong it is.
Examples: Please hand me that pen. Don't touch the stove!

Directions: Write the correct punctuation mark at the end of each sentence below. Then write whether the sentence is a statement, question, exclamation or command.

Example: I didn't have time to finish my homework last night. __statement__

1. Why didn't she come shopping with us? __question__
2. Somebody call an ambulance! or . __command or exclamation__
3. He's been watching TV all morning. __statement__
4. How did you do on the quiz? __question__
5. Go sit in the third row! or . __command or exclamation__
6. I have to go to the dentist tomorrow. __statement__
7. I've never been so hungry! __exclamation__
8. Who tracked mud all over the house? __question__
9. That restaurant is too expensive. or ! __statement or exclamation__

Page 142

Compound Subjects/Compound Predicates

A **compound subject** has two or more nouns or pronouns joined by a conjunction. Compound subjects share the same predicate.
Examples:
  Suki and Spot walked to the park in the rain.
  Cars, buses and trucks splashed water on them.
  He and I were glad we had our umbrella.
A **compound predicate** has two or more verbs joined by a conjunction. Compound predicates share the same subject.
Examples:
  Suki **went** in the restroom **and wiped** off her shoes.
  Paula **followed** Suki **and waited** for her.
A sentence can have a compound subject and a compound predicate.
Example: Tina and Maria went to the mall and shopped for an hour.

Directions: Circle the compound subjects. Underline the compound predicates.

1. (Steve and Jerry) went to the store and bought some gum.
2. (Police and firefighters) worked together and put out the fire.
3. (Karen and Marsha) did their homework and checked it twice.
4. In preschool, the (boys and girls) drew pictures and colored them.

Directions: Write compound subjects to go with these predicates.

5–9. _Answers will vary._ ate peanut butter sandwiches / left early / ...

Directions: Write compound predicates to go with these subjects.

10. A scary bo___
11. My friend's___
12. The shadow___
13. The wind___
14. The runaway car___

Answers will vary.

Page 143

Combining Subjects

Too many short sentences make writing sound choppy. Often, we can combine sentences with different subjects and the same predicate to make one sentence with a compound subject.

Example:
Lisa tried out for the play. Todd tried out for the play.
Compound subject: Lisa and Todd tried out for the play.

When sentences have different subjects and different predicates, we cannot combine them this way. Each subject and predicate must stay together. Two short sentences can be combined with a conjunction.

Examples:
Lisa got a part in the play. Todd will help make scenery.
Lisa got a part in the play, and Todd will help make scenery.

Directions: If a pair of sentences share the same predicate, combine them with compound subjects. If the sentences have different subjects and predicates, combine them using **and**.

1. Rachel read a book about explorers. Eric read the same book about explorers.
   Rachel and Eric read a book about explorers.
2. Rachel really liked the book. Eric agreed with her.
   Rachel really liked the book, and Eric agreed with her.
3. Vicki went to the basketball game last night. Dan went to the basketball game, too.
   Vicki and Dan went to the basketball game last night.
4. Vicki lost her coat. Dan missed his ride home.
   Vicki lost her coat, and Dan missed his ride home.
5. My uncle planted corn in the garden. My mother planted corn in the garden.
   My uncle and my mother planted corn in the garden.
6. Isaac helped with the food drive last week. Amy helped with the food drive, too.
   Isaac and Amy helped with the food drive last week.

Page 144

Combining Predicates

If short sentences have the same subject and different predicates, we can combine them into one sentence with a compound predicate.

Example:
Andy got up late this morning.
He nearly missed the school bus.
Compound predicate: Andy got up late this morning and nearly missed the school bus.

The pronoun **he** takes the place of Andy in the second sentence, so the subjects are the same and can be combined.

When two sentences have different subjects and predicates, we cannot combine them this way. Two short sentences can be combined with a conjunction.

Examples:
Andy got up late this morning. Cindy woke up early.
Andy got up late this morning, but Cindy woke up early.

Directions: If the pair of sentences share the same subject, combine them with compound predicates. If the sentences have different subjects and predicates, combine them using **and** or **but**.

1. Kyle practiced pitching all winter. Kyle became the pitcher for his team.
   Kyle practiced pitching all winter and became the pitcher for his team.
2. Kisha studied two hours for her history test. Angela watched TV.
   Kisha studied two hours for her history test, but Angela watched TV.
3. Jeff had an earache. He took medicine four times a day.
   Jeff had an earache and took medicine four times a day.
4. Nikki found a new hair style. Melissa didn't like that style.
   Nikki found a new hair style, but Melissa didn't like that style.
5. Kirby buys his lunch every day. Sean brings his lunch from home.
   Kirby buys his lunch everyday, but Sean brings his lunch from home.

Page 145

Writing: Using Commas Correctly

A **comma** tells a reader where to pause when reading a sentence. Use commas when combining two or more **complete** sentences with a joining word.

Examples: We raked the leaves, and we put them into bags.
Brian dressed quickly, but he still missed the school bus.

Do not use commas if you are not combining complete sentences.

Examples: We raked the leaves and put them into bags.
Brian dressed quickly but still missed the school bus.

If either part of the sentence does not have both a subject and a verb, do not use a comma.

Directions: Read each sentence below and decide whether or not it needs a comma. If it does, rewrite the sentence, placing the comma correctly. If it doesn't, write **O.K.** on the line.

1. The cat stretched lazily and walked out of the room.
   _O.K._
2. I could use the money to buy a new shirt or I could go to the movies.
   I could use the money to buy a new shirt, or I could go to the movies.
3. My sister likes pizza but she doesn't like spaghetti.
   My sister likes pizza, but she doesn't like spaghetti.
4. Mom mixed the batter and poured it into the pan.
   _O.K._
5. The teacher passed out the tests and she told us to write our names on them.
   The teacher passed out the tests, and she told us to write our names on them.
6. The car squealed its tires and took off out of the parking lot.
   _O.K._
7. The snow fell heavily and we knew the schools would be closed the next day.
   The snow fell heavily, and we knew the schools would be closed the next day.
8. The batter hit the ball and it flew over the fence.
   The batter hit the ball, and it flew over the fence.

Page 146

Run-On Sentences

A **run-on sentence** occurs when two or more sentences are joined together without the correct punctuation. A run-on sentence must be divided into two or more separate sentences.

Example:
Run-on: On Tuesday my family went to the amusement park but unfortunately it rained and we got wet and it took hours for our clothes to dry.
Correct: On Tuesday, my family went to the amusement park. Unfortunately, it rained and we got wet. It took hours for our clothes to dry.

Directions: Rewrite these run-on sentences correctly.

1. I have a dog named Boxer and a cat named Phoebe and they are both well-behaved and friendly.
   I have a dog named Boxer and a cat named Phoebe. They are both friendly and well-behaved.
2. Jacob's basketball coach makes the team run for 20 minutes each practice and then he makes them play a full game and afterwards he makes them do 50 push-ups and 100 sit-ups.
   Jacob's basketball coach makes the team run for 20 minutes each practice. Then he makes them play a full game. Afterwards, he makes them do 50 push-ups and 100 sit-ups.
3. My family members each enjoy different hobbies Mom likes to paint Dad likes to read I like to play sports and my younger sister likes to build model airplanes although I think they are too hard.
   My family members each enjoy different hobbies. Mom likes to paint. Dad likes to read. I like to play sports. My younger sister likes to build model airplanes, although I think they are too hard.

Page 147

Commas

Commas are used to separate items in a series. Both examples below are correct. A final comma is optional.

Examples:
The fruit bowl contains oranges, peaches, pears, and apples.
The fruit bowl contains oranges, peaches, pears and apples.

Commas are also used to separate geographical names and dates.

Examples:
Today's date is January 13, 2000.
My grandfather lives in Tallahassee, Florida.
I would like to visit Paris, France.

Directions: Place commas where needed in these sentences.

1. I was born on September, 21 1992.
2. John's favorite sports include basketball, football, hockey and soccer.
3. The ship will sail on November 16, 2004.
4. My family and I vacationed in Salt Lake City, Utah.
5. I like to plant beans, beets, corn and radishes in my garden.
6. Sandy's party will be held in Youngstown, Ohio.
7. Periods, commas, colons and exclamation marks are types of punctuation.
8. Cardinals, juncos, blue jays, finches and sparrows frequent our birdfeeder.
9. My grandfather graduated from high school on June 4, 1962.
10. The race will take place in Burlington, Vermont.

Directions: Write a sentence using commas to separate words in a series.
11. _Sentences will vary._

Directions: Write a sentence using commas to separate geographical names.
12. _Sentences will vary._

Directions: Write a sentence using commas to separate dates.
13. _Sentences will vary._

Page 148

Commas

Commas are used to separate a noun or pronoun in a direct address from the rest of the sentence. A noun or pronoun in a **direct address** is one that names or refers to the person addressed.

Examples:
John, this room is a mess!
This room, **John,** is a disgrace!
Your room needs to be more organized, **John.**

Commas are used to separate an appositive from the rest of the sentence. An **appositive** is a word or words that give the reader more information about a previous noun or pronoun.

Examples:
My teacher, **Ms. Wright,** gave us a test.
Thomas Edison, **the inventor of the lightbulb,** was an interesting man.

Directions: Place commas where needed in these sentences. Then write **appositive** or **direct address** on the line to explain why the commas were used.

1. Melissa, do you know the answer? _direct address_
2. John, the local football hero, led the parade through town. _appositive_
3. Cancun, a Mexican city, is a favorite vacation destination. _appositive_
4. Please help me move the chair, Gail. _direct address_
5. My great-grandfather, an octogenarian, has witnessed many events. _appositive_
6. The president of the company, Madison Fagan, addressed his workers. _appositive_
7. My favorite book, Anne of Green Gables, is a joy to read. _appositive_
8. Your painting, Andre, shows great talent. _direct address_

GRADE 5

Page 149

Combining Sentences

When the subjects are the same, sentences can be combined by using appositives.

Examples:
Tony likes to play basketball. Tony is my neighbor.
Tony, **my neighbor**, likes to play basketball.

Ms. Herman was sick today. Ms. Herman is our math teacher.
Ms. Herman, **our math teacher**, was sick today.

Appositives are set off from the rest of the sentence with commas.

Directions: Use commas and appositives to combine the pairs of sentences.

1. Julie has play practice today. Julie is my sister.
   Julie, my sister, has play practice today.
2. Greg fixed my bicycle. Greg is my cousin.
   Greg, my cousin, fixed my bicycle.
3. Mr. Scott told us where to meet. Mr. Scott is our coach.
   Mr. Scott, our coach, told us where to meet.
4. Tiffany is moving to Detroit. Tiffany is my neighbor.
   Tiffany, my neighbor, is moving to Detroit.
5. Kyle has the flu. Kyle is my brother.
   Kyle, my brother, has the flu.
6. My favorite football team is playing tonight. Houston is my favorite team.
   My favorite football team, Houston, is playing tonight.
7. Bonnie Pryor will be at our school next week. Bonnie Pryor is a famous author.
   Bonnie Pryor, a famous author, will be at our school next week.
8. Our neighborhood is having a garage sale. Our neighborhood is the North End.
   Our neighborhood, the North End, is having a garage sale.

Page 150

Punctuation

Directions: Add commas where needed. Put the correct punctuation at the end of each sentence.

1. My friend, Jamie, loves to snowboard.
2. Winter sports such as hockey, skiing and skating are fun.
3. Oh, what a lovely view!
4. The map shows the continents of Asia, Africa, Australia and Antarctica.
5. My mother, a ballet dancer, will perform tonight.
6. What will you do tomorrow?
7. When will the plane arrive at the airport?
8. Jason, do you know what time it is?
9. Friends of ours, the Watsons, are coming for dinner.
10. Margo, look out for that falling rock!
11. The young child sat reading a book.
12. Who wrote this letter?
13. My sister, Jill, is very neat.
14. The trampoline is in our backyard.
15. We will have chicken, peas, rice and salad for dinner.
16. That dog, a Saint Bernard, looks dangerous.

Page 151

Quotation Marks

When a person's exact words are used in a sentence, **quotation marks** (" ") are used to identify those words. Commas are used to set off the quotation from the rest of the sentence. End punctuation is placed inside the final quotation mark.

Examples:
"When are we leaving?" Joe asked.
Marci shouted, "Go, team!"

When a sentence is interrupted by words that are not part of the quotation (he said, she answered, etc.), they are not included in the quotation marks. Note how commas are used in the next example.

Example: "I am sorry," the man announced, "for my rude behavior."

Directions: Place quotation marks, commas and other punctuation where needed in the sentences below.

1. "Watch out!" yelled Dad.
2. Angela said, "I don't know how you can eat Brussels sprouts, Ted."
3. "Put on your coats," said Mom. "We'll be leaving in 10 minutes."
4. "Did you hear the assignment?" asked Joan.
5. Jim shouted, "This game is driving me up the wall!"
6. After examining our dog, the veterinarian said, "He looks healthy and strong."
7. The toddlers both wailed, "We want ice cream!"
8. The judge announced to the swimmers, "Take your places."
9. Upon receiving the award, the actor said, "I'd like to thank my friends and family."
10. "These are my favorite chips," said Becky.
11. "This test is too hard," moaned the class.
12. When their relay team came in first place, the runners shouted, "Hooray!"
13. "Where shall we go on vacation this year?" Dad asked.
14. As we walked past the machinery, the noise was deafening. "Cover your ears," said Mom.
15. "Fire!" yelled the chef as his pan ignited.
16. "I love basketball," my little brother stated.

Page 152

Capitalization/Punctuation

Directions: Rewrite the paragraphs below, adding punctuation where it is needed. Capitalize the first word of each sentence and all other words that should be capitalized.

most countries have laws that control advertising in norway no ads at all are allowed on radio or TV in the united states ads for alcoholic drinks, except beer and wine, are not permitted on radio or TV england has a law against advertising cigarettes on TV what do you think about these laws should they be even stricter

Most countries have laws that control advertising. In Norway, no ads at all are allowed on radio or TV. In the United States, ads for alcoholic drinks, except beer and wine, are not permitted on radio or TV. England has a law against advertising cigarettes on TV. What do you think about these laws? Should they be even stricter?

my cousin jeff is starting college this fall he wants to be a medical doctor, so he's going to central university the mayor of our town went there mayor stevens told jeff all about the university our town is so small that everyone knows what everyone else is doing is your town like that

My cousin, Jeff, is starting college this fall. He wants to be a medical doctor, so he's going to Central University. The mayor of our town went there. Mayor Stevens told Jeff all about the university. Our town is so small that everyone knows what everyone else is doing. Is your town like that?

my grandparents took a long vacation last year grandma really likes to go to the atlantic ocean and watch the dolphins my grandfather likes to fish in the ocean my aunt went with them last summer they all had a party on the fourth of july

My grandparents took a long vacation last year. Grandma really likes to go to the Atlantic Ocean and watch the dolphins. My grandfather likes to fish in the ocean. My aunt went with them last summer. They all had a party on the Fourth of July.

Page 153

Capitalization

Directions: Write **C** if capital letters are used correctly or **X** if they are used incorrectly.

X 1. Who will win the election for Mayor in November?
C 2. Tom Johnson used to be a police officer.
X 3. He announced on monday that he wants to be mayor.
C 4. My father said he would vote for Tom.
C 5. Mom and my sister Judy haven't decided yet.
C 6. They will vote at our school.
X 7. Every Fall and Spring they put up voting booths there.
C 8. I hope the new mayor will do something about our river.
X 9. That River is full of chemicals.
C 10. I'm glad our water doesn't come from Raven River.
X 11. In late Summer, the river actually stinks.
X 12. Is every river in our State so dirty?
C 13. Scientists check the water every so often.
C 14. Some professors from the college even examined it.
X 15. That is getting to be a very educated River!

Directions: Write sentences that include:

16. A person's title that should be capitalized.
17. The name of a place that should be capitalized.
18. The name of a time (month, holiday) that should be capitalized.

Answers will vary.

Page 154

"Who" Clauses

A **clause** is a group of words with a subject and a verb. When the subject of two sentences is the same person or people, the sentences can sometimes be combined with a "who" clause.

Examples:
Mindy likes animals. Mindy feeds the squirrels.
Mindy, **who likes animals**, feeds the squirrels.

A "who" clause is set off from the rest of the sentence with commas.

Directions: Combine the pairs of sentences, using "who" clauses.

1. Teddy was late to school. Teddy was sorry later.
   Teddy, who was late to school, was sorry later.
2. Our principal is retiring. Our principal will be 65 this year.
   Our principal, who will be 65 this year, is retiring.
3. Michael won the contest. Michael will receive an award.
   Michael, who won the contest, will receive an award.
4. Charlene lives next door. Charlene has three cats.
   Charlene, who lives next door, has three cats.
5. Burt drew that picture. Burt takes art lessons.
   Burt, who drew that picture, takes art lessons.
6. Marta was elected class president. Marta gave a speech.
   Marta, who was elected class president, gave a speech.
7. Amy broke her arm. Amy has to wear a cast for 6 weeks.
   Amy, who broke her arm, has to wear a cast for 6 weeks.
8. Dr. Bank fixed my tooth. He said it would feel better soon.
   Dr. Bank, who fixed my tooth, said it would feel better soon.

Answer Key   327   Total Basic Skills Grade 5

Page 155

"Which" Clauses

When the subject of two sentences is the same thing or things, the sentences can sometimes be combined with a "which" clause.

Examples:
The guppy was first called "the millions fish." The guppy was later named after Reverend Robert Guppy in 1866.
The guppy, **which was first called "the millions fish,"** was later named after Reverend Robert Guppy in 1866.

A "which" clause is set off from the rest of the sentence with commas.

Directions: Combine the pairs of sentences using "which" clauses.

1. Guppies, which also used to be called rainbow fish, were brought to Germany in 1908.
2. The male guppy, which is about 1 inch long, is smaller than the female.
3. The guppies' colors, which range from red to violet, are brighter in the males.
4. Baby guppies, which hatch from eggs inside the mothers' bodies, are born alive.
5. The young, which are usually born at night, are called "fry."
6. Female guppies, which have 2 to 50 fry at one time, sometimes try to eat their fry!
7. These fish, which have been studied by scientists, actually like dirty water.
8. Wild guppies, which eat mosquito eggs, help control the mosquito population.

Page 156

"That" Clauses

When the subject of two sentences is the same thing or things, the sentences can sometimes be combined with a "that" clause. We use **that** instead of **which** when the clause is very important in the sentence.

Examples:
The store is near our house. The store was closed.
The store **that is near our house** was closed.

The words "**that is near our house**" are very important in the combined sentence. They tell the reader which store was closed. A "that" clause is not set off from the rest of the sentence with commas.

Examples:
Pete's store is near our house. Pete's store was closed.
Pete's store, which is near our house, was closed.

The words "**which is near our house**" are not important to the meaning of the combined sentence. The words **Pete's store** already told us which store was closed.

Directions: Combine the pairs of sentences using "that" clauses.

1. The dog lives next door. The dog chased me.
   The dog that lives next door chased me.
2. The bus was taking us to the game. The bus had a flat tire.
   The bus that was taking us to the game had a flat tire.
3. The fence is around the school. The fence is painted yellow.
   The fence that is around the school is painted yellow.
4. The notebook had my homework in it. The notebook is lost.
   The notebook that had my homework in it is lost.
5. A letter came today. The letter was from Mary.
   A letter that was from Mary came today.
6. The lamp was fixed yesterday. The lamp doesn't work today.
   The lamp that was fixed yesterday doesn't work today.
7. The lake is by our cabin. The lake is filled with fish.
   The lake that is by our cabin is filled with fish.

Page 157

"That" and "Which" Clauses

Directions: Combine the pairs of sentences using either a "that" or a "which" clause.

1. The TV show was on at 8:00 last night. The TV show was funny.
   The TV show that was on at 8:00 last night was funny.
2. *The Snappy Show* was on at 8:00 last night. *The Snappy Show* was funny.
   The Snappy Show, which was on at 8:00 last night, was funny.
3. The Main Bank is on the corner. The Main Bank is closed today.
   The Main Bank, which is on the corner, is closed today.
4. The bank is on the corner. The bank is closed today.
   The bank that is on the corner is closed today.
5. The bus takes Dad to work. The bus broke down.
   The bus that takes Dad to work broke down.
6. The Broad Street bus takes Dad to work. The Broad Street bus broke down.
   The Broad Street bus, which takes Dad to work, broke down.

Page 158

Combining Sentences

Not every pair of sentences can be combined with "who," "which" or "that" clauses. These sentences can be combined in other ways, either with a conjunction or by renaming the subject.

Examples:
I'm couldn't go to sleep. Todd was sleeping soundly.
Tim couldn't go to sleep, **but** Todd was sleeping soundly.

The zoo keeper fed the baby ape. A crowd gathered to watch.
When the zoo keeper fed the baby ape, a crowd gathered to watch.

Directions: Combine each pair of sentences using "who," "which" or "that" clauses, by using a conjunction or by renaming the subject.

1. The box slipped off the truck. The box was filled with bottles.
   The box that was filled with bottles slipped off the truck.
2. Carolyn is our scout leader. Carolyn taught us a new game.
   Carolyn, who is our scout leader, taught us a new game.
3. The girl is 8 years old. The girl called the emergency number when her grandmother fell.
   The girl, who is 8 years old, called the emergency number when her grandmother fell.
4. The meatloaf is ready to eat. The salad isn't made yet.
   The meatloaf is ready to eat, but the salad isn't made yet.
5. The rain poured down. The rain canceled our picnic.
   The rain poured down and canceled our picnic.
6. The sixth grade class went on a field trip. The school was much quieter.
   When the sixth grade class went on a field trip, the school was much quieter.

Page 159

"Who's" and "Whose"

Who's is a contraction for **who is**.
Whose is a possessive pronoun.

Examples:
Who's going to come?
Whose shirt is this?

To know which word to use, substitute the words "who is." If the sentence makes sense, use **who's**.

Directions: Write the correct word to complete these sentences.

who's 1. Do you know who's/whose invited to the party?
whose 2. I don't even know who's/whose house it will be at.
Whose 3. Who's/Whose towel is on the floor?
Who's 4. Who's/Whose going to drive us?
Whose 5. Who's/Whose ice cream is melting?
whose 6. I'm the person who's/whose gloves are lost.
Who's 7. Who's/Whose in your group?
Whose 8. Who's/Whose group is first?
who's 9. Can you tell who's/whose at the door?
Whose 10. Who's/Whose friend are you?
Who's 11. Who's/Whose cooking tonight?
Whose 12. Who's/Whose cooking do you like best?

Page 160

"Their," "There" and "They're"

Their is a possessive pronoun meaning belonging to them.
There is an adverb that indicates place.
They're is a contraction for **they are**.

Examples:
Dan and Sue took **their** dog to the park.
They like to go **there** on Sunday afternoon.
They're probably going back next Sunday, too.

Directions: Write the correct words to complete these sentences.

their 1. All the students should bring their/there/they're books to class.
there 2. I've never been to France, but I hope to travel their/there/they're someday.
their 3. We studied how dolphins care for their/there/they're young.
they're 4. My parents are going on vacation next week, and their/there/they're taking my sister.
There 5. Their/There/They're was a lot of food at the party.
their 6. My favorite baseball team lost their/there/they're star pitcher this year.
they're 7. Those peaches look good, but their/there/they're not ripe yet.
there 8. The book is right their/there/they're on the table.

Page 161

"Teach" and "Learn"

Teach is a verb meaning "to explain something." Teach is an irregular verb. Its past tense is **taught**.

Learn is a verb meaning "to gain information."

Examples:
Carrie will **teach** me how to play the piano.
Yesterday she **taught** me "Chopsticks."

I will **learn** a new song every week.
Yesterday I **learned** to play "Chopsticks."

Directions: Write the correct words to complete these sentences.

1. taught — My brother taught/learned me how to ice skate.
2. learned — With his help, I taught/learned in three days.
3. learn — First, I tried to teach/learn skating from a book.
4. learn — I couldn't teach/learn that way.
5. learn — You have to try it before you can really teach/learn how to do it.
6. teach — Now I'm going to teach/learn my cousin.
7. learned — My cousin already taught/learned how to roller skate.
8. teaching — I shouldn't have any trouble teaching/learning her how to ice skate.
9. taught — Who taught/learned you how to skate?
10. taught — My brother taught/learned Mom how to skate, too.
11. learn — My mother took longer to teach/learn it than I did.
12. teach — Who will he teach/learn next?
13. learn — Do you know anyone else who wants to teach/learn how to ice skate?
14. teach — My brother will teach/learn you for free.
15. learn — You should teach/learn how to ice skate in the wintertime, though. The ice is a little thin in the summer!

Page 162

"Lie" and "Lay"

Lie is a verb meaning "to rest." Lie is an intransitive verb that doesn't need a direct object.

Lay is a verb meaning "to place or put something down." Lay is a transitive verb that requires a direct object.

Examples:
Lie here for a while. (**Lie** has no direct object; **here** is an adverb.)
Lay the book here. (**Lay** has a direct object: **book**.)

Lie and lay are especially tricky because they are both irregular verbs. Notice the past tense of lie is lay!

Present tense	ing form	Past tense	Past participle
lie	lying	lay	has/have/had lain
lay	laying	laid	has/have/had laid

Examples:
I **lie** here today.
I **lay** here yesterday.
I **was lying** there for three hours.

I **lay** the baby in her bed.
I will **be laying** her down in a minute.
I **laid** her in her bed last night, too.

Directions: Write the correct words to complete these sentences.

1. lays — Shelly lies/lays a blanket on the grass.
2. lies — Then she lies/lays down in the sun.
3. lies — Her dog lies/lays there with her.
4. laid — Yesterday, Shelly lay/laid in the sun for an hour.
5. laying — The workers are lying/laying bricks for a house.
6. laid — Yesterday, they lay/laid a ton of them.
7. lay — They lie/lay one brick on top of the other.
8. lay — The bricks just lie/lay in a pile until the workers are ready for them.
9. lie — At lunchtime, some workers lie/lay down for a nap.
10. lay — Would you like to lie/lay bricks?
11. laid — Last year, my uncle lay/laid bricks for his new house.
12. laid — He was so tired every day that he lay/laid down as soon as he finished.

Page 163

"Rise" and "Raise"

Rise is a verb meaning "to get up" or "to go up." Rise is an intransitive verb that doesn't need a direct object.

Raise is a verb meaning "to lift" or "to grow." Raise is a transitive verb that requires a direct object.

Examples:
The curtain **rises**.
The girl **raises** her hand.

Raise is a regular verb. Rise is irregular.

Present tense	Past tense	Past participle
rise	rose	has/have/had risen
raise	raised	has/have/had raised

Examples:
The sun **rose** this morning.
The boy **raised** the window higher.

Directions: Write the correct words to complete these sentences.

1. rises — This bread dough rises/raises in an hour.
2. raise — The landlord will rise/raise the rent.
3. rose — The balloon rose/raised into the sky.
4. raised — My sister rose/raised the seat on my bike.
5. raised — The baby rose/raised the spoon to his mouth.
6. rose — The eagle rose/raised out of sight.
7. raises — The farmer rises/raises pigs.
8. raised — The scouts rose/raised the flag.
9. rose — When the fog rose/raised, we could see better.
10. rose — The price of ice cream rose/raised again.
11. raised — The king rose/raised the glass to his lips.
12. Raise — Rise/Raise the picture on that wall higher.

Page 164

"All Right," "All Ready" and "Already"

All right means "well enough" or "very well." Sometimes **all right** is incorrectly spelled. **Alright** is not a word.

Example:
Correct: We'll be **all right** when the rain stops.
Incorrect: Are you feeling **alright** today?

All ready is an adjective meaning "completely ready."

Already is an adverb meaning "before this time" or "by this time."

Examples:
Are you **all ready** to go?
He was **already** there when I arrived.

Directions: Write the correct words to complete these sentences.

1. all ready — The children are all ready/already for the picnic.
2. already — Ted was all ready/already late for the show.
3. all right — Is your sister going to be all right/alright?
4. already — I was all ready/already tired before the race began.
5. already — Joan has all ready/already left for the dance.
6. all right — Will you be all right/alright by yourself?
7. all ready — We are all ready/already for our talent show.
8. already — I all ready/already read that book.
9. all ready — I want to be all ready/already when they get here.
10. all right — Dad was sick, but he's all right/alright now.
11. all ready — The dinner is all ready/already to eat.
12. already — Cathy all ready/already wrote her report.

Page 166

Writing: Topic Sentences

The topic sentence in a paragraph usually comes first. Sometimes, however, the topic sentence can come at the end or even in the middle of a paragraph. When looking for the topic sentence, try to find the one that tells the main idea of a paragraph.

Directions: Read the following paragraphs and underline the topic sentence in each.

The maple tree sheds its leaves every year. The oak and elm trees shed their leaves, too. Every autumn, the leaves on these trees begin changing color. Then, as the leaves gradually begin to die, they fall from the trees. <u>Trees that shed their leaves annually are called deciduous trees.</u>

When our family goes skiing, my brother enjoys the thrill of going down the steepest hill as fast as he can. Mom and Dad like to ski because it gets them out of the house and into the fresh air. I enjoy looking at the trees and birds and the sun shining on the snow. <u>There is something about skiing that appeals to everyone in my family.</u> Even the dog came along on our last skiing trip!

If you are outdoors at night and there is traffic around, you should always wear bright clothing so that cars can see you. White is a good color to wear at night. If you are riding a bicycle, be sure it has plenty of reflectors, and if possible, headlamps as well. Be especially careful when crossing the street, because sometimes drivers cannot see you in the glare of their headlights. <u>Being outdoors at night can be dangerous, and it is best to be prepared!</u>

Page 167

Writing: Supporting Sentences

A **paragraph** is a group of sentences that tell about one topic. The **topic sentence** in a paragraph usually comes first and tells the main idea of the paragraph. **Supporting sentences** follow the topic sentence and provide details about the topic.

Directions: Write at least three supporting sentences for each topic sentence below.

Example: Topic Sentence: Carly had an accident on her bike.
Supporting Sentences: She was on her way to the store to buy some bread. A car came weaving down the road and scared her. She rode her bike off the road so the car wouldn't hit her. Now, her knee is scraped, but she's all right.

1. I've been thinking of ways I could make some more money after school.

2. In my opinion, cats (dogs, fish, etc.) make the best pets.

3. My life ... older ... sister, younger brother, older sister,

4. I'd like to live next door to a (swimming pool, video store, movie theater, etc.).

Answers will vary.

Page 168

Writing: Building Paragraphs

Directions: Read the groups of topic sentences and questions below. On another sheet of paper, write supporting sentences that answer the questions. Use your imagination! Write the supporting sentences in order, and copy them on this page after the topic sentence.

1. On her way home from school, Mariko made a difficult decision.
   Questions: What was Mariko's decision? Why did she decide that? Why was the decision hard to make?

2. Suddenly, Conrad thought of a way to clear up ...
   Questions: What was the confu... ...? What did he do to clear it up?

3. Bethany used to feel awkward at the school social activities.
   Questions: Why did Bethany feel awkward before? How does she feel now? What happened to change the way she feels?

Answers will vary.

Page 169

Writing: Sequencing

When writing paragraphs, it is important to write events in the correct order. Think about what happens first, next, later and last.

Directions: The following sentences tell about Chandra's day, but they are all mixed up. Read each sentence and number them in the order in which they happened.

- **3** She arrived at school and went to her locker to get her books.
- **7** After dinner, she did the dishes, then read a book for a while.
- **8** Chandra brushed her teeth and put on her pajamas.
- **5** She rode the bus home, then she fixed herself a snack.
- **2** She ate breakfast and went out to wait for the bus.
- **1** Chandra woke up and picked out her clothes for school.
- **4** She met her friend Sarah on the way to the cafeteria.
- **6** She worked on homework and watched TV until her mom called her for dinner.

Directions: Write a short paragraph about what you did today. Use words like **first**, **next**, **then**, **later** and **finally** to indicate the order in which you did things.

Paragraphs will vary.

Page 170

Sequencing

Sequencing means to place events in order from beginning to end or first to last.

Example:
To send a letter, you must:
Get paper, pencil or pen, an envelope and a stamp.
Write the letter.
Fold the letter and put it in the envelope.
Address the envelope correctly.
Put a stamp on the envelope.
Put the envelope in the mailbox or take it to the Post Office.

Directions: Write the sequence for making a peanut butter and jelly sandwich.
- Get out bread, peanut butter, jelly and knife.
- Spread jelly on one slice of bread.
- Spread peanut butter on the other slice of bread.
- Put the two pieces of bread together so peanut butter and jelly sides are together.
- Put away knife, peanut butter and jelly.
- Enjoy your sandwich.

Directions: After you finish, try making the sandwich **exactly** the way you wrote the steps. Did you leave out any steps? Which ones?

Does a particular section ... explanation by adding mi...

Answers will vary.

Page 171

Author's Purpose

Authors write to fulfill one of three purposes: to **inform**, to **entertain** or to **persuade**.
Authors who write to inform are providing facts for the reader in an informational context.
Examples: Encyclopedia entries and newspaper articles
Authors who write to entertain are hoping to provide enjoyment for the reader.
Examples: Funny stories and comics
Authors who write to persuade are trying to convince the reader to believe as they believe.
Examples: Editorials and opinion essays

Directions: Read each paragraph. Write **inform**, **entertain** or **persuade** on the line to show the author's purpose.

1. The whooping crane is a migratory bird. At one time, this endangered bird was almost extinct. These large white cranes are characterized by red faces and trumpeting calls. Through protection of both the birds and their habitats, the whooping crane is slowly increasing in number.
   inform

2. It is extremely important that all citizens place bird feeders in their yards and keep them full for the winter. Birds that spend the winter in this area are in danger of starving due to lack of food. It is every citizen's responsibility to ensure the survival of the birds.
   persuade

3. Imagine being able to hibernate like a bear each winter! Wouldn't it be great to eat to your heart's content all fall? Then, sometime in late November, inform your teacher that you will not be attending school for the next few months because you'll be resting and living off your fat? Now, that would be the life!
   entertain

4. Bears, woodchucks and chipmunks are not the only animals that hibernate. The queen bumblebee also hibernates in winter. All the other bees die before winter arrives. The queen hibernates under leaves in a small hole. She is cold-blooded and therefore is able to survive slightly frozen.
   inform

Page 172

Author's Purpose

Directions: Write a paragraph of your own for each purpose. The paragraph can be about any topic.

1. to inform

2. to persuade

3. to entertain

Answers will vary.

Directions: Reread your paragraphs. Do they make sense? Check for grammar, spelling and punctuation errors and make corrections where needed.

Total Basic Skills Grade 5 — Answer Key

Page 173

Descriptive Sentences

Descriptive sentences give readers a vivid image and enable them to imagine a scene clearly.

Example:
Nondescriptive sentence: There were grapes in the bowl.
Descriptive sentence: The plump purple grapes in the bowl looked tantalizing.

Directions: Rewrite these sentences using descriptive language.

1. The dog walked in its pen.
2. The turkey was almost done.
3. I became upset when my computer wouldn't work.
4. Jared and Michelle went to the ice-cream parlor.
5. The telephone rang.
6. I wrote a letter.
7. The movie was excellent.
8. Dominique was upset that her friend was ill.

Sentences will vary.

Page 174

Writing: Descriptive Details

A writer creates pictures in a reader's mind by telling him/her how something looks, sounds, feels, smells or tastes. For example, compare **A** and **B** below. Notice how the description in **B** makes you imagine how the heavy door and the cobweb would feel and how the broken glass would look and sound as someone walked on it.

A. I walked into the house.
B. I pushed open the heavy wooden door of the old house. A cobweb brushed my face, and broken glass, sparkling like ice, crushed under my feet.

Directions: Write one or two sentences about each topic below. Add details that will help your reader see, hear, feel, smell or taste what you are describing.

1. Your favorite dinner cooking
2. Old furniture
3. Wind blowing in the trees
4.
5. Wearing wet clothes
6. A strange noise somewhere in the house

Sentences will vary.

Page 175

Writing: Descriptive Details

Directions: For each topic sentence below, write three or four supporting sentences. Include details about how things look, sound, smell, taste or feel. Don't forget to use adjectives, adverbs, similes and metaphors.

Example: After my dog had his bath, I couldn't believe how much better he looked. His fur, which used to be all matted and dirty, was as clean as new snow. He still felt a little damp when I scratched behind his ears. The smell from rolling in our garbage was gone, too. He smelled like apples now because of the shampoo.

1. My little cousin's birthday party was almost over.
2. I always keep my grandpa company while he bakes.
3. By th... a mess.
4. Early morning is the best time to go for a bike ride.

Answers will vary.

Page 176

Personal Narratives

A **personal narrative** tells about a person's own experiences.

Directions: Read the example of a personal narrative. Write your answers in complete sentences.

My Worst Year

When I look back on that year, I can hardly believe that one person could have such terrible luck for a whole year. But then again, I should have realized that if things could begin to go wrong in January, it didn't bode well for the rest of the year.

It was the night of January 26. One of my best friends was celebrating her birthday at the local roller-skating rink, and I had been invited. The evening began well enough with pizza and laughs. I admit I have never been a cracker jack roller skater, but I could hold my own. After a few minutes of skating, I decided to exit the rink for a cold soda. Unfortunately, I did not notice the trailing ribbons of carpet which wrapped around the wheel of my skate, yanking my left leg from under me. My leg was broken. It wasn't just broken in one place but in four places! At the hospital, the doctor set the bone and put a cast on my leg. Three months later, I felt like a new person.

Sadly, the happiness wasn't meant to last. Five short months after the final cast was removed, I fell and broke the same leg again. Not only did it rebreak but it broke in the same four places! We found out later that it hadn't healed correctly. Three months later, it was early December and the end of a year I did not wish to repeat.

1. List the sequence of events in this personal narrative.
   January 26: fell while skating and broke leg in four places.
   Three months later: cast removed.
   Five months later: fell and broke leg again in same four places.

2. From reading the personal narrative, what do you think were the author's feelings toward the events that occurred?
   Answers will vary.

Page 177

Personal Narratives

A **narrative** is a spoken or written account of an actual event. A **personal narrative** tells about your own experience. It can be written about any event in your life and may be serious or comical.

When writing a personal narrative, remember to use correct sentence structure and punctuation. Include important dates, sights, sounds, smells, tastes and feelings to give your reader a clear picture of the event.

Directions: Write a personal narrative about an event in your life that was funny.

Narratives will vary.

Page 178

Complete the Story

Directions: Read the beginning of this story. Then complete the story with your own ideas.

It was a beautiful summer day in June when my family and I set off on vacation. We were headed for Portsmouth, New Hampshire. There we planned to go on a whale-watching ship and perhaps spy a humpback whale or two. However, there were many miles between our home and Portsmouth.

We camped at many lovely parks along the way to New Hampshire. We stayed in the Adirondack Mountains for a few days and then visited the White Mountains of Vermont before crossing into New Hampshire.

My family enjoys tent camping. My dad says you can't really get a taste of the great outdoors in a pop-up camper or RV. I love sitting by the fire at night, gazing at the stars and listening to the animal noises.

The trip was going well, and everyone was enjoying our vacation. We made it to Portsmouth and were looking forward to the whale-watching adventure. We arrived at the dock a few minutes early. The ocean looked rough, but we had taken seasickness medication. We thought we were prepared for any kind of weather.

Stories will vary.

Page 179

Answers will vary.

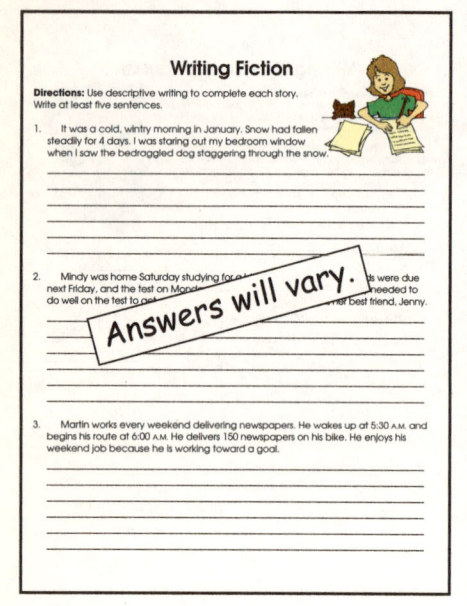

Page 180

Paragraphs will vary.

Page 181

Friendly Letters

A **friendly letter** has these parts: return address, date, greeting, body, closing and signature.

Directions: Read this letter. Then label the parts of the letter.

- return address → 222 West Middle Street, Boise, Idaho 33444
- May 17, 1999 → date
- Dear Blaine, ← greeting
- body → Hello! I know I haven't written in several weeks, but I've been very busy with school and baseball practice. How have you been? How is the weather in Boston? It is finally getting warm in Boise. As I mentioned, I am playing baseball this year. My team is called the Rockets, and we are really good. We have a terrific coach. We practice two nights a week and play games on the weekends. Are you playing baseball?
  I can hardly wait to visit you this summer. I can't believe I'll be flying on an airplane and staying with you and your family for 2 weeks! There is probably a lot to do in Boston. When you write, tell me some ideas you have for the 2 weeks.
- closing → Your friend,
- signature → Mason

Envelopes should follow this format:

Mason Fitch
222 West Middle Street
Boise, ID 33444

  Blaine Morgan
  111 E. 9th Street, Apt 22B
  Boston, MA 00011

Page 182

Letters should follow format given.

Page 183

Paragraphs will vary.

Page 184

Answers will vary.

Page 185

Writing a Summary

A **summary** is a short description of what a selection or book is about.

Directions: Read the following selection and the example summary.

Fads of the 1950s

A fad is a practice or an object that becomes very popular for a period of time. Recent popular fads include yo-yos and Beanie Babies®. In the 1950s, there were many different fads, including coonskin caps, hula hoops and 3-D movies.

Coonskin caps were made popular by the weekly television show about Davy Crockett, which began in December of 1954. Not only did Davy's hat itself become popular but anything with Davy Crockett on it was in hot demand.

Also popular were hula hoops. They were produced by the Wham-O company in 1958. The company had seen similar toys in Australia. Hula hoops were priced at $1.98, and over 30 million hoops were sold within 6 months.

Another fad was the 3-D movie. When television sets began to appear in every American home, the movie industry began to suffer financially. Movie companies rushed to produce 3-D movies, and movie-goers once more flocked to theaters. The first 3-D movie was shown in Los Angeles on November 26, 1952. People loved the special Polaroid® glasses and scenes in the movie that seemed to jump out at them. As with the hula hoop and Davy Crockett, people soon tired of 3-D movies, and they became old news as they were replaced by new fads.

Summary

Over the years, many fads have become popular with the American public. During the 1950s, three popular fads were the hula hoop, Davy Crockett and 3-D movies. Davy Crockett's coonskin cap became a fad with the beginning of the weekly television show. Hula hoops were sold by the millions, and 3-D movies were enjoyed by people everywhere. However, like all fads, interest in these items soon died out.

Page 186

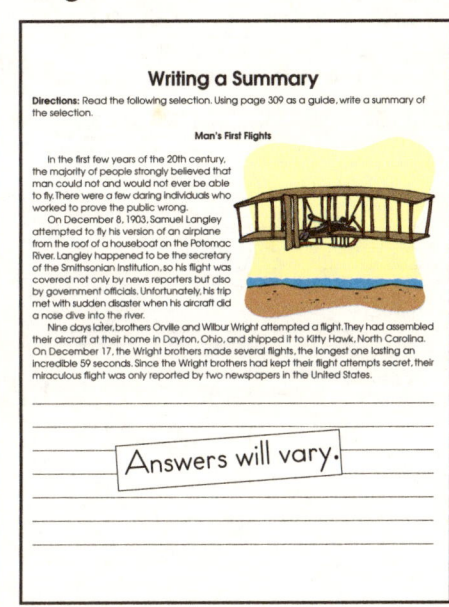

Writing a Summary

Directions: Read the following selection. Using page 309 as a guide, write a summary of the selection.

Man's First Flights

In the first few years of the 20th century, the majority of people strongly believed that man could not and would not ever be able to fly. There were a few daring individuals who worked to prove the public wrong.

On December 8, 1903, Samuel Langley attempted to fly his version of an airplane from the roof of a houseboat on the Potomac River. Langley happened to be the secretary of the Smithsonian Institution, so his flight was covered not only by news reporters but also by government officials. Unfortunately, his trip met with sudden disaster when his aircraft did a nose dive into the river.

Nine days later, brothers Orville and Wilbur Wright attempted a flight. They had assembled their aircraft at their home in Dayton, Ohio, and shipped it to Kitty Hawk, North Carolina. On December 17, the Wright brothers made several flights, the longest one lasting an incredible 59 seconds. Since the Wright brothers had kept their flight attempts secret, their miraculous flight was only reported by two newspapers in the United States.

Answers will vary.

Page 187

Comparing and Contrasting

When writing comparison/contrast essays, it is helpful to write one paragraph which contains all the similarities and another paragraph which contains all the differences.

Directions: Write an essay in response to the prompt.

Writing Prompt: Think of your brother, sister or a friend. What similarities are there between you and this person? What differences are there?

Answers will vary.

Directions: When you finish writing, reread your essay. Use this checklist to help make corrections.

☐ My essay makes sense.
☐ I listed at least two similarities and two differences.
☐ My sentences are correctly written.
☐ I used correct spelling, grammar and punctuation.

Page 188

Advantages and Disadvantages

As in the comparison/contrast essay, it is easiest to put all of the advantages in one paragraph and the disadvantages in another paragraph.

Directions: Write an essay in response to the prompt.

Writing Prompt: Think about what a society would be like if all people had the same skin tone, hair color, eye color, height and weight. What would the benefits of living in such a society be? Would there be any disadvantages? What would they be?

Answers will vary.

Directions: When you finish writing, reread your essay. Use this checklist to help make corrections.

☐ My essay makes sense.
☐ I used correct spelling, grammar and punctuation.
☐ I answered the writing prompt.
☐ I have varied sentence length.

Page 189

Newswriting

Newswriting is a style of writing used by newspaper reporters and other journalists who write for periodicals. **Periodicals** are newspapers, magazines and newsletters that are published regularly.

Magazine and newspaper writers organize their ideas and their writing around what is called "the five W's and the H" — who, what, when, where, why and how. As they conduct research and interview people for articles, journalists keep these questions in mind.

Directions: Read a newspaper article of your choice. Use the information you read to answer the questions.

Who is involved? _____
Who is affected? _____
Who is responsible? _____
What is the event or subject? _____
What exactly has happened? _____

Answers will vary.

Why did it happen? _____
Why will readers care? _____
How did it happen? _____

Page 190

Newswriting: Inverted Pyramid Style

Newspaper reporters organize their news stories in what is called the **inverted pyramid** style. The inverted pyramid places the most important facts at the beginning of the story—called the lead (LEED)—and the least important facts at the end.

There are two practical reasons for this approach:

1) If the story must be shortened by an editor, he or she simply cuts paragraphs from the end of the story rather than rewriting the entire story.

2) Because newspapers contain so much information, few people read every word of every newspaper story. Instead, many readers skim headlines and opening paragraphs. The inverted pyramid style of writing enables readers to quickly get the basics of what the story is about without reading the entire story.

Directions: Read the news story. Then answer the questions.

Cleveland—Ohio State University student John Cook is within one 36-hole match of joining some of amateur golf's top performers. The 21-year-old Muirfield Village Golf Club representative will try for his second straight U.S. Amateur championship Sunday against one of his California golf buddies, Mark O'Meara, over the 6,837-yard Canterbury Golf Club course. Starting times are 8 a.m. and 12:30 p.m.

"Winning the U.S. Amateur once is a great thrill," said Cook after Saturday's breezy 5-3 semifinal decision over Alabama's Cecil Ingram III. "But winning the second time is something people don't very often do."

1. Who is the story about? __John Cook__
2. The "dateline" at the beginning of a news article tells where the event happened and where the reporter wrote the story. Where was the story about John Cook written? __Cleveland__
3. What is Cook trying to accomplish? __win second straight U.S. Amateur Championship__
4. Who did Cook beat on Saturday? __Cecil Ingram III__
5. Which of the above paragraphs could be cut by an editor? __the second one__

Answer Key — 333 — Total Basic Skills Grade 5

Page 191

Writing: Just the Facts

Paragraphs will vary.

Page 192

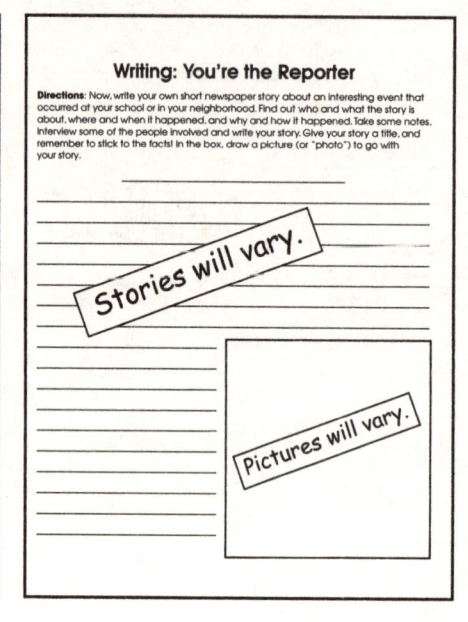

Writing: You're the Reporter

Stories will vary.

Pictures will vary.

Page 193

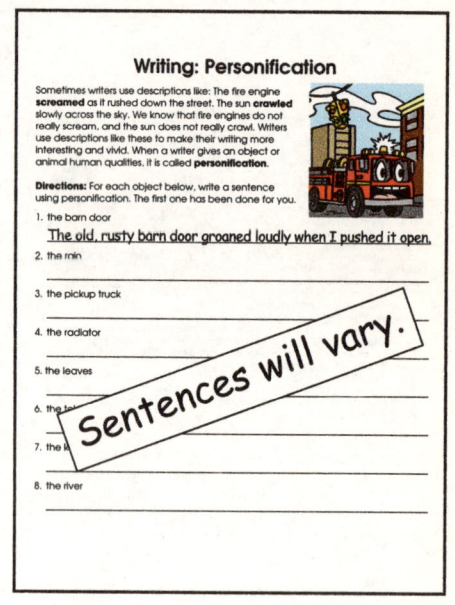

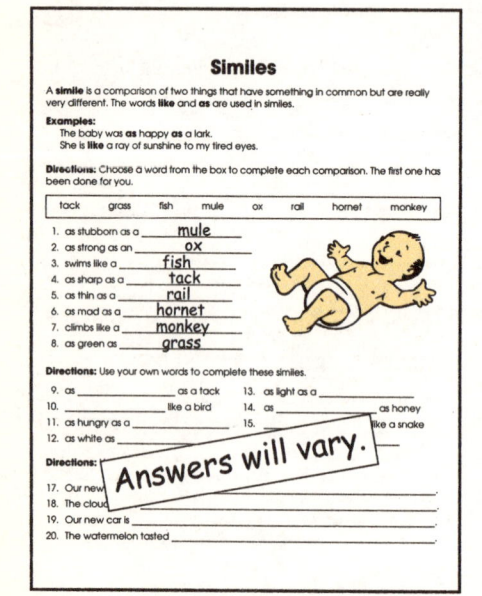

Writing: Personification

1. the barn door
   The old, rusty barn door groaned loudly when I pushed it open.
2. the rain
3. the pickup truck
4. the radiator
5. the leaves
6.–8. Sentences will vary.

Page 194

Similes

1. as stubborn as a **mule**
2. as strong as an **ox**
3. swims like a **fish**
4. as sharp as a **tack**
5. as thin as a **rail**
6. as mad as a **hornet**
7. climbs like a **monkey**
8. as green as **grass**

9.–20. Answers will vary.

Page 195

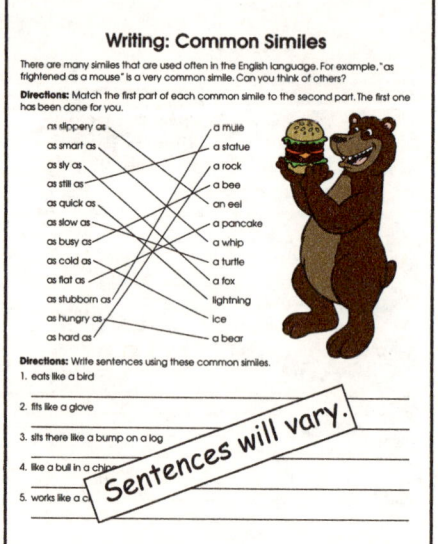

Writing: Common Similes

- as slippery as — an eel
- as smart as — a fox
- as sly as — a fox
- as still as — a statue
- as quick as — lightning
- as slow as — a turtle
- as busy as — a bee
- as cold as — ice
- as flat as — a pancake
- as stubborn as — a mule
- as hungry as — a bear
- as hard as — a rock

Sentences will vary.

Page 196

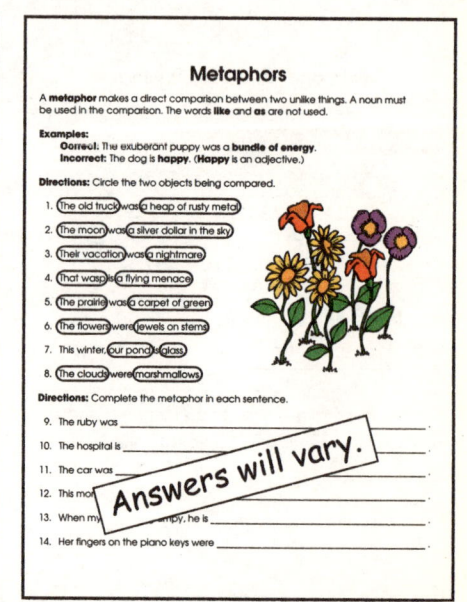

Metaphors

1. The old truck / a heap of rusty metal
2. The moon / a silver dollar in the sky
3. Their vacation / a nightmare
4. That wasp / a flying menace
5. The prairie / a carpet of green
6. The flowers / jewels on stems
7. our pond / glass
8. The clouds / marshmallows

9.–14. Answers will vary.

Answer Key — Grade 5

Page 197 — How to Write a Book Report

1. Which of these introductory sentences is more interesting?
   - ☑ Richie, a 12-year-old runaway, cries himself to sleep every night in the bowling alley where he lives.
   - ☐ Many children run away from home, and this book is about one of them, a boy named Richie.

2. In a report on a fiction book about runaways, where would these sentences go?
   "Richie's mother is dead. He and his father don't get along."
   - ☑ introduction
   - ☐ conclusion

3. In the same report, where would these sentences go?
   "Author Clark Howard has written a sad and exciting book about runaways that shows how terrible the life of a runaway can be. I strongly recommend the book to people of all ages."
   - ☐ body
   - ☑ conclusion

Page 198 — Book Report: A Book I Devoured

Answers will vary.

Page 199 — Library Research

1. Name two general encyclopedias. **Encyclopedia Americana, World Book**
2. Name three special encyclopedias. **Encyclopedia of Education, International Encyclopedia of the Social Sciences, Encyclopedia of Bioethics**
3. Which reference book contains a weekly summary of national and international news? **Facts on File**

Page 200 — Library Research

1. What index should you consult if you're researching an article about water pollution in your town? **a local newspaper index**
2. What is a "clip file"? **folders of articles cut out and saved by librarians**
3. What are two sources of information on people in the news? **Current Biography, Biography Index**

Page 201 — Fiction, Nonfiction and Biographies

Answers will vary.

Page 202 — Reports: Choosing a Topic

1. What is a report? **A report is a written paper based on the writer's research.**
2. Which general topic did you choose? **Answers will vary.**
3. What specific topic will you write about?

Page 203

Reports: Doing Research

1. How many reference sources should you consult before writing your report? **3-4**
2. What are two references that provide statistics and facts? **Facts on File, Editorial Research Reports**
3. Where will you find a listing of magazine articles? **Reader's Guide to Periodical Literature**
4. Where should you look for geographical information? **Rand McNally Contemporary World Atlas**
5. If you're stumped or don't know where to begin, who can help? **the librarian**

Page 204

Reports: Taking Notes

Answers will vary.

Page 205

Encyclopedia Skills: Taking Notes

Answers will vary.

Page 206

Reports: Making an Outline

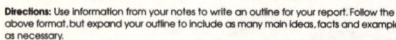

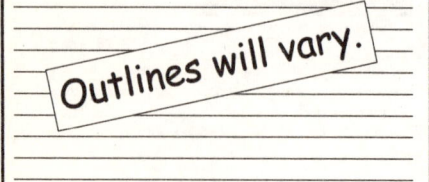

Outlines will vary.

Page 207

Reports: Writing the Paper

Word search answers: topic, facts, outline, introduction, body, conclusion, notes, research, edit

Page 208

Editing

1. T — When you are editing, you should look for correct grammar and spelling.
2. F — Editors do not look for complete sentences.
3. F — Editors do not have to read each word of a story.
4. F — It is best to use both sides of a sheet of paper when writing the rough draft of your report.
5. T — It does not matter how neat your first draft is.
6. T — Editors make sure that sentences are punctuated correctly.

Page 209

Editing

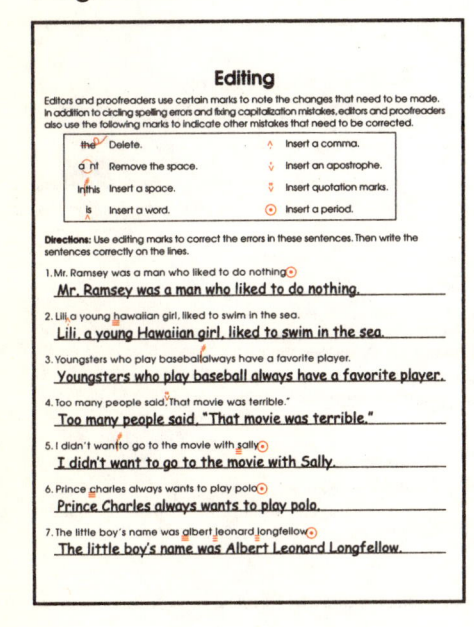

Editors and proofreaders use certain marks to note the changes that need to be made. In addition to circling spelling errors and fixing capitalization mistakes, editors and proofreaders also use the following marks to indicate other mistakes that need to be corrected.

the	Delete.	∧	Insert a comma.
a nt	Remove the space.	∨	Insert an apostrophe.
In this	Insert a space.	∨∨	Insert quotation marks.
∧ is	Insert a word.	⊙	Insert a period.

Directions: Use editing marks to correct the errors in these sentences. Then write the sentences correctly on the lines.

1. Mr. Ramsey was a man who liked to do nothing.
   Mr. Ramsey was a man who liked to do nothing.
2. Lili, a young hawaiian girl, liked to swim in the sea.
   Lili, a young Hawaiian girl, liked to swim in the sea.
3. Youngsters who play baseballalways have a favorite player.
   Youngsters who play baseball always have a favorite player.
4. Too many people said,That movie was terrible."
   Too many people said, "That movie was terrible."
5. I didn't wantto go to the movie with sally.
   I didn't want to go to the movie with Sally.
6. Prince charles always wants to play polo.
   Prince Charles always wants to play polo.
7. The little boy's name was albert leonard longfellow.
   The little boy's name was Albert Leonard Longfellow.

Page 210

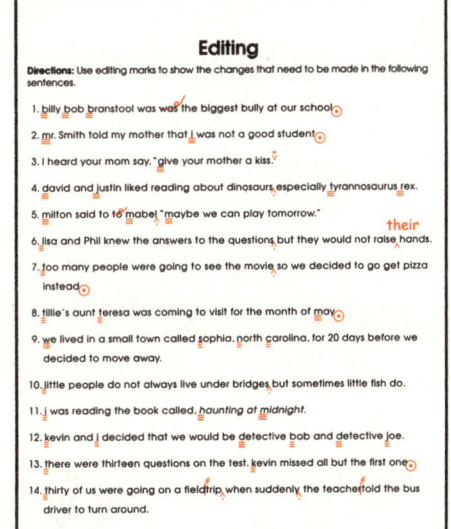

Editing

Directions: Use editing marks to show the changes that need to be made in the following sentences.

1. billy bob branstool was was the biggest bully at our school.
2. mr. Smith told my mother that i was not a good student.
3. I heard your mom say, "give your mother a kiss."
4. david and justin liked reading about dinosaurs, especially tyrannosaurus rex.
5. milton said to to mabel "maybe we can play tomorrow."
6. lisa and Phil knew the answers to the questions, but they would not raise their hands.
7. too many people were going to see the movie so we decided to go get pizza instead.
8. tillie's aunt teresa was coming to visit for the month of may.
9. we lived in a small town called sophia, north carolina, for 20 days before we decided to move away.
10. little people do not always live under bridges but sometimes little fish do.
11. i was reading the book called, haunting at midnight.
12. kevin and i decided that we would be detective bob and detective joe.
13. there were thirteen questions on the test. kevin missed all but the first one.
14. thirty of us were going on a fieldtrip, when suddenly the teacher told the bus driver to turn around.

Page 211

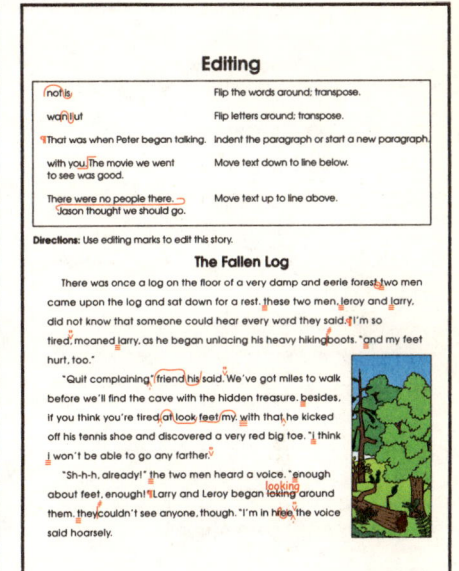

Editing

not is	Flip the words around; transpose.
wantlut	Flip letters around; transpose.
That was when Peter began talking.	Indent the paragraph or start a new paragraph.
with you. The movie we went to see was good.	Move text down to line below.
There were no people there. Jason thought we should go.	Move text up to line above.

Directions: Use editing marks to edit this story.

The Fallen Log

There was once a log on the floor of a very damp and eerie forest. two men came upon the log and sat down for a rest. these two men, leroy and larry, did not know that someone could hear every word they said. "i'm so tired," moaned larry, as he began unlacing his heavy hikingboots. "and my feet hurt, too."

"Quit complaining," friend his said. "We've got miles to walk before we'll find the cave with the hidden treasure. besides, if you think you're tired at look feet my. with that, he kicked off his tennis shoe and discovered a very red big toe. "I think I won't be able to go any farther."

"Sh-h-h, already!" the two men heard a voice. "enough about feet, enough!" Larry and Leroy began looking around them. they couldn't see anyone, though. "I'm in here," the voice said hoarsely.

Page 212

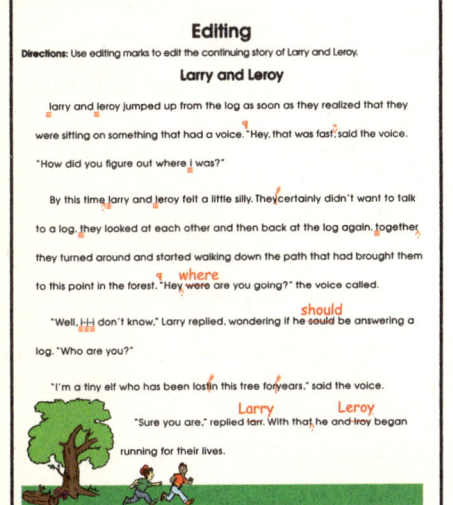

Editing

Directions: Use editing marks to edit the continuing story of Larry and Leroy.

Larry and Leroy

larry and leroy jumped up from the log as soon as they realized that they were sitting on something that had a voice. "Hey, that was fast," said the voice.

"How did you figure out where I was?"

By this time larry and leroy felt a little silly. They certainly didn't want to talk to a log. they looked at each other and then back at the log again. together they turned around and started walking down the path that had brought them to this point in the forest. "Hey, where are you going?" the voice called.

"Well, I-I don't know," Larry replied, wondering if he sould should be answering a log. "Who are you?"

"I'm a tiny elf who has been lostin this tree for years," said the voice. "Sure you are," replied larr Larry. With that, he and lroy Leroy began running for their lives.

Page 213

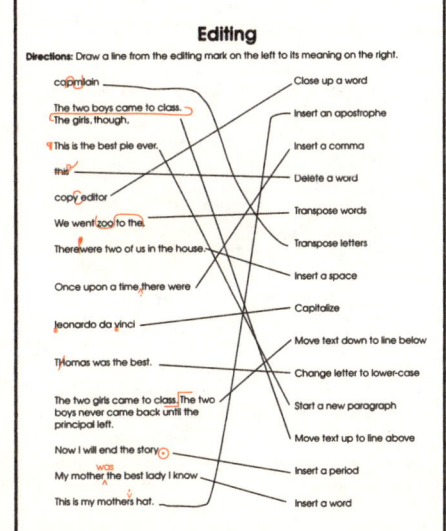

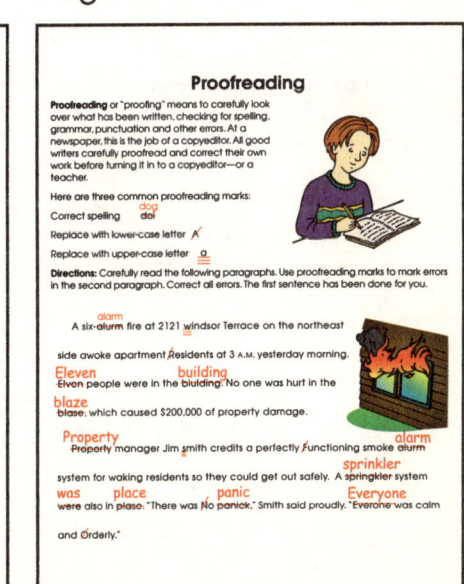

Editing

Directions: Draw a line from the editing mark on the left to its meaning on the right.

caprmplain — Close up a word
The two boys came to class. The girls, though. — Insert an apostrophe
This is the best pie ever. — Insert a comma
that — Delete a word
copy editor — Transpose words
We went zoo to the. — Transpose letters
There were two of us in the house. — Insert a space
Once upon a time there were — Capitalize
leonardo da vinci — Move text down to line below
Thomas was the best. — Change letter to lower-case
The two girls came to class. The two boys never came back until the principal left. — Start a new paragraph
Now I will end the story — Move text up to line above
My mother the best lady I know — Insert a period
This is my mothers hat. — Insert a word

Page 214

Proofreading

Proofreading or "proofing" means to carefully look over what has been written, checking for spelling, grammar, punctuation and other errors. At a newspaper, this is the job of a copyeditor. All good writers carefully proofread and correct their own work before turning it in to a copyeditor—or a teacher.

Here are three common proofreading marks:
Correct spelling   dog dol
Replace with lower-case letter   K
Replace with upper-case letter   a

Directions: Carefully read the following paragraphs. Use proofreading marks to mark errors in the second paragraph. Correct all errors. The first sentence has been done for you.

A six-alarm alarm fire at 2121 windsor Terrace on the northeast side awoke apartment Residents at 3 A.M. yesterday morning. Eleven Elven people were in the building. No one was hurt in the blaze blase, which caused $200,000 of property damage.

Property manager Jim smith credits a perfectly functioning smoke alarm alurm system for waking residents so they could get out safely. A sprinkler system were also in was place. "There was No panic," Smith said proudly. "Everyone Everone was calm and Orderly."

Answer Key — 337 — Total Basic Skills Grade 5

Page 215

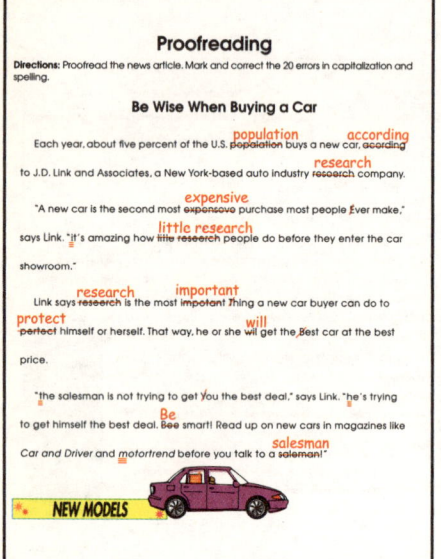

Proofreading

Directions: Proofread the news article. Mark and correct the 20 errors in capitalization and spelling.

Be Wise When Buying a Car

Each year, about five percent of the U.S. *population* buys a new car, *according* to J.D. Link and Associates, a New York-based auto industry *research* company.

"A new car is the second most *expensive* purchase most people *ever* make," says Link. "It's amazing how *little research* people do before they enter the car showroom."

Link says *research* is the most *important* thing a new car buyer can do to *protect* himself or herself. That way, he or she *will* get the best car at the best price.

"The salesman is not trying to get *you* the best deal," says Link. "He's trying to get himself the best deal. *Be* smart! Read up on new cars in magazines like *Car and Driver* and *Motortrend* before you talk to a *salesman*!"

Page 216

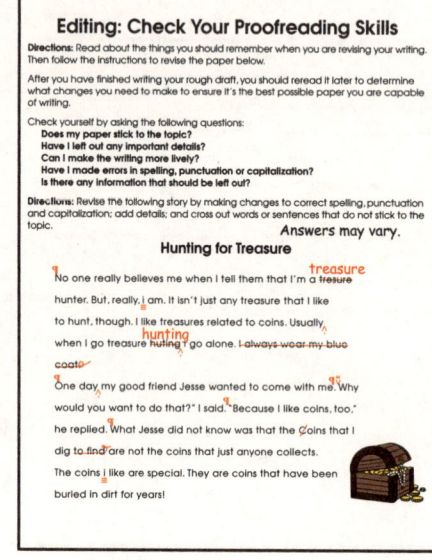

Editing: Check Your Proofreading Skills

Directions: Read about the things you should remember when you are revising your writing. Then follow the instructions to revise the paper below.

After you have finished writing your rough draft, you should reread it later to determine what changes you need to make to ensure it's the best possible paper you are capable of writing.

Check yourself by asking the following questions:
- Does my paper stick to the topic?
- Have I left out any important details?
- Can I make the writing more lively?
- Have I made errors in spelling, punctuation or capitalization?
- Is there any information that should be left out?

Directions: Revise the following story by making changes to correct spelling, punctuation and capitalization; add details; and cross out words or sentences that do not stick to the topic.

Answers may vary.

Hunting for Treasure

No one really believes me when I tell them that I'm a *treasure* hunter. But, really, I am. It isn't just any treasure that I like to hunt, though. I like treasures related to coins. Usually, when I go treasure *hunting*, I go alone. ~~I always wear my blue coat.~~ One day my good friend Jesse wanted to come with me. Why would you want to do that?" I said. "Because I like coins, too," he replied. What Jesse did not know was that the coins that I dig to *find* are not the coins that just anyone collects. The coins I like are special. They are coins that have been buried in dirt for years!

Page 217

Ancient Egypt

Have you ever wished you could visit Egypt for a first-hand look at the pyramids and ancient mummies? For most people, learning about Egypt is the closest they will come to visiting these ancient sites.

Directions: Test your knowledge about Egypt by writing as many of the answers as you can.

1. Write a paragraph describing what you already know about Egypt.
   Answers will vary.

2. Name at least two famous Egyptian kings or queens. **Sample answers: King Tut, Queen Nefertiti**

3. What was the purpose of a pyramid? **Sample answers: to bury Egyptian kings in; to worship the gods**

4. What was the purpose of mummification? **to preserve bodies after death**

5. What major river runs through Egypt? **the Nile**

Page 218

Taking Notes: Egyptian Mummies

Taking notes is the process of writing important points to remember, such as taking notes from material prepared by your teacher or from what is discussed in class or from an article you read. Taking notes is useful when preparing for a test or when writing a report. When taking notes, follow these steps:
1. Read the article carefully.
2. Select one or two important points from each paragraph.
3. Write your notes in your own words.
4. Reread your notes to be sure you understand what you have written.
5. Abbreviate words to save time.

Directions: Read about Egyptian mummies. Select one or two important points from each paragraph. Write your notes in your own words.

After the Egyptians discovered that bodies buried in the hot, dry sand of the desert became mummified, they began searching for ways to improve the mummification...

Sample notes: *Sample answers:*

Paragraph 1: Bodies buried in hot dry sand became mummified. Natron is vital for embalming.

Paragraph 2: Natron is a salt that is found when water from an oasis evaporates, leaving behind salts that were in it.

Paragraph 3: The body was soaked in natron for up to 40 days, causing it to shrink and the skin to become leathery. Natron was used for thousands of years.

Page 219

Outlining

Outlining is a way to organize information before you write an essay or informational paragraph. Outlining helps you understand the information you read.

This sample form will help you get started. When outlining, you can add more main points, more smaller points and/or more examples.

Title
I. First Main Idea
 A. A smaller idea
  1. An example
  2. An example
 B. Another smaller idea
II. Second Main Idea
 A. A smaller idea
 B. Another smaller idea
  1. An example
  2. An example
III. Third Main Idea
 A. A smaller idea
 B. A smaller idea

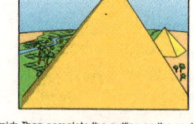

Directions: Read about building pyramids. Then complete the outline on the next page.

The process of building pyramids began as a way to honor a king or queen. Since the Egyptians believed in an afterlife, they thought it only fitting for their kings and queens to have elaborate burial tombs filled with treasures to enjoy in the afterlife. Thus, the idea of the pyramid was born.

At first pyramids were not built as they are known today. In the early stages of the Egyptian dynasty, kings were entombed in a *mastaba*. Mastabas were tombs made of mud-dried bricks. They formed a rectangular tomb with angled sides and a flat roof.

Later, as the Egyptian kingdom became more powerful, kings felt they needed grander tombs. The step pyramid was developed. These pyramids were made of stone rather than mud and were much taller. A large mastaba was built on the ground. Then, four more mastabas (each smaller than the previous) were stacked on top.

Finally, the pyramids took the shape that is familiar today. They were constructed with a flat bottom and four slanting sides which ascended to a final point. One of the tallest is over 400 feet high. These pyramids were also built of stone and were finished with an exterior of white limestone.

Page 220

Outlining: Egyptian Pyramids

Directions: Complete the outline. Then answer the question.

Egyptian Pyramids
(title)

I. Mastabas
 A. made of mud-dried bricks
 B. rectangular tomb
 C. angled sides and a flat roof
II. Step pyramids
 A. made of stone
 B. much taller than a mastaba
 C. large mastaba with four smaller mastabas stacked on top
III. Pyramids
 A. flat bottom and four slanting sides ascending to a final point
 B. tallest is over 400 feet high
 C. built of stone and finished with white limestone exterior

What do you find is the most interesting aspect about the pyramids of ancient Egypt? Why?

Answers will vary.

Page 221

Summarizing

A **summary** includes the main points from an article, book or speech.

Example:
Tomb robbing was an important business in ancient Egypt. Often entire families participated in the plunder of tombs. These robbers may have been laborers, tomb architects or guards, but they all probably had one thing in common. They were involved in the building or designing of the tomb or they wouldn't have had the knowledge necessary to successfully rob the burial sites. Not only did tomb robbing ensure a rich life for the robbers but it also enabled them to be buried with many riches themselves.

Summary:
Tomb robbing occurred in ancient Egypt. The robbers stole riches to use in their present lives or in their burials. Tomb robbers usually had some part in the building or design of the tomb. This allowed them to find the burial rooms where the treasures were stored.

Directions: Read about life in ancient Egypt. Then write a three- to five-sentence summary.

Egyptologists have learned much from the pyramids and mummies of ancient Egypt from the items left by grave robbers.
Women of ancient Egypt wore makeup to enhance their features. Dark colored minerals called *kohl* were used as eyeliner and eye shadow. Men also wore eyeliner. Women used another mineral called ocher on their cheeks and lips to redden them. Henna, a plant which produces an orange dye, tinted the fingernails, the palms of their hands and the soles of their feet.
Perfume was also important in ancient Egypt. Small cones made of wax were worn on top of the head. These cones contained perfume oils. The sun slowly melted the wax, and the perfume would scent the hair, head and shoulders.

Sample answer:
We have learned much from the pyramids and mummies. Women wore makeup made out of the minerals kohl and ocher and a plant called henna. Men wore eyeliner, too. Perfume made out of wax was also important to the ancient Egyptians.

Page 222

Summarizing: King Tut

Directions: Read about King Tut. Then write a five- to seven-sentence summary.

King Tutankhamen (TO-TAN-KO-MEN) became king of Egypt when he was only nine years old. Known today as "King Tut," he died in 1355 B.C. when he was 18. Because King Tut died so young, not much is known about what he did while he was king.
After his death, Tut's body was "mummified" and buried in a pyramid in the Valley of the Kings in Egypt. Many other kings of ancient Egypt were buried there also.
In 1922, King Tut became famous when an Englishman named Howard Carter discovered and explored his tomb. The king's mummy, wearing a gold mask decorated with precious stones, was found intact. Amazingly, all King Tut's riches were still in his tomb. His was the only one in the Valley of the Kings that had not been discovered and robbed.
The King's tomb contained four rooms. One contained his mummy. The other rooms were filled with beautiful furniture, including King Tut's throne. Also found in Tut's tomb were more than 3,000 objects, like clothes, jewelry, wine, food—and a trumpet that could still be played. Obviously, King Tut planned to live royally in the next world!

Sample answers:
King Tut ruled Egypt from age 9 to 18. Because he died so young, not much is known about his life. He was buried in the Valley of the Kings. His tomb was discovered by Howard Carter. All of King Tut's riches were still inside. There were more than 3,000 objects found in the tomb, including his mummy and his throne.

Page 224

Place Value

The place value of a digit or numeral is shown by where it is in the number. In the number 1,234, 1 has the place value of thousands, 2 is hundreds, 3 is tens and 4 is ones.

Example: 1,250,000,000
Read: One billion, two hundred fifty million
Write: 1,250,000,000

Billions	Millions	Thousands	Ones
h t o	h t o	h t o	h t o
1,	2 5 0,	0 0 0,	0 0 0

Directions: Read the words. Then write the numbers.

twenty million, three hundred four thousand _____ 20,304,000

five thousand, four hundred twenty-three _____ 5,423

one hundred fifty billion, eight million, one thousand, five hundred _____ 150,008,001,500

sixty billion, seven hundred million, one hundred thousand, three hundred twelve _____ 60,700,100,312

four hundred million, fifteen thousand, seven hundred one _____ 400,015,701

six hundred ninety-nine million, four thousand, nine hundred forty-two _____ 699,004,942

Here's a game to play with a partner.
Write a ten-digit number using each digit, 0 to 9, only once. Do not show the number to your partner. Give clues like: "There is a five in the hundreds place." The clues can be given in any order. See if your partner can write the same number you have written.

Page 225

Place Value

Directions: Draw a line to connect each number to its correct written form.

1. 791,000 — Three hundred fifty thousand
2. 350,000 — Seventeen million, five hundred thousand
3. 17,500,000 — Seven hundred ninety-one thousand
4. 3,500,000 — Seventy thousand, nine hundred ten
5. 70,910 — Three million, five hundred thousand
6. 35,500,000 — Seventeen billion, five hundred thousand
7. 17,000,500,000 — Thirty-five million, five hundred thousand

Directions: Look carefully at this number: 2,071,463,548. Write the numeral for each of the following places.

8. **6** ten thousands
9. **1** millions
10. **5** hundreds
11. **2** billions
12. **4** hundred thousands
13. **7** ten millions
14. **3** one thousands
15. **0** hundred millions

2,342

Page 226

Addition

Addition is "putting together" two or more numbers to find the sum.

Directions: Add. Fill the backpacks with the right answers.

38+92	71+48	43+62	56+14	87+13
130	119	105	70	100

24+39	15+67	83+47	35+80	17+64
63	82	130	115	81

95+25	54+19	61+77	42+89	37+97
120	73	138	131	134

62+39	18+43	27+94	11+89	48+58
101	61	121	100	106

Page 227

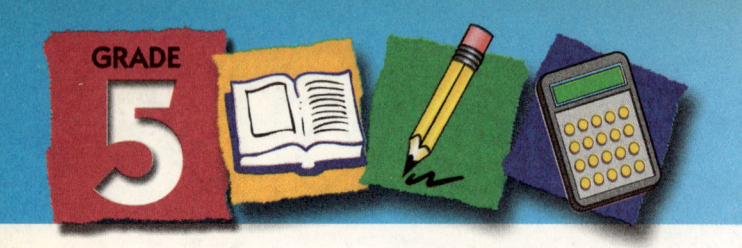

Addition

Teachers of an Earth Science class planned to take 50 students on an overnight hiking and camping experience. After planning the menu, they went to the grocery store for supplies.

Breakfast	Lunch	Dinner	Snacks
bacon	hot dogs/buns	pasta	crackers
eggs	apples	sauce	marshmallows
bread	chips	garlic bread	chocolate bars
cereal	juice	salad	cocoa mix
juice	granola bars	cookies	
$34.50	$52.15	$47.25	$23.40

Directions: Answer the questions. Write the total amount spent on food for the trip.

What information do you need to answer the question? **the total for each meal and snacks added together**

What is the total? **$157.30**

Directions: Add.

462 + 574 = 1,036
918 + 359 = 1,277
527 + 582 = 1,109
386 + 745 = 1,131
295 + 764 = 1,059

397 + 448 = 845
524 + 725 = 1,249
906 + 337 = 1,243
750 + 643 = 1,393
891 + 419 = 1,310

1,568 + 2,341 = 3,909
3,214 + 2,896 = 6,110
5,147 + 4,285 = 9,432
7,259 + 2,451 = 9,710
9,317 + 3,583 = 12,900

Page 228

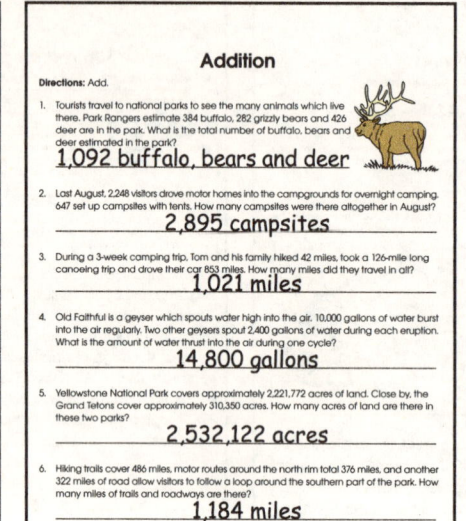

Addition

Directions: Add.

1. Tourists travel to national parks to see the many animals which live there. Park Rangers estimate 384 buffalo, 282 grizzly bears and 426 deer are in the park. What is the total number of buffalo, bears and deer estimated in the park? **1,092 buffalo, bears and deer**

2. Last August, 2,248 visitors drove motor homes into the campgrounds for overnight camping. 647 set up campsites with tents. How many campsites were there altogether in August? **2,895 campsites**

3. During a 3-week camping trip, Tom and his family hiked 42 miles, took a 126-mile long canoeing trip and drove their car 853 miles. How many miles did they travel in all? **1,021 miles**

4. Old Faithful is a geyser which spouts water high into the air. 10,000 gallons of water burst into the air regularly. Two other geysers spout 2,400 gallons of water during each eruption. What is the amount of water thrust into the air during one cycle? **14,800 gallons**

5. Yellowstone National Park covers approximately 2,221,772 acres of land. Close by, the Grand Tetons cover approximately 310,350 acres. How many acres of land are there in these two parks? **2,532,122 acres**

6. Hiking trails cover 486 miles, motor routes around the north rim total 376 miles, and another 322 miles of road allow visitors to follow a loop around the southern part of the park. How many miles of trails and roadways are there? **1,184 miles**

Page 229

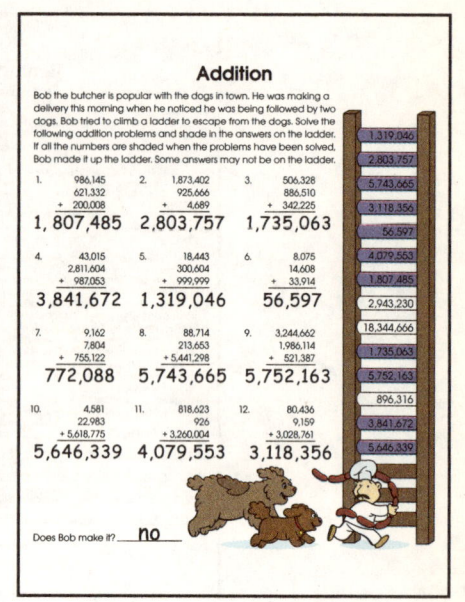

Addition

Bob the butcher is popular with the dogs in town. He was making a delivery this morning when he noticed he was being followed by two dogs. Bob tried to climb a ladder to escape from the dogs. Solve the following addition problems and shade in the answers on the ladder. If all the numbers are shaded when the problems have been solved, Bob made it up the ladder. Some answers may not be on the ladder.

1. 986,145 + 621,332 + 200,008 = **1,807,485**
2. 1,873,402 + 925,666 + 4,689 = **2,803,757**
3. 506,328 + 886,510 + 342,225 = **1,735,063**

4. 43,015 + 2,811,604 + 987,053 = **3,841,672**
5. 18,443 + 300,604 + 999,999 = **1,319,046**
6. 8,075 + 14,608 + 33,914 = **56,597**

7. 9,162 + 7,804 + 755,122 = **772,088**
8. 88,714 + 213,653 + 5,441,298 = **5,743,665**
9. 3,244,662 + 1,986,114 + 521,387 = **5,752,163**

10. 4,581 + 22,983 + 5,618,775 = **5,646,339**
11. 818,623 + 926 + 3,260,004 = **4,079,553**
12. 80,436 + 9,159 + 3,028,761 = **3,118,356**

Ladder values: 1,319,046; 2,803,757; 5,743,665; 3,118,356; 56,597; 4,079,553; 1,807,485; 2,943,230; 18,344,666; 1,735,063; 5,752,163; 896,316; 3,841,672; 5,646,339

Does Bob make it? **no**

Page 230

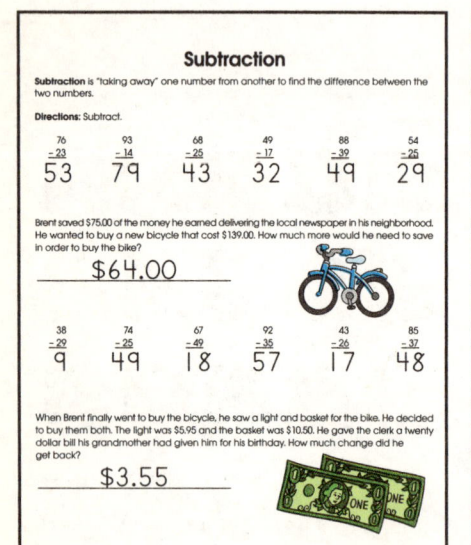

Subtraction

Subtraction is "taking away" one number from another to find the difference between the two numbers.

Directions: Subtract.

76 − 23 = 53
93 − 14 = 79
68 − 25 = 43
49 − 17 = 32
88 − 39 = 49
54 − 25 = 29

Brent saved $75.00 of the money he earned delivering the local newspaper in his neighborhood. He wanted to buy a new bicycle that cost $139.00. How much more would he need to save in order to buy the bike? **$64.00**

38 − 29 = 9
74 − 25 = 49
67 − 49 = 18
92 − 35 = 57
43 − 26 = 17
85 − 37 = 48

When Brent finally went to buy the bicycle, he saw a light and basket for the bike. He decided to buy them both. The light was $5.95 and the basket was $10.50. He gave the clerk a twenty dollar bill his grandmother had given him for his birthday. How much change did he get back? **$3.55**

Page 231

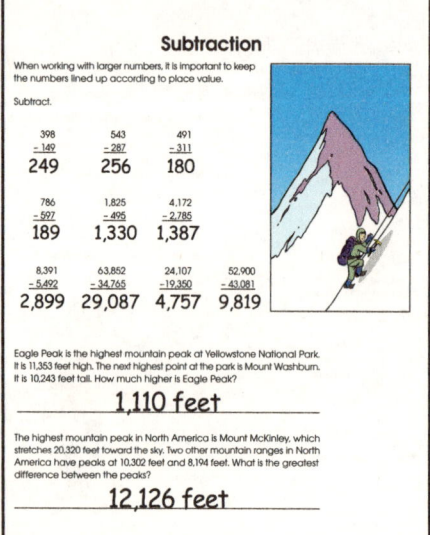

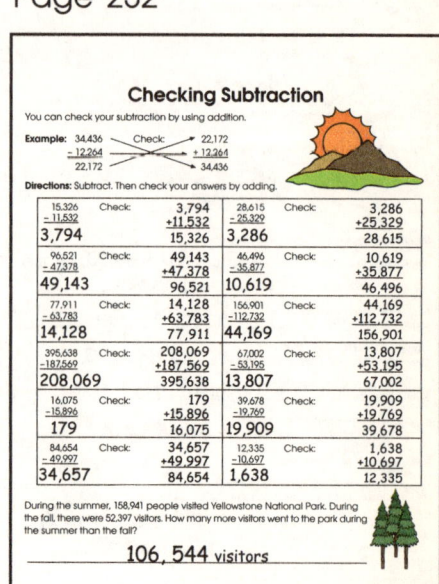

Subtraction

When working with larger numbers, it is important to keep the numbers lined up according to place value.

Subtract.

398 − 149 = 249
543 − 287 = 256
491 − 311 = 180

786 − 597 = 189
1,825 − 495 = 1,330
4,172 − 2,785 = 1,387

8,391 − 5,492 = 2,899
63,852 − 34,765 = 29,087
24,107 − 19,350 = 4,757
52,900 − 43,081 = 9,819

Eagle Peak is the highest mountain peak at Yellowstone National Park. It is 11,353 feet high. The next highest point at the park is Mount Washburn. It is 10,243 feet tall. How much higher is Eagle Peak? **1,110 feet**

The highest mountain peak in North America is Mount McKinley, which stretches 20,320 feet toward the sky. Two other mountain ranges in North America have peaks at 10,302 feet and 8,194 feet. What is the greatest difference between the peaks? **12,126 feet**

Page 232

Checking Subtraction

You can check your subtraction by using addition.

Example: 34,436 − 12,264 = 22,172   Check: 22,172 + 12,264 = 34,436

Directions: Subtract. Then check your answers by adding.

15,326 − 11,532 = 3,794   Check: 3,794 + 11,532 = 15,326
28,615 − 25,329 = 3,286   Check: 3,286 + 25,329 = 28,615

96,521 − 47,378 = 49,143   Check: 49,143 + 47,378 = 96,521
46,496 − 35,877 = 10,619   Check: 10,619 + 35,877 = 46,496

77,911 − 63,783 = 14,128   Check: 14,128 + 63,783 = 77,911
156,901 − 112,732 = 44,169   Check: 44,169 + 112,732 = 156,901

395,638 − 187,569 = 208,069   Check: 208,069 + 187,569 = 395,638
67,002 − 53,195 = 13,807   Check: 13,807 + 53,195 = 67,002

16,075 − 15,896 = 179   Check: 179 + 15,896 = 16,075
39,678 − 19,769 = 19,909   Check: 19,909 + 19,769 = 39,678

84,654 − 49,997 = 34,657   Check: 34,657 + 49,997 = 84,654
12,335 − 10,697 = 1,638   Check: 1,638 + 10,697 = 12,335

During the summer, 158,941 people visited Yellowstone National Park. During the fall, there were 52,397 visitors. How many more visitors went to the park during the summer than the fall? **106,544 visitors**

Total Basic Skills Grade 5 — Answer Key

Page 233

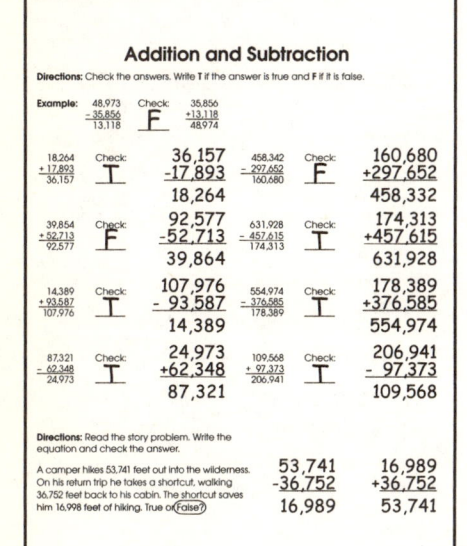

Addition and Subtraction

Directions: Check the answers. Write T if the answer is true and F if it is false.

Example: 48,973 − 35,856 = 13,118 → Check: 35,856 + 13,118 = 48,974 → **F**

18,264 + 17,893 = 36,157 → Check: 36,157 − 17,893 = 18,264 → **T**

458,342 − 297,652 = 160,680 → Check: 160,680 + 297,652 = 458,332 → **F**

39,854 + 52,713 = 92,577 → Check: 92,577 − 52,713 = 39,864 → **F**

631,928 − 457,615 = 174,313 → Check: 174,313 + 457,615 = 631,928 → **T**

14,389 + 93,587 = 107,976 → Check: 107,976 − 93,587 = 14,389 → **T**

554,974 − 376,585 = 178,389 → Check: 178,389 + 376,585 = 554,974 → **T**

87,321 − 62,348 = 24,973 → Check: 24,973 + 62,348 = 87,321 → **T**

109,568 − 97,373 = 206,941 → Check: 206,941 − 97,373 = 109,568 → **F**

Directions: Read the story problem. Write the equation and check the answer.

A camper hikes 53,741 feet out into the wilderness. On his return trip he takes a shortcut, walking 36,752 feet back to his cabin. The shortcut saves him 16,998 feet of hiking. True or **False**?

53,741 − 36,752 = 16,989   16,989 + 36,752 = 53,741

Page 234

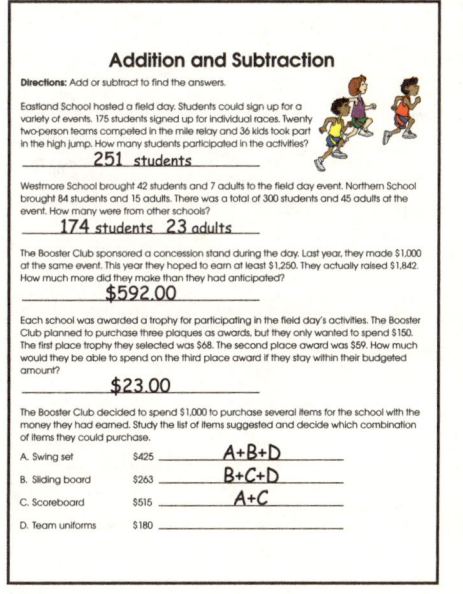

Addition and Subtraction

Directions: Add or subtract to find the answers.

Eastland School hosted a field day. Students could sign up for a variety of events. 175 students signed up for individual races. Twenty two-person teams competed in the mile relay and 36 kids took part in the high jump. How many students participated in the activities?
251 students

Westmore School brought 42 students and 7 adults to the field day event. Northern School brought 84 students and 15 adults. There was a total of 300 students and 45 adults at the event. How many were from other schools?
174 students 23 adults

The Booster Club sponsored a concession stand during the day. Last year, they made $1,000 at the same event. This year they hoped to earn at least $1,250. They actually raised $1,842. How much more did they make than they had anticipated?
$592.00

Each school was awarded a trophy for participating in the field day's activities. The Booster Club planned to purchase three plaques as awards, but they only wanted to spend $150. The first place trophy they selected was $68. The second place award was $59. How much would they be able to spend on the third place award if they stay within their budgeted amount?
$23.00

The Booster Club decided to spend $1,000 to purchase several items for the school with the money they had earned. Study the list of items suggested and decide which combination of items they could purchase.

A. Swing set $425   **A+B+D**
B. Sliding board $263   **B+C+D**
C. Scoreboard $515   **A+C**
D. Team uniforms $180

Page 235

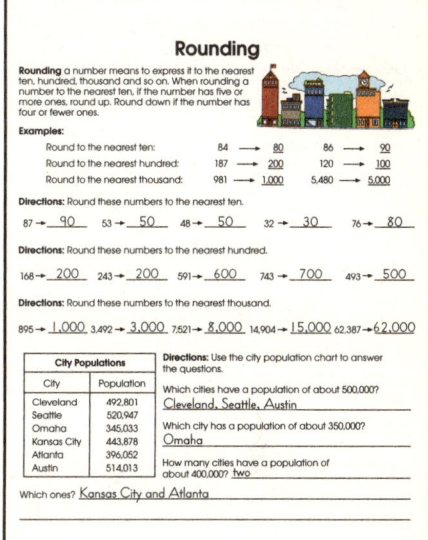

Rounding

Rounding a number means to express it to the nearest ten, hundred, thousand and so on. When rounding a number to the nearest ten, if the number has five or more ones, round up. Round down if the number has four or fewer ones.

Examples:
Round to the nearest ten: 84 → 80   86 → 90
Round to the nearest hundred: 187 → 200   120 → 100
Round to the nearest thousand: 981 → 1,000 5,480 → 5,000

Directions: Round these numbers to the nearest ten.
87 → **90**   53 → **50**   48 → **50**   32 → **30**   76 → **80**

Directions: Round these numbers to the nearest hundred.
168 → **200**   243 → **200**   591 → **600**   743 → **700**   493 → **500**

Directions: Round these numbers to the nearest thousand.
895 → **1,000**   3,492 → **3,000**   7,521 → **8,000**   14,904 → **15,000**   62,387 → **62,000**

City	Population
Cleveland	492,801
Seattle	520,947
Omaha	345,033
Kansas City	443,878
Atlanta	396,052
Austin	514,013

Directions: Use the city population chart to answer the questions.

Which cities have a population of about 500,000?
Cleveland, Seattle, Austin

Which city has a population of about 350,000?
Omaha

How many cities have a population of about 400,000? **two**
Which ones? **Kansas City and Atlanta**

Page 236

Estimating

To **Estimate** means to give an approximate rather than an exact answer. Rounding each number first makes it easy to estimate an answer.

Example:
93 + 48 → 90 + 50 = 140
321 + 597 → 300 + 600 = 900
1,859 − 997 → 2,000 − 1,000 = 1,000

Directions: Estimate the sums and differences by rounding the numbers first.

68 + 34 → 70 + 30 = 100
12 + 98 → 10 + 100 = 110
89 + 23 → 90 + 20 = 110

638 − 395 → 600 − 400 = 200
281 − 69 → 300 − 100 = 200
271 − 126 → 300 − 100 = 200

1,532 − 998 → 2,000 − 1,000 = 1,000
8,312 − 4,789 → 8,000 − 5,000 = 3,000
6,341 + 9,286 → 6,000 + 9,000 = 15,000

Bonnie has $50 to purchase tennis shoes, a tennis racquet and tennis balls. Does she have enough money? **yes**

Page 237

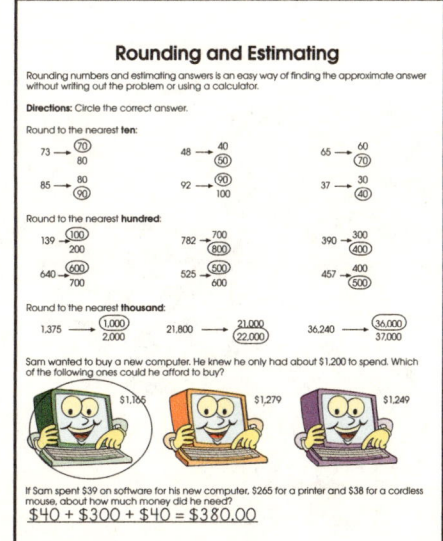

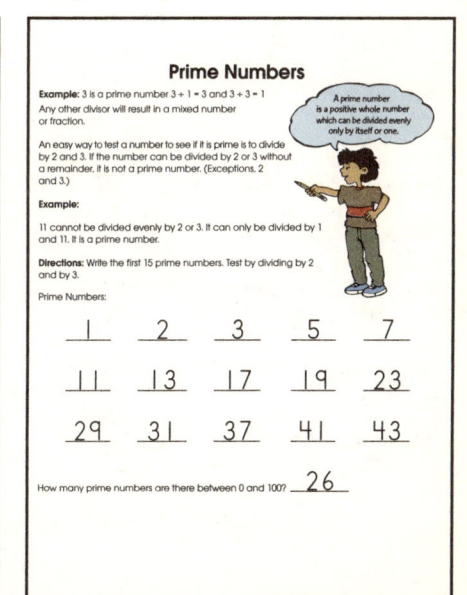

Rounding and Estimating

Rounding numbers and estimating answers is an easy way of finding the approximate answer without writing out the problem or using a calculator.

Directions: Circle the correct answer.

Round to the nearest ten:
73 → **70**, 80
48 → 40, **50**
65 → 60, **70**
85 → 80, **90**
92 → **90**, 100
37 → 30, **40**

Round to the nearest hundred:
139 → **100**, 200
782 → 700, **800**
390 → 300, **400**
640 → **600**, 700
525 → **500**, 600
457 → 400, **500**

Round to the nearest thousand:
1,375 → **1,000**, 2,000
21,800 → **21,000**, 22,000
36,240 → **36,000**, 37,000

Sam wanted to buy a new computer. He knew he only had about $1,200 to spend. Which of the following ones could he afford to buy? **$1,165** $1,279 $1,249

If Sam spent $39 on software for his new computer, $265 for a printer and $38 for a cordless mouse, about how much money did he need?
$40 + $300 + $40 = $380.00

Page 238

Prime Numbers

Example: 3 is a prime number 3 ÷ 1 = 3 and 3 ÷ 3 = 1
Any other divisor will result in a mixed number or fraction.

An easy way to test a number to see if it is prime is to divide by 2 and 3. If the number can be divided by 2 or 3 without a remainder, it is not a prime number. (Exceptions, 2 and 3.)

Example:
11 cannot be divided evenly by 2 or 3. It can only be divided by 1 and 11. It is a prime number.

Directions: Write the first 15 prime numbers. Test by dividing by 2 and by 3.

Prime Numbers:
1   2   3   5   7
11   13   17   19   23
29   31   37   41   43

How many prime numbers are there between 0 and 100? **26**

Page 239

Prime Numbers

Directions: Circle the prime numbers.

(71)	(3)	82	20	(43)	69
128	(97)	(23)	111	75	51
(13)	44	(137)	68	171	(83)
(61)	21	77	(101)	34	16
(2)	39	92	(17)	52	(29)
19	156	63	99	27	147
121	25	88	12	87	55
57	(7)	(139)	91	9	(37)
(67)	183	(5)	(59)	(11)	95

Page 240

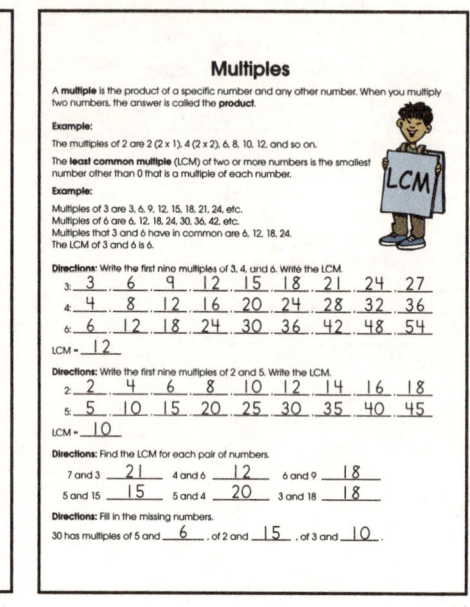

Multiples

A **multiple** is the product of a specific number and any other number. When you multiply two numbers, the answer is called the **product**.

Example:
The multiples of 2 are 2 (2 × 1), 4 (2 × 2), 6, 8, 10, 12, and so on.
The **least common multiple** (LCM) of two or more numbers is the smallest number other than 0 that is a multiple of each number.

Example:
Multiples of 3 are 3, 6, 9, 12, 15, 18, 21, 24, etc.
Multiples of 6 are 6, 12, 18, 24, 30, 36, 42, etc.
Multiples that 3 and 6 have in common are 6, 12, 18, 24.
The LCM of 3 and 6 is 6.

Directions: Write the first nine multiples of 3, 4, and 6. Write the LCM.
3: 3, 6, 9, 12, 15, 18, 21, 24, 27
4: 4, 8, 12, 16, 20, 24, 28, 32, 36
6: 6, 12, 18, 24, 30, 36, 42, 48, 54
LCM = 12

Directions: Write the first nine multiples of 2 and 5. Write the LCM.
2: 2, 4, 6, 8, 10, 12, 14, 16, 18
5: 5, 10, 15, 20, 25, 30, 35, 40, 45
LCM = 10

Directions: Find the LCM for each pair of numbers.
7 and 3 21   4 and 6 12   6 and 9 18
5 and 15 15   5 and 4 20   3 and 18 18

Directions: Fill in the missing numbers.
30 has multiples of 5 and 6, of 2 and 15, of 3 and 10.

Page 241

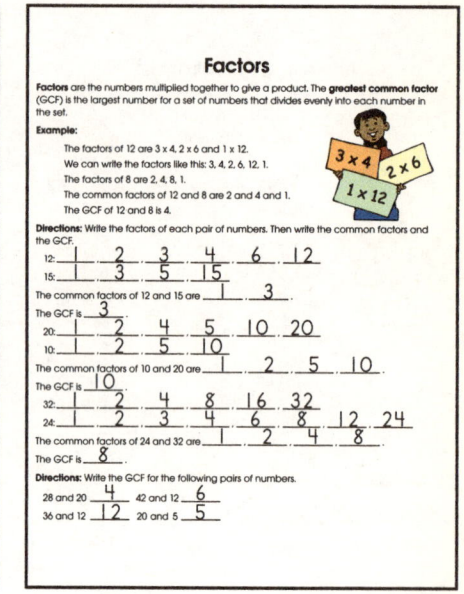

Factors

Factors are the numbers multiplied together to give a product. The **greatest common factor** (GCF) is the largest number for a set of numbers that divides evenly into each number in the set.

Example:
The factors of 12 are 3 × 4, 2 × 6 and 1 × 12.
We can write the factors like this: 3, 4, 2, 6, 12, 1.
The factors of 8 are 2, 4, 8, 1.
The common factors of 12 and 8 are 2 and 4 and 1.
The GCF of 12 and 8 is 4.

Directions: Write the factors of each pair of numbers. Then write the common factors and the GCF.

12: 1, 2, 3, 4, 6, 12
15: 1, 3, 5, 15
The common factors of 12 and 15 are 1, 3.
The GCF is 3.

20: 1, 2, 4, 5, 10, 20
10: 1, 2, 5, 10
The common factors of 10 and 20 are 1, 2, 5, 10.
The GCF is 10.

32: 1, 2, 4, 8, 16, 32
24: 1, 2, 3, 4, 6, 8, 12, 24
The common factors of 24 and 32 are 1, 2, 4, 8.
The GCF is 8.

Directions: Write the GCF for the following pairs of numbers.
28 and 20 4   42 and 12 6
36 and 12 12   20 and 5 5

Page 242

Factor Trees

A **factor tree** shows the prime factors of a number. A prime number, such as 7, has for its factors only itself and 1.

Example: 30 = 3 × 2 × 5. 3, 2, and 5 are prime numbers.

Directions: Fill in the numbers in the factor trees.

18 = 6 × 3 = 3 × 2 × 3
30 = 15 × 2 = 3 × 5 × 2
45 = 15 × 3 = 3 × 5 × 3
20 = 4 × 5 = 2 × 2 × 5
18 = 9 × 2 = 3 × 3 × 2
40 = 10 × 4 = 5 × 2 × 2 × 2

Page 243

Factor Trees

Directions: Fill in the numbers in the factor trees. The first one has been done for you.

13,720 = 140 × 98 = 10 × 14 × 7 = 5 × 2 × 2 × 7 × 7

192 = 8 × 24 = 2 × 4 × 6 = 1 × 2 × 2 × 3

1,125 = 75 × 15 = 15 × 5 × 3 = 3 × 5 × 1 × 3

Page 244

Greatest Common Factor

Directions: Write the greatest common factor for each set of numbers.

10 and 35 5
2 and 10 2
42 and 63 21
16 and 40 8
25 and 55 4
12 and 20 4
14 and 28 14
16 and 20 4
6 and 27 3
15 and 35 5
18 and 48 6

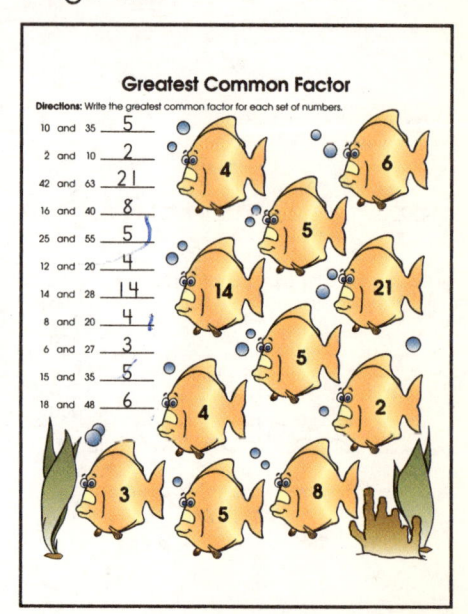

4, 6, 14, 21, 5, 3, 8, 2

Page 245

Least Common Multiple

Directions: Write the least common multiple for each pair of numbers.

12 and 7 **84**
2 and 4   **4**
22 and 10 **44**
6 and 10 **30**
3 and 7   **21**
6 and 8   **24**
5 and 10 **10**
8 and 12 **24**
9 and 15 **45**
7 and 5   **35**
3 and 8   **24**
9 and 4   **36**

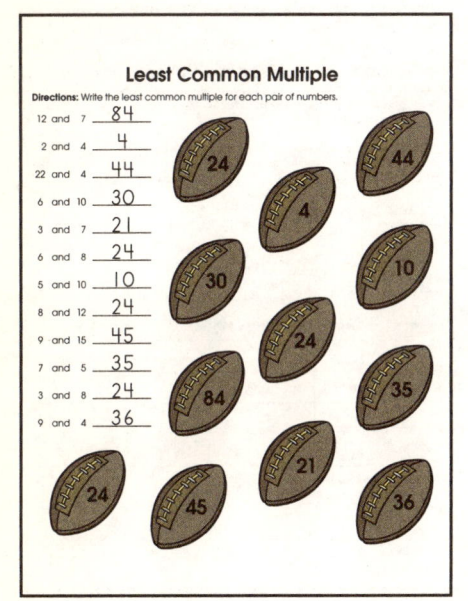

Page 246

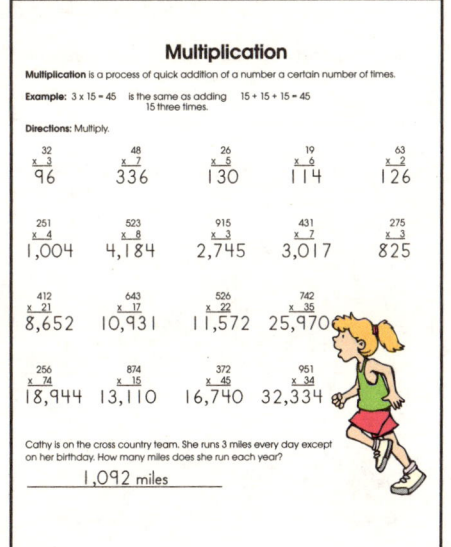

Multiplication

Multiplication is a process of quick addition of a number a certain number of times.

Example: 3 × 15 = 45 is the same as adding 15 + 15 + 15 = 45, 15 three times.

Directions: Multiply.

32 × 3 = **96**
48 × 7 = **336**
26 × 5 = **130**
19 × 6 = **114**
63 × 2 = **126**

251 × 4 = **1,004**
523 × 8 = **4,184**
915 × 3 = **2,745**
431 × 7 = **3,017**
275 × 3 = **825**

412 × 21 = **8,652**
643 × 17 = **10,931**
526 × 22 = **11,572**
742 × 35 = **25,970**

256 × 74 = **18,944**
874 × 15 = **13,110**
372 × 45 = **16,740**
951 × 34 = **32,334**

Cathy is on the cross country team. She runs 3 miles every day except on her birthday. How many miles does she run each year? **1,092 miles**

Page 247

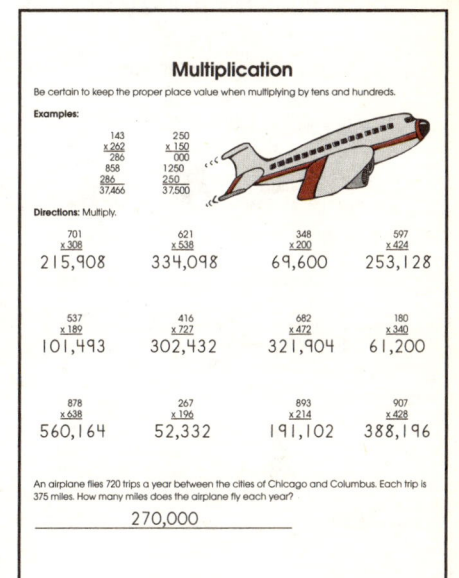

Multiplication

Be certain to keep the proper place value when multiplying by tens and hundreds.

Examples:
143 × 262 = 286 / 858 / 286 / 37,466
250 × 150 = 000 / 1250 / 250 / 37,500

Directions: Multiply.

701 × 308 = **215,908**
621 × 538 = **334,098**
348 × 200 = **69,600**
597 × 424 = **253,128**

537 × 189 = **101,493**
416 × 727 = **302,432**
682 × 472 = **321,904**
180 × 340 = **61,200**

878 × 638 = **560,164**
267 × 196 = **52,332**
893 × 214 = **191,102**
907 × 428 = **388,196**

An airplane flies 720 trips a year between the cities of Chicago and Columbus. Each trip is 375 miles. How many miles does the airplane fly each year? **270,000**

Page 248

Division

Division is the reverse of multiplication. It is the process of dividing a number into equal groups of smaller numbers.

Directions: Divide.

Greg had 936 marbles to share with his two brothers. If the boys divided them evenly, how many will each one get? **312 marbles**

The marbles Greg kept were four different colors: blue, green, red and orange. He had the same number of each color. He divided them into two groups. One group had only orange marbles. The rest of the marbles were in the other group. How many marbles did he have in each group? orange **78** others **234**

The **dividend** is the number to be divided by another number. In the problem 28 ÷ 7 = 4, 28 is the dividend.
The **divisor** is the number by which another number is divided. In the problem 28 ÷ 7 = 4, 7 is the divisor.
The **quotient** is the answer in a division problem. In the problem 28 ÷ 7 = 4, 4 is the quotient.
The **remainder** is the number left over in the quotient of a division problem. In the problem 29 ÷ 7 = 4 r1, 1 is the remainder.

Directions: Write the answers.

In the problem 25 ÷ 8 = 3 r1 ...
What is the divisor? **8**   What is the remainder? **1**
What is the quotient? **3 r1**   What is the dividend? **25**

Directions: Divide.

9)2,025 = **225**
6)2,508 = **418**
3)225 = **75**
5)400 = **80**
2)1,156 = **578**

Page 249

Division

The remainder in a division problem must always be less than the divisor.

Example:
26)6,367 = 244 r 23

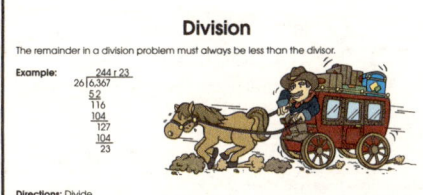

Directions: Divide.

53)1,220 = **23 r1**
37)1,528 = **41 r11**
83)6,270 = **75 r45**
26)3,618 = **139 r4**

14)389 = **27 r11**
29)2,645 = **91 r6**
60)8,010 = **133 r30**
57)5,406 = **94 r48**

35)2,546 = **72 r26**
43)492 = **11 r19**
83)4,608 = **55 r43**
19)185 = **9 r14**

The Oregon Trail is 2,197 miles long. How long would it take a covered wagon traveling 20 miles a day to complete the trip? **110 days**

Page 250

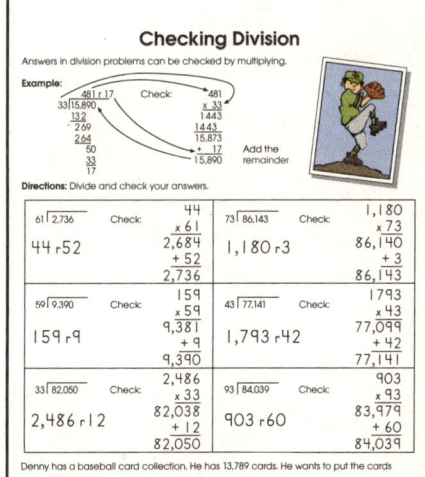

Checking Division

Answers in division problems can be checked by multiplying.

Example:
33)15,890 = 481 r 17   Check: 481 × 33 = 1443 / 1443 / 15,873 + 17 = 15,890

Directions: Divide and check your answers.

61)2,736 = **44 r52**   Check: 44 × 61 = 2,684 + 52 = 2,736
73)86,143 = **1,180 r3**   Check: 1,180 × 73 = 86,140 + 3 = 86,143

59)9,390 = **159 r9**   Check: 159 × 59 = 9,381 + 9 = 9,390
43)77,141 = **1,793 r42**   Check: 1,793 × 43 = 77,099 + 42 = 77,141

33)82,050 = **2,486 r12**   Check: 2,486 × 33 = 82,038 + 12 = 82,050
93)84,039 = **903 r60**   Check: 903 × 93 = 83,979 + 60 = 84,039

Denny has a baseball card collection. He has 13,789 cards. He wants to put the cards in a scrapbook that holds 15 cards on a page. How many pages does Denny need in his scrapbook? **920**

Page 251

Multiplication and Division

Directions: Multiply or divide to find the answers.

Brianne's summer job is mowing lawns for three of her neighbors. Each lawn takes about 1 hour to mow and needs to be done once every week. At the end of the summer, she will have earned a total of $630. She collected the same amount of money from each job. How much did each neighbor pay for her summer lawn service? **$210**

If the mowing season lasts for 14 weeks, how much will Brianne earn for each job each week? **$15**

If she had worked for two more weeks, how much would she have earned? **$720**

Brianne agreed to shovel snow from the driveways and sidewalks for the same three neighbors. They agreed to pay her the same rate. However, it only snowed seven times that winter. How much did she earn shoveling snow? **$315**

What was her total income for both jobs? **$945**

Directions: Multiply or divide.

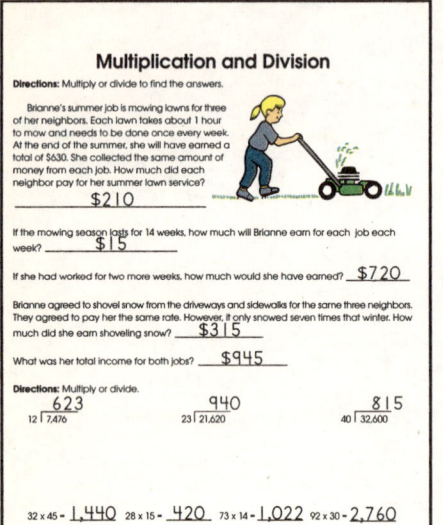

12 ⟌ 7,476 = **623**   23 ⟌ 21,620 = **940**   40 ⟌ 32,600 = **815**

32 × 45 = **1,440**   28 × 15 = **420**   73 × 14 = **1,022**   92 × 30 = **2,760**

Page 252

Adding and Subtracting Like Fractions

A **fraction** is a number that names part of a whole. Examples of fractions are $\frac{1}{2}$ and $\frac{1}{3}$. **Like fractions** have the same **denominator**, or bottom number. Examples of like fractions are $\frac{1}{4}$ and $\frac{3}{4}$.

To add or subtract fractions, the denominators must be the same. Add or subtract only the **numerators**, the numbers above the line in fractions.

Example:
numerators / denominators $\frac{5}{8} - \frac{1}{8} = \frac{4}{8}$

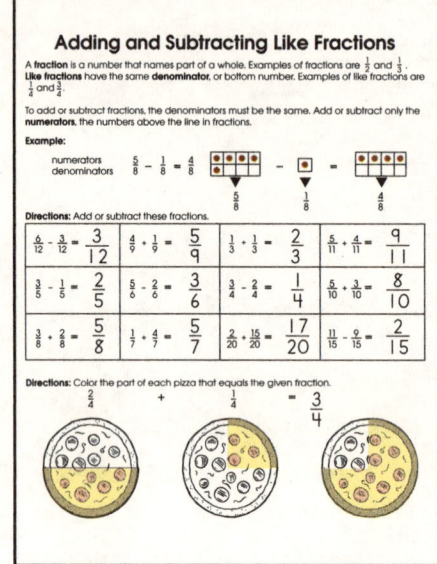

Directions: Add or subtract these fractions.

$\frac{6}{12} - \frac{3}{12} = \frac{3}{12}$	$\frac{4}{9} + \frac{1}{9} = \frac{5}{9}$	$\frac{1}{3} + \frac{1}{3} = \frac{2}{3}$	$\frac{5}{11} + \frac{4}{11} = \frac{9}{11}$
$\frac{3}{5} - \frac{1}{5} = \frac{2}{5}$	$\frac{5}{6} - \frac{2}{6} = \frac{3}{6}$	$\frac{3}{4} - \frac{2}{4} = \frac{1}{4}$	$\frac{5}{10} + \frac{3}{10} = \frac{8}{10}$
$\frac{3}{8} + \frac{2}{8} = \frac{5}{8}$	$\frac{1}{7} + \frac{4}{7} = \frac{5}{7}$	$\frac{2}{20} + \frac{15}{20} = \frac{17}{20}$	$\frac{11}{15} - \frac{9}{15} = \frac{2}{15}$

Directions: Color the part of each pizza that equals the given fraction.

$\frac{2}{4} + \frac{1}{4} = \frac{3}{4}$

Page 253

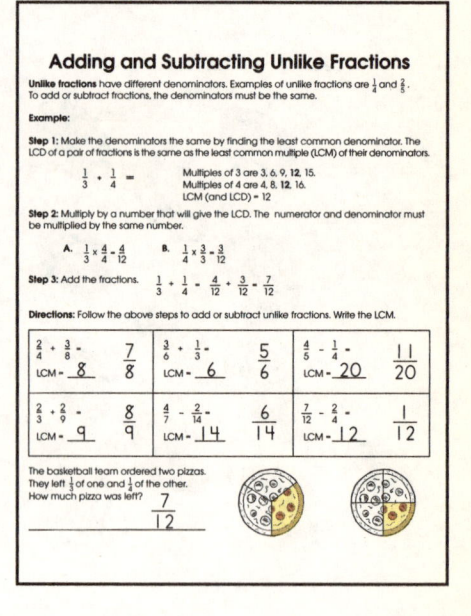

Adding and Subtracting Unlike Fractions

Unlike fractions have different denominators. Examples of unlike fractions are $\frac{1}{4}$ and $\frac{2}{5}$. To add or subtract fractions, the denominators must be the same.

Example:
Step 1: Make the denominators the same by finding the least common denominator. The LCD of a pair of fractions is the same as the least common multiple (LCM) of their denominators.

$\frac{1}{3} + \frac{1}{4} =$ Multiples of 3 are 3, 6, 9, **12**, 15.
Multiples of 4 are 4, 8, **12**, 16.
LCM (and LCD) = 12

Step 2: Multiply by a number that will give the LCD. The numerator and denominator must be multiplied by the same number.

A. $\frac{1}{3} \times \frac{4}{4} = \frac{4}{12}$ B. $\frac{1}{4} \times \frac{3}{3} = \frac{3}{12}$

Step 3: Add the fractions. $\frac{1}{3} + \frac{1}{4} = \frac{4}{12} + \frac{3}{12} = \frac{7}{12}$

Directions: Follow the above steps to add or subtract unlike fractions. Write the LCM.

$\frac{2}{4} + \frac{3}{8} = \frac{7}{8}$ LCM = **8**	$\frac{3}{6} + \frac{1}{3} = \frac{5}{6}$ LCM = **6**	$\frac{4}{5} - \frac{1}{4} = \frac{11}{20}$ LCM = **20**
$\frac{2}{3} + \frac{2}{9} = \frac{8}{9}$ LCM = **9**	$\frac{4}{7} - \frac{2}{14} = \frac{6}{14}$ LCM = **14**	$\frac{7}{12} - \frac{2}{4} = \frac{1}{12}$ LCM = **12**

The basketball team ordered two pizzas. They left $\frac{1}{3}$ of one and $\frac{1}{4}$ of the other. How much pizza was left? **$\frac{7}{12}$**

Page 254

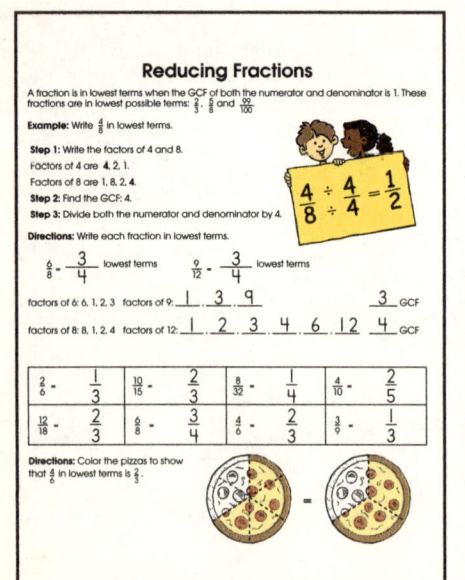

Reducing Fractions

A fraction is in lowest terms when the GCF of both the numerator and denominator is 1. These fractions are in lowest possible terms: $\frac{2}{3}$, $\frac{5}{8}$ and $\frac{29}{100}$.

Example: Write $\frac{4}{8}$ in lowest terms.

Step 1: Write the factors of 4 and 8.
Factors of 4 are **4**, 2, 1.
Factors of 8 are 1, 8, 2, **4**.
Step 2: Find the GCF: **4**.
Step 3: Divide both the numerator and denominator by 4.

$\frac{4}{8} \div \frac{4}{4} = \frac{1}{2}$

Directions: Write each fraction in lowest terms.

$\frac{6}{12} = \frac{3}{4}$ lowest terms $\frac{9}{12} = \frac{3}{4}$ lowest terms

factors of 6: 6, 1, 2, 3   factors of 9: **1, 3, 9**   **3** GCF
factors of 8: 8, 1, 2, 4   factors of 12: **1, 2, 3, 4, 6, 12**   **4** GCF

$\frac{2}{6} = \frac{1}{3}$	$\frac{10}{15} = \frac{2}{3}$	$\frac{8}{32} = \frac{1}{4}$	$\frac{4}{10} = \frac{2}{5}$
$\frac{12}{18} = \frac{2}{3}$	$\frac{6}{9} = \frac{2}{3}$	$\frac{3}{4} = \frac{2}{4}$	$\frac{1}{3}$

Directions: Color the pizzas to show that $\frac{4}{6}$ in lowest terms is $\frac{2}{3}$.

Page 255

Improper Fractions

An **improper fraction** has a numerator that is greater than its denominator. An example of an improper fraction is $\frac{7}{2}$. An improper fraction should be reduced to its lowest terms.

Example: $\frac{5}{4}$ is an improper fraction because its numerator is greater than its denominator.

Step 1: Divide the numerator by the denominator: 5 ÷ 4 = 1, r1
Step 2: Write the remainder as a fraction: $\frac{1}{4}$

$\frac{5}{4} = 1\frac{1}{4}$ $1\frac{1}{4}$ is a mixed number—a whole number and a fraction.

Directions: Follow the steps above to change the improper fractions to mixed numbers.

$\frac{9}{8} = 1\frac{1}{8}$	$\frac{11}{5} = 2\frac{1}{5}$	$\frac{5}{3} = 1\frac{2}{3}$	$\frac{7}{6} = 1\frac{1}{6}$	$\frac{8}{7} = 1\frac{1}{7}$	$\frac{4}{3} = 1\frac{1}{3}$
$\frac{21}{5} = 4\frac{1}{5}$	$\frac{9}{4} = 2\frac{1}{4}$	$\frac{7}{6} = 1\frac{1}{6}$	$\frac{5}{2} = 1\frac{1}{2}$	$\frac{25}{4} = 6\frac{1}{4}$	$\frac{8}{3} = 2\frac{2}{3}$

Sara had 29 duplicate stamps in her stamp collection. She decided to give them to four of her friends. If she gave each of them the same number of stamps, how many duplicates will she have left? **1**

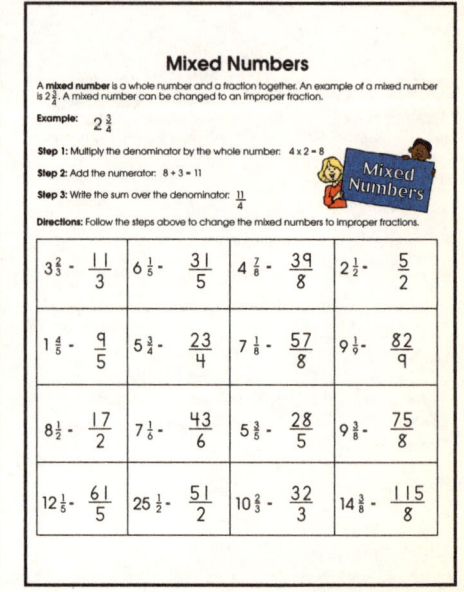

Name the improper fraction in this problem. **$\frac{29}{4}$**

What step must you do next to solve the problem? **change to a mixed number**

Write your answer as a mixed number. **7 1/4**

How many stamps could she give each of her friends? **7**

Page 256

Mixed Numbers

A **mixed number** is a whole number and a fraction together. An example of a mixed number is $2\frac{3}{4}$. A mixed number can be changed to an improper fraction.

Example: $2\frac{3}{4}$

Step 1: Multiply the denominator by the whole number: 4 × 2 = 8
Step 2: Add the numerator: 8 + 3 = 11
Step 3: Write the sum over the denominator: $\frac{11}{4}$

Directions: Follow the steps above to change the mixed numbers to improper fractions.

$3\frac{2}{3} = \frac{11}{3}$	$6\frac{1}{5} = \frac{31}{5}$	$4\frac{7}{8} = \frac{39}{8}$	$2\frac{1}{2} = \frac{5}{2}$
$1\frac{4}{5} = \frac{9}{5}$	$5\frac{3}{4} = \frac{23}{4}$	$7\frac{1}{8} = \frac{57}{8}$	$9\frac{1}{9} = \frac{82}{9}$
$8\frac{1}{2} = \frac{17}{2}$	$7\frac{1}{6} = \frac{43}{6}$	$5\frac{3}{5} = \frac{28}{5}$	$9\frac{3}{8} = \frac{75}{8}$
$12\frac{1}{5} = \frac{61}{5}$	$25\frac{1}{2} = \frac{51}{2}$	$10\frac{2}{3} = \frac{32}{3}$	$14\frac{3}{8} = \frac{115}{8}$

Page 257

Adding Mixed Numbers

$8\frac{1}{2} + 7\frac{1}{4} = 15\frac{3}{4}$

$5\frac{1}{4} + 2\frac{3}{8} = 7\frac{5}{8}$

$9\frac{1}{10} + 7\frac{2}{5} = 16\frac{1}{2}$

$8\frac{1}{5} + 6\frac{7}{10} = 14\frac{9}{10}$

$4\frac{4}{5} + 3\frac{9}{10} = 8\frac{1}{10}$

$3\frac{1}{2} + 7\frac{1}{4} = 10\frac{3}{4}$

$4\frac{1}{2} + 1\frac{1}{3} = 5\frac{5}{6}$

$6\frac{1}{2} + 3\frac{1}{3} = 9\frac{5}{6}$

$5\frac{1}{3} + 2\frac{2}{9} = 7\frac{2}{3}$

$6\frac{1}{3} + 2\frac{1}{12} = 8\frac{11}{15}$

$2\frac{2}{7} + 4\frac{1}{14} = 6\frac{5}{14}$

$3\frac{1}{2} + 3\frac{1}{4} = 6\frac{3}{4}$

Boys and girls picked apples: **9**

Page 258

Subtracting Mixed Numbers

$2\frac{3}{7} - 1\frac{1}{14} = 1\frac{5}{14}$

$7\frac{2}{3} - 5\frac{1}{4} = 2\frac{13}{24}$

$6\frac{3}{4} - 2\frac{3}{12} = 4\frac{1}{2}$

$9\frac{5}{12} - 5\frac{9}{24} = 4\frac{1}{24}$

$5\frac{1}{2} - 3\frac{1}{3} = 2\frac{1}{6}$

$7\frac{3}{4} - 5\frac{1}{6} = 2\frac{5}{24}$

$8\frac{3}{4} - 6\frac{1}{2} = 1\frac{23}{24}$

$11\frac{5}{6} - 7\frac{1}{12} = 4\frac{3}{4}$

$9\frac{3}{5} - 7\frac{1}{3} = 2\frac{8}{15}$

$4\frac{4}{5} - 2\frac{1}{4} = 2\frac{11}{20}$

$9\frac{2}{3} - 4\frac{1}{6} = 5\frac{1}{2}$

$14\frac{3}{8} - 9\frac{3}{16} = 5\frac{3}{16}$

Rodriguez Farm more acres: $2\frac{1}{6}$

Page 259

Comparing Fractions

$\frac{1}{2} > \frac{1}{3}$ $\frac{2}{5} < \frac{3}{7}$ $\frac{3}{8} < \frac{2}{4}$

$\frac{3}{4} = \frac{6}{8}$ $\frac{2}{3} < \frac{4}{5}$ $\frac{3}{9} = \frac{1}{3}$

$\frac{3}{12} = \frac{1}{4}$ $\frac{2}{14} = \frac{1}{7}$ $\frac{5}{15} < \frac{2}{3}$

Kelly had left: **7/15**

Holly and Deb each got: **1/6**

Page 260

Ordering Fractions

Least to Largest:
$\frac{1}{2}, \frac{2}{7}, \frac{4}{5}, \frac{1}{3}, \frac{2}{7}, \frac{1}{3}, \frac{1}{2}, \frac{4}{5}$

$\frac{3}{12}, \frac{3}{6}, \frac{3}{12}, \frac{3}{6}, \frac{3}{4}$

$\frac{2}{5}, \frac{4}{15}, \frac{5}{15}, \frac{4}{15}, \frac{5}{15}, \frac{2}{5}, \frac{3}{5}$

$3\frac{4}{5}, 3\frac{2}{5}, 3\frac{1}{5}, \frac{9}{5}, 3\frac{1}{5}, 3\frac{2}{5}, 3\frac{4}{5}$

$9\frac{1}{3}, 9\frac{2}{3}, 9\frac{1}{12}, 8\frac{3}{5}, 8\frac{2}{3}, 9\frac{1}{3}, 9\frac{2}{3}, 9\frac{9}{12}$

$5\frac{2}{3}, 5\frac{5}{6}, 5\frac{4}{24}, 5\frac{3}{12}, 5\frac{4}{24}, 5\frac{5}{12}, 5\frac{3}{6}, 5\frac{8}{12}$

$4\frac{3}{5}, 5\frac{7}{15}, 6\frac{2}{5}, 5\frac{1}{5}, 4\frac{3}{5}, 5\frac{1}{5}, 5\frac{7}{15}, 6\frac{2}{5}$

Winner: **Dog A** $(3\frac{4}{5})$

Dog B $3\frac{2}{3}$ Dog C $3\frac{5}{15}$ Dog D $3\frac{9}{12}$

Page 261

Multiplying Fractions

$\frac{3}{4} \times \frac{1}{6} = \frac{1}{8}$

$\frac{1}{2} \times \frac{5}{8} = \frac{5}{16}$

$\frac{2}{3} \times \frac{1}{6} = \frac{1}{9}$

$\frac{3}{2} \times \frac{1}{2} = \frac{1}{3}$

$\frac{5}{6} \times 4 = 3\frac{1}{3}$

$\frac{3}{8} \times \frac{1}{16} = \frac{3}{128}$

$\frac{1}{5} \times 5 = 1$

$\frac{7}{8} \times \frac{3}{4} = \frac{21}{32}$

$\frac{7}{11} \times \frac{1}{3} = \frac{7}{33}$

$\frac{2}{9} \times \frac{9}{4} = \frac{1}{2}$

$\frac{1}{3} \times \frac{1}{3} = \frac{1}{27}$

$\frac{1}{8} \times \frac{1}{4} \times \frac{1}{2} = \frac{1}{64}$

Jennifer's pets:
Cats = 4
Fish = 5
Dogs = 1

Page 262

Multiplying Mixed Numbers

$4\frac{1}{4} \times 2\frac{1}{8} = 9\frac{7}{20}$	$1\frac{1}{3} \times 3\frac{1}{4} = 4\frac{1}{3}$	$1\frac{1}{9} \times 3\frac{3}{5} = 4$
$1\frac{2}{7} \times 4\frac{1}{2} = 8\frac{5}{14}$	$2\frac{3}{4} \times 2\frac{3}{5} = 7\frac{3}{20}$	$4\frac{2}{3} \times 3\frac{1}{7} = 14\frac{2}{3}$
$6\frac{2}{5} \times 2\frac{1}{8} = 13\frac{3}{5}$	$3\frac{1}{7} \times 4\frac{5}{8} = 14\frac{15}{28}$	$7\frac{3}{8} \times 2\frac{1}{9} = 15\frac{41}{72}$

Stalls for cows: **30**
Stalls for horses: **20**

Page 263

Dividing Fractions

To divide fractions, follow these steps:

$\frac{3}{4} \div \frac{1}{4} =$

Step 1: "Invert" the divisor. That means to turn it upside down.

$\frac{3}{4} \quad \frac{4}{1}$

Step 2: Multiply the two fractions:

$\frac{3}{4} \times \frac{4}{1} = \frac{12}{4}$

Step 3: Reduce the fraction to lowest terms by dividing the denominator into the numerator.

$12 \div 4 = 3$

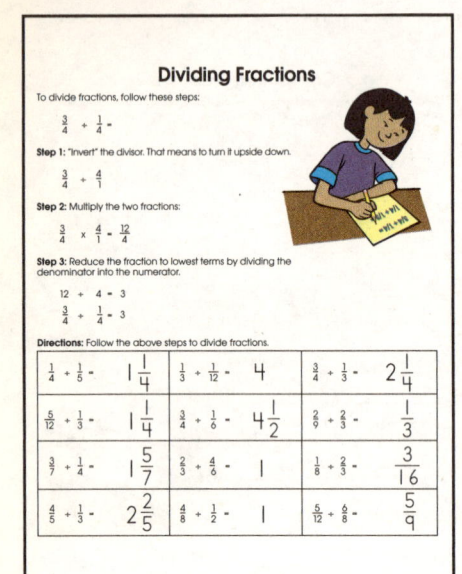

$\frac{3}{4} \div \frac{1}{4} = 3$

Directions: Follow the above steps to divide fractions.

$\frac{1}{4} \div \frac{1}{5} = 1\frac{1}{4}$	$\frac{1}{3} \div \frac{1}{12} = 4$	$\frac{3}{4} \div \frac{1}{3} = 2\frac{1}{4}$
$\frac{5}{12} \div \frac{1}{4} = 1\frac{2}{3}$	$\frac{3}{4} \div \frac{1}{6} = 4\frac{1}{2}$	$\frac{2}{9} \div \frac{2}{3} = \frac{1}{3}$
$\frac{3}{7} \div \frac{1}{4} = 1\frac{5}{7}$	$\frac{2}{3} \div \frac{4}{6} = 1$	$\frac{1}{8} \div \frac{2}{3} = \frac{3}{16}$
$\frac{4}{5} \div \frac{1}{3} = 2\frac{2}{5}$	$\frac{4}{8} \div \frac{1}{2} = 1$	$\frac{5}{12} \div \frac{6}{8} = \frac{5}{9}$

Page 264

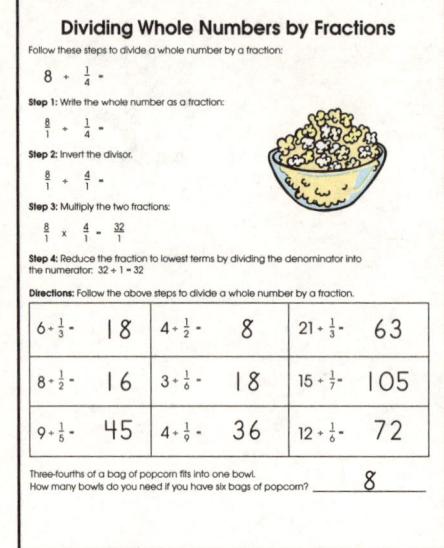

Dividing Whole Numbers by Fractions

Follow these steps to divide a whole number by a fraction:

$8 \div \frac{1}{4} =$

Step 1: Write the whole number as a fraction:

$\frac{8}{1} \div \frac{1}{4} =$

Step 2: Invert the divisor.

$\frac{8}{1} \quad \frac{4}{1} =$

Step 3: Multiply the two fractions:

$\frac{8}{1} \times \frac{4}{1} = \frac{32}{1}$

Step 4: Reduce the fraction to lowest terms by dividing the denominator into the numerator: $32 \div 1 = 32$

Directions: Follow the above steps to divide a whole number by a fraction.

$6 \div \frac{1}{3} = 18$	$4 \div \frac{1}{2} = 8$	$21 \div \frac{1}{3} = 63$
$8 \div \frac{1}{2} = 16$	$3 \div \frac{1}{6} = 18$	$15 \div \frac{1}{7} = 105$
$9 \div \frac{1}{5} = 45$	$4 \div \frac{1}{9} = 36$	$12 \div \frac{1}{6} = 72$

Three-fourths of a bag of popcorn fits into one bowl. How many bowls do you need if you have six bags of popcorn? __8__

Page 265

Decimals

A **decimal** is a number with one or more places to the right of a decimal point.

Examples: 6.5 and 2.25

Fractions with denominators of 10 or 100 can be written as decimals.

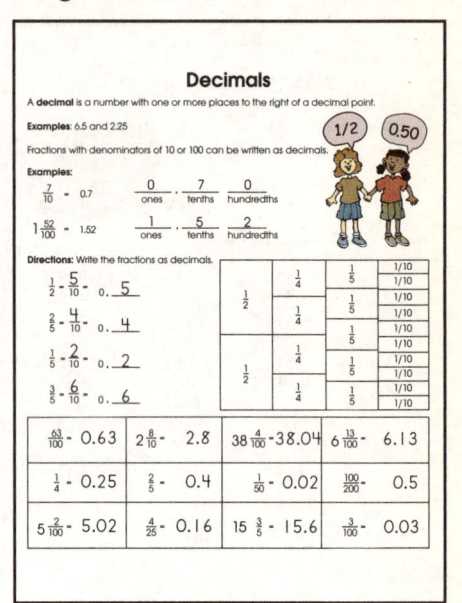

Examples:

$\frac{7}{10} = 0.7$ → 0 ones . 7 tenths 0 hundredths

$1\frac{52}{100} = 1.52$ → 1 ones . 5 tenths 2 hundredths

Directions: Write the fractions as decimals.

$\frac{1}{2} = \frac{5}{10} = 0.5$

$\frac{2}{5} = \frac{4}{10} = 0.4$

$\frac{1}{5} = \frac{2}{10} = 0.2$

$\frac{3}{5} = \frac{6}{10} = 0.6$

$\frac{1}{2}$	$\frac{1}{4}$	$\frac{1}{5}$	1/10
$\frac{1}{2}$	$\frac{1}{4}$	$\frac{1}{5}$	1/10
$\frac{1}{2}$	$\frac{1}{4}$	$\frac{1}{5}$	1/10
$\frac{1}{2}$	$\frac{1}{4}$	$\frac{1}{5}$	1/10

$\frac{63}{100} = 0.63$	$2\frac{8}{10} = 2.8$	$38\frac{4}{100} = 38.04$	$6\frac{13}{100} = 6.13$
$\frac{1}{4} = 0.25$	$\frac{2}{5} = 0.4$	$\frac{1}{50} = 0.02$	$\frac{100}{200} = 0.5$
$5\frac{2}{100} = 5.02$	$\frac{4}{25} = 0.16$	$15\frac{3}{5} = 15.6$	$\frac{3}{100} = 0.03$

Page 266

Decimals and Fractions

Directions: Write the letter of the fraction that is equal to the decimal.

0.25 = G
0.5 = L
0.7 = O
0.8 = N
0.37 = J
0.2 = K
0.65 = C
0.75 = B
0.6 = D
0.12 = E
0.33 = A
0.95 = F
0.24 = M
0.3 = I
0.4 = H

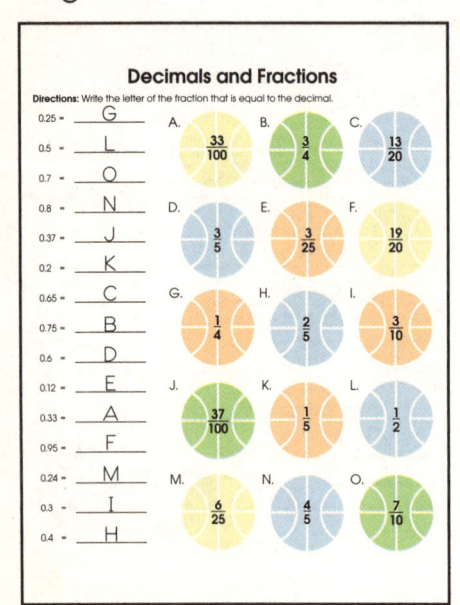

A. $\frac{33}{100}$
B. $\frac{3}{4}$
C. $\frac{13}{20}$
D. $\frac{3}{5}$
E. $\frac{3}{25}$
F. $\frac{19}{20}$
G. $\frac{1}{4}$
H. $\frac{2}{5}$
I. $\frac{3}{10}$
J. $\frac{37}{100}$
K. $\frac{1}{5}$
L. $\frac{1}{2}$
M. $\frac{6}{25}$
N. $\frac{4}{5}$
O. $\frac{7}{10}$

Page 267

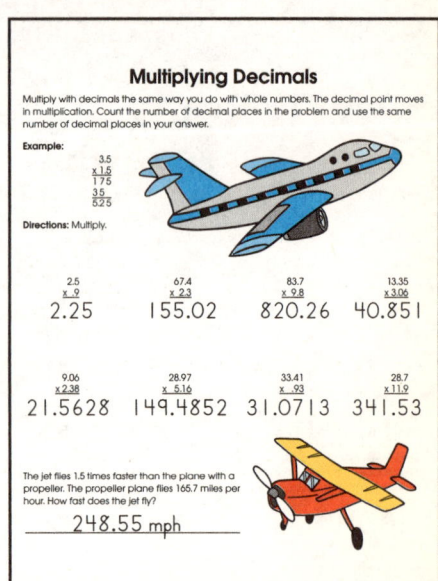

Adding and Subtracting Decimals

Add and subtract with decimals the same way you do with whole numbers. Keep the decimal points lined up so that you work with hundredths, then tenths, then ones, and so on.

Directions: Add or subtract. Remember to keep the decimal point in the proper place.

0.5 + 0.8 = 1.3
0.35 + 0.25 = 0.60
47.5 − 32.7 = 14.8
85.7 − 9.8 = 75.9

13.90 + 4.23 = 18.13
9.53 − 8.16 = 1.37
72.8 − 63.9 = 8.9
6.43 + 4.58 = 11.01

638.07 − 19.34 = 618.73
811.060 + 78.430 = 889.490
521.09 − 148.75 = 372.34

916.635 + 172.136 = 1,088.771
287.768 − 63.951 = 223.817
467.05 − 398.19 = 68.86

Sean ran a 1-mile race in 5.58 minutes. Carlos ran it in 6.38 minutes. How much less time did Sean need? __0.8 minutes__

Page 268

Multiplying Decimals

Multiply with decimals the same way you do with whole numbers. The decimal point moves in multiplication. Count the number of decimal places in the problem and use the same number of decimal places in your answer.

Example:

3.5 × 1.5 = 175; 35; 5.25

Directions: Multiply.

2.5 × .9 = 2.25
67.4 × 2.3 = 155.02
83.7 × 9.8 = 820.26
13.35 × 3.06 = 40.851

9.06 × 2.38 = 21.5628
28.97 × 5.16 = 149.4852
33.41 × .93 = 31.0713
28.7 × 11.9 = 341.53

The jet flies 1.5 times faster than the plane with a propeller. The propeller plane flies 165.7 miles per hour. How fast does the jet fly? __248.55 mph__

Total Basic Skills Grade 5 — Answer Key

Answer Key

Page 269

Dividing With Decimals

When the dividend has a decimal, place the decimal point for the answer directly above the decimal point in the dividend. The first one has been done for you.

3 | 12.5 / 37.5
4 | 8.6 / 34.4
2 | 15.8 / 31.6
3 | 43.8 / 131.4

5 | 37.5 / 187.5
7 | 25.9 / 181.3
6 | 56.8 / 340.8
9 | 32.7 / 294.3

3 | 45.2 / 135.6
5 | 52.9 / 264.5
2 | 67.3 / 134.6
8 | 94.3 / 754.4

5 | 7.05 / 35.25
7 | 11.35 / 79.45
9 | 3.19 / 28.71
36 | 5.54 / 199.44

Page 270

Dividing Decimals by Decimals

0.3 | 9.3 / 27.9
0.6 | 7 / 42.6
0.9 | 91 / 81.9
0.7 | 119 / 83.3

0.4 | 58 / 23.2
0.7 | 81 / 56.7
1.2 | 9 / 10.8
2.2 | 63 / 138.6

12.6 | 450 / 5,670
4.7 | 120 / 564
8.6 | 98 / 842.8
3.7 | 543 / 2,009.1

5.9 | 325 / 1,917.5
4.3 | 320 / 1,376
2.9 | 318 / 922.2
2.7 | 2079 / 5613.3

Page 271

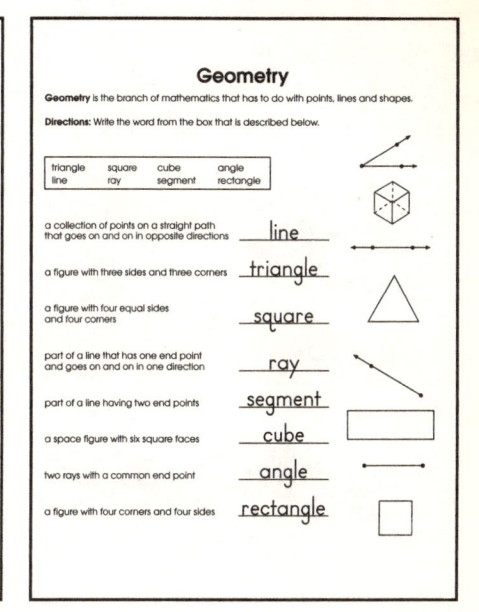

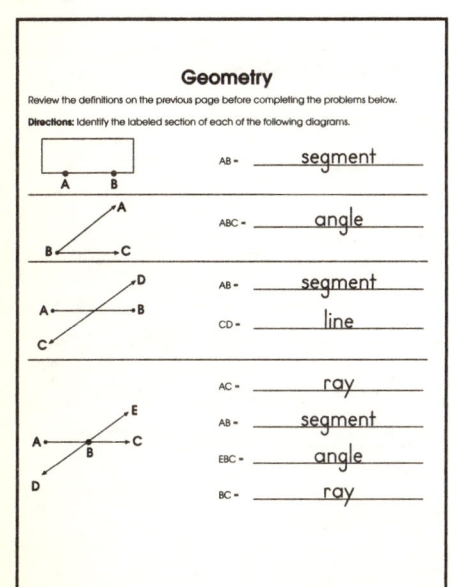

Geometry

- a collection of points on a straight path that goes on and on in opposite directions — **line**
- a figure with three sides and three corners — **triangle**
- a figure with four equal sides and four corners — **square**
- part of a line that has one end point and goes on and on in one direction — **ray**
- part of a line having two end points — **segment**
- a space figure with six square faces — **cube**
- two rays with a common end point — **angle**
- a figure with four corners and four sides — **rectangle**

Page 272

Geometry

- AB = **segment**
- ABC = **angle**
- AB = **segment**
- CD = **line**
- AC = **ray**
- AB = **segment**
- EBC = **angle**
- BC = **ray**

Page 273

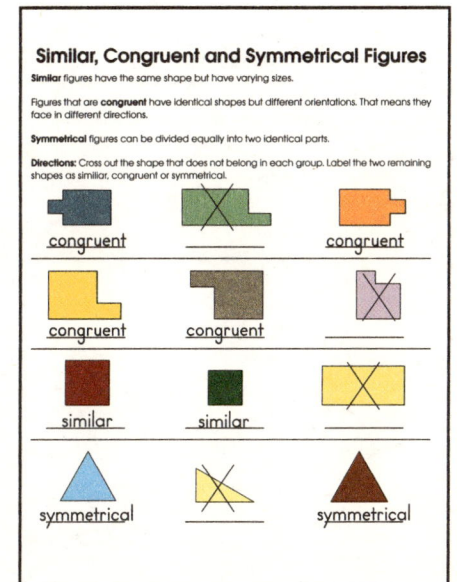

Similar, Congruent and Symmetrical Figures

congruent, congruent
congruent, congruent
similar, similar
symmetrical, symmetrical

Page 274

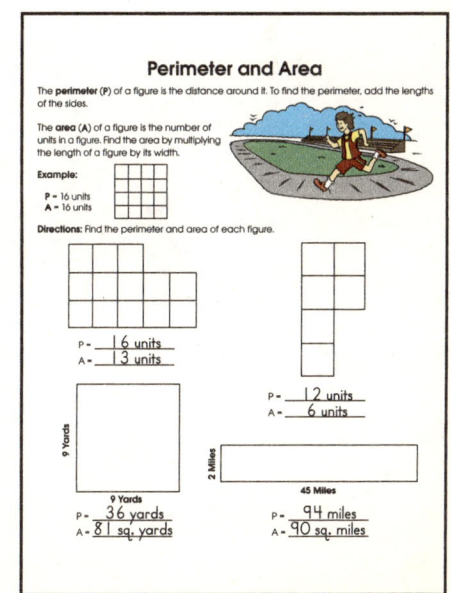

Perimeter and Area

P = 16 units
A = 13 units

P = 12 units
A = 6 units

P = 36 yards
A = 81 sq. yards

P = 94 miles
A = 90 sq. miles

Page 275

Volume

The formula for finding the volume of a box is length times width times height (L x W x H). The answer is given in cubic units.

Directions: Solve the problems.

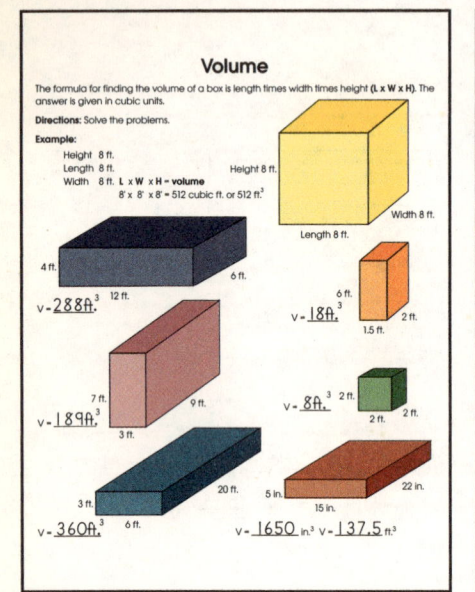

Example:
Height 8 ft.
Length 8 ft.
Width 8 ft. L x W x H = volume
8' x 8' x 8' = 512 cubic ft. or 512 ft.³

V = 288 ft.³
V = 18 ft.³
V = 189 ft.³
V = 8 ft.³
V = 360 ft.³
V = 1650 in.³
V = 137.5 ft.³

Page 276

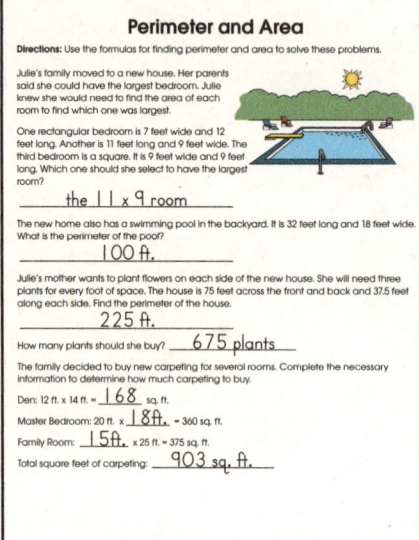

Perimeter and Area

Directions: Use the formulas for finding perimeter and area to solve these problems.

Julie's family moved to a new house. Her parents said she could have the largest bedroom. Julie knew she would need to find the area of each room to find which one was largest.

One rectangular bedroom is 7 feet wide and 12 feet long. Another is 11 feet long and 9 feet wide. The third bedroom is a square. It is 9 feet wide and 9 feet long. Which one should she select to have the largest room?

the 11 x 9 room

The new home also has a swimming pool in the backyard. It is 32 feet long and 18 feet wide. What is the perimeter of the pool?

100 ft.

Julie's mother wants to plant flowers on each side of the new house. She will need three plants for every foot of space. The house is 75 feet across the front and back and 37.5 feet along each side. Find the perimeter of the house.

225 ft.

How many plants should she buy? 675 plants

The family decided to buy new carpeting for several rooms. Complete the necessary information to determine how much carpeting to buy.

Den: 12 ft. x 14 ft. = 168 sq. ft.
Master Bedroom: 20 ft. x 18 ft. = 360 sq. ft.
Family Room: 15 ft. x 25 ft. = 375 sq. ft.

Total square feet of carpeting: 903 sq. ft.

Page 277

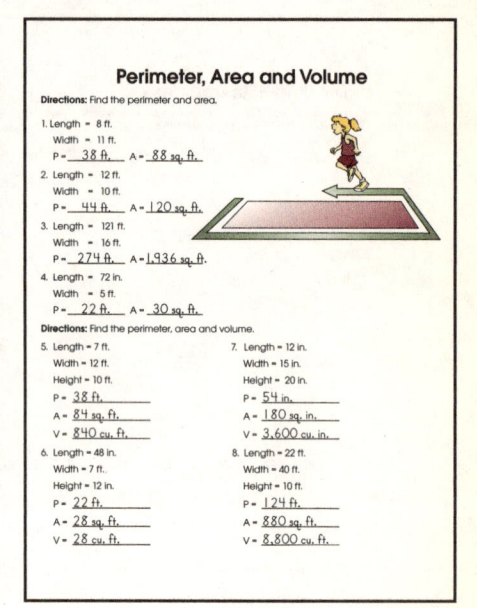

Perimeter, Area and Volume

Directions: Find the perimeter and area.

1. Length = 8 ft.
   Width = 11 ft.
   P = 38 ft. A = 88 sq. ft.

2. Length = 12 ft.
   Width = 10 ft.
   P = 44 ft. A = 120 sq. ft.

3. Length = 121 ft.
   Width = 16 ft.
   P = 274 ft. A = 1,936 sq. ft.

4. Length = 72 in.
   Width = 5 in.
   P = 22 ft. A = 30 sq. ft.

Directions: Find the perimeter, area and volume.

5. Length = 7 ft.
   Width = 12 ft.
   Height = 10 ft.
   P = 38 ft.
   A = 84 sq. ft.
   V = 840 cu. ft.

6. Length = 48 in.
   Width = 7 in.
   Height = 12 in.
   P = 22 ft.
   A = 28 sq. ft.
   V = 28 cu. ft.

7. Length = 12 in.
   Width = 15 in.
   Height = 20 in.
   P = 54 in.
   A = 180 sq. in.
   V = 3,600 cu. in.

8. Length = 22 ft.
   Width = 40 ft.
   Height = 10 ft.
   P = 124 ft.
   A = 880 sq. ft.
   V = 8,800 cu. ft.

Page 278

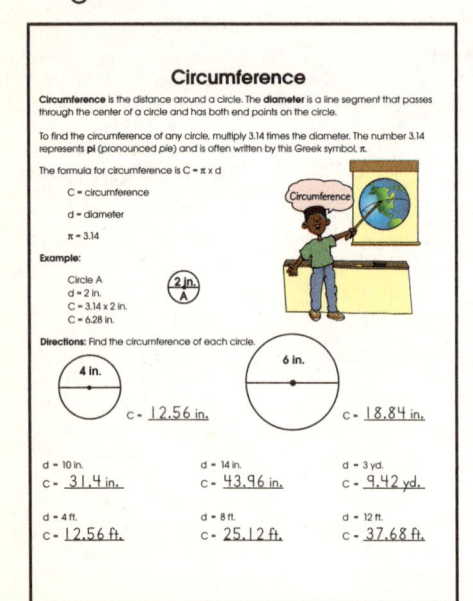

Circumference

Circumference is the distance around a circle. The **diameter** is a line segment that passes through the center of a circle and has both end points on the circle.

To find the circumference of any circle, multiply 3.14 times the diameter. The number 3.14 represents **pi** (pronounced pie) and is often written by this Greek symbol, π.

The formula for circumference is C = π x d

C = circumference
d = diameter
π = 3.14

Example:
Circle A
d = 2 in.
C = 3.14 x 2 in.
C = 6.28 in.

Directions: Find the circumference of each circle.

4 in. C = 12.56 in.
6 in. C = 18.84 in.

d = 10 in. C = 31.4 in.
d = 14 in. C = 43.96 in.
d = 3 yd. C = 9.42 yd.

d = 4 ft. C = 12.56 ft.
d = 8 in. C = 25.12 ft.
d = 12 ft. C = 37.68 ft.

Page 279

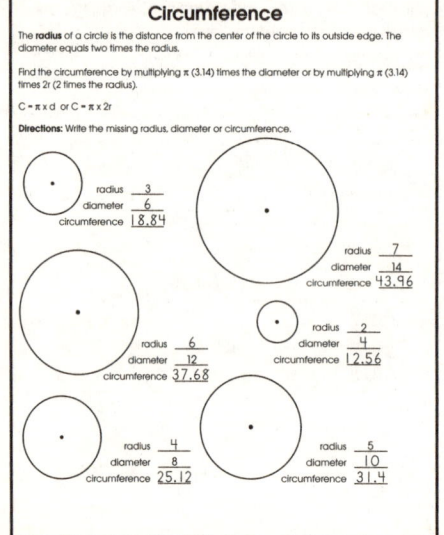

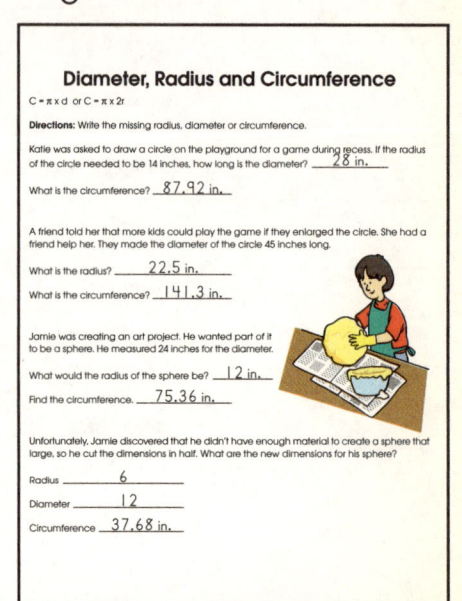

Circumference

The **radius** of a circle is the distance from the center of the circle to its outside edge. The diameter equals two times the radius.

Find the circumference by multiplying π (3.14) times the diameter or by multiplying π (3.14) times 2r (2 times the radius).

C = π x d or C = π x 2r

Directions: Write the missing radius, diameter or circumference.

radius 3
diameter 6
circumference 18.84

radius 7
diameter 14
circumference 43.96

radius 6
diameter 12
circumference 37.68

radius 2
diameter 4
circumference 12.56

radius 4
diameter 8
circumference 25.12

radius 5
diameter 10
circumference 31.4

Page 280

Diameter, Radius and Circumference

C = π x d or C = π x 2r

Directions: Write the missing radius, diameter or circumference.

Katie was asked to draw a circle on the playground for a game during recess. If the radius of the circle needed to be 14 inches, how long is the diameter? 28 in.

What is the circumference? 87.92 in.

A friend told her that more kids could play the game if they enlarged the circle. She had a friend help her. They made the diameter of the circle 45 inches long.

What is the radius? 22.5 in.
What is the circumference? 141.3 in.

Jamie was creating an art project. He wanted part of it to be a sphere. He measured 24 inches for the diameter.

What would the radius of the sphere be? 12 in.
Find the circumference. 75.36 in.

Unfortunately, Jamie discovered that he didn't have enough material to create a sphere that large, so he cut the dimensions in half. What are the new dimensions for his sphere?

Radius 6
Diameter 12
Circumference 37.68 in.

Page 281

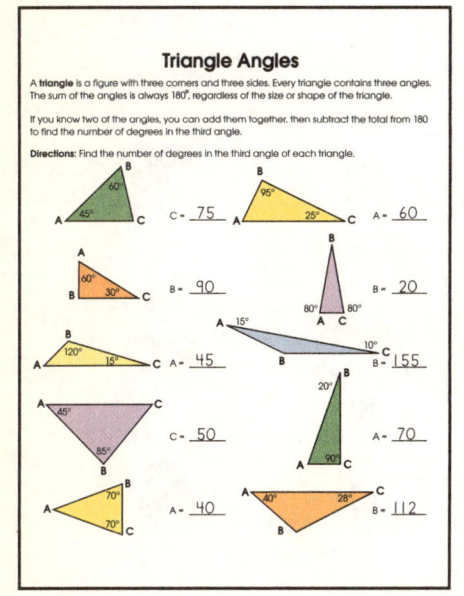

Triangle Angles

A **triangle** is a figure with three corners and three sides. Every triangle contains three angles. The sum of the angles is always 180°, regardless of the size or shape of the triangle.

If you know two of the angles, you can add them together, then subtract the total from 180 to find the number of degrees in the third angle.

Directions: Find the number of degrees in the third angle of each triangle.

C = 75   A = 60
B = 90   B = 20
A = 45   B = 155
C = 50   A = 70
A = 40   B = 112

Page 282

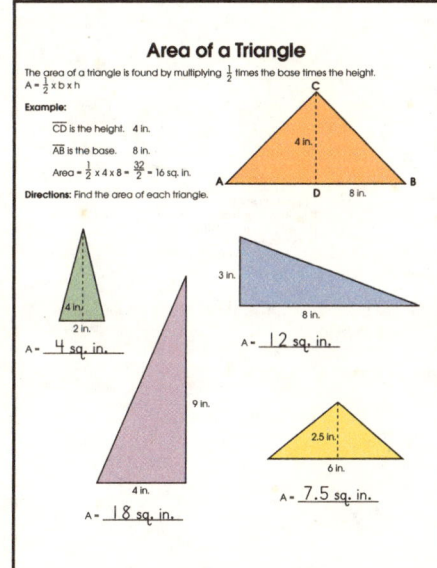

Area of a Triangle

The area of a triangle is found by multiplying $\frac{1}{2}$ times the base times the height.
A = $\frac{1}{2}$ × b × h

Example:
$\overline{CD}$ is the height. 4 in.
$\overline{AB}$ is the base. 8 in.
Area = $\frac{1}{2}$ × 4 × 8 = $\frac{32}{2}$ = 16 sq. in.

Directions: Find the area of each triangle.

A = 4 sq. in.
A = 12 sq. in.
A = 18 sq. in.
A = 7.5 sq. in.

Page 283

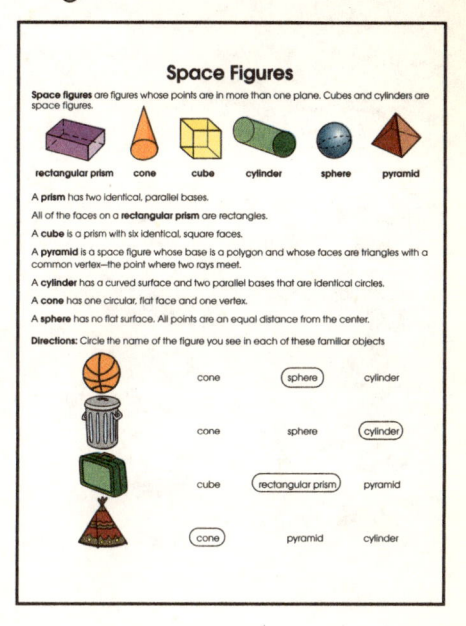

Space Figures

Space figures are figures whose points are in more than one plane. Cubes and cylinders are space figures.

rectangular prism   cone   cube   cylinder   sphere   pyramid

A **prism** has two identical, parallel bases.
All of the faces on a **rectangular prism** are rectangles.
A **cube** is a prism with six identical, square faces.
A **pyramid** is a space figure whose base is a polygon and whose faces are triangles with a common vertex—the point where two rays meet.
A **cylinder** has a curved surface and two parallel bases that are identical circles.
A **cone** has one circular, flat face and one vertex.
A **sphere** has no flat surface. All points are an equal distance from the center.

Directions: Circle the name of the figure you see in each of these familiar objects

cone   (sphere)   cylinder
cone   sphere   (cylinder)
cube   (rectangular prism)   pyramid
(cone)   pyramid   cylinder

Page 284

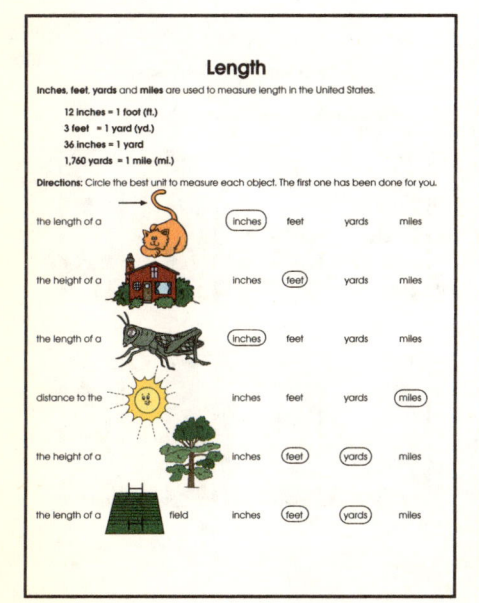

Length

Inches, feet, yards and **miles** are used to measure length in the United States.

12 inches = 1 foot (ft.)
3 feet = 1 yard (yd.)
36 inches = 1 yard
1,760 yards = 1 mile (mi.)

Directions: Circle the best unit to measure each object. The first one has been done for you.

the length of a cat — (inches) feet yards miles
the height of a house — inches (feet) yards miles
the length of a grasshopper — (inches) feet yards miles
distance to the sun — inches feet yards (miles)
the height of a tree — inches (feet) yards miles
the length of a field — inches (feet) yards miles

Page 285

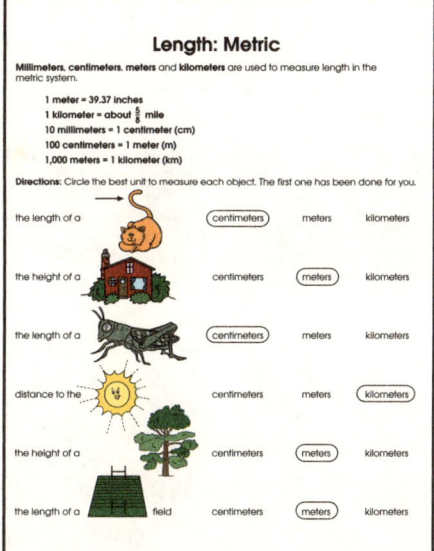

Length: Metric

Millimeters, centimeters, meters and **kilometers** are used to measure length in the metric system.

1 meter = 39.37 inches
1 kilometer = about $\frac{5}{8}$ mile
10 millimeters = 1 centimeter (cm)
100 centimeters = 1 meter (m)
1,000 meters = 1 kilometer (km)

Directions: Circle the best unit to measure each object. The first one has been done for you.

the length of a cat — (centimeters) meters kilometers
the height of a house — centimeters (meters) kilometers
the length of a grasshopper — (centimeters) meters kilometers
distance to the sun — centimeters meters (kilometers)
the height of a tree — centimeters (meters) kilometers
the length of a field — centimeters (meters) kilometers

Page 286

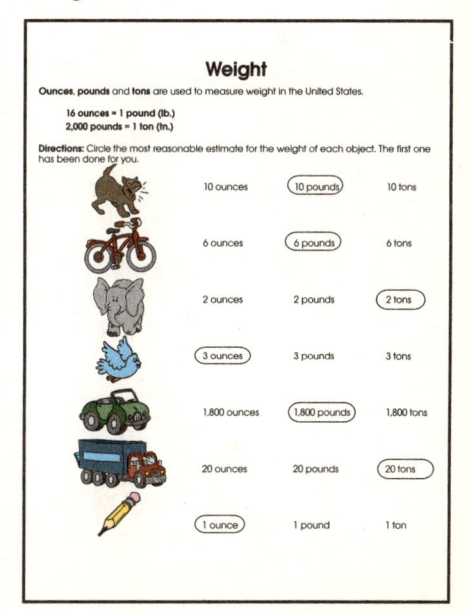

Weight

Ounces, pounds and **tons** are used to measure weight in the United States.

16 ounces = 1 pound (lb.)
2,000 pounds = 1 ton (tn.)

Directions: Circle the most reasonable estimate for the weight of each object. The first one has been done for you.

10 ounces   (10 pounds)   10 tons
6 ounces   (6 pounds)   6 tons
2 ounces   2 pounds   (2 tons)
(3 ounces)   3 pounds   3 tons
1,800 ounces   (1,800 pounds)   1,800 tons
20 ounces   20 pounds   (20 tons)
(1 ounce)   1 pound   1 ton

Page 287

Weight: Metric

Grams and **kilograms** are units of weight in the metric system. A paper clip weighs about 1 gram. A kitten weighs about 1 kilogram.

1 kilogram (kg) = about 2.2 pounds
1,000 grams (g) = 1 kilogram

Directions: Circle the best unit to weigh each object.

- squirrel: (kilogram) / gram
- flower: kilogram / (gram)
- bicycle: (kilogram) / gram
- truck: (kilogram) / gram
- leaf: kilogram / (gram)
- elephant: (kilogram) / gram
- car: (kilogram) / gram
- pencil: kilogram / (gram)
- bird: kilogram / (gram)
- weightlifter: (kilogram) / gram

Page 288

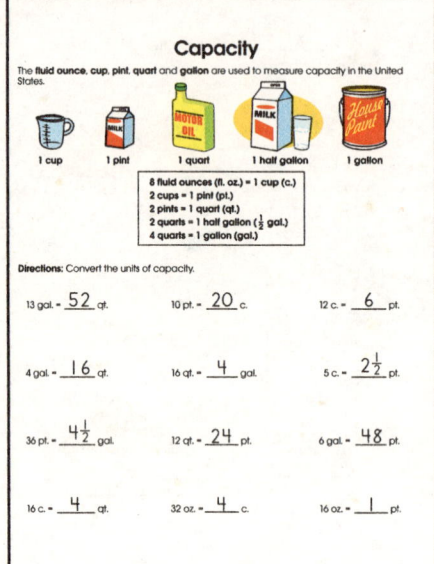

Capacity

The **fluid ounce**, **cup**, **pint**, **quart** and **gallon** are used to measure capacity in the United States.

8 fluid ounces (fl. oz.) = 1 cup (c.)
2 cups = 1 pint (pt.)
2 pints = 1 quart (qt.)
2 quarts = 1 half gallon (½ gal.)
4 quarts = 1 gallon (gal.)

Directions: Convert the units of capacity.

13 gal. = __52__ qt.   10 pt. = __20__ c.   12 c. = __6__ pt.

4 gal. = __16__ qt.   16 qt. = __4__ gal.   5 c. = __2½__ pt.

36 pt. = __4½__ gal.   12 qt. = __24__ pt.   6 gal. = __48__ pt.

16 c. = __4__ qt.   32 oz. = __4__ c.   16 oz. = __1__ pt.

Page 289

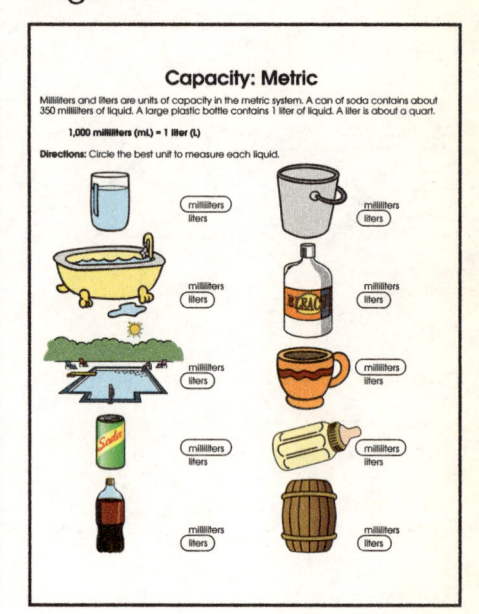

Capacity: Metric

Milliliters and liters are units of capacity in the metric system. A can of soda contains about 350 milliliters of liquid. A large plastic bottle contains 1 liter of liquid. A liter is about a quart.

1,000 milliliters (mL) = 1 liter (L)

Directions: Circle the best unit to measure each liquid.

- bathtub: milliliters / (liters)
- bucket: milliliters / (liters)
- puddle: (milliliters) / liters
- bottle: milliliters / (liters)
- soda can: (milliliters) / liters
- baby bottle: (milliliters) / liters
- soda bottle: milliliters / (liters)
- barrel: milliliters / (liters)

Page 290

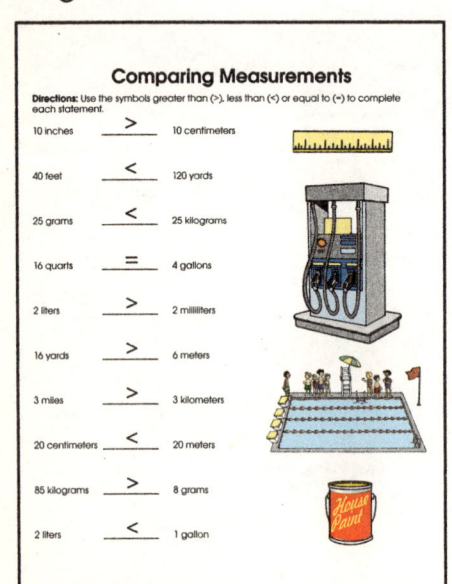

Comparing Measurements

Directions: Use the symbols greater than (>), less than (<) or equal to (=) to complete each statement.

- 10 inches __>__ 10 centimeters
- 40 feet __<__ 120 yards
- 25 grams __<__ 25 kilograms
- 16 quarts __=__ 4 gallons
- 2 liters __>__ 2 milliliters
- 16 yards __>__ 6 meters
- 3 miles __>__ 3 kilometers
- 20 centimeters __<__ 20 meters
- 85 kilograms __>__ 8 grams
- 2 liters __<__ 1 gallon

Page 291

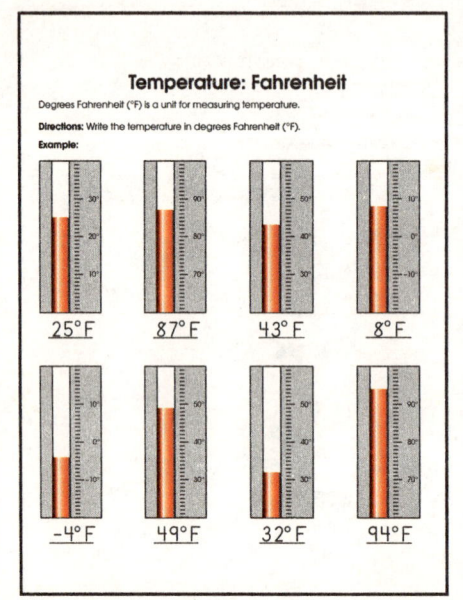

Temperature: Fahrenheit

Degrees Fahrenheit (°F) is a unit for measuring temperature.

Directions: Write the temperature in degrees Fahrenheit (°F).

__25__°F   __87__°F   __43__°F   __8__°F

__-4__°F   __49__°F   __32__°F   __94__°F

Page 292

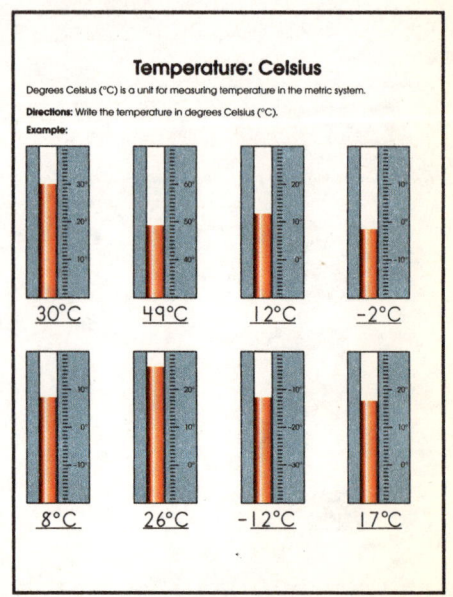

Temperature: Celsius

Degrees Celsius (°C) is a unit for measuring temperature in the metric system.

Directions: Write the temperature in degrees Celsius (°C).

__30__°C   __49__°C   __12__°C   __-2__°C

__8__°C   __26__°C   __-12__°C   __17__°C

Page 293

Review

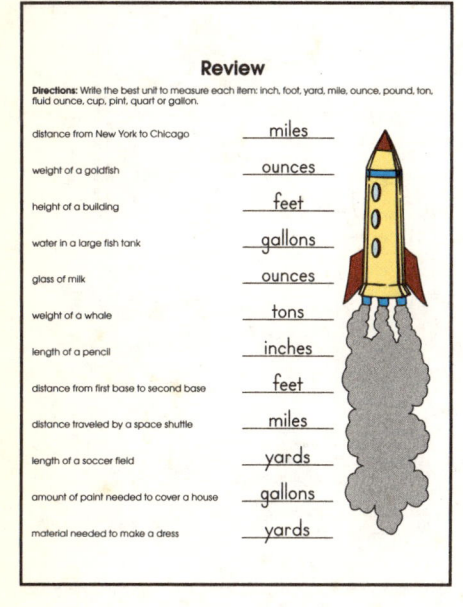

Directions: Write the best unit to measure each item: inch, foot, yard, mile, ounce, pound, ton, fluid ounce, cup, pint, quart or gallon.

distance from New York to Chicago	miles
weight of a goldfish	ounces
height of a building	feet
water in a large fish tank	gallons
glass of milk	ounces
weight of a whale	tons
length of a pencil	inches
distance from first base to second base	feet
distance traveled by a space shuttle	miles
length of a soccer field	yards
amount of paint needed to cover a house	gallons
material needed to make a dress	yards

Page 294

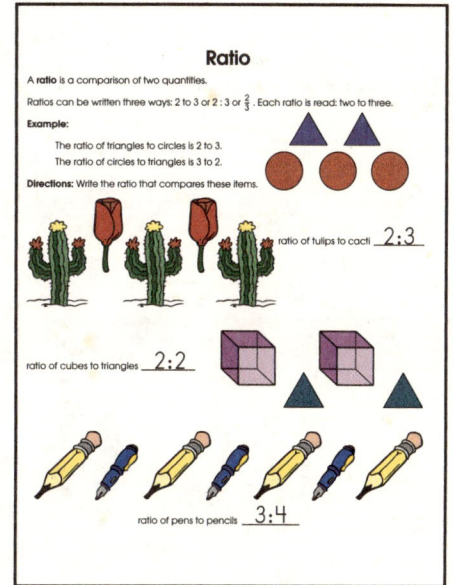

Ratio

A **ratio** is a comparison of two quantities.
Ratios can be written three ways: 2 to 3 or 2 : 3 or $\frac{2}{3}$. Each ratio is read: two to three.

Example:
The ratio of triangles to circles is 2 to 3.
The ratio of circles to triangles is 3 to 2.

Directions: Write the ratio that compares these items.

ratio of tulips to cacti 2:3

ratio of cubes to triangles 2:2

ratio of pens to pencils 3:4

Page 295

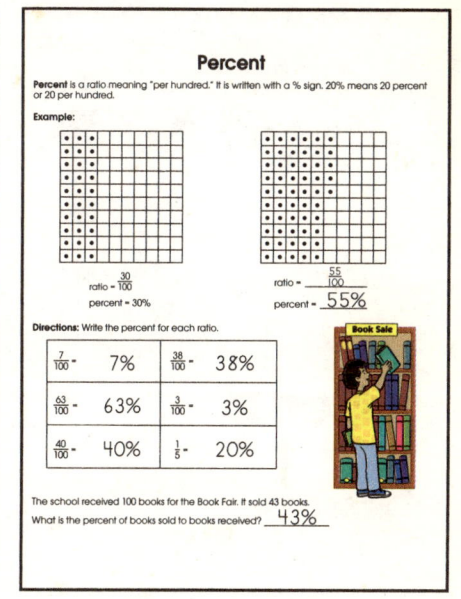

Percent

Percent is a ratio meaning "per hundred." It is written with a % sign. 20% means 20 percent or 20 per hundred.

Example:

ratio = $\frac{30}{100}$ percent = 30%

ratio = $\frac{55}{100}$ percent = 55%

Directions: Write the percent for each ratio.

$\frac{7}{100}$ =	7%	$\frac{38}{100}$ =	38%
$\frac{63}{100}$ =	63%	$\frac{3}{100}$ =	3%
$\frac{40}{100}$ =	40%	$\frac{1}{5}$ =	20%

The school received 100 books for the Book Fair. It sold 43 books. What is the percent of books sold to books received? 43%

Page 296

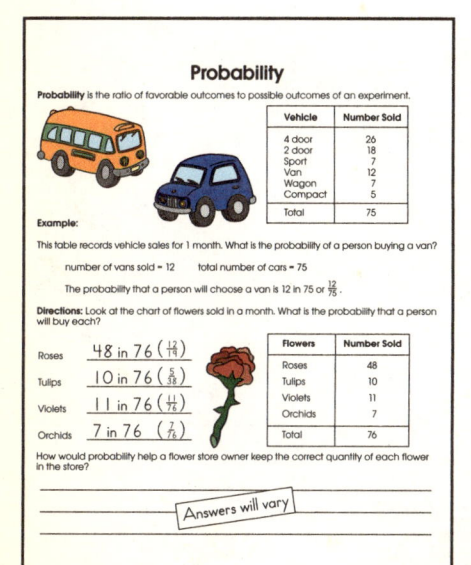

Probability

Probability is the ratio of favorable outcomes to possible outcomes of an experiment.

Vehicle	Number Sold
4 door	26
2 door	18
Sport	7
Van	12
Wagon	7
Compact	5
Total	75

Example:
This table records vehicle sales for 1 month. What is the probability of a person buying a van?
number of vans sold = 12   total number of cars = 75
The probability that a person will choose a van is 12 in 75 or $\frac{12}{75}$.

Directions: Look at the chart of flowers sold in a month. What is the probability that a person will buy each?

Flowers	Number Sold
Roses	48
Tulips	10
Violets	11
Orchids	7
Total	76

Roses   48 in 76 ($\frac{12}{19}$)
Tulips   10 in 76 ($\frac{5}{38}$)
Violets 11 in 76 ($\frac{11}{76}$)
Orchids 7 in 76 ($\frac{7}{76}$)

How would probability help a flower store owner keep the correct quantity of each flower in the store? Answers will vary

Page 297

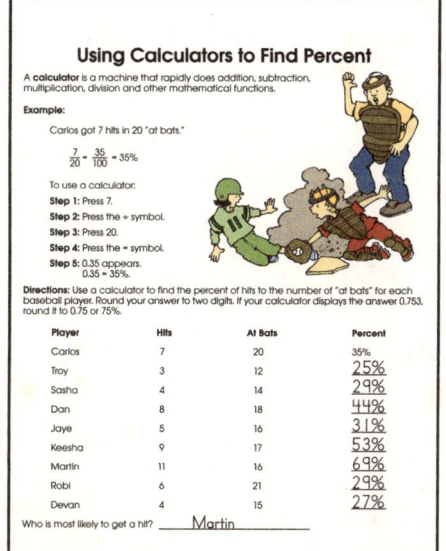

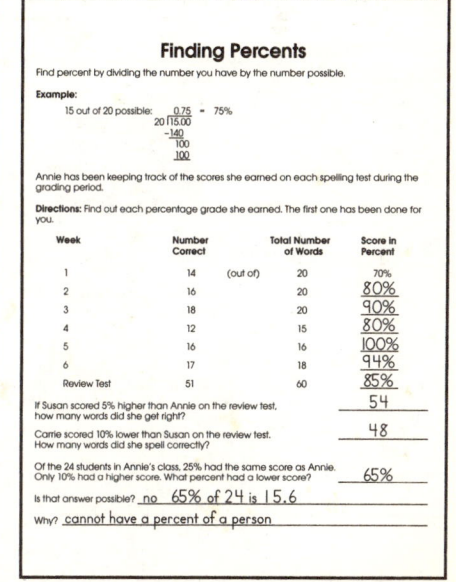

Using Calculators to Find Percent

A **calculator** is a machine that rapidly does addition, subtraction, multiplication, division and other mathematical functions.

Example:
Carlos got 7 hits in 20 "at bats."
$\frac{7}{20} = \frac{35}{100} = 35\%$

To use a calculator:
Step 1: Press 7.
Step 2: Press the ÷ symbol.
Step 3: Press 20.
Step 4: Press the = symbol.
Step 5: 0.35 appears.
0.35 = 35%.

Directions: Use a calculator to find the percent of hits to the number of "at bats" for each baseball player. Round your answer to two digits. If your calculator displays the answer 0.753, round it to 0.75 or 75%.

Player	Hits	At Bats	Percent
Carlos	7	20	35%
Troy	3	12	25%
Sasha	4	14	29%
Dan	8	18	44%
Jaye	5	16	31%
Keesha	9	17	53%
Martin	11	16	69%
Robi	6	21	29%
Devan	4	15	27%

Who is most likely to get a hit? Martin

Page 298

Finding Percents

Find percent by dividing the number you have by the number possible.

Example:
15 out of 20 possible: $\frac{0.75}{20 \overline{)15.00}} = 75\%$
$\quad\quad -140$
$\quad\quad\quad 100$
$\quad\quad\quad 100$

Annie has been keeping track of the scores she earned on each spelling test during the grading period.

Directions: Find out each percentage grade she earned. The first one has been done for you.

Week	Number Correct	Total Number of Words	Score in Percent
1	14	(out of) 20	70%
2	16	20	80%
3	18	20	90%
4	12	15	80%
5	16	16	100%
6	17	18	94%
Review Test	51	60	85%

If Susan scored 5% higher than Annie on the review test, how many words did she get right? 54

Carrie scored 10% lower than Susan on the review test. How many words did she spell correctly? 48

Of the 24 students in Annie's class, 25% had the same score as Annie. Only 10% had a higher score. What percent had a lower score? 65%

Is that answer possible? no 65% of 24 is 15.6
Why? cannot have a percent of a person

Answer Key   351   Total Basic Skills Grade 5

Page 299

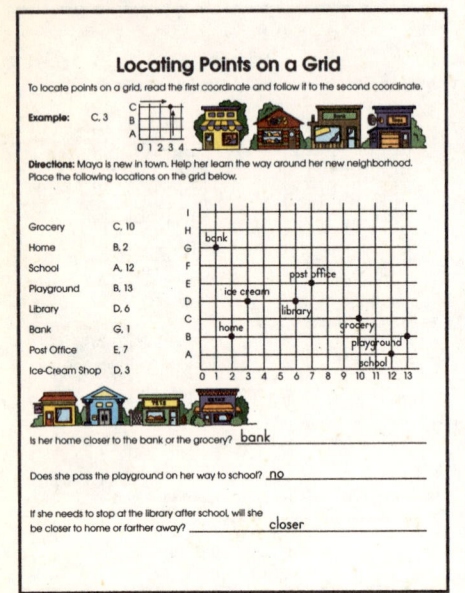

Locating Points on a Grid

To locate points on a grid, read the first coordinate and follow it to the second coordinate.

Example: C, 3

Directions: Maya is new in town. Help her learn the way around her new neighborhood. Place the following locations on the grid below.

Grocery	C, 10
Home	B, 2
School	A, 12
Playground	B, 13
Library	D, 6
Bank	G, 1
Post Office	E, 7
Ice-Cream Shop	D, 3

Is her home closer to the bank or the grocery? **bank**

Does she pass the playground on her way to school? **no**

If she needs to stop at the library after school, will she be closer to home or farther away? **closer**

Page 300

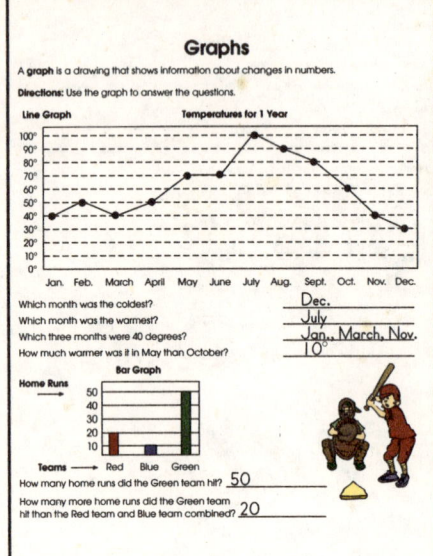

Graphs

A **graph** is a drawing that shows information about changes in numbers.

Directions: Use the graph to answer the questions.

Line Graph — Temperatures for 1 Year

Which month was the coldest? **Dec.**
Which month was the warmest? **July**
Which three months were 40 degrees? **Jan., March, Nov.**
How much warmer was it in May than October? **10°**

Bar Graph — Home Runs

How many home runs did the Green team hit? **50**
How many more home runs did the Green team hit than the Red team and Blue team combined? **20**

Page 301

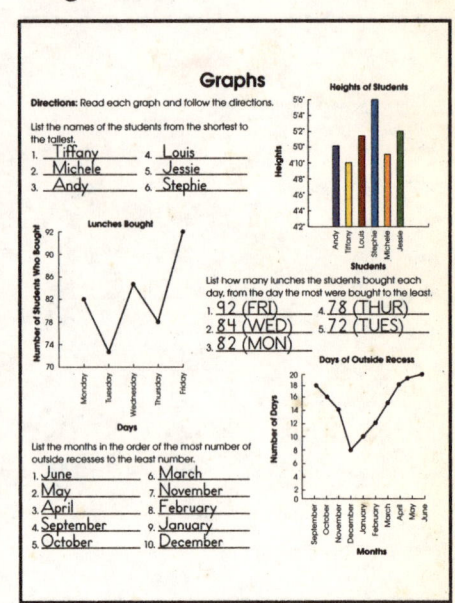

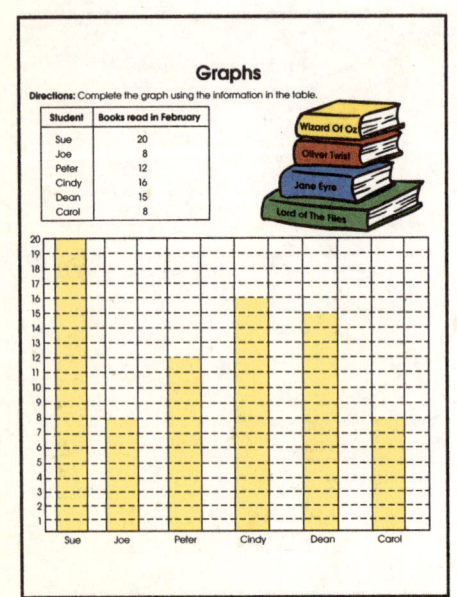

Graphs

Directions: Read each graph and follow the directions.

List the names of the students from the shortest to the tallest.
1. Tiffany
2. Michele
3. Andy
4. Louis
5. Jessie
6. Stephie

List how many lunches the students bought each day, from the day the most were bought to the least.
1. 92 (FRI)
2. 84 (WED)
3. 82 (MON)
4. 78 (THUR)
5. 72 (TUES)

List the months in the order of the most number of outside recesses to the least number.
1. June
2. May
3. April
4. September
5. October
6. March
7. November
8. February
9. January
10. December

Page 302

Graphs

Directions: Complete the graph using the information in the table.

Student	Books read in February
Sue	20
Joe	8
Peter	12
Cindy	16
Dean	15
Carol	8

Ready Reference Misspelled Words

Frequently Misspelled Words

about	children	getting	no one	thorough
affect/effect	chimney	goes	o'clock	though
again	chocolate	grammar	often	thought
allowed	Christmas	grateful	once	threw/through
a lot	close/clothes	guarantee	people	tired
all right	college	guess	please	to/too/two
already	coming	handkerchief	present	together
always	congratulations	Halloween	pretty	tomorrow
ancient	couldn't	happen	principal	tonight
angle	courtesy	heard	probably	tried
animals	cousin	height	quite	truly
another	decided	hello	really	until
answer	didn't	holiday	receive	upon
are/our	different	horrible	remember	usually
around	doctor	horse	right	very
asked	doesn't	hospital	rough	visitor
aunt/ant	eighth	humorous	said	weather
awhile	elementary	icicle	school	weight
baggage	especially	innocent	secretary	weird
balloon	every	instead	skiing	welfare
beautiful	everybody	interesting	something	were
because	exactly	into	sometimes	we're
before	except	island	start	when
beginning	experience	jewelry	straight	where
believe	family	knew	summer	which
birthday	favorite	know	suppose	while
bought	February	league	surely	whole
brother	finally	likely	surprise	with
brought	first	little	swimming	women
business	foreign	many	teacher	world
buy	found	maybe	than/then	would
calendar	friend	money	that's	writing
canyon	frightened	morning	their/there/they're	yellow
captain	from	mother	themselves	yesterday
caught	geography	neighbor	think	you're

Proofreading Symbols

∧	Insert	⌒	Close up one space	↑	Add a comma
ℯ	Delete	◡	Close up entirely	⊙	Add a period
stet	Let it stand	~ tr	Transpose	∨	Add an apostrophe
#	Add a space	≡ cap	Capitalize	∨∨	Add quotation marks
¶	New paragraph	/ lc	Lowercase		

Grade 5 Ready Reference Grammar Guide

Punctuation Rules

A period is used…
- at the end of declarative sentences and mild imperatives.
- after initials and abbreviations.
- only once for a sentence ending with an abbreviation.

A question mark is used…
- at the end of an interrogative sentence.

An exclamation mark is used…
- after a word, phrase, or sentence showing strong feeling.

A comma is used…
- to separate two or more adjectives of equal rank.
- to set off a direct quotation.
- to separate three or more words, phrases, or clauses in a series.
- to separate two independent clauses in a compound sentence.
- to set off a word, phrase, or dependent clause at the beginning of a sentence.

A semicolon is used…
- to separate independent clauses very close in meaning but not separated by *and, but, or, nor, for,* or *yet*.
- to separate items in a series when the series already contains commas.

A colon is used…
- before a list of items or details.
- before a statement that summarizes the original statement.
- before a long, formal quotation or statement.

Parentheses are used…
- to set off words, phrases, clauses, or sentences which are independent of the main part of the sentence.

Quotation marks are used…
- to set off a direct quotation. (Single quotation marks are used for quotes within quotes.)
- to set off words, phrases, or sentences referred to in the sentence.
- to set off slang and foreign words or phrases.

Pronoun-Antecedent Agreement

- A personal pronoun must agree with its antecedent in person, number, and gender.
- Collective nouns are singular when the group is acting as a single unit.
- Collective nouns are plural when the members of the group are acting independently.
Example:
  The orchestra disagree on the selections for the concert.

Subject-Verb Agreement

- Normally, when two or more subjects are connected by and, the subject is plural and requires a plural verb.
  Fred and Dave like this class.

- If the two subjects form a unit, the subject is then singular and requires a singular verb.
  Chicken and dumplings is my favorite meal.

- Two singular subjects joined by *or* are considered singular and require a singular verb.

- When one of the subjects is singular and the other is plural, the verb agrees with the subject that is nearer.

- The subject of the sentence is never affected by intervening phrases that might come between it and the verb.

- A collective noun that is singular requires a singular verb.

- If the collective noun indicates by its usage that the individual members are acting separately, then a plural verb is required.

- A plural noun that shows *weight, extent,* or *quantity* is singular and takes a singular verb.
  Ten dollars is the price of this tape.

Rules for Titles

- All principal words in titles are capitalized. Do not capitalize prepositions, coordinating conjunctions, and articles unless they begin the title.
- Underline the titles of books, magazines, newspapers, and films. (Italics may take the place of underlining if you are using a word processor capable of doing it.)
- Quotation marks are used to enclose the titles of magazine articles, chapters of books, names of songs, and titles of poems.

Capitalization Rules

- Capitalize names of particular persons, places, and things.
- Capitalize titles of rank when they come before a person's name.
- Do not capitalize the names of the seasons of the year unless they are personified.
- The words *north, south, east,* and *west* are capitalized only when they refer to sections of the country, not directions.
- The names of school subjects are not capitalized unless they are names of languages.
- All words that refer to a specific deity and sacred books are capitalized.

The "Of" Error

- Do not substitute the preposition *of* for the auxiliary verb *have*. Common error forms are:
  could of
  should of
  You should use:
  could have
  should have